MATTHEW AND THE DIDACHE

Huub van de Sandt (ed.)

MATTHEW AND THE DIDACHE

Two Documents from the Same Jewish-Christian Milieu?

2005
Royal Van Gorcum, Assen
Fortress Press, Minneapolis

This volume is a cooperative venture of Royal Van Gorcum and Fortress Press.

© 2005 Koninklijke Van Gorcum BV, P.O. Box 43, 9400 AA Assen, The Netherlands

ISBN   90 232 4077 4 (Royal Van Gorcum)

0 8006 3722 4 (Fortress Press)

Printed in The Netherlands by Royal Van Gorcum, Assen, The Netherlands

Contents

V

Introduction

In modern scholarship a new consensus is emerging which dates the Didache at about the turn of the First Century C.E. At the same time, significant agreements between the Didache and the gospel of Matthew have been detected as these writings share words, phrases and motifs. There seems to be an increasing reluctance, however, to support the thesis that the Didache used Matthew. And, indeed, such a close relationship might equally suggest that both documents were created in the same historical and geographical setting, for example in the Greek-speaking part of Syria. In the study *The Didache. Its Jewish Sources and its Place in Early Judaism and Christianity* (CRINT III/5; Van Gorcum / Fortress, 2002), the late David Flusser and I substantiated the evidence supporting the emergence, transmittance, and growth of both writings in a common environment.

Among our arguments suggesting a common environment are that the community of both the Didache and the gospel of Matthew was probably composed of Judaeo-Christians from the outset, though each manuscript shows indications of a congregation which appears to have alienated itself from its Jewish background. Additionally, the Two Ways teaching (*Did.* 1-6) may well have served in some form as a pre-baptismal instruction within the community of the Didache and Matthew. Furthermore, the correspondence of the Trinitarian baptismal formula in the Didache and Matthew (*Did.* 7 and Matt 28:19) as well as the similar shape of the Lord's Prayer (*Did.* 8 and Matt 6:5-13) apparently reflect the use of resembling oral forms of church traditions. Finally, both the community of the Didache (*Did.* 11-13) and Matthew (Matt 7:15-23; 10:5-15, 40-42; 24:11,24) were visited by itinerant apostles and prophets, some of whom were illegitimate.

In order to invite discussion and exchange ideas on this fundamental issue, an international conference was organized by the Tilburg Faculty of Theology. During 7-8 April 2003, a group of approximately 55 participants from around the globe gathered at the Tilburg University campus. Scholars of related fields (New Testament, Second Temple Judaism, Liturgy, Patristic Studies) were brought together to debate about the matter in the light of their diverse specialisms and previous research. This volume contains the edited proceedings of the expert meeting. Instead of looking at the Didache as a subject of study belonging to Patristics only, the document is considered part of a larger environment of Jewish and Christian religious history. If the Didache and Matthew did indeed emanate from the same geographical, social and cultural setting, new questions arise. Who were the Christians standing behind the Didache and Matthew? Can we trace the developing interests of the respective community or communities in the different textual layers of the Didache and Matthew? Is it possible to frame the congregation(s) within the social history of Jews and Jewish believers-in-Jesus in First-Century Syria? What stage of development or separation between Christians, Jewish Christians and Jews is envisaged?

The way the agreements between the Didache and the Matthean gospel are comprehended and explained clearly affects the way one creates the framework for understanding early Christian communities, their belief structures, and their relations. Similarly, the background against which Matthew and the Didache are viewed has an immediate effect on the interpretation of both documents. If the Didache may be treated as a window on Matthew, through which a picture emerges of the social world the gospel wishes to address, and if the gospel of Matthew may be used as a window through which we can catch glimpses of the Didache community, we may find a way out in several redactional-critical problems of distinguishing between tradition and redaction in the two documents.

There is little doubt, for example, that the author of the gospel of Matthew by recasting the traditional source materials of the life of Jesus also tells the story of Jesus in the light of his own experience. The sharp disagreement between Jesus and the Pharisees, deepened into intense controversies through Matthean redaction may represent the worsening relations between local Jewish communities and the Christian communities. The gospel of Matthew can be used this way as a window through which the critic might catch glimpses of the society, culture, and history of the Matthean community. On the other hand, however, this assumption poses the problem of the gospel being not a literary but a documentary source. Although Matthew allegedly provides the interpreter with a direct view of the historical situation, the latter is usually unable to demonstrate that he has displayed the correct and faithful historical and social world behind the text. Other data, not derived from the gospel itself, may help to overcome this weakness. If the Didache is not dependent on the gospel of Matthew but reflects materials used by Matthew, it would mean that we have in the Didache a window on the social and religious milieu out of which the gospel of Matthew arose. As a 'primitive' teaching manual, largely unaffected by theological developments, it could be particularly interesting in this respect since it might corroborate, readjust, or dismiss a conjectural picture of the historical situation behind the text. Two windows may provide the transparency needed to reach more insight into the situation of the community.

This volume is divided into three major parts. *Part One* is about the conceivable setting or milieu in which Matthew and the Didache could have originated. Here the predominant scholarly view is adopted, which situates Matthew and the Didache in some Greek-speaking part of Syria. The two opening essays deal with the development of both Judaism and Christianity in Syria in the period after 70 of the Common Era. *Bas ter Haar Romeny* examines the character and make-up of the communities behind the Didache and Matthew. In his opinion, the Didache and Matthew may have been written "in each other's neighbourhood." His interest centers, however, on the question of getting a reliable picture of the communities behind these documents. Should we describe the Matthean and Didache groups as "Christian" as opposed to "Jewish?" He emphasizes the paucity of relevant sources and the tendentious character of those available. From the Edessa example he derives that we must not view these communities as specifically Jewish or Jewish-Christian with their own elaborate theology. A self-aware distinction between sharply defined groups even after 70 C.E. is anachronistic. The emergence of Christianity and rabbinic Judaism as distinct entities was a gradual process of dissimilarity and definition. Whereas literary sources, especially ideological or doctrinal, tend to stress differentiation, it is the epigraphic evidence which suggests a far wider range of common life among Jews and Christians.

Clayton N. Jefford is even more specific with regard to the geographical setting for Matthew and the Didache. He recognizes a relationship between these documents and Ignatius. Ignatius, bishop of Antioch, wrote several letters that are likely to have had a bearing on the Antiochian situation. Jefford not only points to the Syrian Antioch as the setting of the work of the bishop Ignatius, but also identifies this city as the location where Matthew and the Didache achieved their final form. In this context, a problem arises as a result of the specific nature of the respective materials. While the Didache incorporates Jewish traditions and displays a concern for Judaism, Ignatius represents a Pauline, non-Jewish perspective on what it meant to be a Christian. Jefford considers these opposing views as reflecting the diversity of the Antiochian church. They represent tensions at work within the Christian community of Antioch. In his opinion, the Matthean gospel preserving both the Jewish roots and adding missionary materials may have served as a binding element between the two conflicting poles.

In *Part Two* it is again the provenance and origin of the Didache and Matthew which is central but now the starting point is the distinct texts of the writings themselves. The authors move from the literary world of the documents to the real world to which they refer. *Wim Weren* explores the ways in which Matthew reshaped the traditions at his disposal. He distinguishes three phases in the history of the Matthean community corresponding to three stages in the development of the gospel. Interestingly, he connects two remarkable phenomena. Firstly, after the Jewish War (ca. 70-80 C.E.), the community moved from its place of origin in the border area between Lower and Upper Galilee to the district of Caesarea Philippi, to the Golan and the southern part of Syria, where gentile Christianity began. This change of location may have been occasioned by ongoing and intensive conflicts with the Pharisees. Second, the community's relationship to Judaism was changing. While Matthew's community is still embedded within Judaism in the first phase and also during the bitter conflicts with the Pharisees in the penultimate stage of the community's history, it gradually distanced itself from Judaism in the youngest stage (ca. 80-90 C.E.).

Aaron Milavec underlines the essential and intentional unity of Didache as a "well-integrated and self-contained religious system." He looks at the unity of the manual against the cultural background of its time and dates the text to the mid-first century C.E. In his view, the Didache represents a training program for gentile converts who had decisively and irrevocably broken with their previous lifestyle in Graeco-Roman society. The conversion of a gentile who became an adherent of the Jesus movement would involve a process of complete rejection of his or her original social and religious context and a corresponding acquisition of new values, rules and attitudes. According to Milavec, however, the training program reflected in the Didache does not reveal any coherence with Matthew's gospel. In his view, the Didache and Matthew represent two different religious systems. The framers of the Didache might not only have been unaware of the gospel itself but also of those traditions that guided Matthew's community.

In *Part Three* the subject is handled thematically, by consideration of a number of relevant topics in the order of presentation in the Didache. The introduction to these essays is far from comprehensive, but hopefully one which highlights some of the significant content and debate which characterized the Tilburg conference. *Kari Syreeni* compares the Sermon on the Mount (Matt 5-7) and the Two Ways section in *Did.* 1-6. He argues that Chaps. 1-6 in the Didache function as pre-baptismal catechetical instructions for gentiles entering the church. They are exhorted to leave behind traditional gentile standards of morality and instead embrace a more highly developed ethical behaviour. In his opinion, the Doctrina/Didache version and the Barnabas text of the Two Ways may be Christian products without guarantee that their immediate ancestors were purely Jewish documents. Syreeni shows that there are important traditional-historical links between Matthew and the Didache but he, at the same time, ascertains that the paucity of common material in the Sermon on the Mount and *Did.* 1-6 does not support the hypothesis that Matthew might have known some form of the Two Ways tradition. He thinks it unlikely that Matthew's gospel and the Didache were written in the same community in about the same period.

John S. Kloppenborg examines the sayings of Jesus in what is called the *sectio evangelica* of the Didache (*Did.* 1:3b-2:1). Unlike the greater part of the first six chapters of the Didache, this section is a late addition to the Two Ways source of the Didache. The specific themes of this passage remind us of sayings in the Sermon on the Mount in Matthew. The question is whether this evangelical section in the Didache draws on Q, on the Synoptic gospels or on an independent Jesus tradition, that is, material of a Matthean type not derived from the gospels as we have them. No consensus of scholarly opinion has emerged as yet. Kloppenborg applies the insights of recent years in determining what is redactional and what is source material in a gospel, before he reaches conclusions concerning the relationship between the evangelical section of the Didache, the finished gospel and the material behind the gospel. He argues that *Did.* 1:4 evidences Didache's knowledge of Luke's redaction of Q. The verse provides sufficient indication that the compiler of the Didache might have been aware of Q and of the distinctively Lukan transformations of this source. This conclusion has a bearing on the dating of the evangelical section. Its insertion into the Two Ways tradition cannot have occurred much "before the early to mid-second century, when Luke's gospel was in circulation." All this leaves the possibility open, however, that in other cases (*Did.* 8:2; 9:5b; 15:3,4; 16) the Didache might have used pre-synoptic material, resting on a source or sources common to both the Didache and Matthew.

Peter J. Tomson deals with the halakhot concerning fasting and praying in *Did.* 8 and Matt 6. Halakhot reflect a standard of one's behaviour and, in that quality, define one's identity as a Jew. In *Did.* 8 the composer of the Didache denounces a group of opponents before proceeding to the Eucharist prayers of his community. This polemical demarcation *vis à vis* the "hypocrites", which is also found in Matthew, probably reflects the schism between the Didache community and Rabbinic Judaism. The disparaging term "hypocrites" referring to the Pharisees, represents the feelings of animosity in the community of the Didache and Matthew against their adversaries. We are facing a rupture in halakha between two Jewish groups here. The conflict comes down to two points. Firstly, Didache choses Wednesdays and Fridays as fasting days and this position varies from the Pharisees and rabbis, who favoured Mondays and Thursdays. Secondly, both the Didache and Matthew maintain an alternative Jewish tradition as to which prayer was to be recited three times a day. They require the Lord's Prayer to be recited. Tomson points out that in the light of the almost identical versions of the Lord's Prayer in an analogous polemical context, *Did.* 8 and Matt 6:1-18 may well represent the rules of one and the same community at a certain stage in history.

Gerard Rouwhorst focusses his attention on the eucharistic prayers in *Did.* 9-10. He asks how the Eucharist of the Didache relates to the institution narratives in the New Testament. Many scholars dispute the contention that the prayers of *Did.* 9-10 are eucharistic prayers as they do not include the words of institution. The idea, however, that an institution account must be present if a ritual is to be assessed as indisputably eucharistic is merely a preconceived theory of historical development based on common, but later, practice. For what is most common is not necessarily most ancient. According to Rouwhorst, the development of the Eucharist can no longer be reconstructed with the help of indications borrowed from the New Testament institution narratives. This may also be the reason that he did not find striking similarities between the ritual pattern of the meal underlying *Did.* 9-10 and the gospel of Matthew. In any case, it certainly is worth keeping his conclusion in mind that though many passages in the Didache display a clear resemblance with Matthew, this does not hold for the meal prayers of the Didache.

André Tuilier considers the apostles, prophets and teachers appearing in *Did.* 11-13 and in Matthew. He situates the Didache in the period that the three charismatic leadership roles gradually disappeared and an innovation of offices took place at ca. 70-75 C.E. Two considerations are important. First of all, there is the relationship between Matthew and the Didache. Matthew's gospel was an Aramaic compilation of the *logia* (words) of the Lord at the outset. In a later stage, the collection was translated for the sake of the Christian mission to the Greek-speaking peoples in the Hellenistic East. Since the Greek translation of this collection is likely to have initially circulated in various forms, the editor of the Didache, without knowing our canonical gospel of Matthew, may well have had one of these versions at his disposal. This explains the Didache's divergence from readings in Matthew with regard to the Jesus traditions. Another point which requires attention is the following. The decline of the authority and reputation of the itinerant charismatics is, according Tuilier, due to the growing diffusion of the gospel of Matthew. At first, the Aramaic and Greek copies of the gospel supported and supplemented the mission of the charismatics but as time went by, it ultimately was the increasing spread of this gospel which brought about a gradual cessation of the charismatic ministries. The internal dynamics of the gospel radiating the belief in God, altruistic love, confidence in the Spirit and, at the same time, its directives against undisciplined wandering teachers and prophets ushered in a new era where the visiting charismatics became scarce and lost importance.

Huub van de Sandt establishes that the reproof passages in *Did.* 15:3 and Matt 18:15-17 reflect a community's reworking of a kind of rule which has a special parallel in the Manual of Discipline (1QS), a major manuscript found among the Dead Sea Scrolls. A comparison of the correspondences between 1QS 5:23b-6:1b and our reproof passages shows that Matt 18:15-17 and *Did.* 15:3 are connected collaterally, through their dependence on this or a similar Jewish ancestor. Two things are significant. Firstly, the reproof passage in the Didache seems to represent an earlier setting in the development of the tradition than the one in Matthew. The evidence surveyed shows that the Didache and 1QS present similar materials in the same sequence in relatively extensive passages (*Did.* 14:1-15:3 // 1QS 5:10a-6:1) while both writings have almost identical wordings in the clauses with which we are directly concerned (*Did.* 15:3a = 1QS 5:24b-25). Secondly, the materials in Matthew and the Didache represent a revised form of the tradition which is closely related to the one reflected in 1QS. The revised form of the tradition was not due to the peculiar views of the individual authors. The fact that Matthew and the Didache both independently transmuted and rewrote a Jewish reproof tradition akin to Qumran thought was a result of the immediate ties they had with the community where this tradition was transmitted. The injunction may have been altered and adapted within Jewish or Jewish-Christian circles, which maintained highly refined ethical standards.

Joseph Verheyden examines the relationship of *Did.* 16 with the eschatological discourse in Matt 24-25. The hypothesis that the Didache had access to the gospel of Matthew cannot be built upon a mere listing of the parallels, as has sometimes been done in the past. Like Kloppenborg, Verheyden too considers the presence or absence of redactional materials in the Synoptics as decisive for the assessment whether the Didache is familiar with the finished gospels or with traditions behind these gospels. With respect to *Did.* 16 he argues in favour of the Didachist's dependence on the gospel of Matthew and explores the implications of this conclusion for the explanation of the eschatological scenario of Didache's final chapter. Verheyden's reading of *Did.* 16 with an eye on Matthew shows that we are not dealing here with gospel materials that have been cut loose from their original context and freely reused in a variety of ways. He comes to an opposite conclusion. In his opinion, it is difficult to escape the impression that the composer of *Did.* 16 was inspired by Matthew's eschatological scenario to a much greater extent than one would gather from the verbal parallels only.

Jonathan A. Draper's study covers the Didache as a whole. In his opinion, there existed no monolithic, uniform, orthodox Judaism at the end of the first century but rather diverse Judaisms. There was no fundamental distinction between the Didache and Matthew on the one hand and a single unitary Judaism on the other. The word "hypocrite" in *Did.* 8:1-2 is not directed against Judaism but expresses opposition of a Jewish community against the practice of the nascent rabbinic movement. It points to an inner Jewish quarrel. This understanding is crucial in appreciating the next step of Draper's argument. In his opinion, the strong agreements between Matthew and the Didache indicate that these documents come from the same Jewish community at a different stage of development. He settles the question of evolution from one to the other on the basis of internal evidence. Six key terms are analysed which are used with a different valuation in Didache and Matthew. As a result, Draper finds that both documents in their final form represent different stages of development in the process of alienation from Israel. He discovers a gradual transition from a predominantly Jewish-Christian community in the Didache to an increasingly gentile community in Matthew. Moreover, while little polemic against nascent Rabbinism is found in the Didache, the Matthean gospel shows a growing tension felt by the community over the infringement of Pharisaic authority putting them on the sideline. The final rift with Israel has not yet occurred in Didache and Matthew, but the chasm is so deep that "it is certainly on the horizon, even inevitable."

It remains to briefly offer some final observations. Nearly all papers presented in this volume concur that the Didache has significant words, phrases and motifs in common with the gospel of Matthew. As one could have imagined, however, they convey no uniform solution to these similarities. A main obstacle in an attempt to assign Matthew and the Didache to the same milieu appears to be the question whether the composer of the Didache was familiar with the finished gospel of Matthew and other Synoptics *or* with traditions underlying these gospels. Some papers argue that at least some passages in the Didache are dependent on the canonical Matthew and/or Luke (Kloppenborg, Syreeni, Verheyden) while others contend that the Didache and Matthew are related in their dependence on common tradition (Tomson, Tuilier, Van de Sandt, Draper). This issue is important since the second option would provide us with a direct view into a given historical situation or even into the development of the community behind Matthew and the Didache. Once one accepts the Didache's independence of canonical gospel sources, the Didache might reproduce an earlier, simultaneous or later *Sitz im Leben* of the same community as the one reflected in Matthew.

The essays in this volume of course do not agree with all points Flusser and I made in *The Didache*. I will not here respond to, let alone refute, the questions and objections raised by scholars in this volume, since they often do not touch upon the subject. However, one diverging view calls for comment. I refer to those scholars who argue that the community of the Didache (Tomson) or the community of both the Didache and Matthew (Draper) is to be viewed as still embedded within Judaism by the time these writings were edited. Their argument, briefly put, runs as follows. Matthew and the Didache were probably composed after the Jewish war. This is the period when the influence of the rabbis, the successors of the Pharisees, became stronger. The rise of Rabbinism in this period is coupled with the consolidation of the rabbinic academy in Yavne (Jamnia) and occasions the promulgations of legal decisions which laid claim to religious authority. But the decisions made in Yavne were not held as normative everywhere. On the contrary, it is quite conceivable that the members in the community of Matthew and the Didache felt bitter about this attempt of the Jewish central authority to manage their lives and resented the rabbis gaining control of the public sphere. The label "hypocrites" in the polemic sections of Matt 23 and *Did.* 8 is likely to be directed against this particular Jewish group. The best background for interpreting the tension and sense of crisis in the Didache and Matthew is therefore the conflict between this community and emergent Rabbinism.

At first sight, this historical context is a plausible and appealing reconstruction for understanding the disagreement expressed in Matthew and the Didache. Whereas before the Jewish war Judaism exhibited a degree of pluralism which permitted Jewish Christians to exist as one group among many, a fierce tendency toward uniformism appeared in post-70 Judaism under leadership of the rabbis. And indeed, the rabbinic measures in the post-war years were to have a great effect on Judaism as it redefined itself. But how far along was the rabbinic process of unification by the time that the gospel of Matthew and the Didache were written? At the end of the first and the beginning of the second century C.E. the Yavne academy seems to have enjoyed the highest esteem and its decrees probably were accepted by most Israelites as valid and binding.[1] Moreover, at this time the Birkat Ha-Minim, the benediction against the heretics, appears to have been inserted into the liturgy. Jewish Christians are likely to have been a major target of this synagogue denouncement.[2] Is it not possible, then, that at this stage the community of the gospel of Matthew and the Didache shared a consciousness of their views being suppressed by coalescing Judaism in general?

To be more specific, as far as Matthew is concerned, scholarly opinions are much divided in assessing its social setting. For there are indications in the gospel of Matthew displaying a "parting of the ways" between its community and the "synagogue."[3] Matthew sometimes seems to draw a sharp distinction between himself and his community on the one hand and the 'Jews over there' on the other. Nonetheless, the failure to reach unanimity in this respect draws attention to the complexity of the material and to the difficulty of distinguishing sharply delineated groups. We should be alert to the risk of literary sources, especially ideological or doctrinal, tending to stress differentiation and boundaries of separation as a way of keeping the tensions alive (Ter Haar Romeny). Similarly, it is not easy to obtain scientifically justifiable criteria for the evaluation of the evidence in the Didache. Was the community of the Didache a competing group within the larger fabric of Judaism in its day? Or does the term "hypocrites" in this manual reflect the deteriorated relations between the particular Didache community and the Jewish opponents in general?

In my view, the ritual of *Did.* 9-10, which belongs to the same liturgical section (Chaps. 7-10) as the antecedent polemic against the "hypocrites", may shed light on this puzzle in the Didache. It probably expresses practices and beliefs that were commonly accepted within the community. Now, if we pay close attention to the eucharistic prayers, rendered here, a peculiar phenomenon is found. According to a wide scholarly consensus these eucharistic prayers are grafted on the Birkat Ha-Mazon, the Jewish meal prayer. The supplication for the triumphant reunion of the church in *Did.* 9:4 and 10:5 is bound up with the biblical expectation of salvation for the people of Israel. In this respect, the Didache prayer echoes the third benediction of the Birkat Ha-Mazon, in which the people of Israel and the city of Jerusalem are central. The desire for a concrete historical return to Jerusalem was characteristic of the belief of Jews inside and outside the Land of Israel. Jews, though scattered throughout the ancient world, maintained the bond with the motherland and the holy city. Surprisingly, however, the elements like "Israel, your people," "Jerusalem, your city," "Zion," "your altar," "your temple," which constitute the substance of the supplication in the Birkat Ha-Mazon, do not return in the Didache prayer. Apparently, the Christian longing for a gathering of the dispersed church into the kingdom as reflected in the eucharistic

---

[1] See Schürer, *The History of the Jewish People* 1, 524-26.

[2] See Gafni, "The Historical Background," 17-18; Tomson, "The Halakhic Evidence," in this volume, p. 140.

[3] See in this volume the papers of Weren, pp. 53, 62; Tomson, p. 141 and n. 52 and Draper, 221-22 (in his reference to Graham Stanton).

prayers of *Did.* 9-10 does not include the Jewish hope for a restoration of Israel and Jerusalem.[4]

The liturgy of the Didache thus shows indications of a community which has ceased to consider itself a variety of Judaism. What may have caused the congregation to move away from its roots? The Didache obviously was composed for the initiation of gentiles into their community. This already becomes clear in the supplementary long title of the Didache (*Doctrine of the Lord [brought] to the Nations by the Twelve Apostles*) and in the rules concerning baptism. Similarly, the Two Ways doctrine of Chaps. 1-6 apparently is intended as a prescriptive code principally for gentiles who had grown up in households in which pagan gods and pagan standards of morality abounded. In Syria, and particularly in Antioch, a mixture of different peoples, religions and traditions was found. Since the gathering of the church into God's kingdom no longer has any connection with the gathering of Israel in the Didache liturgy, it is not far-fetched to suppose that the conversion of gentiles may have affected the community in the last stage of the development of the Didache, even to the extent of becoming a separate movement. By the time the Didache was composed, many of them were already baptized and adopted in the community.

I would like to acknowledge my indebtedness to Mrs. Eveline Schortinghuis who helped me organize the conference and assisted me in preparing this volume. She has devoted much of her time to the laborious task of creating the Index of Sources. My thanks are also due to Clayton N. Jefford who gave a first evaluation of the conference during the Plenary Session. His contribution has been helpful to me in writing this introduction. I also appreciate the assistance of Alan J.P. Garrow who enthusiastically volunteered to replace one of the speakers unable to attend the conference for health reasons. He recently wrote a dissertation entitled *The Gospel of Matthew's Dependence on the Didache* which has been published as a volume in the JSNT Supplement series.

In the same context, it is appropriate to mention the institutions who provided support and resources. I am grateful to the Tilburg Faculty of Theology for the financial and material support of the conference. Other sponsors whom I am indebted to were the Royal Netherlands Academy of Arts and Sciences (KNAW), the Netherlands Organization for Scientific Research (NWO), and the Netherlands School for Advanced Studies in Theology and Religion (NOSTER).

Huub van de Sandt

---

[4] See Van de Sandt, "The Gathering of the Church in the Kingdom" and compare also Van de Sandt-Flusser, *The Didache*, 33-34, 325-29.

I   Milieu

Chapter One

Hypotheses on the Development of Judaism and Christianity in Syria in the Period after 70 C.E.

Bas ter Haar Romeny *

Faculty of Theology, Leiden University (The Netherlands)

The editor of this volume, Huub van de Sandt, appropriately asked me to write not about "Judaism and Christianity in Syria after 70," but about "theses" or even "hypotheses". The problem of the subject is the lack of direct sources from the period after 70 until about 200. Most descriptions of the period tend to rely to some extent on rabbinic texts and the Church Fathers as sources. However, the church historian who seems to serve us best, Eusebius of Caesarea, wrote his Historia Ecclesiastica at the beginning of the fourth century, at least 200 years after the events. Even the Mishna was not compiled before the beginning of the third century. But the main problem is perhaps not so much the distance in time, but the fact that all sources, also those from the period itself, are written from a certain perspective. This is the perspective of the winning parties: the rabbinic form of Judaism that became prevalent, and the form of Christianity that was adopted as orthodox in the synods called together by Constantine and his successors in the fourth century. Even the ecclesiastical authors from the time before the synods write from this same perspective: others were simply not handed down to us.

This article will discuss some of the difficulties in forming a reliable picture of Jewish and Christian communities in the area and period under review. The search for contemporary evidence that can be connected directly to a city in the area will bring us eventually to the example of Edessa. The situation in this city – and especially the extent of its Hellenization and the origins of the local Church – has been the subject of debate for over a century. However, some recent publications point to additional evidence from an unexpected[1] source, the Syriac translation of the Old Testament. This evidence leads to an adjustment of the hypothesis of a predominantly pagan origin for Edessan Christianity, as it attests to a significant Jewish influence. Together with information from other sources, including some long-neglected inscriptions, it helps us understand the complex reality of life in the small cities of Syria, in which separation from others was an impossible and even undesirable ideal.

---

* The investigations were funded by the Netherlands Organization for Scientific Research (NWO).
[1] That is, the evidence is likely to be overlooked by those who are not at home in the discussions on the origins of the Syriac Bible. Thus the latest treatment of early Christianity and Edessan culture completely ignores it: Ross, *Roman Edessa*, Chapter 6.

The Perspective of the Winners, Other Views, and External Data

The information that we have on perspectives other than those of orthodox Christianity or rabbinic Judaism is based on refutations of such perspectives by other writers, on lucky finds of texts in the dry sand of the desert or jars in caves in the Dead Sea area, and on the pragmatic character of some of the scribes involved in the tradition process. Thus we have Bardaisan's *Dialogue on Fate* (from the beginning of the third century), with its striking combination of Christianity, astrology, and a cosmology in which classical philosophy and Persian ideas seem to come together. This work survived simply because it contained so much information on the laws and customs of different peoples. It would have been a waste to burn it. Its new title, *The Book of the Laws of Countries*, attests to the new interest taken in this "heretical" work. Some other works have come down to us in similar ways. I am thinking in particular of certain Pseudepigrapha and Apocrypha. The problem with all such material, however, is that we often lack a framework for it. It is clear that Judaism, and later also Christianity, consisted in a number of varieties, but how exactly they related to each other, what the sizes of certain movements were, how and when they started or came to an end, or where we should situate them geographically, we often do not know.[2] We have some pieces of a large jigsaw puzzle, but we hardly even know which corner they belong in.

In addition to the problem of how to relate the different movements to each other, there is the problem of anchoring the religious and social development of Jewish and Christian communities in data outside the known corpora of Jewish and Christian literature. Fergus Millar describes the difficulty of finding such data for rabbinic Judaism in the archaeological or documentary record or in references by external observers. For instance, the mixture of city and village names in Syria Palaestina (Judaea) or the Golan is not very different from what we find in the limestone massif of Northern Syria or in the Hauran.[3] It is the negative evidence of the lack of rural temples, together with the emergence of "rabbi", used as a specific title, in inscriptions, and the presence of public buildings that can be identified as Jewish, that helps us out. However, as Goodman observes, if we relied merely on such evidence (as we do for other religions in the Roman Empire), we would remain unaware of any variety within Judaism.[4] For Christian groups in Palestine and Syria, there is hardly any archaeological evidence from before 350[5] – the possibility of a church house at Capernaum being one of the

---

[2] Some questions of method with regard to this variety in Judaism are dealt with by Goodman, *Josephus and Variety*.

[3] Millar, *The Roman Near East*, 379–382.

[4] Goodman, *Josephus and Variety*, 12, and idem, "Jews, Greeks, and Romans," 3–14.

[5] In architecture this can be explained from the fact that before the fourth century, Christian congregations mostly used private houses; only after Christianity became *religio licita* could the basilica form become popular: Tsafrir, "The Development of Ecclesiastical Architecture in Palestine," 1–16. Cf. Sodini, "Les églises de Syrie du Nord," 347–72, and Restle, "Les monuments chrétiens de la Syrie du Sud," 373–84.

few exceptions.[6] In funerary inscriptions, people often showed they had a classical culture without professing or even hinting at their faith.[7]

The problem of connecting texts that give evidence of certain groups or trends to a given place and time is of course not only a problem of lacking external data. The texts themselves are often not very helpful either. For their suggestion of a geographical location for the Didache in rural Syria, Van de Sandt and Flusser have no more to go on in the text itself than an indication of the presence of mountains, an apparent lack of water, the presence of itinerant Christian preachers, the rudimentary character of the community's organizational structure, and an affinity with sayings in the gospel of Matthew.[8] The reference to Matthew is only a relocation of the problem, however. Discussions of the place and time of origin of this gospel often pair speculation with simplification. Thus Kümmel denies a Palestinian origin because the author had intended the work for Greek-speaking Christians.[9] However, what we know about the linguistic situation of Palestine at the end of the first century does not warrant this denial.[10] The arguments for an Antiochene origin, put together by Davies and Allison, form a rather pitiful collection of circumstantial evidence, which impresses the reader more because of its size than its content – as the authors themselves seem to realize.[11] Especially their portrayal of the author as "some sort of scholar," on which basis they make a connection with such legendary figures as Lucian of Antioch, of whom they still suppose that he "had a good command of Hebrew," shows how limited the actual evidence is.[12]

The Importance of the Year 70

My account thus far contains nothing new, but I found it important to start with the above remarks, if only because our picture of history is still so much influenced by the later selection and re-interpretation of the facts and events. Even an issue such as the significance of the year 70, which is relevant to our theme, will reveal that one of the few sources that can be attached to a place and time within the period under discussion has often been read in the light of later re-interpretations. I refer to Josephus' Bellum judaicum and Antiquitates judaicae. Written by a Jew at the end of the first century, the works were quickly adopted by Christian writers who used them for their

---

[6] The identification of a building in Capernaum as a church house is defended in the archaeological report of Corbo, *Cafarnao 1. Gli edifici della città*, 59–111.

[7] Thus, for the Hauran, Sartre-Fauriat, "Culture et société dans le Hauran," 223. See also the discussion of Edessan inscriptions below.

[8] Van de Sandt-Flusser, *The Didache*, 51–52.

[9] Kümmel, *Einleitung in das Neue Testament*, 89–90.

[10] Cf. the surveys of Mussies, "Greek in Palestine and the Diaspora," 1040–64, and Barr, "Hebrew, Aramaic and Greek in the Hellenistic Age," 79–114.

[11] Davies-Allison, *The Gospel according to Saint Matthew* 1, 143–147.

[12] A critical review of sources on Lucian can already be found in: Dörrie, "Zur Geschichte der Septuaginta," 69–87. Cf. the survey of Brennecke, "Lucian von Antiochien," 474–79.

own purposes. Thus we see that Origen (d. ca. 254) developed a clearly anti-Jewish interpretation of the fall of Jerusalem, for which purpose he re-interpreted a number of suitable passages from the *A.J.*[13] His message is that the Jews lost their homeland and their Temple on account of their crimes and their rejection of Jesus. Eusebius of Caesarea (d. ca. 340) followed Origen, but added considerably to the picture. In his book, the events of 70 C.E. have become the proof of the truth of Christianity, and he states that after this year the Jews fell into collective servitude. Eusebius used Josephus' account, carefully selecting the passages that served his purpose and omitting information that did not fit in. The reality is, as we know, that the Jews did suffer disadvantages, especially after the Bar Kokhba revolt, but they were never denied the status of *religio licita*.

Interestingly, it was not only among Christians that the idea took root that the year 70 was a watershed in history. This also happened in rabbinic sources; but as in the case of the Christian sources, we find the idea only long after the actual events. Günter Stemberger recently published a study on the reactions to the destruction of the Temple, paying due attention to the dating of the sources. His conclusion is that earlier sources, including the Mishna and Tosefta, hardly deal with the events of 70. It is mainly in the Talmudim and later Midrashim that the theme of the destruction is given more coverage.[14] There it appears to fit well into the foundation legend of the rabbinic movement. The year 70 not only saw the end of the Temple and its cult (as a result of a number of sins), but also that of the sects. A picture was sketched of a reunited Jewry under rabbinic leadership. It received the consent of Rome and established its own new academy at Yabne.[15] Several institutions could now be defined as replacements of original Jerusalem institutions: thus the council of 72 Elders appeared as the replacement of the Sanhedrin. Prayer had already become important in Judaism, but eventually it came to be seen even as a substitute for the offerings at the Temple.[16] Though it is clear from such later views that the movement of Yabne was a tremendous success, we should keep in mind that its final victory came only much later than the year 70.

Many textbooks still follow the traditional interpretation of the events. A good example is the way the English Schürer[17] deals with the end of the cult in Jerusalem. It sums up the evidence for the cult's continuation: the Letter to the Hebrews, Clement of Rome, the Letter to Diognetus, and Josephus all suggest, for example through their use of the present tense, that in their time – after the destruction of the Temple – the sacrificial cult is still practised. In the end, however, it is declared that in spite of all this,

---

[13] See Schreckenberg, "The Works of Josephus," 315–324, with further references, as well as his detailed study in Schreckenberg-Schubert, *Jewish Historiography and Iconography*, 1–138.

[14] Stemberger, "Reaktionen auf die Tempelzerstörung," 207–236.

[15] A discussion of the formation of these traditions (with an eye to the sociological processes involved) can be found in Overman, *Matthew's Gospel and Formative Judaism*, 35–71.

[16] Cf. Reif, *Judaism and Hebrew Prayer*, 95–102.

[17] Schürer, *The History of the Jewish People* 1, 521–23, which adds "even more direct" statements from the Babylonian Talmud, as well as a reference to Justin (which in my opinion would fit with the standard Christian interpretation of events).

we can be sure that the cult did indeed end in 70. After all, the Mishna *explicitly* states as much (*m. Taʿan.* 4:6). Now if we consider that the Mishna was concluded around 220, and that it had some interest in portraying affairs as it does, this conclusion seems to have been drawn rather hastily. It is clear that Josephus and the other contemporary witnesses also had considerable interests to defend, but I do not see how these could affect the casual remarks just mentioned. It would seem that we should give precedence in this case to the witness of someone who lived at the time rather than to the Mishna – even though it means that we raise a number of new questions: who were those who continued the offerings and where did they do so?[18]

We are dealing with a question of method here. Sources present a perspective on the past and the present. They do give reliable information, in the first place, on how things were *perceived* by the author at the time of writing. A New Testament example: if we see that Matthew points to the Pharisees as Jesus' main enemies, whereas his sources more generally indicate "a crowd," Jews, or at least Sadducees and Pharisees, this does not necessarily mean that he has different information. It shows rather that in Matthew's own situation, the Pharisees were the main adversaries.[19]

Even if newer textbooks become more aware of the vested interests of later Jewish and Christians who wrote history with the intention of portraying themselves as the true and only followers of the ancient tradition, I am afraid that these "interpretations of the winners" will still affect students and scholars, if only because nowadays many people rely on translations, and these translations may be coloured by them. A case in point is the rendering of ἀποδόσθαι in Josephus' Bellum judaicum 7:216. On the basis of Thackeray's translation, it would seem that the emperor "farmed out" all captured Jewish land in Judaea after 70. Also the English Schürer, in its discussion of the instance, talks about "farming out" or "leasing" the land, suggesting that the area was held in possession by the emperor, who would not allow Jews to acquire property any longer.[20] Benjamin Isaac has now shown that the correct interpretation is "to dispose of, to sell" – a much more common meaning of the verb – , and that there is no reason to assume that Jews were not able to buy property as well.[21] Communities and individuals who had not taken part in the revolt were probably not punished: the Romans would not have alienated themselves from everybody. At least not then: it seems that the image of the situation after the Bar Kokhba revolt was projected onto the period between 70 and 132.

I do not, of course, wish to deny that the capture of Jerusalem and the destruction of the Temple had any significance whatsoever. It is clear that changes took place, but as far as we can see, these were more gradual. The diversity within Judaism that leads some scholars to speak even of Judaisms, in the plural, did not immediately come to an

---

[18] In fact, past precedents show that cessation of the cult was not the inevitable consequence of the destruction of the Temple; cf. Guttmann, "The End of the Jewish Sacrificial Cult," 137–48, who assumes at least private sacrifices after 70.

[19] Samples in Overman, *Matthew's Gospel and Formative Judaism*, 78-86.

[20] Schürer, *The History of the Jewish People* 1, 512. 520.

[21] Isaac, "Judaea after A.D. 70," 44–50 / 112–121.

end. There is a growing consensus that outside Palestine it may not have been until the fourth century that the rabbinic Patriarch gained a certain degree of control over the Jewish communities.[22] Justinian's *Novel* 146, issued in 553 and establishing – against the opposition of those who insisted on Hebrew – the option of reading translations in Greek or other languages in synagogues,[23] may be interpreted as an indication that even as late as the sixth century there was considerable opposition to (or within) the rabbinic movement, which had developed a clear preference for Hebrew and Aramaic.

The Example of Edessa

The dearth of archaeological evidence and external sources from before 350 for Christian and Jewish groups in Palestine and Syria forces us to try to interpret the written sources that we have, while proceeding with due caution. What I propose to do here is to look at the situation in the city of Edessa.[24] This is the only town to which we can link, with a reasonable degree of probability, a good number of different sources from the second century and the beginning of the third.[25]

The first question is of course whether the situation in Edessa can serve as a model for other towns in Syria. Though every city was different in its geographical position, its history, and the composition of its population, one should not stress this uniqueness too much. Over the centuries, a number of strong unifying forces had been at work. I am not referring here to the Neo-Babylonian, Persian, Hellenistic, or Roman administrations as such. These empires did not engender the sense of belonging together that we associate with the modern nation state. They functioned more like tax-gathering and conscription systems. However, the way they resettled populations did help to blur regional boundaries. More important still were the trade routes. Edessa was situated at a junction of roads connecting it with Antioch in the west, Nisibis and Singara in the east, and Armenia in the north. From Nisibis the ancient silk road continued to the Far East.[26] Steven Ross voices doubts as to whether the position of Edessa in the silk trade was really very important in the first century.[27]

[22] Dunn, *The Partings of the Ways*, 232 with further references (especially in note 6). Cf. also Alexander, "The Parting of the Ways," 21, and Goodman, "Diaspora Reactions," 28–29.

[23] See Linder, *The Jews in Roman Imperial Legislation*, no. 66, especially section 1.

[24] One of the main sources for Christian Antioch in this period, Ignatius of Antioch, is discussed in Clayton N. Jefford's contribution to this volume. The choice for Edessa excludes the book of Acts as a source; on the contribution of the traditions of this text to our knowledge of the development of Early Christianity, see now the articles in Nicklas-Tilly, *The Book of Acts as Church History*.

[25] A full listing of sources for early Edessan Christianity is found in Brock, "Eusebius and Syriac Christianity," 221–26. See the discussion in the next section. For the town's history in its Roman period, cf. also Fergus Millar's very useful survey "Materials for the History of Roman Edessa and Osrhoene, AD 163–337," in his *The Roman Near East*, 553–62, with, among other things, a reconstruction of the king-list for this period.

[26] On the geographical position of Edessa and the trade routes, cf. Drijvers, *Cults and Beliefs at Edessa*, 9–10, with further references.

[27] Ross, *Roman Edessa*, 15–17.

He reminds us that at the beginning of the Common Era, Isidore of Charax stresses the importance of the route from Zeugma down the Euphrates to Seleucia-Ctesiphon, and from there eastwards. I would counter that the fact that Isidore stressed one route does not necessarily mean that another is less important. It is hard to believe that Edessa could maintain its status as an independent buffer state between the Parthian and Roman Empires without an income generated by trade.[28]

The fact that in Edessa another language was used – Syriac, an Eastern form of late Aramaic, of which the written language was a continuation of Standard Literary Aramaic – should not make us assign a separate position to this town either. Though the use of Syriac was by no means limited to the city of Edessa itself, it is possible to speculate on the use of Syriac as a political instrument, stressing independence from Rome and perhaps a certain allegiance to Parthia. After all, when the influence of Rome increased, it was Maʿnu "Φιλορώμαιος" who from the sixties of the second century minted coins that carried Greek legends, replacing the Syriac coins of his predecessor.[29] From a cultural point of view, however, the use of languages did not mark a boundary in this early period. As in the other cities of the Syrian-Mesopotamian desert, bilingualism must have been widespread, and extensive translation work from Greek to Syriac and from Syriac to Greek was carried out from early days.

The use of the Syriac language is one of the issues in a wider debate on the question of whether Edessa can be considered a Hellenized town. Warwick Ball has recently stated that its Hellenization "was never more than skin deep," that "the city and region remained fundamentally Semitic in character," and that it was "a counterbalance of the Hellenic culture of Antioch."[30] However, such a simplistic scheme – either Hellenic or Semitic – does not do justice to reality. Ball can only maintain it by leaving important data out of consideration. Thus he calls the Edessan thinker Bardaisan "one of the most important philosophers of the Semitic East," without telling us that what we know about his thought betrays a local philosophical milieu with substantial knowledge of Greek philosophy.[31] The *Book of the Laws of Countries* mentioned above is actually written in the form of a Platonic dialogue. Fergus Millar's characterization of Edessan culture as a "non-Mediterranean descendant of Greek culture," which was severely criticized by Ball, is therefore much closer to the truth.[32] With this classification, Millar does not deny the importance of non-Greek elements in Edessan culture. Such elements, whether indicative of cultural continuity or of the importation of new elements from

---

[28] On the basis of the fact that Edessa's wealth is best visible in archaeological evidence from the period of Abgar VIII and his successor, we may perhaps conclude that their reign was a golden era, as Ross does (see also *Roman Edessa*, 84); it does not prove, however, that Edessa was doing less well under Abgar V.

[29] A full discussion of Edessa's coins is found in an appendix to Ross' *Roman Edessa*.

[30] Ball, *Rome in the East*, 89. 92.

[31] Unfortunately, this is not the only problem that mars this book. All sorts of anachronistic concerns and ideas pop up even in the most unlikely places. Is Ball serious when on page 2 of *Rome in the East* he calls Trajan "a Spaniard" and when in note 266 to page 93 (on p. 464) he suggests that "the Jewish lobby" were behind Abgar V aiding Nabataea against Herod Antipas?

[32] Millar, *The Roman Near East*, 472. Ball (*Rome in the East*, n. 238 to p. 89, on p. 464) criticizes Millar for distorting Daniel Schlumberger's phrase "descendants non-méditerranéens de l'art grec;" however, Millar clearly indicates that he is adapting the phrase and that Schlumberger refers to art only.

Parthia or from the desert,[33] are clearly present. The point is precisely that Hellenism as it emerges in sources after the Hellenistic period in the strict sense is characterized by a symbiosis of elements. Greek thought could be expressed in a Semitic language, as is the case with Bardaisan, and adherence to non-Greek religions could equally be expressed in Greek. Such a coexistence, or even a mix, of traits was found in Edessa as it was in other parts of Syria and also in Galilee, the variety of forms stemming from the emphasis given to one ingredient or the other in the cultural fusion.[34] In this sense we may indeed call Edessa "as Hellenized as the rest of Syria," as Han Drijvers did.[35]

Though less extreme, Steven Ross' criticism of Drijvers' characterization is ultimately also based on an "either-or" scheme, just like Ball's criticism of Millar. Ross speaks of a cultural orientation either towards the West or the East, and concludes that for all Hellenistic influences, "in language and in outlook Edessa remained a Mesopotamian city for many years after officially becoming a 'Roman' one." Only under Abgar VIII did a "wave of what might be called 'Westernization'" begin, and did the communion "with the peoples of the desert and elsewhere in the Semitic Middle East" become less important.[36] It is true that our main evidence for the public and private use of Greek in Edessa dates from after the sixties of the second century.[37] There is, however, no evidence for a separate "Mesopotamian" culture before that time. The city was re-founded by Seleukos I Nicator. The allegiance to the Parthians did not imply a total breach with the past: the structure of Seleucid rule and probably various elements of their culture were retained. Besides, as Ross himself concedes, Edessa had always been dominated to some extent by Antioch, even before the political border was erased.[38] And if Bardaisan's work suggests "the existence of a tradition of Edessan literature probably extending over much of the second century and even earlier," as Ross says,[39] one might wonder where Bardaisan picked up his knowledge of Greek thought, if not in a likewise already existing school system.

With Ross, we can therefore conclude that neither the political barrier between the Roman and Parthian spheres of influence, nor the regional dominance of Syriac as both official language and vernacular, constituted a hindrance to the interchange of ideas.[40] The intellectual developments that took place in the Graeco-Roman area could reach Edessa via the trade routes, just as ideas from Edessa could travel back to Antioch and other places in Western Syria. The universalist tendencies in Judaism and Christianity themselves make it even more difficult to restrict developments within these religions to certain places in the Fertile Crescent. What we can learn from the example of Edessa might therefore help us to understand the situation elsewhere in Syria.

---

[33] On the difficulties of determining the nature of the culture of Syrian cities of the Achaemenid and Hellenistic age, see Millar's "The Problem of Hellenistic Syria," 110–133.
[34] Goodman, *State and Society in Roman Galilee*, 175.
[35] Drijvers, "Syrian Christianity and Judaism," 139.
[36] Ross, *Roman Edessa*, 115–117.
[37] Brock, "Greek and Syriac in Late Antique Syria," 151–52.
[38] Ross, *Roman Edessa*, 116; cf. also 123.
[39] *Ibid.*, 137.
[40] *Ibid.*, 123

Judaism and the Origins of Christianity in Edessa: Drijvers' Reconstruction

The fact that we have a number of sources for Edessan Christianity in the second century does not mean, unfortunately, that there is agreement even on the general framework in which they should fit. The widespread opinion is that Christianity in Edessa had close links with Judaism. It would have been through the Jewish communities that Christianity spread eastward. This idea is sometimes formulated in a down-to-earth fashion, sometimes in a more romantic way. Representatives of the latter approach are Vööbus and Murray, who suggest that Syriac Christianity was an island in splendid isolation from Hellenism, preserving a pure and untouched original form of Christianity.[41] The matter-of-fact approach can be found, for example, in the works of Jacob Neusner. He suggests that the two new groups formed in the heart of Palestinian Judaism, rabbinic Judaism and Christianity, competed to win over the Jews of the oriental diaspora, spreading eastward along the same channel of the trade route.[42] A different opinion is found mainly in the works of Han Drijvers. He advocates the opinion that Syriac-speaking Christianity in Edessa and further to the East was mainly of gentile origin: the Jews are hardly mentioned in the earliest sources.[43] Let us have a look at these ourselves.

The first person we could mention is Tatian, a pupil of Justin Martyr, who returned from Rome to his homeland Syria in 177. In his Oratio ad Graecos 42[44] he describes himself as someone who "philosophizes in the manner of the barbarians, born in the land of the Assyrians, educated first on your principles, secondly in what I now profess." This sentence shows that self-defining statements are sometimes difficult to decode. The barbarian philosophy must be Christianity, and the word "Assyrians" refers simply to the inhabitants of the province of Syria.[45] The education this man with his Latin name received was clearly Hellenistic. Whether he came from Edessa itself cannot be ascertained; there is no doubt, however, that his ideas and his work exerted a considerable influence there.[46] Significant for his theology is the idea that salvation can be reached through austere sexual asceticism, ἐγκράτεια. This is the way to undo the fall and regain immortality.[47] This was also the guiding principle in the composition

---

[41] Vööbus, *History of Asceticism in the Syrian Orient*, 4; Murray, for instance in "The Characteristics of the Earliest Syriac Christianity," 3–16.

[42] Neusner, *A History of the Jews in Babylonia* 1, 166–69, and Idem, *Aphrahat and Judaism*, 1–2.

[43] Drijvers advocates this opinion in a number of articles. Below I follow mainly his latest full statement on the issue, "Syrian Christianity and Judaism". His more recent review of some publications dealing with the matter is also of importance: "Early Syriac Christianity," 159–177.

[44] Text in Whittaker (ed.), *Tatian: Oratio ad Graecos*, 76.

[45] Thus Millar, *The Roman Near East*, 227. 460, following Nöldeke, " Ἀσσύριος Σύριος Σύρος," 465. A different view is found in Beyer, *Die aramäischen Inschriften*, 7, who still assumes that the indication "Assyrian" refers to an eastern Mesopotamian origin, but gives no arguments to support this position.

[46] On the popularity of the Diatessaron in Syria, cf. Petersen, *Tatian's Diatessaron*, 432–33.

[47] Drijvers, "Syrian Christianity and Judaism," 129–30. Emily J. Hunt (*Christianity in the Second Century*, 144–75) may be right in denying Tatian's membership of an Encratite *sect*; his ascetic ideals, she admits, are indisputable. Whether these belonged to a general "spirit of asceticism" in second century Syriac Christianity, as she contends, or formed the source of inspiration of such spirit, can in my opinion no longer be established. Note, however, that Bardaisan is not known as an ascetic.

– perhaps in Greek, but more probably in Syriac[48] – of his Diatessaron, in which the four gospels are made into one story.

The Diatessaron is witness to the fact that Marcionism was a very strong force in Syria. Tatian's work is an effort to smooth out contradictions between the four gospels and to offer an alternative to the selection made by Marcion himself, who retained only parts of Luke and the Pauline letters.[49] I would add that the problem of the position of the Old Testament, made acute by Marcion, dominated exegesis for quite a long time in the whole area. On the basis of our textbooks, it might seem that Marcionism was something that came up in the beginning of the second century and was dealt with within that century. The truth is, however, that Theodoret of Cyrrhus in the fifth century was still preoccupied with the Marcionite communities in the villages around Antioch.[50] On the one hand, the Old Testament was necessary: it showed that Christianity was not something completely new. Judaism was an ancient and therefore venerable religion, and it was also recognized as a *religio licita*. It was important for Christians to prove to the authorities, but also to Jews and non-Jews attracted to Judaism who might be won over (or had been won over but might lapse), that they stood in this tradition, and were in fact the only true followers of it. On the other hand, much of the content matter of the Old Testament seemed either to have been superseded by the gospel, or to be no longer compatible with the Hellenistic world-view that pre-dominated even in the remotest corners of Palestine and Syria. Moreover, especially the prescription of circumcision was impractical for winning over possible converts.

The work of Bardaisan (154–222), already mentioned above, also attests to the strength of Marcionism in Syria. In a Platonic dialogue, Bardaisan explains the role of free will. There is one God, who is at the same time creator and saviour. As a good God, he had to grant humankind a free will that was stronger than fate (as indicated in the stars) and the laws of nature. He is not to blame for the fact that people did not use this free will according to his desire, which was that man's conduct should be good and just. Therefore, the creator is not an evil deity. In Bardaisan's view, Jesus is the divine logos that was the main agent in the creation. At the same time he is the divine teacher who explains how to use free will in the right manner. As in the theology of Tatian, who also stressed the possibility of free will undoing what went wrong at the beginning, incarnation and crucifixion play no role.[51]

---

[48] Petersen, *Tatian's Diatessaron*, 384–97. 428.

[49] Drijvers, "Syrian Christianity and Judaism," 130–31. Cf. also his "Marcionism in Syria," 153–72.

[50] Cf. Von Harnack, *Die Mission und Ausbreitung des Christentums*, 931–32.

[51] Drijvers, "Syrian Christianity and Judaism," 131–32. Unfortunately, recent publications show a trend of unwarranted simplification when dealing with Bardaisan. The assessment of the different sources for Bardaisan's teaching was the subject of what Drijvers calls a "paper war" between him and Taeke Jansma, who wrote the study *Natuur, lot en vrijheid* in reply to Drijvers' *Bardaiṣan of Edessa*. For this point, see Drijvers, "Early Syriac Christianity: Some Recent Publications," 169, with further references. One cannot dismiss Ephrem's evidence out of hand as Emily Hunt does (*Christianity in the Second Century*, 166–68), even though one readily accepts her suspicion of heresiologists. Ross' discussion of Bardaisan (*Roman Edessa*, 119–23. 126–27) is only slightly more profound.

It is possible, and according to Drijvers even probable, that also the Acts of Judas Thomas and even the gospel of Thomas were connected with Edessa. Their asceticism and many theological concepts, including the stress on abstinence from sex as the key to immortality, are in the style of Tatian, and the New Testament quotations in the *Gos. Thom.* have been related to his Diatessaron.[52]

It appears, then, that Marcionites, followers of Bardaisan, and Encratite Christians dominated Christianity in the Edessa region in the second century.[53] These groups were either clearly anti-Jewish, like the Marcionites, or simply did not mention any connection with the Jews in their writings. Then where does the idea of a Jewish connection come from? In part, it is a remnant of an older theory that connected the beginnings of Syriac Christianity with the Jewish Kingdom of Adiabene, further to the East. This theory found confirmation in the so-called *Chronicle of Arbela*. Nowadays, however, this chronicle is considered problematic, if not simply the product of a falsification. Newer theories connect Edessa itself with Judaism, and more precisely, with Jerusalem. This idea is based on the Abgar legend, which was first attested in Eusebius of Caesarea's Historia Ecclesiastica, but which found its final form in the fifth-century *Doctrina Addai*.[54]

The legend uses the motif of the conversion of the King. King Abgar (the name of many of Edessa's kings) is ill, and decides to send an embassy to Jerusalem to ask Jesus to come and heal him. In Edessa there is room enough for Jesus, and he would be safe from the Jews. The messengers find Jesus in the house of the High Priest in Jerusalem. Jesus replies that he is awaited in Heaven, but promises to arrange for a disciple to be sent to Abgar. This indeed happens: after the Ascension, Judas Thomas sends the apostle Addai (Thaddaeus in Eusebius, who did not know of any Addai among the 70). When he arrives in Edessa, he stays with Tobias, a Jew from Palestine, until Abgar hears of his arrival and invites him to the court. Addai heals the King and some of his nobles, and is granted the opportunity to deliver a speech to the full population of Edessa. As a result, many people convert to Christianity, including a number of pagan priests and Jews. The legend as we find it in the *Doctrina Addai* seems to have propagandistic aims relevant to the fifth century.[55] According to Drijvers, however, the original version

---

[52] Drijvers, "Syrian Christianity and Judaism," 132–33. Drijvers assumes a dependence of the gospel of Thomas on the Diatessaron. This was also suggested by Baarda, "Thomas and Tatian," 49. A strong plea for the idea is now found in Perrin, *Thomas and Tatian*. According to William Petersen, the dependence of the Diatessaron on *Gos. Thom.* or of *Gos. Thom.* on the Diatessaron is a puzzle that still defies solution: *Tatian's Diatessaron*, 298–300.

[53] Drijvers builds on Bauer's partial reversal of the traditional sequence unbelief – orthodoxy – heresy, as "heresy" apparently comes before "orthodoxy". Cf. Bauer, *Rechtgläubigkeit und Ketzerei*, esp. 6–48 on Edessa. Note, however, that Drijvers does not agree with the way Bauer applies the terms of orthodoxy and heresy in a normative-doctrinal way to the historical evidence, with the details of Bauer's construction of early Edessan Christianity, nor with the role given to Rome as sponsor of orthodoxy; see Drijvers, "Rechtgläubigkeit und Ketzerei," 291–308.

[54] Drijvers, "Syrian Christianity and Judaism," 138–39; see also Idem, "Edessa und das jüdische Christentum," 30–31.

[55] These interests include the position of Edessan nobility and a link with the see of Rome, according to Brock, "Eusebius and Syriac Christianity," 227–28. Alain Desreumaux, however, thinks of Monophysite concerns: "La doctrine d'Addaï," 73–79. See now Griffith, "The Doctrina Addai as a Paradigm of Christian Thought."

was an anti-Manichaean tract.[56] Addai was one of Mani's main apostles in the third century. The legend redefines him as a Christian. The link with Jerusalem and the High Priest helps to show that Christianity is older and therefore more prestigious than Manichaeism. The Jews play a double role in the legend, Drijvers explains: on the one hand they are the crucifiers, on the other hand, the contention is made, through the High Priest, the Jew Tobias, and the conversions, that Christianity is connected with Judaism in a positive sense. It is this positive connection that is at the basis of the theory of the Jewish origin of Christianity in Edessa. The trouble is, however, that these remarks may very well be a case of propaganda, the intended audience being Jews or, more probably, Christians attracted to Judaism. The legend shows them that Jesus was staying with the High Priest himself – so what could be wrong with him? – and that wise Jews converted after hearing the gospel.[57]

A second argument for the assumed close connection between Judaism and Edessan Christianity can be found in the Jewish traditions in the later literature of the Syriac Church.[58] One could refer to the various Apocrypha and Pseudepigrapha handed down in Syriac. It is difficult to say, however, when exactly these were translated and by whom. Though in general it seems that the translations were made before the fourth century, from Greek originals, this does not tell us much about their reception. There are always exceptions to the rule, of course: thus the Syriac Wisdom of Solomon betrays the kind of Encratite Christian milieu already mentioned.[59] The *Cave of Treasures*, which quotes from Jewish Adam literature and various other non-rabbinic traditions, may go back to a Jewish-Christian milieu, but its present, probably sixth-century form does not enable us to conclude anything with regard to the whereabouts and period of activity of this group.

More pertinent data can be found in writers such as Ephrem and Aphrahat: in these fourth-century Syriac writers we find a number of Jewish traditions with parallels in rabbinic texts, as well as some comparable material possibly originating in non-rabbinic Jewish sources.[60] The genre of Ephrem's commentary is also noteworthy. It has more in common with the Genesis Apocryphon of Qumran than with the rabbinic midrashim[61] or the Christian commentaries from the Antiochene School.[62] Another case in point is perhaps Aphrahat's Christology. In one statement, Jesus is portrayed as a man, comparable to Moses or Solomon. William Petersen has argued that this points to Jewish-Christian traditions, such as we find also in the Pseudo-Clementine Recognitions.[63] Both Aphrahat and Ephrem also employ phraseology known from the Palestinian Targum tradition, as do the Syriac Old Testament, the Diatessaron and the Vetus Syra.[64] Ephrem and others even have a number of quotations that go against the Peshitta, the Syriac translation of the Bible, but agree with one or more Targumim.[65]

[56] Drijvers, "Facts and Problems," 157–75; and Idem, "Addai und Mani," 171–85.

[57] Drijvers, "Jews and Christians at Edessa," 88–102; cf. also his "Syrian Christianity and Judaism," 139.

[58] Drijvers, "Syrian Christianity and Judaism," 140.

[59] Drijvers, "The Peshitta of Sapientia Salomonis," 15–30.

[60] Cf. Brock, "Jewish Traditions in Syriac Sources," 212–32.

[61] See Janson, *De Abrahamcyclus in de Genesiscommentaar*, 240–41.

[62] Van Rompay, "Antiochene Biblical Interpretation," 101–23.

[63] Petersen, "The Christology of Aphrahat," 241–56; Idem, "Constructing the Matrix," 126–44.

[64] Brock, "A Palestinian Targum Feature in Syriac," 271–82.

[65] See on these Targum readings now Weitzman, *The Syriac Version of the Old Testament*, 137–39, with further references.

Drijvers seems to have no problem in incorporating such use of Jewish or Jewish-Christian traditions in his theory of a predominantly gentile origin of Edessan Christianity. The Christian minority group that resisted Marcion's solution of the problem of the position of the Old Testament was simply compelled to deal with Jewish material without identifying themselves with Judaism, he argues. There was an urge to adapt the Old Testament and other Jewish traditions to their own ideological concepts.[66] Sebastian Brock noted a number of objections, however.[67] His first point, the fact that Palestinian Targum features can be found as early as the Diatessaron, would not seem to hurt Drijvers' theory: in the latter's opinion, the Diatessaron was part of the anti-Marcionite efforts. The later occurrences, in Aphrahat and Ephrem, are somewhat more problematic because of the antagonistic relations between Jews and Christians in the fourth century. Against this point, Drijvers has argued that this antagonism, at least until the end of the fourth century, did not prevent Christians from initiating contacts with Jews.[68] It is Brock's third objection that brings Drijvers into serious trouble: it may be true that the Christians of Edessa needed a version that was different from the Hebrew text and the Aramaic Targumim which were in use among the Jews; it is, however, very unlikely that gentile Christians would have been able to produce the Old Testament Peshitta, a version based on the Hebrew text rather than the Greek Septuagint.

The Community behind the Peshitta: Weitzman's Theory

The origin of the Peshitta is a matter of debate. Already at the beginning of the fifth century, Theodore of Mopsuestia was complaining that the translator was unknown, and that he invented a lot of stories.[69] The fact that one had to guess where the Peshitta came from might betray that the real origin was not within the orthodox Syrian Christian community itself. Over the past two centuries, some scholars have defended Jewish authorship, others Christian, whereas the famous linguist Theodor Nöldeke came up with the compromise that Jewish Christians were behind the work.[70] Drijvers suggests Christian authorship, but this idea is based on the translation of the Wisdom of Solomon, which may have been done at a later stage, from a Greek text. The main problem for Drijvers' theory is the fact that the Peshitta Old Testament was a direct translation from a proto-Masoretic Hebrew original. It even betrays an excellent knowledge of the language.

[66] Drijvers, "Syriac Christianity and Judaism," 140–41.
[67] Brock, "A Palestinian Targum Feature in Syriac," 281–82.
[68] Drijvers, "Jews and Christians at Edessa," 97–102
[69] Ter Haar Romeny, "The Peshitta and its Rivals," 21–31.
[70] A survey of the discussion with further references can be found in Dirksen, "The Old Testament Peshitta," 261–64. For the idea of a Jewish-Christian translation, see also Van der Kooij, *Die alten Textzeugen des Jesajabuches*, 273–77.

The Christian authors we are familiar with did not know Hebrew: Origen did not, and neither did Eusebius of Emesa (d. ca. 359), the first ecclesiastical author to posit the idea of *Hebraica veritas*, in the fourth century. He thought that the Syriac Bible, which he knew from his youth in Edessa, would help him to correct the Septuagint, as Syriac was, in his words, "a neighbour of Hebrew."[71] Jerome was really an innovator and an exception in that he took up this idea and followed it through.[72] He probably learned Hebrew in Chalcis in the Syrian desert. Among Jews in the Greek diaspora of Egypt and Italy, knowledge of Hebrew was already very limited or even absent in the first century. Even the Bible commentaries of a learned man like Philo do not betray a knowledge of Hebrew. So how would Christians of the second century – the Peshitta is already quoted in the Diatessaron, it would seem[73] – have been able to translate the Hebrew Bible in this way? And why did they not translate the Septuagint, as did all other non-Greek churches? On the other hand, if Jews made the translation, why do Jewish scholars not quote it until the end of the Middle Ages?

The most thorough and innovative discussion of the origin of the Peshitta is that of the late Michael Weitzman. In his *Introduction* to this Syriac version he defends the idea that the Peshitta was translated from 150 onwards by a non-rabbinic Jewish group that clearly identified themselves with Judaism, but neglected some elements of ritual in favour of a more personal belief, in which prayer played an important role.[74] They emphasized faith and hope rather than observance. Weitzman's main arguments come from the translation of Chronicles. It happens that most of the Peshitta is a very literal translation that hardly betrays its origin. In Chronicles, however, we find some instances that are completely different from the Hebrew text as we know it. Weitzman suggests that the translator or translators had to deal with a damaged manuscript. Here and there, the *Vorlage* was simply unreadable, which forced them to fill the gaps themselves, thus bringing in their own ideas and concerns. As Chronicles was probably the last book to be translated, its seems reasonable to attribute the whole translation to this group, rather than the first parts to Christians and only the latter part to this Jewish group.

Weitzman reconstructs the history of the version as follows. Instead of assuming a Jewish group that lapsed from some pre-existing rabbinic standard, he thinks the origins of the translators' religion go back to biblical times. Sacrifice was prescribed twice daily in the Pentateuch, and prayer was not prescribed. It is possible, however, that Levites developed an independent prayer-cult "evening and morning and noon-day," as Ps 55:18 (17) has it. If this cult was already established in the provinces before the exile, it may have been accompanied by sacrifice, but this must have been abolished later on. In any

---

[71] Ter Haar Romeny, *A Syrian in Greek Dress*.

[72] Kamesar, *Jerome, Greek Scholarship, and the Hebrew Bible*.

[73] Brock, "Limitations of Syriac in Representing Greek," 97–98. This position is strongly advocated by Joosten, "The Old Testament Quotations," 55–76. Shedinger, *Tatian and the Jewish Scriptures*, pleads against it. In his review of the latter book William L. Petersen assumes a neutral position (*Hugoye* [http://syrcom.cua.edu/hugoye] 6.2 [2003], par. 3), though he makes it clear that Shedinger's work cannot be considered a serious contribution to the discussion on the issue.

[74] Weitzman, *The Syriac Version of the Old Testament*, 206–62.

case, the book of Daniel, where Daniel is said to have prayed in the direction of Jerusalem "three times a day" (Dan 6:11), and Chronicles, which traces psalmody and the Levitical choirs back to David, at the origin of the Temple, indicate that the importance of regular prayer was recognized in the period of the Second Temple.[75]

Forms of prayer-cult that were meant as a substitute for the sacrificial cult, as in Qumran and rabbinic Judaism, were aligned with the intervals within which the sacrifices had to be offered.[76] Therefore prayer was offered only twice a day in these communities. The original prayer-cult – three times a day at specified hours, without connection to sacrifice, as Weitzman claims – survived especially in the Diaspora.[77] It appealed to God-fearers and full converts among the gentiles, and also became the rule among Christians, for whom it is recorded as early as in the Didache (8:3). The fact that Acts 10:30 ascribes praying at the ninth hour to Cornelius, at that moment a God-fearer rather than a Christian, would confirm that the Christian observance of fixed hours originated in certain non-rabbinic currents of Judaism.[78] It is also this system that is central to the Peshitta. Weitzman holds the opinion that it tended to depreciate not only sacrifice, but also ritual in general. Instead, it emphasizes inward faith. Weitzman sees the beginnings of this movement in the book of Proverbs in the Hebrew Bible. Independently, the translators of the Peshitta introduced more passages reflecting the same attitude, especially in Chronicles. Weitzman goes on to suggest that a Jewish community that confined itself in its obedience to the law to the prayer-cult could have adopted Christianity. With many Christians they shared a high appreciation for prayer, charity, and faith. This would then explain how a Jewish translation came to be transmitted by the Eastern Churches, and why it was not received among rabbinic Jews.[79]

Though I share Weitzman's view that non-rabbinic Jews must have been responsible for the translation, I think we should make at least one adjustment to his reconstruction. He suggests that these Jews belonged to a community of a certain non-rabbinic signature, "estranged from the Jewish people as a whole."[80] The question is, however, whether it is at all possible to distinguish such a separate community. As Reif stresses with regard to the development of Jewish liturgy: we should think more in terms of dominant religious trends than of watertight, discrete groups occupying separate contexts. There was a variety of forms which were never mutually exclusive or beyond reciprocal influence.[81] As noted above, outside Palestine it may not have been until the fourth century that the rabbinic Patriarch gained a certain degree of control over the Jewish communities, and

---

[75] *Ibid.*, 258–59.

[76] The evidence for Qumran does indeed appear to corroborate Weitzman's picture of prayer twice a day as a replacement for Temple sacrifice, cf. Falk, *Daily, Sabbath, and Festival Prayers*, 47. 87. 123–124; and Nitzan, "The Dead Sea Scrolls and the Jewish Liturgy," 198 and 207. For rabbinic Judaism, the picture seems to be more complicated. It must be conceded that it took a number of centuries for the precise injunctions regarding prayer to be finally settled; rabbinic Judaism was not monolithic, and certainly not in its first centuries (see Reif, *Judaism and Hebrew Prayer*, 66–68. 88–121).

[77] Weitzman, *The Syriac Version of the Old Testament*, 212–14.

[78] *Ibid.*, 213.

[79] *Ibid.*, 258–62.

[80] *Ibid.*, 246.

[81] Reif, *Judaism and Hebrew Prayer*, 61.

even after that all sorts of non-rabbinic trends could remain active. Thus if one follows Weitzman's theory, it is not necessary to think in terms of a community that was clearly separated from other Jews of Edessa. Before we conclude, however, we should examine the evidence for the presence of Jews in Edessa. It will appear that this may lead to a further modification of the picture.

The Evidence from Inscriptions: An Alternative Hypothesis

The main evidence for the presence of Jews in Edessa in our period is formed by four rather neglected funerary inscriptions found at Kırk Mağara, close to the city itself.[82] On the basis of the ratio between pagan and Jewish funerary inscriptions, Drijvers suggests that about ten percent of the population was Jewish.[83] The inscriptions in Old Syriac from the region are all pagan, it seems.[84] As far as we can see, Jews who could afford a burial site with an inscription used the square Jewish Aramaic script that was also used for Hebrew,[85] while adding, in one case, a Greek inscription. The Aramaic[86] used shows on the one hand a feature shared by Old and Classical Syriac (the demonstrative pronoun *hn'*), on the other hand also a form typical of Jewish Babylonian Aramaic (the construct state *by* for *byt*, "house"[87]). One would stretch the limitations of the evidence much too far if one assumed that Jews were using a dialect different from that of pagans and Christians – as was the case in more recent days in some regions of northern Iraq, north-west Iran, south-eastern Turkey, Armenia, and Georgia, where Jews and Christians used different dialects of North-Eastern Neo-Aramaic.[88] The choice for the Jewish script is significant, however. In contrast to other

---

[82] Pognon, *Inscriptions sémitiques de la Syrie*, nos. 40–43 with pl. XXII; re-edited by Frey, *Corpus inscriptionum iudaicarum*, nos. 1415–1418. The dating of these inscriptions cannot be established with certainty. Their context would seem to suggest that they are from different dates in the second century and perhaps the beginning of the third. Pognon cautiously leaves a wider margin: from the first to the fourth century.

[83] Drijvers, "Jews and Christians at Edessa," 90; in "Syrian Christianity and Judaism" he mentions a figure of 12 percent; on the basis of the known numbers of inscriptions, 7 or 8 percent would be more realistic.

[84] One inscription bears the name John (*ywḥnn*): As10:2, 5, in Drijvers-Healey, *The Old Syriac Inscriptions of Edessa and Osrhoene*. The editors rightly remark that this does not prove that the text is Christian. The content of most inscriptions gives no certainty with regard to the religious background of the person who commissioned them, as we have seen above; the same is true, however, for their names. One of the persons mentioned in the inscriptions is called Seleukos, son of Izates – not a typically Jewish name. At the same time, we find the (Jewish or Christian) name Jacob in graffiti in pagan temples in Dura-Europos: Kraeling-Welles, *The Christian Building*, 111.

[85] On this script, see Klugkist, *Midden-Aramese Schriften*, 206–10, and Naveh, *Early History of the Alphabet*, 162–72. The script is best comparable to that of nos. IV (Murabba'at 42) and VI (liturgical fragment on parchment, Dura-Europos) of fig. 77 in the former work.

[86] J.B. Segal assumed – probably on the basis of the script – that the texts were in Hebrew: *Edessa: "The Blessed City"*, 27. 30. 42. He was followed by Drijvers, "Edessa und das jüdische Christentum," 11; "Jews and Christians at Edessa," 90; "Syrian Christianity and Judaism," 138; "Early Syriac Christianity: Some Recent Publications," 174.

[87] Also found in Hatran and in one Old Syriac inscription (As59:3). In earlier Aramaic *by* is sometimes found as the absolute state.

[88] Khan, "Some Remarks on Linguistic and Lexical Change," 179–80.

scripts, the Jewish script was not connected with a certain region or language, but with a religious group. Though it is theoretically possible that there were also Jews who adopted the Syriac script, we have clear evidence that there were at least some who chose to indicate their religious identity in this way in their funerary inscription, while one Jewish family simultaneously professed its allegiance to Greek culture by adding a Greek version of the text.

From the Classical Syriac as we know it from later Christian sources, we may infer that Edessan Christians adopted the Old Syriac dialect and script that were used by the pagans, rather than the Jewish script. This confronts us with the paradox of a translation that must have been made by Jews but was not written in the Jewish script. Was the Peshitta a gentile project, after all, or should we assume that, perhaps together with an update of the language, the translation was recast in Syriac script? I would suggest an alternative: the translators may have been Jewish Christians from the start.[89] Weitzman deals with this possibility in only two sentences: he says the sorrow at the plight of the Jews in exile as expressed in some passages in Chronicles, is unlikely for a Jewish Christian. Furthermore, he contends that Jewish Christianity is characterized by the retention of Jewish law, which is not typical of Peshitta Chronicles, rather than by what he calls "Jewish national identification."[90] I am not convinced. Peshitta Chronicles does not argue against the law as such; it just shows indifference to rabbinic halakha. The idea that the law retains its value but should be interpreted in a different way would fit very well in a community such as that of Matthew. The identification with the Jewish people, which is found in combination with a strongly negative attitude towards the body of Israel that has not followed the right teaching, as well as the positive attitude towards the nations and to proselytes, would all fit in. In fact, the pattern of prayer three times a day at set hours (the third, sixth, and ninth hours) would perhaps fit better in a Christian community than in a Jewish one: it is in Christian sources that we find this pattern for the first time in its full form.[91] The evidence that Weitzman gives for the occurrence of the pattern in Second Temple Judaism is rather thin: the statement in Dan 6:11 that Daniel prays three times a day may be meant as a proof that Daniel is a pious man; the "evening and morning and noon" of Ps 55:18 (17) may simply indicate "all the time;" and Acts 10:30, though ascribing praying at the ninth hour to a God-fearer rather than a Christian, is itself a Christian source. Besides, it does not mention the third and the ninth hour.

Returning to the question of the community behind the Peshitta, we can conclude that either some of the Jews of Edessa or one of its Christian groups felt the need of a version in the dialect of the town. What Weitzman calls the "theological profile" of the translators is compatible with either possibility, as long as we do not think in terms of the ideal types of rabbinic Judaism and later Christianity. Moreover, both those who defined themselves as Jews and those who called themselves Christians had a motive:

---

[89] Defining Jewish Christianity is a very problematic issue; see Carleton Paget, "Jewish Christianity", 733–42. Here, I do not want to indicate more than "Jews who came to believe that Christ brought salvation".

[90] Weitzman, *The Syriac Version of the Old Testament*, 209.

[91] Compare the discussion of various theories regarding Jewish and Christian times of prayer by Falk, "Jewish Prayer Literature," 293–98.

for Jews it may simply have been a matter of dialect, for Christians the translation may also have played a role in their polemics with Marcionites, which made it necessary for them to have their own version of the Old Testament.[92] The use of the Syriac script, however, points solely in the direction of Christians. Whatever the case may be, it should be granted that the actual translation work was done by Jews, be they converted to Christianity before (my position) or after (Weitzman) the production of the Peshitta. The occurrence of conversions points not only to close contacts between Jews and Christians, as do the use of phraseology from the Palestinian Targum tradition and even full Targum readings in Christian authors, it also indicates that at least some Christians had a Jewish rather than a pagan background.

We may now safely say that if Drijvers found that Jews were rarely mentioned or even completely ignored by such early Christians as Tatian and Bardaisan, this does not mean that they were not there. Tatian may have quoted the Peshitta, and Bardaisan is actually seen referring to a reading of Gen 9:6 known from Targum Onqelos.[93] There was, then, an influence, and even an inflow of new believers, from the Jewish community of Edessa. The fact that Jews are not mentioned as such is interesting, though, and needs to be explained. In my view it could point to something other than the absence of Jews among the earliest Edessan Christians. As religious texts tend to stress the boundaries, we may well ask whether the earliest Christians saw a clear demarcation between them and the Jews. In any case, it appears that they were not seen as a threat, as in the fourth-century texts of Ephrem. This brings us to the question of the separation between Judaism and Christianity.

James Dunn argues that the period between the two Jewish revolts, or more precisely, the first thirty to thirty-five years of the second century, was decisive for the parting of the ways between Jews and Christians.[94] At the end of that period "Christian and Jew were clearly distinct and separate," he contends. I would say that the evidence from Edessa shows that the process may have started in the second century. On the Jewish side, at least, we could mention the use of the square script. However, the separation was not in any way "clear-cut and final" in 135, as Dunn would have it. One of his main arguments is the establishment of rabbinic Judaism, which in a sense formed a kind of orthodoxy. Now as Dunn himself already admitted, it took rabbinic Judaism a very long time to gain control over the Diaspora. Dunn also mentions the fact that Jewish Christianity appears in the Fathers as a group of heretical sects that was already detached from mainstream Christianity and could not maintain the continuity of the spectrum between the diverging currents. The relevant evidence does not go back further than the last decade of the second century, however.[95] A stronger point,

---

[92] Drijvers, "Early Syriac Christianity: Some Recent Publications," 174–75, mentions the Christian motives, but, answering to an earlier formulation of Weitzman's theory, he questions whether Edessan Jews would really need a Syriac version, considering that they used Hebrew. His main argument for this is formed by the Jewish inscriptions. As we have seen above, however, these are in Aramaic rather than in Hebrew. The knowledge of Hebrew among Edessan Jews may have been limited to a small group.

[93] Jansma, "The Book of the Laws of Countries," 409–14. A different explanation is found in Van der Kooij, "Peshitta Genesis 6," 43–51.

[94] Dunn, *The Partings of the Ways*, 238–43.

[95] See the collection also quoted by Dunn: Klijn-Reinink, *Patristic Evidence for Jewish-Christian Sects*.

though essentially an argument from silence, is the observation that the stream of Judaeo-Greek documents, which were preserved in the Church rather than in Jewish tradition, dried up after 100 C.E. Either there were no more non-rabbinic Jewish writings available after this date or, more probably, the diminishing contacts between the entailed a diminished impulse to take over newer non-rabbinic writings.[96]

All in all, it would seem that the following picture is most compatible with the evidence. Via the trade routes,[97] the Christian message reached Edessa in different forms. There it attracted the attention of Jews and pagans. In the second half of the second century we can discern various Christian groups, among which at least Marcionites, followers of Bardaisan, and Christians with a strongly ascetic ideal who may have been related with Tatian or his followers. We may assume that these groups met in house churches, such as the one identified among the ruins of Dura-Europos. The groups tried to reach the same public and therefore competed with each other. This implies that the boundaries between them were far from watertight. There is no evidence of a separate Jewish-Christian group that continued practices such as circumcision. It is clear, though, that the Bardesanite and "Tatianic" groups were in contact with Jews. These contacts included more than the interaction "at the margins" that Dunn would allow for this period. Among Edessan Jews, who shared a Hellenistic culture with the rest of the population, there were those who were less interested in observance, and emphasized faith, hope, and the importance of prayer. For such Jews, and certainly also for God-fearers, it was easy to take the step towards the new religion (especially if one considers the rather "light" Christologies of Tatian and Bardaisan, in which crucifixion and incarnation played no role of importance). Through these converts, but also through contacts with Jews who had not accepted any form of Christianity, the group around Bardaisan and those associated with Tatian had access to Targum readings and certain phraseology. Converts eventually also prepared a full new translation of the Hebrew Bible into the town's dialect, following the pagan writing tradition.

We may assume that in the course of the second century, people started stressing the boundaries. The fact that some Jews and God-fearers took up the belief that Jesus was a source of salvation must have stirred a reaction. However, the reality of everyday life in the small and bustling towns did not allow these boundaries to be kept.[98] Ideas travelled from one group to the other, even against the will of the leaders. Church Fathers were complaining about Christians visiting synagogues and magic texts show that Jewish, Christian, and gentile ideas could appear in a mixture as late as the fifth and sixth century. Those who sought healing went to a magician, who could be a rabbi, a monk, or a gentile sorcerer. Both Miriam Taylor[99] and Judith Lieu[100] criticize

---

[96] For this point, see also Goodman, "Diaspora Reactions", 29–30.

[97] On the possible role trade routes played in the spread of Christianity, see now Harrak, "Trade Routes and the Christianization of the Near East," 46–61.

[98] On this point, see the important notes of Drijvers, "Rechtgläubigkeit und Ketzerei", 294–96, as well as his "Syrian Christianity and Judaism," 128–29.

[99] Taylor, *Anti-Judaism and Early Christian Identity*.

[100] Lieu, *Image and Reality*.

Marcel Simon's stress on Jewish proselytizing[101] as an explanation for anti-Judaic statements in Christian texts and rightly point to self-definition as a major factor. However, in Taylor's work the categories of "Jews" and "Christians", if not coloured by later standards, appear at least as monolithic entities facing each other, without making contact.[102] And perhaps even Lieu still sees the exchange of ideas too much as a conscious process in a kind of market-place for religious ideas, in which one can choose to participate or not. Reality was more complex: people's place in society was determined by a web of overlapping and conflicting loyalties, of which they were not always fully conscious. This is perhaps best illustrated by the fact that all inhabitants of Edessa took part in a pagan religious feast until at least the end of the fifth century.[103]

Conclusion

To conclude, we can say that Han Drijvers was right in stating the importance of the gentile element in the forms of Christianity found at Edessa, as against the traditional consensus that Christianity had a Jewish origin. There is also no reason to doubt that Christianity came from Antioch via the trade routes. However, via the same route, it did not reach only gentiles, but also Jews. Even if we do not follow Michael Weitzman's reconstruction of the community behind the Peshitta of the Old Testament in all respects, it is clear that the version was made by Jews who converted before or after they translated their version. Their "theological profile" warns us not to be too hasty when assuming a definitive parting of the ways. Neither Judaism nor Christianity was a single, unified movement, even after the year 70. The changes usually connected to this year did not take effect immediately. Especially in the Diaspora it took the rabbinic movement a very long time to establish its authority over all Jews. People may have had an idea of whether they were Jew, Christian, or pagan, but these ideal categories did not correspond to separated compartments in the historical reality of the Middle Eastern town. Though the idea of two different ways may have come up early, the spectrum between the two was unbroken for a longer time than we may think.

On the basis of the connection between Didache and Matthew it may be suggested that these works were written somewhere in each other's neighbourhood, closer to Palestine, perhaps even in Galilea. The example of Edessa, however, shows us that even after 70 C.E. there were people in the larger area of Palestine and Syria who in terms of kinship and religious background would have defined themselves as Jews, but differed from the rabbinic interpretation of the law and had come to believe that Jesus brought salvation, while their culture was as Hellenistic as that of their pagan neighbours. Here, there are no grounds for assuming a separate Jewish sect or Jewish-Christian group with its own elaborate theology. We should understand that most of the extant

---

[101] Simon, *Verus Israel.*
[102] For a fuller assessment and critique of Taylor's book, see now Carleton Paget, "Anti-Judaism and Early Christian Identity," 195–225.
[103] Drijvers, "The Persistence of Pagan Cults," 39.

literary sources tend to hide the complexity, precisely because of their aim: in order to strengthen the identity of their own group, they stress the differences and minimize the points which their group has in common with others. For our understanding of the background of the communities that were responsible for such texts as the gospel of Matthew and the Didache, this means, among other things, that the question of whether these texts were written *intra* or *extra muros* (of Judaism) comes down to the application of deductive concepts rather than to an inductive description of reality.

Chapter Two

The Milieu of Matthew, the Didache, and Ignatius of Antioch: Agreements and Differences

Clayton N. Jefford

Saint Meinrad School of Theology, St. Meinrad, Indiana (USA)

The late professor of historical theology, John E. Steely, introduced me to the Didache in the early 1980s. It was his professional opinion that in order to understand the text fully one must first resolve the confusing question of the provenance of the tradition that lies behind the work. During my subsequent studies in Claremont, California and after that time when I had determined that the focus of my dissertation research would be devoted to the relationship between the sayings tradition of the Didache and that of the gospel of Matthew, it was one of my New Testament professors, Burton Mack, who approached me with this very same question. When I replied that I felt that the text and its traditions were perhaps best placed in the region of Antioch, he responded, "Antioch – surely you can find a more interesting site than that. Everybody puts everything in Antioch!"

I have a very great sympathy for Mack's retort to my response. And yet, the fact that so many early Christian sources that are associated with ancient gospel and ecclesiastical traditions seem to be inextricably tied in one way or another to Syrian Antioch is perhaps, at the same time, the most reasonable basis for any decision to place the Didache there as well. Of course, on the other hand, the responsible student is ultimately challenged to explain how the presence of so many different sources in a single geographical region during the same historical moment could have evolved. And in many respects, it is this secondary question that has driven so much of my subsequent research into the text and traditions of the Didache.

With the site of Syrian Antioch provided as a basic presupposition for what follows, let me offer the following observation. Any serious discussion of a common milieu for the gospel of Matthew, the manual of instruction that is known as the Didache, and the authentic epistles of Ignatius of Antioch is perhaps best served from the outset by an agreement concerning three basic assertions. First, there is likely no greater issue that remains within modern research on the Didache about which less is known and more is assumed than is the question of the provenance of the text. Further, if we are to be quite honest, the question of the provenance of the gospel of Matthew stands tenuously in a situation that is very similar to that of the Didache.[1] Finally, and much more happily, the setting of the work of the bishop Ignatius seems unchallenged and

---

[1] Thus, I hereby acknowledge that a variety of sites have been proposed for the setting of Matthew with admirable argument, including most popularly the general regions of Syria and northern Galilee.

secure, since no reasonable objection to his location as bishop has been endorsed either by patristic or modern literature.

I have convinced myself that these three sources of early Christian literature were spawned from within the same historical and geographical milieu, that is, the setting of Antioch. In order to hold this position, basic assumptions must be made, some of which are more easily argued than are others. The easiest assumption is that the Didache and Matthew share a common literary tradition. Many scholars have held this view during the last century of biblical research, though the rationales for their perspective have varied widely. Arguments that the Didachist actually is dependent upon some edition of Matthew are no longer the majority view but, instead, scholars now tend to believe that the two authors have drawn from a common collection of local, Jewish-Christian materials.

A second postulation that students of early Christian literature can typically accept with only slightly more difficulty is the view that Ignatius made use of Matthew as a text that was prevalent within the church community of Antioch. It is true that Ignatius spends no great amount of time in an effort to quote from the text. So too, the specifically Jewish nature of Matthew has been studiously omitted in the Ignatian correspondence. Yet it seems relatively certain that the Matthean gospel is indeed his tradition of choice, particularly when compared with other gospel traditions of the period. This observation is offered with the full recognition that Ignatius, like other early patristic commentators, was primarily dependent upon oral sources and traditions. It is affirmed here, at least, that the sources that he recognizes as valid were known to and employed by the author of the gospel of Matthew as well.

The last supposition, and clearly the most difficult, is the recognition that Ignatius knew the tradition of the Didache in some form. I find no particular reason to argue that the bishop of Antioch made any specific use of the text of the Didache itself, and he may in fact have never known any form of our single Greek manuscript that might be considered as a reasonable parallel to the final version of the text. Yet, it seems quite tenable, contrary to what an initial survey of the perspectives of the Didachist and Ignatius might suggest, to believe that these two mindsets, that is, the bishop Ignatius and the Didachist, worked within the same ecclesiastical community. And this observation, while highly tentative, remains crucial, that is, that Ignatius was familiar with the texts and arguments that are preserved in the Didache but chose not to reference them in the few letters that remain from his hand.

My argument for a common milieu behind these early Christian sources is focused here upon the text of the Didache itself. It is my intention merely to suggest a general framework, if perhaps not ultimately determinative, for how a single ancient city could have produced such a text, while at the same time having spawned the diverse efforts of the author of Matthew and the bishop Ignatius. The evidence for this argument is largely circumstantial, of course, and would not be expected to convince lawyers or juries beyond any reasonable doubt. At the same time, when a broad survey of the evidence is gathered, I myself am convinced that no better alternative can be offered.

Antioch as Provenance

Only three primary locations have ever seriously been suggested for the provenance of the Didache since the rediscovery of the text in 1873: Egypt, Palestine, and Asia Minor. These locations each have some claim for consideration, but no choice is ultimately determinative on its own. Nor is there any particularly good reason to argue against other geographical options based upon the evidence at hand.

With respect to Egypt, several arguments have been offered.[2] From the beginning, scholars have made mention of the various Egyptian manuscript traditions that have reflected the Didache, including *POxy* 1782, the Coptic edition of 10:3b-12:2a, and some probable knowledge of the text by Clement of Alexandria and Athanasius. In addition, the supposed dependence of the Two Ways tradition in the Didache upon the parallel materials of Barnabas 18-20, a view that most students of the text once held, originally was believed to add further support to this position. Ultimately, of course, scholars generally came to endorse a new vision that the Didachist and the author of Barnabas worked from independent Two Ways sources, while the presence of an Egyptian tradition for the text simply indicates that the text was known in North Africa, not necessarily that it was written there.

More recently, no less a scholar than Kurt Niederwimmer has indicated specific aspects of the text that suggest an Egyptian provenance, primarily the use of the word κλάσμα ("bread") as a derivative of Egyptian liturgical sources and the correspondence between the doxology of the Lord's Prayer at 8:2 with the Sahidic translation of Matt 6:13. Yet ultimately even he does not find such limited evidence to be persuasive for an Egyptian provenance.[3]

The region of Palestine is also a consideration, though perhaps a minority view among scholars. I say "minority view," since such is the case today. In fact, the tendency to place the Didache somewhere in the general region of Palestine was very early a preference among British scholars. We find that the idea dates as far back as 1885 with the work of Philip Schaff,[4] who opted for the city of Jerusalem specifically, and Canon Spence,[5] who preferred the site of Pella. These are but two examples of a general late nineteenth-century trend, of course. More recently one may refer to the work of Georg Schöllgen, whose brief review of the "first-fruits" motif in *Did.* 13:3-7 suggests a large metropolitan milieu. Among his numerous suggested sites he lists the probability of Caesarea Maritima, though he includes Rome, Alexandria, Carthage, and even Antioch in his list of possibilities.[6]

---

[2] See from the beginning of the discussion, the work of Farrar, "The Bearing of the 'Teaching'," 81-91; Wohlenberg, *Die Lehre der zwölf Apostel*, 91-94; and Von Harnack, *Lehre der zwölf Apostel*, 168-70.

[3] Niederwimmer, *The Didache*, 52-54. 134-38. 149-52.

[4] Schaff, *The Oldest Church Manual*,119-25.

[5] Spence, *The Teaching of the Twelve Apostles*, 87-100.

[6] Schöllgen, "Die Didache," 140-43. See also the generalizations of Vielhauer, *Geschichte der urchirstlichen Literatur*, 737; Koester, *Introduction to the New Testament* 2, 157-60 (who refutes the option of Antioch because the local theology of cross and resurrection that arose there is not found in the Didache); and Wengst, *Didache (Apostellehre)*, 61-63.

What is more typically true about the suggestion of a Palestinian origin today is the common inclination among scholars to move at least the final form of the text away from Palestine toward Syria. This is evident in numerous studies of the Didache, including the 1987 conclusions of Wolf-Dietrich Köhler,[7] who points to the general region of Syria-Palestine in a somewhat hazy indication of only a broad provenance. Typical of these suggestions is the age-old idea that the text stems only generally from the region or province of Syria, and even then not from any particularly well-populated area within those environs. This specific conclusion, which rejects a city setting, is focused primarily upon the weak suggestion that the apparently unique traditions of the text, having no exact parallels in the New Testament or elsewhere in early Christian literature, must have survived in an isolated region whose faith community was not in touch with the evolving tradition of the growing universal church. While the region of Syria certainly holds a primary possibility, the rejection of any city context in preference for an isolated, agrarian setting should perhaps now be rejected based upon our growing realization that "unique within the extant literature" does not necessarily imply "isolated within the early Christian community."

We must ask ourselves, then, what makes Antioch the city of choice, not only for the Didache, but for the gospel of Matthew as well? There is a strong scholarly tradition that places the two texts in this region.[8] Perhaps the most clearly stated understanding of the tradition is found in John Meier's 1983 review of ancient Christian Antioch.[9] He envisions the development of a faith community within the city that evolved through three separate stages from the writings of Paul, to the text of Matthew, and finally culminating in the rule of Ignatius and the production of the Didache. Within this development Meier discusses the rise of local traditions, the influence of outside Christian groups and sources, and the transition of the local church from a Jewish community to a non-Jewish population.

I have great sympathy for this general view of the situation. At the same time, however, the evolutionary development that is suggested in this study does not seem to be quite so clean as one might wish. And to be certain, the details of the texts themselves are inadequately addressed. It is to a limited consideration of some of those details that I now wish to address my attention.

---

[7] Köhler, *Die Rezeption des Matthäusevangeliums*, 29-30.

[8] Support for Antioch as the home of the *Didache* may be found among authors such as Greyvenstein, *The Original 'Teaching,'* 123-30; Telfer, "The *Didache* and the Apostolic Synod," 133-46; and Audet, *La Didachè*, 187-210, to name but a few. Support for Antioch as the home of the gospel of Matthew is widespread and traditional, of course, having the support of such authors as Streeter, *The Four Gospels*, 500-11; Meier, *Matthew*, xii; Beare, *The Gospel According to Matthew*, 8-9; Johnson, *The Writings of the New Testament*, 177, and numerous others.

[9] See Meier's section on Antioch in Brown-Meier, *Antioch and Rome*, 12-86.

Between Matthew and the Didache

Recent publications by Jonathan Draper have offered some interesting insights into both the compilation and presentation of the Didache based upon the hypothetical text of "Q". Draper agrees that the city of Antioch should be considered the eventual provenance of the text. At the same time, however, he presents the Didache as the product of a certain "Q community" perspective, with the association of the Didache and the "Q" tradition forming a significantly complex relationship whose geographical circumstances remain uncertain.[10] One is immediately led to the general observation that is held by scholars of the "Q" hypothesis that the roots of this tradition, whether in oral or written form, were developed while in geographical motion. In other words, the "Q" tradition formed through the process of accumulation, gathering sayings and teachings along the way. In this particular instance, one assumes that "along the way" means from Palestine to Syria.

An intriguing conundrum is thus presented to the student of early patristic literature. This is to say that within the Didache there appear to be two types of material: the first type represents the living, working tradition of a community that is geographically mobile; the second type reflects a settled community that has attempted to shape and reshape the first type of materials in an effort to provide its tradition with specific parameters and limitations. Our primary concern as a result, of course, is to recognize that within the Didache there exist a variety of traditions and sources whose origins have come to a settled community from other venues. This is perhaps not a new and startling revelation, but a primary assumption of most students of the text.

What is intriguing, however, is that this is in essence the very perspective of the gospel of Matthew, for it is in Matthew that we find a presentation of the hypothetical "Q" source by definition, thus to indicate that the text is to some extent dependent upon an outside, traveling faith community. The nature of that community is not so certain, of course, despite the best efforts of various biblical scholars in the field. But for those who accept the "Q" hypothesis, we must at least acknowledge by definition that the materials of that community are now evident throughout the text of Matthew.

At the same time, it is also in Matthew that we hear warnings about false prophets and times of confusion within the community. This is evident both in the Sermon on the Mount and in numerous specific injunctions about how to settle disputes within an established faith community. Indeed, the need to blend a tradition that accepts the witness of traveling Christian prophets and their texts together with the local authority of a settled community is present in a similar fashion both in Matthew and in the Didache. This is the very sort of concern that provoked the analysis of Palestinian Christianity that Gerd Theissen initiated in the late 1970s.[11] And it was in this same vein that Niederwimmer undertook much of his early study of the Didache community, of course. Numerous other scholars have joined the hunt for wandering charismatic prophets and settled communities ever since.

[10] See, e.g., Draper, "Torah and Troublesome Apostles," 347-72, and Id., "Wandering Charismatics and Scholarly Circularities" and "Recovering Oral Performance from Written Text in Q," in Horsley-Draper, *Whoever Hears You Hears Me*, 29-45 and 175-94 (respectively).
[11] See Theissen, *Sociology of Early Palestinian Christianity*.

At the same time, there does not seem to be any particular evidence to support the view that the Didache has been constructed upon the foundation of our "Q" materials, as was so meticulously argued by Richard Glover in 1958.[12] While there is little doubt that some later editor, or perhaps the reworking of the text by the Didachist himself, has provided the materials of 1:3b-2:1 that reveal a marked dependence upon specific sayings from Matthean and Lukan materials that appear in the Sermon on the Mount and Plain respectively,[13] there is no particular reason to suspect that the materials of "Q" served as a foundational source for the Didache otherwise. So too, there is no particular evidence to suggest that the Didachist made use of any specific New Testament gospel writing, based either upon the sayings traditions or upon the liturgical and ecclesiastical materials that appear throughout the text.

What is most often observed is the close similarity between the content of specific texts in the Didache and their parallels in the gospel of Matthew.[14] I am perfectly content to accept the thesis of Helmut Koester's Marburg dissertation that the connection here is to be attributed to oral sources[15] versus the likelihood that the Didachist had the text of Matthew at his disposal.[16] This is not to argue that the Didachist has incorporated a sayings tradition that, while quite similar to, was separate from that which the author of Matthew used. Instead, a careful review of the materials suggests just the opposite, that is, that the two authors (or editors) have drawn upon the same set of core materials. Included here is the famous Two Ways statement of the Didachist that is combined with the well-known commandments about love of God and love of neighbor, as well as the so-called "golden rule."[17] While these texts are not combined in Matthew, it is only with the presentation of these sayings in Matthew's parallels, and in a form that appears only in these two passages, that the materials are offered as the fulfillment of "the law and the prophets."[18] Though this idea may have been broadly acknowledged within Jewish circles in general, it seems more likely that the author of Matthew and the Didachist have drawn from a collection of materials that share a common perspective.

So too, the Didachist provides us with a variety of sayings that have parallels only in Matthew, including the beatitude concerning the meek who will inherit the earth, the clear reference to a Trinitarian formula, the more complete form of the Lord's Prayer, and the warning against giving holy elements to dogs.[19] There is a real sense

[12] Glover, "The 'Didache's' Quotations," 12-29.

[13] In support of this observation, see the most persuasive and now famous study of Layton, "The Sources, Date and Transmission," 343-83, though Crossan, *The Birth of Christianity*, appendix 7, no longer accepts such a position, in a reversal of his earlier support of the view when he wrote *The Historical Jesus*.

[14] Numerous studies have endeavored to show this association, including those of Court, "The Didache," 109-20, and my own *The Sayings of Jesus*, 22-92 (see also the related chart of comparisons on pp. 160-61).

[15] *Synoptische Überlieferung*, 159-241.

[16] See, e.g., Massaux, *The Influence of the Gospel* 3, 144-82.

[17] Though, admittedly, in different forms with Matthew having been influenced by "Q" and the *Didache* reflecting the more common negative version, presumably from Jewish tradition.

[18] Matt 22:40 and 7:12; see Jefford, *The Sayings of Jesus*, 31-38. I argue specifically that the Two Ways concept that has a parallel in Luke 6:31 is in fact only a "two ways" concept in Matthew, not in Luke; cf. pp. 146-59.

[19] So Matt 5:3 (5); 28:19; 6:9-13; 7:6 (respectively).

in which many of the core materials of the Didache reflect sayings traditions that are recognized by scholars of the synoptic tradition as "M" materials, texts that are specific to the community from which the author of Matthew drew much that is unique to the Matthean tradition. I would argue, then, that it does not seem unlikely that the Didachist, having drawn from the same storehouse of material, has worked within the same community as well.

The difficulty, of course, is in the dating of such materials. For example, while on the one hand one may believe that specific sayings that are quite Jewish in form and function may be extremely old, other materials, such as the Trinitarian formula, undoubtedly are much more recent. The suggestion is that both the Didache and Matthew are the production of traditions and practices that cover a variety of dates and circumstances. This point is significant, because this suggests that neither the Didache nor the gospel of Matthew represents a single moment in time that reflects a complete perspective from an entire early Christian community. In other words, it seems unlikely that we should continue to assume that either author represents the total view of an individual community's world but, instead, a single perspective from within a larger community experience.

The bulk of studies that have been devoted to the similarity of sayings between the Didache and Matthew have to some extent, whether limited or more extensively, offered specific comment upon the way in which the Didachist and the author of Matthew have utilized parallel materials within divergent contexts. In certain cases, as with the saying about not giving what is holy to dogs (*Did.* 9:5; Matt 7:6) and with respect to the use of the word "hypocrite" (*Did.* 8:1-2; Matt 6:1-18), it seems that our two authors have applied their source materials to diametrically opposed circumstances. Contemporary scholars have often argued, then, that this indicates two separate provenances for our texts. And indeed, such a conclusion may be warranted. At the same time, it is not required. Indeed, the reality that I myself accept is that these two authors, operating from within the same community, have drawn from a common storehouse of sources and then applied those materials in divergent ways and in dissimilar contexts. This hardly seems unreasonable and is, in fact, typical of any circumstances of living, either ancient or modern. The issue here is one of perspective, not of provenance.

To the question of the collection of specific sayings traditions, we might well add the issue of liturgical and ecclesial traditions, of course. Naturally, the situation is clearly more complex here and requires some care in approach. The Didache has long been recognized as a virtual treasure trove of ancient Christian materials that defy the standard formulas and liturgical positions that are endorsed by scripture. What is widely recognized about these materials, as one would expect, is that they are both Jewish in nature and beyond Jewish in scope. For example, the admonitions concerning baptism are traditionally Jewish in structure and concern (7:1-4). At the same time, however, our author has included exceptions to the rules concerning baptism in cold, running water, thus to indicate a certain pastoral concern for the one who is to be baptized. So too, while the audience of the text is challenged "to bear the whole yoke of the Lord" (6:2), some exception is acceptable dependent upon the abilities of the listener.

Such holds true in the later admonitions about the acceptance of strangers who travel as prophets of Christ as well (12:1-5). The traditional Semitic practice of accepting and welcoming those who are in need is recognized, though limits to this approach are dictated according to the specific limitations of the Didachist's community. The common conclusion of scholars, of course, is that the Didache has incorporated materials that are highly Jewish in nature, and yet has adapted them to a function that stands beyond the bounds of a strictly Jewish perspective.

Needless to say, this is only a cursory review of what is typically Jewish about the materials of the Didache, particularly when compared with the same concerns as those of the author of Matthew. In such a short space as this I am hardly at liberty to survey the entire corpus of parallels, nor do I need to do so beyond a mere illustration of the principle that is involved. Fortunately, we are now in a position to consult the recent survey and conclusions of Huub van de Sandt and the late David Flusser for an exceptional investigation into such matters.[20]

Antioch and the Influence of Paul

To conclude that the Didache is a combination of Jewish materials with a supra-Jewish perspective is not surprising since this process was the very nature of the rise of ancient Christianity. And it is here that what is perhaps the most crucial piece of evidence for providing a provenance must come into play, that is, the influence of the apostle Paul. This is not to suggest that evidence either of the letters of Paul or the traditions that he endorsed as he traveled throughout the eastern Mediterranean region are to be detected within the Didache. Indeed, quite the opposite seems to be true. Instead, what the witness of Paul suggests is that there were cities in antiquity that contained the seeds of both Jewish and non-Jewish Christianity. On the surface this seems obvious, since it presumably applies to most Mediterranean cities. But what makes Antioch particularly attractive in this respect is that we possess the textual evidence to indicate that, as a threshold of early Christian development, the city was the location of heated debate between the bizarre, liberal views of messianic Judaism that Paul endorsed as freedom "in Christ" from the restraints of Jewish cultic boundaries and the views of those whom he labeled as the so-called "circumcision party," namely, the very traditional, messianic Jews of Palestine who, under the leadership of Cephas and James the Lord's brother, came to wield significant influence upon the Christian community of Syrian Antioch. This debate is well known, both from the evidence of Acts 15 and from Paul himself in Galatians 2.

The implications of the struggle are highly significant for us in this context because they indicate that Antioch was a community that, while typically hospitable to a variety of ancient religious creeds and faiths, in actuality was the home of numerous perspectives within nascent Christianity itself.[21] Thus, it is in Antioch, perhaps beyond

[20] Van de Sandt-Flusser, *The Didache.*
[21] This was suggested already by the work of Grant, "The Early Antiochene Antiphon," 91-94; see also his "Jewish Christianity at Antioch," 97-108.

all other ancient cities, that the grounds for a multifaceted form of Christianity took shape. At least this is what is suggested by the literature, namely, by the writings of Paul and the witness of Acts. What is clearly and broadly acknowledged about Antioch is that the city flourished as the home of a Pauline form of Christianity that eventually became embodied within the figure of the bishop Ignatius, whose letters to local bishops of the region are recognized by two primary concerns. The first of these concerns is the bishop's constant insistence upon the need for a structured three-tiered hierarchy among the churches that places the overseer of the community (the bishop) at the top level of authority in the symbolic position of God the Father. This role is to be followed thereafter by the presbyters and deacons in the position of Christ and the apostles. The second of these concerns is the incessant concern of Ignatius about the so-called "Judaizers" whom he perceived as opponents to the freedom in Christ that his hero, Paul, had espoused so freely in his own correspondence.

We are free to argue with the bulk of scholarly tradition concerning Ignatius that he represented what became the foundation of later Christian understanding of hierarchy and a flagrant break with the church's Jewish roots. On the other hand, it is perhaps a wonder that Ignatius had to protest so loudly on these issues. Indeed, was he speaking from the comfort level of a bishop who was assured and firmly supported by a home community that agreed with his views or, instead and more likely, did he stand as an estranged voice within the early Christian community?[22] In many respects it seems that Antioch was clearly not only the home of Pauline theology and ecclesiastical perspective, but was the home of Petrine and more typically Jewish visions of what it meant to be a Christian as well. This is suggested by the New Testament materials to be sure, but it is confirmed a century and a half later with the writings of the bishops Theophilus and Serapion, both of whom seem to have endured their own struggles with the Jewish faction of the Antiochian faith community.[23]

We should not mislead ourselves, then, into the naïve assumption that with the advent of Ignatius to the throne of the Antiochian church that Judaism and its influence among the Christians of the city were eliminated. Quite the contrary, what Ignatius had undoubtedly hoped to settle within Christianity, that is, the tension between Jewish and non-Jewish influences upon second-century Christianity, was hardly resolved through his influence. Indeed, when he writes to the Philadelphians that through their "prayer and compassion" he has heard that the church in Antioch is now at peace,[24] we must wonder if a primary part of the resolution of the problems there cannot be attributed to the fact that he, by virtue of his forced march to presumed martyrdom in Rome, had now been removed from the city! It is perhaps not by coincidence that we are never informed with respect to who arranged for his arrest and removal. As one may surmise, once the thorn has been removed, the wound may heal! And so it may have been with Ignatius, a thorn of the church in Antioch.[25]

[22] For an alternative perspective on the tenuous nature of the position that Ignatius may have held, see my essay "Ignatius of Antioch," 25-39.

[23] See my "Reflections on the Role," 147-67.

[24] Ign. *Phld.* 10:1.

[25] A la Paul's "thorn in the flesh;" see 2 Cor 12:7.

At the bare minimum, then, we may rest assured that the Christians in Antioch formed a community of faith that existed in great tension. On the one hand, this is represented by the role that Ignatius assumed as the heir of Pauline perspective. His rise to power and his virtual "hero worship" of the apostle of the risen Christ seemingly did not draw the ire of Christendom that was subsequently visited upon Marcion of Sinope, of course. But then, Marcion was so bold as to challenge ecclesiastical standards and to claim an entire tradition of Christian faith for himself through his actions. Ignatius, on the other hand, worked within the rising framework of church hierarchy and presumably took hold of the institution from within its own structure. History provides us with no real clues here.

Matthew, Didache, and Ignatius

The key to the Ignatian situation in Antioch for our present purposes is perhaps found in some recognition of the particular gospel text that he acknowledged as authoritative. There is some literature on this issue, and the conclusions that we might draw are instructive.[26] From the outset, a survey of the sources that Ignatius employed quickly reveals his limited use of traditional Jewish materials. There are only three actual quotations, two from Proverbs and one from Isaiah, in addition to a handful of scriptural allusions that draw upon Proverbs, Psalms, Isaiah, and Deuteronomy. It seems that his corpus of Hebrew scriptures is both brief and limited.

We must ask ourselves whether this is the result of his limited awareness of Jewish texts or, perhaps, his reluctance to draw upon such sources within the context of a heated Jewish-gentile debate. My guess is that the latter situation is the more likely.

What is more interesting is the choice of gospel text that he makes. First, there is no evidence that he knew or used the gospel of Mark. In addition and unlike Marcion only slightly later, he does not appear to have any particular affinity for the gospel of Luke, to which he perhaps appeals only once, though this singular instance may have been drawn from a broader tradition.[27] This is intriguing in the light of the bishop's attraction to the works and theology of Paul. While he has consciously patterned his letters upon Paul's own writings,[28] he has not chosen to include the gospel text that is most closely linked with Paul by common tradition. Further, Ignatius reveals some acquaintance with various Johannine themes, but here too shows no particular dependence upon the text of the gospel of John itself.

This brings us then to the gospel of Matthew. And it is here that most scholarly work has been undertaken.[29] There seems to be little question that Ignatius knew

---

[26] One might see here my own "Did Ignatius of Antioch Know?," 330-51.

[27] See Ign. *Smyrn.* 3:2-3 (Luke 24:39-43).

[28] This is surely evident in a comparison of the Pauline (or deutero-Pauline) letter to the Ephesians when compared with the letter of Ignatius to that same church.

[29] See, e.g., Koester, *Synoptische Überlieferung*, 24-61; Massaux, *The Influence of the Gospel*, 1, 85-120; Köhler, *Die Rezeption des Matthäusevangeliums*, 73-96.

and used Matthew as his primary gospel.[30] Indeed, he seems to have been intimately familiar with the text and was comfortable that his readers knew it as well. He employs the gospel as the foundation for important theological and ethical opinions without quoting extensively from the text so much as to use it as a platform from which to launch his arguments. Thus, imagery from Matthew arises consistently throughout the letters of Ignatius, constantly serving as the basis by which he illustrates his perspective. And yet even here, while it is reasonably clear that Ignatius is primarily dependent upon Matthew or at least the Matthean tradition as his gospel source, he is hesitant to quote from the gospel in large sections. To some extent, we might argue that he does not recognize the ultimate authority of the gospel of Matthew as a scriptural canon. But what is much more likely is that he hesitates to utilize this source as his ultimate authority because of the Jewish nature and tendencies that Matthew represents, tendencies that he himself does not share.

This leads us to the relationship between Ignatius and the Didache, if in fact there is one. No less a scholar than B.H. Streeter, who recognized that both Ignatius and the Didachist had a close relationship to the text of Matthew, has offered us the comment that these two authors "stand to Matthew as the preacher to his text."[31] Streeter assumed, of course, that both authors had made specific use of the finished text of the gospel, an assumption that I do not hold with respect to the Didachist. At the same time, he did not suppose that both authors had worked within the same religious community, namely, Antioch, but only within the same general region of Syria.

I have argued elsewhere that various passages in the Didache find a close parallel in the writings of Ignatius, materials that include ideas such as the Two Ways motif, the command to honor visitors "as the Lord," sharing in what is immortal, and the "day of the Lord" concept.[32] These parallels are perhaps not surprising since most of them circulated widely in late Jewish and early Christian circles. What is particularly instructive here, however, is that both Ignatius and the Didache share so many ideas between them. On the one hand, there seems to be no special reason to think that Ignatius knew or used the materials of the Didache. At the same time, as with the relationship of the Didache and the gospel of Matthew, it is entirely possible, if not probable, that the Didachist and the bishop have drawn upon the same storehouse of common community materials.

We are left, then, with a resulting matrix of logical challenges that must be confronted. In the first instance, the Didache and the gospel of Matthew share materials and traditions that are primarily Jewish in nature and are largely aligned with the so-called "M" tradition as identified by the four-source solution to the classic "synoptic problem." In parallel to this observation, the Didache does not seem to be dependent upon Matthew itself, but upon certain materials that are known only in Matthew. In the second place, the bishop Ignatius is highly dependent upon the gospel of Matthew,

---

[30] This conclusion is shared by Schoedel, *Ignatius of Antioch, 9.*
[31] Streeter, *The Four Gospels*, 511 for the quotation (see 504-11 for the argument).
[32] See *Did.* 1:1a (Ign. *Magn.* 5:1); 4:1 (Ign. *Eph.* 6:1); 4:8 (Ign. *Eph.* 20:2); 14:1 (Ign. *Magn.* 9:1) respectively; as argued in Jefford, "Did Ignatius of Antioch Know?"

despite his aversion to Jewish Christianity. Presumably this is true because Matthew is the gospel of choice, not only for him, but for the community of faith in Antioch that he serves as well. Finally, Ignatius has not made use of the Didache, though he does seem to be aware of various materials that find a parallel within the text of the Didache. Either he does not know the text in the form in which it survives today or, instead, he has chosen not to use the text. What is especially curious is that he does show an awareness of certain of the traditions that the Didache contains, despite the fact that he offers no indication that he wishes to support the Jewish dimension of early Christianity.

Admittedly, to some extent the matrix that is proposed here is less than firmly established and is, in fact, highly speculative. At the same time, however, if such a hypothesis may be supported for the sake of argument, then the city of Antioch would be a more than suitable location for this proposed relationship among the texts of the Didache, the gospel of Matthew, and the work of Ignatius.

What we know about ancient Antioch is extensive, if not complete.[33] The background of the city gives clear indication that the population was diverse, revealing the influence of political power and reconstruction as a populated colony of Roman imperialism. As a crucial component of this colony, a large body of Jewish influence survived within the city from the third century B.C.E. The scattered history of the region reveals the ebb and flow of tension that existed in the area as the non-Jewish populace struggled with the presence of Jewish culture and influence, resulting in sporadic violence and rioting throughout the period of early Christianity's rise. Because there was a general struggle within the common populace, there is no reason to assume that a similar tension did not exist within the Antiochian church itself. Indeed, the witness of Paul's letter to the Galatians, the Acts of the Apostles, and the letters of Ignatius firmly establish that Antioch was not only a city of primary importance for the early Christian mission, but was also a location in which the divergent tendrils of rising church consciousness came into constant conflict.

Perhaps the most obvious question that should be offered in response to the situation is why some other ancient Mediterranean city should not be considered to be as likely a site for the provenance of our texts and their authors. To this end, one might suggest suitable locations among any metropolis that contained a sizable population base, a divergent ethnic culture that included a significant and influential Jewish presence, a known center for the presence of early Christian activities, the influence of our particular texts or of their authors, and evidence of the traditions and tendencies of the materials that are under consideration here. In this collection of options one might easily envision that cities like Alexandria, Caesarea Maritima, Damascus, Athens, Rome, Carthage, or any of the numerous cities whose names were associated with the Pauline missions might suffice. The particular difficulty is to find a site in which all three of our sources might find a suitable resting point.

---

[33] See Downey, *A History of Antioch*, and Kraeling, "The Jewish Community in Antioch," 130-60. I am extremely sorry not to have the forthcoming work of Magnus Zetterholm, *The Formation of Christianity in Antioch* available to me when this essay was written. This also goes for the volume of Michelle Slee, *The Church in Antioch in the First Century CE.*

The gospel of Matthew was clearly the most widely respected and utilized gospel text of the Mediterranean church. Its text was widely quoted and referenced by theologians, apologists, heresiologists, bishops, and church historians in all geographic regions. Subsequently, use of Matthew provides only the broadest framework into which to find a common provenance.

Our remaining two texts are the primary problem it seems. The works and influence of Ignatius reduce the options considerably. And in this respect we find ourselves limited primarily to the cities of Asia Minor, and perhaps Macedonia. In the same respect, knowledge of the Didache limits us even further. The use of this text by both Syrian and Egyptian traditions suggests that we must be restricted mostly to these regions, though we may easily include Palestine as the buffer region between the two areas.

Summary and Conclusions

Scholarly consensus suggests that if there is to be any literary-historical relationship between the origins of the Didache and the gospel of Matthew, then it must be restricted to the region from northern Egypt to southern Asia Minor and Syria. Suitable arguments have been offered to indicate the possibility of numerous sites within this realm. The city of Antioch is a primary suspect, yet the presence of Ignatius at the turn of the century raises some doubt.

The basic problem that results for most students of early patristic literature is that the Didache and the gospel of Matthew are representatives of a parallel tradition of Jewish-Christian texts, though each one tends to apply those materials to divergent scenarios and applications. At the same time, Ignatius seems to be distinctly uncomfortable with such materials, and tends to avoid them whenever possible. The solution to this problem is perhaps best found in the realization of the complex diversity of the Antiochian church community, an ecclesiastical forum in which staunchly Jewish views of the Christian faith as represented by the work of the Didachist came into bitter conflict with resilient non-Jewish perspectives about Christianity as represented by the leadership of Ignatius. Between these two poles stood the pastoral sensitivity of the author of the gospel of Matthew, an individual who stood with one foot in the Jewish roots of Christian diversity and one foot turned in the direction of the evolving church, the mission field of the nations. The differences among our authors are hardly significant in this situation, except to indicate the perspective of individual authors and theologians at work. It is the few commonalities of what their writings preserve that suggest a core of sources and traditions which each author knew, respected, and utilized for the benefit of their selected audiences within the local community.

II The Two Documents: Their Provenance and Origin

Chapter Three

The History and Social Setting of the Matthean Community

Wim Weren

Faculty of Theology, Tilburg University (The Netherlands)

Introduction

Where, when, and for whom was the gospel of Matthew written? In this paper, I will make an attempt to gain new insight into the history and social setting of Matthew's community. This will not be an easy task. Owing to the lack of sufficiently reliable external data,[1] we must go on the information that this gospel itself has to offer. A further complication is that Matthew's book belongs to a particular literary genre, which we usually refer to with the term "gospel" and which is modelled on ancient biography. It is characteristic of a gospel that it offers a story of the life of Jesus *in illo tempore*, but such a text has been deeply influenced by the situation of the community within which it originated and for which it was originally meant.

For the purpose of this paper, I define "community" as a number of affiliated or rather loosely confederated Christian groups, in a wide geographical area, that feel connected in the sense that they largely hold the same religious views and adhere to the same ethical values. The groups in this network need not have had the same history or have found themselves in the same stage of development, nor is it certain from the start that these groups were always located in the same region.

The gospel according to Matthew is the fruit of a long maturing process. It contains traces of traditions of days long past. The tension between the older and younger layers can be clearly discerned in the final product. It is therefore inadvisable to relate all the data contained in this gospel, and which are often difficult to reconcile with each other, to one particular moment in the life of one particular group.[2] Redaction-critical studies often suffer from this malady. They focus one-sidedly on the situation in the 80s of the first century C.E., at the time of the final redaction of the book. Taking the tension between tradition and redaction as a point of departure, I want, instead, to try

---

[1] See Papias' statements on Matthew in Eusebius (*Historia Ecclesiastica*, III, 39,16): Ματθαῖος μὲν οὖν ʽΕβ-ραΐδι διαλέκτῳ τὰ λόγια συνετάξατο, ἡρμήνευσεν δ᾽αὐτὰ ὡς ἦν δυνατὸς ἕκαστος; cf. Schwartz, *Eusebius II: Die Kirchengeschichte* 1, 292. See also Irenaeus, *Adversus Haereses* III, 1,2; III, 11, 7-9.

[2] Cf. Stanton, "Revisiting Matthew's Communities," 378-79: "We should stop supposing that the gospel reflects the evangelist's close relationship with one group of Christians in one house church in one particular urban geographical location."

and form a picture of the history of the Matthean community, or groups belonging to it, over a longer period of time.

In my reconstruction, I will distinguish three phases.[3] The first phase takes us back to the period prior to 70 C.E. and brings us into contact with the Jewish disciples of Jesus, who still considered themselves full members of the Jewish community, which had become strongly fragmented in those days. In the second phase (between 70 and 80), these Christian Jews came into conflict with the Pharisees, who were devoted to finding new, common ground on the basis of which various Jewish factions could unite. In this unification process, the Jewish followers of Jesus became a minority group within their original home front. In the third phase (between 80 and 90), these Jewish Christians increasingly came into contact with Christian groups which had gone through a different development and which, in addition to Jews in the Diaspora, also counted many non-Jews among their members. In this last phase, the gospel of Matthew achieved its final redactional form. With his book, the final redactor tried to offer a foundation to his community which had become strongly estranged from Judaism.

It will be obvious that my reconstruction is hypothetical in nature and that the three phases which I distinguish partly overlap. It is especially between the second and third phases that it is hardly possible to draw a sharp distinction. The gradual and continuing estrangement from Jewish groups led by Pharisees (phase 2), advanced an increasing openness of Matthew's community for other local Christian communities and for the gentile world (phase 3).

The phases I distinguish in the history of Matthew's community correspond to three stages in the development of Matthew's gospel.[4] The oldest layer of the gospel we can touch upon, is the material that is unparalleled in Mark or Q. The major part of this material consists of sayings by Jesus. When these are isolated from their present literary context it becomes evident that these sayings are profoundly Jewish in character. It is a moot point whether they initially constituted a unity and ought to be attributed to a special source (M).

The second stage in the development of Matthew's gospel is more easily to be recovered. To my judgment, material derived from Mark or Q should be ascribed to this layer. I presume that groups around Matthew became acquainted with these documents because of increasing contacts with visiting missionaries. This second layer shows a mixture of both tradition and redaction. Many textual elements are

---

[3] To a certain extent, the results of my reconstruction are similar to the proposal concerning the history of Matthew's community formulated by Luz ("Der Antijudaismus im Matthäusevangelium," 311): "Die matthäische Gemeinde ist, so denke ich, eine judenchristliche Jesusgemeinde, die aus Palästina stammt, dort früher Israelmission betrieben hat, daran gescheitert ist, schließlich, wahrscheinlich im Vorfeld des jüdischen Krieges 66-70, sich von der Synagoge trennen und Israel verlassen mußte, in Syrien eine neue Bleibe fand und dort anfing, Heidenmission zu betreiben." My reconstruction differs from Luz's view on two points: 1. the mission to Israel continues when the Matthean community embarks on a mission among gentiles; 2. the parting away from "the synagogue" is not to be dated as early as Luz suggests. See also Luz, *The Theology*, 17-21.

[4] Cf. Tomson, *"If this be from Heaven..."*, 255-89.

derived from Mark or Q, but at the same time Matthew felt free to adapt them to his community's situation. Matthew's thorough redaction is determined by new developments following the year 70 C.E., that were well remembered by both redactor and community, and still had their influence on the community's life in the eighties of the first century C.E.

The last and youngest stage of the development of Matthew's gospel is in line with the second stage. During this stage Matthew's final redaction took place probably by the end of the eighties. In this stage, old traditions were adapted to the circumstances that had changed, and new textual elements were added. An important consideration to distinguish the second and third stages is that in the youngest we can detect a community that is gradually separating itself from (Pharisaic) Judaism and taking a position *extra muros*, whereas the bitter conflicts with the Pharisees, during the penultimate stage, rather point to a community that was still *intra muros*.

First Phase (prior to 70): Christian Jews formed a Robust Group within the Multiform Judaism of the Time

Characteristics
In the years before 70 C.E., many Jewish followers of Jesus considered themselves full members of the Jewish community, which formed a multi-form whole with many other sub-groups and movements at the time.[5] They were accepted by other Jews without any substantial problems. Following Antony Saldarini and David Sim, I will refer to this group as "Christian Jews."[6] The term "Jews" indicates that, both ethnically and religiously, this group completely belonged to the larger Jewish context and that the group did not perceive itself as taking the lead in a new religious movement. With the term "Christian", I refer to a specific characteristic of this group: its members considered Jesus as their core symbol but, in their minds, this did not detract from their Jewishness. On the contrary, they experienced their belief in Jesus as the most authentic way to express their Jewish identity.

Textual Evidence
Our image of this oldest stage is based on ancient traditions which probably originated in Israel; we can still find traces of them in the Matthean *Sondergut*. Linking up with Stephenson Brooks' study on Matthew's special sayings material, I draw the following picture.[7] The Christian Jews considered Jerusalem as the holy city (4:5), they paid

---

[5] That is why present-day scholars use the term "Judaisms". See Metzger-Coogan, *The Oxford Companion*, 391: "[...] the picture that has emerged is of multiple Judaisms, distinct Jewish religious systems, yet with connecting threads, indicators that they share a common legacy."

[6] Saldarini, *Matthew's Christian-Jewish Community*; Sim, *The Gospel of Matthew*. According to these authors the community still kept its Christian-Jewish character at the time of Matthew's writing. Contrary to this opinion I will argue that there was a significant change in the community's attitude during the eighties of the first century.

[7] Brooks, *Matthew's Community*, 120-22.

temple tax (17:24-27), and participated without criticism in temple rites and other religious meetings (5:23-24). The Torah, to them, was normative (5:17-19) and therefore they abided – although not without discussion – by provisions concerning purification and the sabbath. By differentiating between weightier rules and less weighty ones (23:23; 5:18-19), they could emphasise certain parts of the Torah without having to fully reject other elements. They lived pious lives, characterised in 6:1-18 by the three cardinal works of religious life: giving alms, praying, and fasting.

Like many other Jews, they associated with gentiles who had converted to Judaism and had renounced their heathen past but, for the sake of their Jewish identity, they were strongly opposed to adopting the behaviour patterns of the gentiles (5:47; 6:7,32; 7:6; 20:35).

The Christian Jews tried to win others over to Jesus but, in conformity to their master (15:24), they exclusively targeted the house of Israel (10:6). Like those in apocalyptic circles, they looked forward to the imminent return of the Son of Man and they expected this event to transpire before they had visited all the towns on their mission through Israel (10:23).

Time and Place

The situation presented here fits best in the period before the destruction of the temple in the year 70. In that period, there was not yet one dominant Jewish group that could, or wanted to, channel the life of the community into one particular direction. It is more difficult to determine the whereabouts of the Christian Jews. Various urban centres with their surrounding areas qualify, such as Caesarea Maritima[8], Sepphoris[9], or Pella on the eastern side of the Jordan[10], but since it is strongly emphasised in Matthew that Capernaum functioned as the operating base for Jesus' activities in a wider region, I am thinking particularly of the border area between the Lower and Upper Galilee, where towns like Capernaum, Chorazin, and Bethsaida were located. Jesus reproaches these three towns that they have not repented (11:23-24). This strong rebuke may indicate that the Christian Jews may initially have had their home front in these centres, but that they were later compelled to leave these towns because of tensions with the rest of the Jewish population.

Second Phase (ca. 70-80): The Christian Jews are forced into the Margin within a Jewish Community that was Renewing Itself

Characteristics

The history of Judaism in the first century C.E. was strongly defined by the colonial aspirations of the Roman Empire. The capture of Jerusalem by Titus in the year 70 was a heavy blow to Jewish life. The destruction of the temple meant the loss

---

[8] Viviano, "Where was the Gospel ... Written?," 533-46.
[9] Overman, *Matthew's Gospel and Formative Judaism*, 159.
[10] Slingerland, "The Transjordanian Origin," 18-28.

of an important focus of religious life. Multi-formity decreased because groups like the Sadducees and the Qumran community disappeared. Urgent reorientation was necessary. Apocalyptic movements flourished again and other groups also made efforts to redefine the social and religious identity of Judaism and to curb internal disunity.[11] This revitalisation process did not proceed everywhere in the same way and was not so much coordinated from one central position as later rabbinic sources, that see Yavne as the centre, would have us believe. It is certain, however, that the Pharisees made an important contribution to this process.[12] They had great expertise in the field of the Torah, and since they had already advocated the promotion of purity *outside* the temple, they could easily take the lead in the reconstruction of a Jewish community that was no longer centred around the temple cult. The Pharisees were mainly active in the Lower Galilee, where they had much leverage with the local population and had secured the support of local scribal groups.

Textual Evidence
This new coalition is reflected in passages from Matthew that show a redactional processing of material from Mark or Q. The redactor often links "(the) scribes and (the) Pharisees" to form a fixed combination (5:20; 12:38; 23:2,13, 15, 23, 25, 27, 29).[13] The Pharisees are mentioned a total of 29 times. A very negative portrait is painted of this group: they are evil (12:34, 35, 39, 45), blind (15:14; 23:16,17,19, 24, 26), and hypocritical (15:7; 22:18; 23:13,15, 23, 25, 27, 29); they were not planted by God (15:13), but are like weeds sown by the devil that will be burned at the end of the age (13:40); the kingdom of God will be taken away from them because of their lack of productivity (21:43). The tirade against the scribes and Pharisees culminates in 23:13-39, a passage that is uncommonly fierce in tone.

This negative picture may be accounted for by the collisions between the Christian Jews and the Pharisees in the 70s. The Christian Jews knew themselves backed by Jesus, who had also disputed Pharisaic interpretations of the Torah on a number of points.

Initially, the Christian Jews were inclined to support the Pharisees's authority as interpreters of Mosaic law (23:2-3a), but, as a result of their increasing claims to domination, loyalty to them soon began to wane (16:12; 23:16, 18). The power ambitions of the opposing party forced the Christian Jews to emphasise that God had given all power to Jesus (11:27; 28:18) and that Jesus had special authority (7:29; 8:8-9; 21:23-27). Their opponents protested that Jesus was an impostor (27:63) and that he was not inspired by God's Spirit but by Beelzebul (9:34; 12:24, 27; cf. 10:25).

[11] Following Jacob Neusner, Overman (*Matthew's Gospel and Formative Judaism*, 35) talks about "formative Judaism" (= "a new religious synthesis and the process of its construction and emergence in the post-70 period").
[12] According to Schürer (*The History of the Jewish People* 1, 524), the Pharisees were the predominant party in the period following the year 70 CE (see also 2, 369. 402-03).
[13] In Matt 15:1 it says "Pharisees and scribes," in accordance with the order in Mark 7:1,5. In Luke, we come accross "the scibes and the Pharisees" in 5:21; 6:7; 11:53.

Feelings could run so high because the two parties adhered to the same basic values. Both were interested in halakhic issues concerning divorce (5:27-32; 19:3-9), the purity rules (15:1-9), and observance of the sabbath (12:1-14). Both parties appealed to the Scriptures (9:13; 12:3-7; 19:4-5, 7-8) to justify their points of view. On the basis of formula quotations, the Christian Jews tried to show that their innovative movement was deeply rooted in tradition. They presented their views as normative and had the pretension that, in choosing for Jesus, they met the highest ideals, which should in fact hold for the entire Jewish community. This feeling of superiority is articulated in 5:20, where it says that the righteousness of Jesus' disciples must exceed that of the scribes and the Pharisees.

The opposition between the own group and the opposing party was formulated pointedly by means of apocalyptic material, in which the good and the bad are sharply contrasted. References to the final judgement were a fixed element of the diatribes against the opponents: God will take the kingdom away from them (21:43), but He will generously reward the repressed minority group for its ideological choices and its righteous life.

Internal Relations

As a result of collisions with other groups within their milieu, the Christian Jews were increasingly thrown on their own resources. Within the larger Jewish context, they became a sect that deviated from what slowly emerged as the mainstream.[14] Despite their fondness for expressing relations in terms of family relationships – they saw God as their only Father, they considered themselves each others' (23:8-9) and Jesus' (12:46-50; 28:10) brothers and sisters – they began to set up an organisation of their own and adopted disciplinary measures that correspond to the rules from the Dead Sea Scrolls, and which provided that any person who undermined the internal social unity could be expelled from the community (18:15-18). Such strict discipline is characteristic of a sectarian group which clearly wants to dissociate itself from the outside world, which it considers to be hostile.[15]

In order to make their organisation more efficient, they appointed certain individuals from their midst as leaders. In 23:34, we find the following threesome: prophets, wise men, and scribes. The function of the prophet is also mentioned in 10:41, and we also come across the Christian scribe in 13:52. With the function of scribe, the Christian Jews adopted a form of leadership that also existed in the opposing party. It may have been the case that some Christian scribes actually came from the enemy camp and that, having been won over to Jesus's side, they had to join battle with their former colleagues.

[14] Being influenced by studies of E. Troeltsch and M. Weber, L.M. White proposes that a sect is "a deviant or separist movement within a cohesive and religiously defined dominant culture. Thus despite expressed hostilities and exclusivism, the sect shares the same basic constellation of beliefs or 'worldview' of the dominant idiom." ("Shifting Sectarian Boundaries," 14).

[15] Cf. 1QS 5,24-6,1; CD 9,2-8. See García Martínez, "Brotherly Rebuke in Qumran," 221-232. Cf. also H. van de Sandt's contribution in the present volume.

The function of scribe is represented by Peter, who plays a prominent role in Matthew. From the Christian-Jewish circles, Matthew derives the tradition, preserved in 16:17-19, in which Peter is charged with the task of making sure that the community, when developing a new halakha, will remain faithful to Jesus' interpretation of the Torah.[16] As such, he is a model for the entire group and for its leaders.

It was an innovative step that the Christian Jews founded the forms of leadership which they gradually developed on a task received from Jesus (cf. 23:34: "I send") and that they encouraged their leaders to distinguish themselves from their counterparts in the other camp by refusing to be addressed as rabbi, father, or instructor (23:8-12). They were to acknowledge their bond with God, the only Father, and to Jesus, the only rabbi and instructor. With these references to God and Jesus, the Christian Jews put the forms of leadership they established into perspective.

Time and Place

Towards the end of the second phase, the Christian Jews increasingly withdrew from the Pharisees' sphere of influence. There was growing social and geographical distance. A number of Christian Jews left the Lower Galilee, where the Pharisaic influence was greatest and the conflicts most intensive. They took refuge in the sparsely populated Upper Galilee, the district of Caesarea Philippi, to the Golan, and the southern part of Syria (Syria is explicitly referred to in 4:24).[17] Owing to the large number of administrative reorganisations in the recent past, the borders between these areas were not clearly demarcated; they formed a coherent region with villages and a number of towns, which engaged in agriculture and maintained trade relations with a wider area.[18] The relocation of the Christian Jews was also dictated by the fact that they were subject to persecution because of their ties with Jesus ("on my account:" 5:11; 10:18, 39; 16:25; "for my name's sake:" 19:29), even in the synagogues (23:34). The fact that their mission among the house of Israel had not proven to be very successful also played a role. They turned their backs upon the cities of Lower Galilee and, in Southern Syria, they came into contact, in addition to Diaspora Jews, with a non-Jewish population.

---

[16] Matt 16:17-19 is without parallel in Mark. These verses are an addition by Matthew. Language and style point to Matthew having inserted a tradition, which was slightly altered and modified by his specific vocabulary. See Hoffmann, "Der Petrus-Primat im Matthäusevangelium," 96-98; Kähler, "Zur Form- und Traditionsgeschichte," 36-46; Robinson, "Peter and His Successors," 96; Lambrecht, "Du bist Petrus," 21-24.

[17] U. Luz (*Das Evangelium nach Matthäus* 1, 75) calls "eine größere syrische Stadt, deren lingua franca Griechisch war" as its place of origin; he considers Antioch on the Orontes as "nicht die schlechteste Hypothese" (*Ibid.*, 74). Arguments in favour of Antioch as the place of composition of Matthew are given by J.P. Meier, "Antioch," in Brown-Meier, *Antioch and Rome*, 22-27. Cf. Streeter, *The Four Gospels*, 500-523.

[18] White, "Crisis Management and Boundary Maintenance," 228-38.

Third Phase (ca. 80-90): Christian Jews within a Multi-Cultural Network of Christian Communities

Characteristics

In the second phase, the Christian Jews continued to perceive the Jewish community as their spiritual home front; they were still *intra muros*. In the third phase, however, they gradually detached themselves from this social framework and came into contact with a broad multi-cultural network of Christian communities. I call this network multi-cultural because it consisted of communities to which both Jews and non-Jews belonged. In this environment, Matthew's Christian Jews gradually developed into Jewish Christians, into a Jewish branch within a Jesus movement that was not exclusively linked to a particular people.[19]

Some Terms

That the community began to occupy its own position next to, and partly even separate from, the Jewish community is revealed by some of the terms that Matthew uses.

- In 28:15, the author warns his readers about a bad rumour that allegedly persisted until his own time "among Jews" (he does not say: "among *the* Jews"). The choice of this term shows that the author and his readers no longer considered themselves Jews, even though they in fact still were.
- Matthew reserves the word ἐκκλησία for Christian groups and the term συναγωγή for the domain dominated by the Pharisees.[20] This dichotomy becomes even more prominent when we look at the possessive pronouns. Matthew regularly refers to *"their* synagogues" (4:23; 9:35; 10:17; 12:9; 13:54; cf. 23:34: *"your* synagogues"), whereas he calls the Christian branch the church of Jesus (*"my* church:" 16:18). Thus, the two communities are terminologically distinguished; they are two coexisting entities.[21]

---

[19] "Jewish Christians" might not be the best designation, since nowhere in the gospel according to Matthew, we find any support for the fact that Jesus' followers called themselves Christians (Χριστιανοί; cf. Acts 11:26; in the New Testament the word Χριστιανός is found only in Acts 11:26; 26:28 and 1 Peter 4:16). Despite this I will use the designation "Christians", because the community in question not only considers Jesus' words its foundation (7:24-25) but also understands itself as belonging to the church that is built on the confession that Jesus is the Messiah, the Son of God (16:16-17).

[20] Matthew is the only evangelist who uses the word ἐκκλησία (16:18 and 18:17 [twice]). The expression has a twofold meaning: a "community" is a small local congregation (18:17), yet together such small communities constitute the one community around Jesus (16:18). In Ancient Greek texts ἐκκλησία refers to duly summoned assemblies of a political nature (Liddell-Scott-Jones, *A Greek-English Lexicon*, 509). Matthew, however, is more influenced by the Septuagint, in which ἐκκλησία is the Greek rendering of the Hebrew קהל, which is occasionaly also translated as συναγωγή (Cf. Lust-Eynikel-Hauspie, *A Greek-English Lexicon* 1, 136). This confirms the close relationship of the ἐκκλησία to Israel as a religious community. Different from the Septuagint, in Matthew's gospel the words ἐκκλησία and συναγωγή are not used interchangeably.

[21] The original meaning of συναγωγή is "gathering (of people), congregation, assembly." It was only later that this word came to mean "synagogue, house of meeting." That synagogues as distinct architectural entities were not wide-spread in the Galilee of the first century C.E. is clear from archaeological evidence. See *Anchor Bible Dictionary* 6, 251-60.

- In 8:11-12, the expression "the children of the kingdom" is an honorary name for the people of Israel, but in 13:38 this appellation is attributed to the followers of Jesus. The Matthean community thus appropriates a title which previously applied to Israel as a whole.

These terms confirm that the Matthean community was efficiently alienating itself from its Jewish origins. This process did not happen in the same way in the various local groups which together formed the community. The division was probably not complete and definitive everywhere. In any case, Matthew nowhere calls his community the people of God (λαός) and neither does he refer to it as the new or the true Israel. Still, relations had suffered badly. The breach with the dominant group, led by Pharisees, was beyond repair and this movement was completely devalued by Matthew from a theological point of view. A case in point is the text of 21:43, in which it is announced that God will take away the kingdom from them and will give it to a people that produces the fruits of that kingdom. This statement is aimed against the Pharisees (cf. 21:45: "he was speaking about *them*"). We therefore may not read it as a statement condemning the entire Jewish people. The considerably vague term "people" does not necessarily refer to a people other than Israel, nor must that people be identified with the church or with the gentiles; if that had been the case, Matthew would have chosen the term ἐκκλησία or τὰ ἔθνη.[22]

Mission

The independent position vis-à-vis the Jewish community involved that the Matthean community became a closer partner of the other Christian communities within but also outside the same region. Relations between local house churches were well developed, as appears from the fact that Q and Mark were adopted and used by the group around Matthew soon after they were completed. Owing to the excellent infrastructure of the Roman Empire, great distances could be covered in a short time. The *Pax Romana* and the use of Koine Greek were also conducive to the communication.

Contacts with other Christian communities forced the circle around Matthew to again reflect on its mission strategy. Thus far, this community had exclusively targeted the Jews in Israel and in the near Diaspora. Other communities had experienced an entirely different development and had opened up to newcomers from a non-Jewish background at an early stage. As a result of this, they were more moderate on such essential parts of the Torah as circumcision and the purification laws. In the third phase, the groups around Matthew also began to aim at recruiting non-Jews and developed more flexible interpretations of those provisions from the Torah that proved to be obstacles to contact between Jews and gentiles. It is remarkable that these more liberal interpretations are attributed to Jesus, who advocates a radical option in a number of passages (15:1-20; 17:24-26; 18:21-22); in the same passages, a more moderate position is taken by Peter, who is more oriented towards continuity with Judaism. The

---

[22] Cf. Saldarini, *Matthew's Christian-Jewish Community*, 58-63.

effect of Jesus' criticism of Peter's position is that his leadership could be more readily accepted by Christians with a gentile background.[23]

What remains is the question of whether the orientation toward the gentiles entailed that the missionary activities among the house of Israel (10:5b-6) were stopped. In my view, this was not the case. In the third phase, the Christians around Matthew still saw Jews as potential members of their community. The extension to include πάντα τὰ ἔθνη (= all peoples, including Israel) is not an entirely new step in comparison to the mission discourse.[24] The restricted radius of action referred to in 10:5b-6 is already put in perspective within that same discourse, since, according to this text, the testimony of those who are sent to the cities of Israel will also reach the gentiles (10:18). Furthermore, I observe that, in 10:23, the same temporal limit is set as in 28:20: the mission lasts until "the coming of the Son of Man" or "the end of the age." Therefore, we cannot speak of two subsequent phases (Israel first and then the gentiles). The conversion activities among Jews which had been undertaken before continued undiminished when Matthew's community decided in favour of participation in the mission among non-Jews.

As a result of the broadened strategy, the community became a multi-coloured society, a "corpus mixtum," not in an ethical but in an ethnical sense,[25] consisting of people from various cultural backgrounds. With his story about Jesus, Matthew tried to give these subgroups a common ideological foundation and to inspire them to live honourable lives.[26] He stimulates them not to give offence (18:6-9), paying particular attention to the little ones in the community, who are vulnerable because they have chosen the virtue of humility with a view to the kingdom.

Worship
In the third phase, the Christians around Matthew no longer participated in meetings in the synagogues, but convened liturgical gatherings in private homes, which, according to archeological research, offered room for approximately 50 to 60 persons.[27] Matthew's community consisted of a large number of such small home churches spread over towns and villages in the Upper Galilee, the Golan, and the Southern part of Syria.

In their meetings, they celebrated the Supper of the Lord (26:26-29) and prayed the Lord's Prayer (6:9-13) in a version which, except for a few details, is identical to the one from the Didache (8:2-3). New members were received into the community by means of an initiation ritual, baptism, which was administered while invoking

---

[23] See Syreeni, "Peter as Character and Symbol," 151: "Peter's lack of understanding in halachic and disciplinary matters suggests that the author indirectly questions the Jewish-Christian understanding and application of the law."

[24] In the view of Hare-Harrington, "Make Disciples," 359-69, πάντα τὰ ἔθνη in 28:19 should be translated 'all the Gentiles', whereas Meier, "Nations or Gentiles," 94-102, opts for an inclusive interpretation. He demonstrates that the phrase includes both Jews and pagans.

[25] Luomanen, *Entering the Kingdom of Heaven*, 262-82.

[26] Cf. Stanton, *A Gospel for a New People*, 378: "Matthew wrote his gospel as a 'foundation document' for a cluster of Christian communities, probably in Syria in the mid 80s."

[27] Avigad, *The Herodian Quarter*, 75.

the names of God, Jesus, and the Holy Spirit (28:19). This ritual was performed after a brief period of elementary instruction ("making them disciples"). After their baptism, the new members were further initiated in the teachings of Jesus for a longer period.[28]

False Prophets

A serious problem in the third phase was that Matthew's community was threatened by the appearance of false prophets (7:15-23; 24:11, 24). Prophets frequently visited sister churches. During their travels, they depended for food and accommodation on the hospitality of communities where they stopped on their way. According to Matthew, they had a right to a cordial reception, given the nature of their position (10:41). However, in the busy traffic between local churches, it was difficult to distinguish the true prophets from the false ones. This problem did not only arise in Matthew's circle but is also discussed in the Didache.

It is not immediately clear why Matthew brands particular figures as false prophets. At first sight, they did not differ much from other members of the community. After all, they called Jesus their Lord (7:21) and performed charismatic activities while invoking his name (7:22), as others were also able to do (17:20). Although certain parts of their teachings deserved criticism (24:23, 26), their greatest fault was in another area. They distinguished themselves from others by their uncharitable way of life, they were guilty of immorality (7:23; 24:12).[29] What this entailed is explained by the allegation that they were ravenous (7:15). This term indicates that they took advantage of the hospitality offered them, that they lived off the community, or asked a fee for their charismatic deeds. One result of their egocentric attitude was that the love of the community grew cold, which had an adverse effect on the position of "the little ones."

Matthew's criticism of the false prophets finds many parallels in his controversy against the scribes and the Pharisees. In both cases, Matthew censures the contrast between their words and their deeds (7:15-23; 23:3); they appear different outwardly from what they are inside (7:15; 23:25, 27, 28); both groups are warned by means of statements that relate to the final judgment, because, on that occasion, a person's acts will be decisive (7:23; 21:43). Here we see that the weapons that were used in the second phase against the Pharisaic movement were employed against certain leaders in Matthew's own circle in the third phase.

---

[28] This can be inferred from the order of the participles in 28:19-20 (βαπτίζοντες αὐτοὺς [...] διδάσκοντες αὐτοὺς...). See Scheuermann, *Gemeinde im Umbruch*.

[29] Here, ἀνομία is the refusal to obey the law and does not mean antinomianism which is a denial of the enduring validity of the Torah.

Conclusion

In this paper, I have tried to give a dynamic picture of Matthew's community. The innovative element here is the focus on the phases that preceded the period in which the gospel of Matthew achieved its final form. Two main tendencies emerged in the development described above. The first is that, as a result of the historical circumstances, the community increasingly distanced itself from the Jewish community; with his book, Matthew wanted to legitimize this process. The second tendency is that, owing to its special developmental process, the community was continuously subject to internal tension; Matthew tried to stimulate the social cohesion in his community by uniting the various subgroups around the interpretation of the Torah offered by Jesus and further cultivated by the community's local leaders. By publishing his own story of Jesus' life, he provided his community with a new and firm foundation. In view of the close contacts with sister churches, both within and outside the same region, it is likely that, from the start, his book was also meant for a wider circle of readers.[30] For them, too, Matthew saw the road his community had taken as the road to life.

---

[30] Cf. Bauckham, *The Gospels for All Christians.*

Chapter Four

When, Why, and for Whom Was the Didache Created? Insights into the Social and Historical Setting of the Didache Communities

Aaron Milavec

Research Fellow, 2002-2003, CSRS, University of Victoria (BC, Canada)

My ideas regarding the Didache have changed many times in the course of the last fifteen years. During this period, three convictions have emerged that have guided my studies:

1 *Unity of the Didache* – Up to this point, a unified reading of the Didache has been impossible because the prevailing assumption has been that the Didache was created in stages with the compiler splicing together pre-existing documents with only a minimum of editing. The end result, therefore, was a complex (or even a haphazard) collage that joined together bits and pieces of traditional material coming from unidentified communities and unknown authors. Thanks to the impact of Jacob Neusner during our 1988 summer seminar on "Religious Systems," I have slowly come to the conviction that the Didache has a intentional unity from beginning to end which, up to this point, has gone unnoticed.

2 *Independence of the Didache from the gospels* – The Didache has been widely understood as citing either Matthew's gospel or some combination of the Matthean or Lucan traditions. From this vantage point, it followed that the date of composition had to be set beyond the 80s and that the Synoptic material could be used to help interpret and understand the Didache. Thanks to my work with Willy Rordorf during the summers of 1990 and 1992, I came to an early appreciation of the possibility that the Didache might have been created without any dependence upon any known gospel. My extensive study of this issue demonstrates that the internal logic, theological orientation, and pastoral practice of the Didache runs decisively counter to what one finds within the received gospels.[1] The repercussions of this conclusion are enormous: (a) I am encouraged to return to a mid-first century dating for the Didache, and (b) I am prohibited from using Matthew's gospel by way of clarifying the intent of the Didache.

---

[1] Aaron Milavec, *The Didache*, 693-740; Id., "Synoptic Tradition in the Didache Revisited."

3 *The Didache's Oral Character* – Given the manifest clues of orality[2] within the Didache itself, one can be quite certain that it was originally composed orally and that it circulated on the lips of the members of this community for many years before any occasion arose that called for a scribe to prepare a textual version. The Didache was created in "a culture of high residual orality"[3] wherein "oral sources" attached to respected persons were routinely given greater weight and were immeasurably more serviceable than "written sources."[4] Furthermore, recent studies have demonstrated that oral repetition has a measure of socially maintained stability but not the frozen rigidity of a written text.[5] As such, any methodology circumscribed by the bias of textuality and ignorant of orality can no longer be relied upon to explain the origin, the internal structures, and the use of the Didache.

Recovering the Orality of the Didache

To test this "orality" on the part of the Didache, I decided some dozen years ago to memorize it. Linda Bartholomew and other members of the National Organization

---

[2] Within the Didache, the vocabulary and the linguistic structure itself displays a one-sided preference for orality. Thus, the Didache defines the Way of Life and immediately goes on to specify the "training" required for the assimilation "of these *words*" (1:3). The novice is told to honor "the one *speaking* to you the *word* of God" (4:1) thereby signaling that oral training was presupposed. Moreover, the novice trembles "at the *words* that you have *heard*" (3:8).

In every instance where the Didache cites specific mandates from the Hebrew Scriptures, the oral aspect (as opposed to the written) is highlighted: "It has been *said*" (1:6); "The Lord has likewise *said*" (9:5); "This is the thing having been *said* by the Lord" (14:3); "As it has been *said*" (16:7). The same thing can be presumed to hold true when citing the "good news" (8:2; 11:3; 15:3; 15:4; see Milavec, *The Didache*, Chap. 11, box e). Accordingly, the Didache gives full attention to speaking rightly (1:3b; 2:3, 5; 4:8b, 14; 15:3b) and entirely neglects false or empty writing. At the baptism, the novice is immersed in water "having *said* all these things beforehand" (7:1). Thus, when the novice is warned to watch out for those who "might make you wander from this way of training" (6:1), one surmises that defective words rather than defective texts are implied. The same holds true, when later in the Didache, the baptized are warned only to receive him/her who "should train you in all the things *said* beforehand" (11:1) indicating that even the Didache was being heard. Finally, faced with the end time, each one is alerted to the importance of frequently being "gathered together" (16:2). This enforces an earlier admonition to "seek every day the presence of the saint in order that you may rest upon their *words*" (4:2) – thereby signaling once again how verbal exchange was paramount when "seeking the things pertaining to your souls" (16:2). The one misbehaving, accordingly, was reproved "not in anger [i.e., angry words], but in peace" (15:3). Those unable to abide by the reproof received were cut off from hearing or being discussed by community members: "Let no one *speak* to him/her, nor let anyone *hear* from you about him/her until he/she should repent" (15:3).

From beginning to end, therefore, the vocabulary and linguistic structure of the Didache reinforce oral performance. The literary world of seeing, reading, writing, and editing are entirely passed over in silence. Accordingly, the Didache was created, transmitted, interpreted, and transformed in "a culture of high residual orality which nevertheless communicated significantly by means of literary creations" (Achtemeier, "Omne verbum sonat," 9-19, 26-27). See Draper, "Confessional Western Text-Centered Biblical Interpretation," 59-77; Henderson, "Didache and Orality," 295-299 and Milavec, *The Didache*, 715-725.

[3] Achtemeier, "Omne verbum sonat," 3.

[4] Achtemeier, *ibid.*, 9-11 and Ong, *The Presence of the Word*, 52-53.

[5] Achtemeier, *ibid.*, 27 and Ong, *The Presence of the Word*, 231-234.

of Biblical Storytellers gave me some practical hints on how to do this. For my part, I was skeptical. Let's face it, I had become thoroughly habituated to making, consulting, and relying upon written records – in everything from analyzing texts to shopping for groceries. Once I began, however, I surprised myself. By abandoning the norms of linear logic that structure written texts, I gradually found that I was able to intuit the oral logic that structured the Didache. Once this happened, I memorized the Didache with great ease.

Once the whole of the Didache was in my bones, I took every opportunity to perform it. Before my students. Before my faculty. At regional meetings of learned societies. As word got around, I was even invited to perform it before a Jewish audience. With each performance, I was adjusting my translation and expanding my understanding of the narrative until, in gradual steps, I finally felt assured that my narrative performance revealed the flow of topics and the marvelous unity hidden below the surface from beginning to end. The suspicion that overcame me, therefore, is that I had recovered the same thread that those who originally recited the Didache relied upon for ordering their recitation.

In my seminars, consequently, I perform segments of the Didache so that participants can take in the oral feel before they read it on the page. I furthermore invite participants to make a tape of the Didache that they can listen to as they go to sleep at night or as they travel back and forth in their cars.[6]

The Organizational Unity of the Didache in a Nutshell

The object of my thousand-page commentary[7] is to reconstruct the pastoral genius of the framers of the Didache. In a nutshell, this pastoral genius consisted in establishing a comprehensive, step-by-step program of formation that would transform the settled habits of perceiving and of judging of gentile candidates seeking perfection in their new religious movement. Throughout, the framers of the Didache gave detailed norms and practical descriptions of what was to be done. Behind these particulars, however, lie the concerns and the anxieties, the experience and the successes of senior mentors who, over a period of time, worked with candidates and fashioned a training program which transmitted, in measured and gradual steps, the operative values and theological underpinnings which knit together their individual and collective lives. Undoubtedly the framers of the Didache were well aware that any community that did not effectively pass on its values, its rites, its way of life would flounder and eventually perish from the face of the earth. The Didache was the insurance policy that this was not going to happen to them!

---

[6] For those hesitant to create their own oral recording, *EasyGreek Software* has reproduced, at a nominal cost, my oral presentation (20 min.) and, on the reverse side, has recorded a feminist adaptation by Deborah Rose-Milavec. Portions of this cassette might even find a suitable use in the classroom. See *www.Didache.info* for details.

[7] Milavec, *The Didache*.

In the next pages, I will reconstruct some of the hidden dynamics of this training program in order to allow you to glimpse something of its organic unity. I will also reflect upon the key importance of selecting and testing an origination hypothesis by way of resolving the perplexing question of why the Didache was created and how it was used. Finally, I will reflect on how the date and provenance of the Didache shift once one establishes its independence from Matthew's gospel.

The Way of Life as Implying an Apprenticeship

After defining the Way of Life, the Didache turns its attention to "the training [required for the assimilation] of these words" (1:3). The Greek word διδαχή makes reference to the training that a master-trainer (διδάσκαλος) imparts to apprentices or disciples. In classical Greek, basket weaving, hunting with a bow, and pottery making represent typical skills transmitted under the term διδαχή.[8] For our purposes here, it is significant to note that the verb διδάσκειν – customarily translated as "to teach" – was normally used to refer to a prolonged apprenticeship under the direction of a master:

> Thus διδάσκειν is the word used more especially for the impartation of practical or theoretical knowledge when there is continued activity with a view to gradual, systematic, and therefore all the more fundamental assimilation.[9]

This usage finds confirmation from modern studies of how the rudiments of a scientific, artistic, or religious tradition are passed on from one generation to the next. Michael Polanyi, more especially, has noted that all deep knowing implies a way of being in one's body and a way of being in the world that cannot be transmitted by a mere telling in words.[10] For an adult to learn the ways of a master, a novice has to submit to a prolonged apprenticeship. Polanyi notes that, even during an apprenticeship, learning depends upon a certain sympathy that exists between the novice and the master. This sympathy begins in the spontaneous admiration that prompts the novice to establish a master-apprentice

---

[8] See Rengstorf, "διδάσκω, διδάσκαλος, νομοδιδάσκαλος, κτλ." 135

[9] Rengstorf, *ibid.*

[10] Polanyi repudiates the ideal of critical, detached knowing as unrealized and unrealizable (both in science as well as in religion), and he explains that this is so by virtue of the fact that all knowledge is embodied knowledge relying upon tacit skills:

> If we know a great deal that we cannot tell, and if even that which we know and can tell is accepted by us as true only in view of its bearing on a reality beyond it . . .; if indeed we recognize a great discovery, or else a great personality, as most real, owing to the wide range of its yet unknown future manifestations: then the idea of knowledge based on wholly identifiable grounds collapse, and we must conclude that *the transmission of knowledge from one generation to the other must be predominantly tacit* (Polanyi, *The Tacit Dimension*, 61).

Given the tacit character of all deep knowing, Polanyi insists that no scientific, artistic, or religious enterprise can be entirely analyzed, dissected, and expressed in plain language such that a detached observer could discern and affirm the foundational principles involved and, through progressive steps in clear logic, arrive at the same tacit skills presupposed by the master.

relationship in the first place. This sympathy operates throughout the apprenticeship itself, giving the novice the means to enter into and to assimilate the performance skills exhibited by his/her trusted master.[11] The authority of a master, consequently, is directed toward progressively enlarging the performance skills of novices such that they, in the end, demonstrate that they understand his/her words because they share the way of being and doing that is upheld and prized by the community to which they belong.

Remembering One's Mentor, the Presence of the Lord, and "Trembling"

The internal clues of the Didache demonstrate that the Way of Life was not received as mere information. Mentors understood themselves as "speaking to you the word of God" (4:1); hence, they were honored "as the Lord for where the dominion of the Lord is spoken of, there the Lord is" (4:1). Faced with this realization, the Didache notes, in passing, that the novice became someone "trembling through all time at the words that you have heard" (3:8). This was the way that Israel originally experienced the word of the Lord from Mt. Sinai (Exod 19:16) and the way that the prophets came to discover the transforming power of their own callings (e.g., Ezra 9:4; Isa 66:2; Hab 3:16).

The temptation might exist to trivialize "trembling" and to imagine that here one finds only a pious metaphor. On the other hand, those of you who have studied the phenomenology of scientific knowing by Michael Polanyi[12] or those of you who have

---

[11] Michael Polanyi notes that the success of any given master-apprentice relationship either succeeds or falters on the basis of the quality of the sustained admiration and sympathy operative within the apprenticeship itself:

> The pupil must presume that a teaching which appears meaningless to start with has in fact a meaning which can be discovered by hitting on the same kind of indwelling as the teacher is practicing. Such an effort is based upon accepting the teacher's authority (Polanyi, *The Tacit Dimension*, 61).

Authority within the context of an apprenticeship is not to be confused with authoritarianism. The master of a craft does not intend to accept the compliance and admiration of disciples in order to rule over them but rather to transform them into skilled performers. The authority of a master, consequently, is directed toward progressively enlarging the performance skills of novices such that they, in the end, demonstrate that they understand his/her words because they share the way of being and doing that is upheld and prized by the community to which they belong.

Applying this to the Didache, it becomes clear that novices were not intent upon entering an authoritarian system where they were simply told what to do and what not to do. Rather, novices came forward intent upon achieving for themselves the way of being and of doing (the wisdom) exemplified by those mentors whom they admired. This demanded an interior transformation that could only be achieved due to trusting person-to-person contacts over an extended period of time in what Polanyi would describe as an apprenticeship.

[12] Polanyi, *Personal Knowledge*. Polanyi insisted that the ideal of objective knowing based upon facts and experimentation alone was a misleading ideal that could never be put into practice. As suggested earlier, the personal calling of a scientist followed by long years of apprenticeship under admired masters reveals the personal dynamics that make all deep and transformative learning possible. Even later, those collaborating within a research program continue to be guided by the tacit skills and overarching ideals learned from their mentors: "The riches of mental companionship between two equals can be released only if they share a convivial passion for others greater than themselves, within a like-minded community – the partners must belong to each other by participating in a reverence for a common superior knowledge" (378). All this applies, with even a greater force, to the bonds within the Didache communities.

first-hand experience of being transformed by an apprenticeship under the direction of a beloved mentor might well imagine that this is the stuff of which the Didache speaks.

Consider, for example, the case of Malcolm X. In his autobiography, Malcolm recalls how he trembled at reading Elijah Mohammed's words during his time in prison.[13] This was so, not because someone had told him to do so, but because the words of his spiritual master were liberating him from his former way of death and opening him up to embrace his true destiny and calling as a Black Muslim.

> I went to bed every night ever more awed. If not Allah, who else could have put such wisdom into that little humble lamb of a man from the Georgia fourth grade and sawmills and cotton patches. . . . My adoration of Mr. Muhammad grew. . . . My worship of him was so awesome that he was the first man whom I had ever feared – not fear such as of a man with a gun, but the fear such as one has of the power of the sun (210, 211, 212).[14]

This is what the Didache means when it speaks of "remember[ing] night and day the one speaking to you the word of God" (4:1) and "trembling at all times at the words that you have received" (3:8). This same phenomenology existed among the classical rabbis where it was commonplace to find disciples listening to their masters "with awe and fear, with trembling and trepidation" (*b.Ber.* 22a).

Whether Each Novice had a Single Spiritual Mentor

The Didache offers evidence suggesting that each novice was paired off with a single spiritual master. The principal clue for this is the fact that the entire training program (save for 1:3) addresses a single novice using the second-person singular. If, under normal circumstances, a single spiritual master were assigned the training of many or all the novices within a community, one would have expected that the second-person plural would have been used throughout. Furthermore, within the Way of Life training program, the novice is instructed to actively remember and mull over the life and the training of "the one speaking to you the word of God" (4:1). This use of the singular here points in the direction of each novice having a single master. So, too, when regulations are put forward for choosing the water for baptism (7:2-3) and for ordering "the one being baptized to fast beforehand" (7:4), in each case the singular is used – again confirming the expectation that each candidate was baptized individually by a single individual – presumably the one who was their spiritual mentor and parent.

---

[13] *Autobiography of Malcolm X*, 170.
[14] Elijah Mohammed represented a way of life that powerfully attracted Malcolm. Through letters, and later, through personal contacts, Malcolm gradually discovered his own calling "to remove the blinders from the eyes of the black man [woman] in the wilderness of North America" (210). This calling emerged for Malcolm within the spontaneous awe and fear that he felt for his teacher. For more details, see Milavec, *The Didache*, Chap. 1, box h.

Since women in the ancient world were accustomed to be trained by other women (#1g, #2b),[15] and since it would have been a source of scandal for a man to be alone for prolonged periods with a woman unrelated to him, it would be presumed that, save for special circumstances, women were appointed to train female candidates, and men were appointed to train male candidates.

Whether the Didache Envisioned Training Women

Matthew 5-8 provides an illustration of a training program directed to men. Phrases like "angry with his brother" (5:22) and "your brother has something against you" (5:23) and "eye of your brother" (7:4) reflect the mediterranean world in which men inhabited the public spaces and settled their concerns. The women in the courtyards, meanwhile, are silently passed over. Jesus' observations about the one "looking at a woman lustfully" or "divorcing his wife" (5:28, 31) again captures exclusively the male point of view.

In contrast, while the Didache focuses upon issues that apply particularly to women,[16] other aspects apply particularly to men.[17] The household codes of *Did.* 4:9-11 are noticeably inclusive. In fact, my gender-inclusive translation[18] makes it evident that women and women's issues were being addressed throughout the Didache. Furthermore, the Greek expression τέκνον μου (3:1-6) literally signifies "my offspring" without regard for age or sex. In this context, it cannot be supposed that the master-trainer is the biological father or mother of the novice. Within the Septuagint, τέκνον μου is already used metaphorically as an intimate form of address (Gen 43:29) or to denote a novice in relationship to his trainer and mentor (1 Sam 3:16; 26:17). This gender-inclusive term aptly captures the fact that the Didache addresses women and their concerns.

[15] In Milavec, *The Didache*, one finds over three hundred extended discussions bearing upon particular aspects of the social, historical, and religious world in which the Didache communities took shape. These discussions provide information and sources that are placed in boxes (defined by shaded areas) that are scattered throughout the book. For purposes of brevity, these sources will be henceforth presented in the text in abbreviated form. Thus, #1g refers to box g in Chapter 1 of Milavec. #2b refers to box b in Chapter 2.

[16] In the revised decalogue of the Didache, the injunctions against practicing magic, making potions, and murdering offspring by means of abortion (2:2) apply principally to women. So, too, references to training "sons and daughters . . . in the fear of God" (4:9) also addresses a sphere largely relegated to women. When it comes to offering first fruits of the dough being made into bread (13:5), one has here a sphere of activity entire dominated by women. *Did.* 13:6-7 might apply equally to men and women.

[17] In the revised decalogue of the Didache, the injunctions against adultery, corrupting boys, and illicit sex (2:2) apply principally to men. In the ancient world, a husband could commit adultery only by having intercourse with the wife of another man; if he had sexual relations with a slave, a prostitute, a concubine, or a divorced or widowed woman, this did not constitute adultery. Outside of pederasty which Jews particularly abhorred (Josephus, *C. Ap.* 1:199; Philo, *Spec. Leg.* 3:37 and *Contempl.* 52:57-61), one cannot know to what degree the prohibition of "illicit sex" (πορνεία) excluded men from having sexual relations with slaves, prostitutes, and concubines. When it comes to offering first fruits of the wine vat and the threshing floor (13:5), one has here a sphere of activity entire dominated by men. *Did.* 13:6-7 might apply equally to men and women.

[18] Milavec, *The Didache*, 12-45. The Greek of the Didache is very much gender-inclusive. This quality, however, is practically entirely lost in English, French, and German translations that are forced, by rules of grammar, to give preference to the male gender. To my knowledge, Milavec is the first person to provide a gender-inclusive translation.

In contrast, Jewish wisdom literature normally addresses the gendered "my son" and then proceeds to warn against being intoxicated by loose women (e.g., Prov 5:20). The Didache, therefore, stands apart from most first century instructional material by deliberately offering training to women (#1e, #1f, #1k, #2n). Such training insures that women within the Didache communities were expected to be active participants within community affairs.[19] As Deborah Rose-Gaier rightly notes, nowhere in the Didache does one find "a household code whereby wives are subordinated to their husbands."[20]

First Rule – Praying for Enemies and Turning the Other Cheek

Seen from the vantage point of an orderly progressive of topics, the initial section dealing with praying for enemies and turning the other cheek would appear to be placed at the head of the training program because new recruits had to be immediately prepared to receive abusive treatment (1:3-4). When examined in detail, the "enemies" envisioned by the Didache were not highway robbers or Roman soldiers, but relatives and friends who had become antagonists due to the candidate's new religious convictions.[21] Thus, praying and fasting (#4c) for such "enemies" functioned to sustain a non-violent surrender to the abusive family situations[22] hinted at in *Did.* 1:4.

---

[19] The only function specifically reserved for men was the one in which negotiations with outsiders (nearly always men) was mandatory (15:1). Kurt Niederwimmer interprets *Did.* 15:1-2 to mean "that the local officials, together with the prophets and teachers (or, to the extent that the last two groups are absent, they alone) lead the worship service that formerly was in the hands of the prophets and teachers alone" (*The Didache*, 202). Willy Rordorf, for his part, reads *Did.* 15:1-2 in a more radical manner: "the bishops and deacons are charged to replace them" (*La doctrine des douze apôtres*, 228) as presiders at the Eucharist. Georg Schöllgen, in contrast, takes the position that "these matters remain in the dark" ("The Didache as a Church Order," 59). Going beyond Schöllgen, I would argue that the Didache provides sufficient evidence to decide that neither the prophets nor the bishops presided at the Eucharist (see #6o and #9f). From my reading of the evidence, the presider at the first Eucharist would have been the presider at the baptism, namely, the mentor who had "fathered" or "mothered" the candidate. Space prohibits me from developing this topic here. One can be sure, however, that if women were being trained by women, then the logic of the text and the social reconstruction of the rite would lead us to surmise that these same women were baptizing and eucharistizing.

[20] Deborah Rose-Gaier, "The Didache: A Community of Equals," a paper presented in the "Women and the Historical Jesus" session of the Society of Biblical Literature's 1996 Annual Meeting. Highlights summarized in Crossan, *The Birth of Christianity*, 369-373. Citation from p. 371.

[21] Cf. Milavec, "The Social Setting," 131-143. Kloppenborg, in his paper in this volume, continues to think of the Didache as using Luke 6:29-30 and imagining the social setting of a robbery. In the Synoptic gospels, meanwhile, one finds what John Dominic Crossan refers to as "an almost savage attack on family values" (*Jesus: A Revolutionary Biography*, 58). Sayings such as "I have come to set a man against his father . . " (Matt 10:35-36) and "Call no one your father on earth" (Matt 23:9) serve to illustrate how inter-generational strife arose as parents endeavored to use their authority to block the conversion of their adult children. See n. 34 below for further illustrations.

[22] Among other things, the abusive family situation envisioned the forcible seizure of the novice's goods (1:4). The candidate was instructed to yield completely to such hostile acts and, at the same time, to surrender his goods to beggars (1:5), not due to any compulsion, but simply because his/her "Father" wished it. What emerges here is the contrast between a natural father seizing assets and the Father in heaven who generously gives to everyone in need and invites imitation. The text will return to this shortly.

Just as the Didache omits subordinating wives to their husbands, it likewise omits the Lord's commandment requiring children to honor their parents. Gentiles could hardly be trained to honor their parents (Exod 20:12) when that "filial piety" so highly prized by Romans would have made the desertion of ancestral gods and the abandonment of their parental upbringing unthinkable save in those instances wherein an entire patriarchal household converted to the Lord as a group (e.g., as in the case of the household of Cornelius in Acts 10). Given the implications of *Did.* 1:3-4, it became impossible to honor their parents and, at the same time, to honor the God of Israel. Accordingly, novices preparing to enter the community were directed to honor God as their true Father (1:5; 9:2-3; 10:2) and to accept their mentors as their true parent (4:8). Not even God can require two contradictory commitments.

The Great Difference between the Two Rules of Giving

Within the training program, the issue of giving is taken up at the very beginning and, again, near the very end. The first giving (1:4) is presented in the present imperative and represents the kind of giving the candidate was expected to practice immediately upon entering upon his/her apprenticeship. The second section on giving (4:5-8), however, is much more than a reinforcement of the earlier giving. Now everything (save for 4:5) is presented in the future tense and the focus is on the routine "taking and giving" and the much more extensive "partnering" of all one's resources "with your brother [or sister]" (4:8) (#2m, #2o). The future tense used here could function as a mild imperative (as in English) but then this would leave the awkward situation whereby two diverse rules of giving are provided and no attempt is made to harmonize them. On the other hand, if one examines the second set of rules for giving, one discovers that this later giving involves sharing one's resources with members of the community – a situation that would prevail only after the time the candidate had gained admittance as a full member of the movement through baptism.

Consider the character of the first kind of giving (1:5). The novice is taught to yield "to anyone asking you for anything" simply because "the Father wishes to give these things from his own free gifts" (1:5). This is the first instance where the fatherhood of God is introduced within the pragmatic theology of *imitatio dei* ("the imitation of God"). God gives freely; hence, in imitation of the one who has blessed the novice with the necessities of life, the novice acts in a parallel fashion.[23] Acting as a faithful steward or broker, the novice dispenses not his / her own resources but the Father's "free gifts." In so doing, the novice is prohibited from feeling proud or generous in the act of giving since whatever he or she gives belongs to the Father to begin with. The one receiving, meanwhile, need not feel humiliated or indebted to the one giving (namely, "do not

---

[23] The Didache is the oldest known Christian document that makes it clear that, in the act of giving, what is given has been freely received from the Father. This evaluation of personal possessions finds clear expression in other Christian and Jewish documents as well (see #2d).

ask for it back") since, in point of fact, the recipient is receiving what belongs to the Father.[24]

Roman society placed great emphasis upon the inviolability of private ownership and upon economizing; hence, Romans felt no moral or civic obligation to come to the aid of the poor or destitute.[25] There were public benefactors, to be sure, who erected monuments, subsidized festivals, and provided short-term relief in the face of emergencies. Such persons, however, did so with the motive of promoting themselves and their families as "benefactors". In contrast, the rule of giving advanced by the Didache is calculated to break down and replace these very instincts. To enforce this, the novice is further prevented from even examining the worthiness or honesty of the one asking (1:5). This final examination is left in God's hands. Thus, by this rule of action, the former stubborn instincts governing possessions is broken down and replaced by the notion of stewardship, gratitude, and *imitatio dei*. Those incapable of implementing the rule of *Did.* 1:5 would have to be sent away since, in the end, such persons would be incapable of practicing a lifelong responsiveness to the needs of "brothers" and "sisters" within the community they aspired to join. The opening rule of giving, consequently, now appears as the absolutely indispensable training grounds for the economic partnership that comes later. And this is only the first of eight pragmatic reasons accounting for this rule.[26]

The Progressive Training Implied in the Two Ways Schema

When one examines how material is set out in the Way of Life, one discovers that a progressive training program is implied. For example, notice how the negative prohibitions (2:2-7) come first. Then, once this foundation is in place, "fences" (3:1-6) can be introduced by way of supplying a framework whereby grave infractions are prevented by avoiding minor infractions. Finally, once minor infractions are checked, then positive virtues can be cultivated (3:7-10). Any mentor who would scramble this propaedeutic order would clearly be building on sand and risking disaster.

[24] The *Derekh Erets Zuta*, a third-century training manual for rabbinic students, echoes this same theology:

> If you did a great favor [for someone], regard it as small,
> and do not say, "I did this good act with my own [money]."
> Rather it was [from what God] had graciously given you,
> and you should offer thanks to Heaven (2:10).

[25] Cf. De Sainte Croix, *The Class Struggle*, 194-197; Hamel, *Poverty and Charity in Roman Palestine*, 219 and Reid, "Charity, Almsgiving (Roman)," 391-92.

[26] Milavec, *The Didache*, 190-198. The eight effects of implementing the rule of 1:5 are as follows:
  1. Preparing for a Lifetime of Sharing Everything with One's Brothers
  2. Breaking Addiction to Increased Economic Productivity
  3. Developing the Habit of Acting in Imitation of God
  4. Relieving the Debt of Gratitude for the Knowledge and Life Received
  5. Tasting the Benefit of Almsgiving as Ransoming One's Sins
  6. Beginning a Prophetic Witness to God's Future Designs
  7. Preparing to Publicly Account for One's New Commitments
  8. Breaking Down the Bond between the Candidate and his Biological Family

The Art of Reconciliation Revealed by Degrees

From 4:2 onward, everything is framed in the simple future tense. Herein one hears the novice being trained for future eventualities that will emerge only after baptism when community life becomes a possibility. The Didache first holds out the future promise of finding "rest" among the "saints" (4:2), and then it addresses the darker side of community life: "dissention" and "fighting" (4:3). The novice is trained to anticipate the obligation of intervening in these latter instances. The details of this intervention, however, are kept for later when the practice of "reproving" and "shunning" are spelled out in detail (15:3). From this case, one can learn that the ordering of materials does not stop with the end of the Way of Life but continues throughout the whole of the Didache. One might suspect, therefore, that whenever the same issue shows up in two places, this might have been done deliberately in order to respect the condition of the candidate and to implement the principle of gradualism.

As another instance of this, consider the confession of failings. Training in the Way of Life closes with the injunction that "in church [i.e., in the assembly], you will confess your failings" (4:14). The novice is thus alerted that all the particulars of the Way of Life would be used for an examination of conscience and a public admission of failures. For the moment, the candidate is entirely unfamiliar with the eucharistic meal; hence, neither the time, place, or the character of this confession are presented. This will come later at *Did.* 14:1-3. It suffices that the novice be forewarned that a confession will take place so that "you will not go to your prayer with a bad conscience" (4:14). This general rubric suffices and, in due course, will give way to a theology of sacrifice once the Eucharist is experienced. Again, the condition of the candidate is respected and the principle of gradualism prevails.

The Nature of the Perfection Required by the Didache

In 1987, David Flusser argued that those preparing for baptism were told to observe as much of the Torah as possible, including food regulations, "in order to strengthen the ties of gentile Christians believers with Jews believing in Christ who were 'all zealous of the Law [Torah]' (Acts 21:20)."[27] Four years later,[28] Jonathan Draper, who has always impressed me with his creative and insightful scholarship, championed a similar position seemingly independent of Flusser's study. Draper concludes that "the Didache allows the proselyte flexibility about the timetable, but at the end of the day, it is required of him/her that he/she become a full Jew in order to attain salvation."[29]

---

[27] Flusser, "Paul's Jewish-Christian Opponents,"(1987) 86.

[28] Jefford, in his *The Sayings of Jesus*, proposed that the Didachist "did not seek to replace the 'yoke of the Torah' with the 'yoke of Jesus' (cf. *Did.* 6:2) but instead . . . was anxious to weld the two yokes into a single system" (102). The details of Jefford's thesis were largely undeveloped; yet, in effect, Jefford offered a variant of Flusser's thesis (without mentioning him).

[29] Draper, "Torah and Troublesome Apostles," (1991) 368. See also Draper's paper in this volume where his earlier position is reenforced.

Draper's thesis has been enthusiastically received in some circles.[30] Finally, with the collaboration of Huub van de Sandt and Flusser, a modified version of Flusser's 1987 thesis has been proposed in a book that will surely give it wide circulation.[31] While both Flusser and Draper are very persuasive and very keen to exploit every clue available to support their positions, I believe they are fundamentally mistaken and risk misinterpreting a foundational issue, namely, the centrality of the Way of Life as defining the perfection required of gentile proselytes in preparation for the coming of the Lord (16:2).[32]

My own reading of 6:2 begins by taking seriously 4:13 where the novice is warned just prior to the end of his/her training:

> You will not at all leave behind the rules of the Lord,
> but you will guard the things you have received
> neither adding anything nor taking away.

The "rules of the Lord" here clearly look backward to the training received in the Way of Life. To be sure, the novice would be rightfully distressed if, in the very next session, he/she were told that everything received up to this point was only propaedeutic for

---

[30] See, for example, Mitchell, "Baptism in the Didache," 231-232.

[31] Van de Sandt-Flusser, *The Didache.*

[32] In my book, *The Didache,* I devote an entire chapter to examining this position (769-782). In brief, my position on this matter is as follows:

1. To begin with, it is extraneous to make appeals to Acts 15:20 or to the Noahide Covenant by way of resolving the background for interpreting *Did.* 6:2-3. The framers of the Didache knew nothing of Acts 15:20. In fact, the very formulation of the Way of Life for gentiles clearly goes way beyond both Acts 15:20 and the requirements of the Noahide Covenant. Flusser, more especially, repeatedly downplays or ignores historical development within Jewish sources. David Novak, on the other hand, demonstrates that the very notion of the Noahide Covenant did not emerge within formative Judaism until the time of the Tosefta (*The Image of the Non-Jew,* 5-8).

2. The same thing can be said relative to uses of Paul and of Matthew. Both Draper and Flusser identify those "apostles" coming with the intention of "tearing down" (*Did.* 11:2) with Pauline Christians (Draper, "Torah and Troublesome Apostles," 372; Flusser, "Paul's Jewish-Christian Opponents," 71-90 and Van de Sandt-Flusser, *The Didache,* 239. 268). It follows that the "lawlessness" (*Did.* 16:4: ἀνομία) characterizing "false-prophets and corrupters" (*Did.* 16:3) just prior to the Lord's coming can be identified as the Pauline doctrine that the gentiles are saved through faith in Christ without observing Torah (Draper, p. 370)! Here, again, careful analysis demonstrates that the framers of the Didache took no notice of Paul; hence, it is hazardous to suppose that Paul or his theology is the *bête noire* which is being fended off by the Didache. The same holds for Matthew's gospel.

3. Flusser, given his ahistorical predispositions, easily associates "yoke of the Lord" with the Mosaic Torah (Van de Sandt-Flusser, *The Didache,* 241). Draper, being more careful, notes that the phrase "yoke of the Lord" does not appear within the early rabbinic material. While "yoke of the Torah" is used, Draper cites its usage in a text that also uses "yoke of the [Roman] kingdom" and "yoke of worldly care" (*m. Abot* 3:5). This demonstrates that, as late as the early third century, "yoke" was a far-reaching metaphor that found applications to areas of existence quite apart from Torah ("Draper, Torah and troublesome Apostles," 364). Even if "yoke of the Lord" had some consistent use in both the Christian Scriptures and in the rabbinic sources, however, it would still have to be examined whether the internal rhetoric and logic of the Didache support that meaning. See also Kari Syreeni's contribution in this volume, nn. 45 and 46.

learning/doing what Maimonides would later enumerate as the 613 prescriptions of Torah. "Hey, wait a minute!" the novice might object, "Didn't you just get finished telling me that nothing was to be added?" And, indeed, his distress would be right on target.

The γάρ-clause in 6:2 serves to explain what has gone before. Flusser gets off track because he mistakenly links 6:2 with the food prohibition of 6:3 that follow. When 6:2 looks backward to 6:1, it becomes clear that the novice is to hold fast to "this way of training" because, anyone able to entirely bear it "will be perfect" (6:2). Those unable to bear it, on the other hand, are urged to do what they can for, by and by, they will gradually become capable of bearing "the whole yoke of the Lord" (6:2).

Note that the framers of the Didache show themselves to be uncompromising on some points and lenient on others. When it comes to defining what constitutes "the rules of the Lord" (4:13) and "the way of training" (6:1), no room is allowed for confusion or half measures. When it comes to achieving these things, however, allowance is made for failure and for gradualism. Thus, the intent of *Did.* 6:1 is to define and to conserve the Lord's standards of excellence *even if and when* it is evident that not every novice will be able to perfectly meet these standards prior to baptism. Given the practice of the confession of failings, the novice will soon discover (a) that even professed members are striving for perfection and (b) that no one can continue to confess the same failing week after week without being stimulated by shame and urged on by fraternal love to correct that failing. This then is the pastoral genius of the Didache – being firm when it comes to defining the standards of the Lord while being lenient when it comes to embracing persons who fail and humbly return week after week acknowledging their failure.

In the end, contrary to Flusser and Draper, I therefore hold that the Way of Life is the only standard of perfection within the Didache. As Paula Fredriksen so capable puts it, the scandal of the gentile mission is that the Lord has made provisions for the *salvation of the gentiles in the end times without requiring them to become Jews:* "Gentiles are saved as gentiles: they do not, eschatologically, become Jews."[33] In fact, Fredriksen reminds us that this is, first and foremost, a Jewish perception of things and not a Christian invention that departs from Judaism. Matthew formulated this doctrine in his way; the framers of the Didache did it in theirs. Neither knew of the other. Neither was the enemy of the other.

The Mysterious Placement of the Food Prohibitions

The absolute prohibition against eating "the food sacrificed to idols" (6:3) occurs at the beginning of what has frequently been accepted as the beginning of the "liturgical section." How or why this would be an introduction to a liturgical document never made sense to me. On the other hand, it is possible that the placement of this important and absolute injunction may have evolved in order to address a very practical purpose.

[33] "Judaism, the Circumcision of Gentiles," 547.

As long as candidates were in training, they were obliged to refrain from attending the sacred community meals (9:5). This we know. Of necessity, therefore, most candidates would have been constrained to take part in family and community meals wherein, either regularly or periodically, offerings were made to the household gods as part of the meal or some portion of the meats served had been previously offered at a public altar.[34] Only with baptism a few days away, therefore, could the candidate be bound by this final rule.

The Key Significance of Pre-baptismal Fasting

Baptism marked a turning point. Social bonds were being broken, and new ones were being forged. Following baptism, every day would be spent visiting the saints and "rest[ing] upon their words" (4:2). Prior to baptism, however, most candidates probably felt the keen anticipation of entering into their new way of life along with the anxiety attendant upon the irreversible step that would cut them off from most of their family and friends.[35] During these few days, it is no accident that the candidate

---

[34] A novice would be expected to receive invitations from friends and extended family members to give thanks to the gods on the occasion of important moments in their lives: the birth, coming of age, or marriage of a child, success in business, returning safe from a long voyage, etc. Such meals were not, in and of themselves, pagan rites. Nor was there necessarily any notion that eating of the food constituted some sort of sacramental union with a god (Willis, *Idol Meat in Corinth*, 21-62 w/r 1 Cor 10:20). The Didache, after all, regarded the gods as "dead" (6:3). Nonetheless, those who joined in the meal would be expected to tacitly acknowledge that the feast was being celebrated in thanksgiving for a particular blessing received from a particular god (Willis, *Idol Meat in Corinth*, 39-42). Thus eating any meal offered to idols constituted a denial that "apart from [the true] God, nothing happens" (3:10). Hence, such food was off limits.

[35] Anticipation and anxiety dulled their desire to eat (#3f). Paul, for example, following his unsettling experience on the road to Damascus, "was without sight, and neither ate nor drank" (Acts 9:9) for three days. More pointedly, the book of *Joseph and Aseneth* (100 B.C.E.) describes how Aseneth, the beautiful and virtuous daughter of an Egyptian priest, converted to Judaism and went on to become the fitting bride of Joseph who had gained great favor with the Pharaoh in Egypt. Upon first encountering Joseph, the narrator describes how "she wept bitterly, and she repented of her gods she used to worship" (9:2). As a result, "she was listless and wept until sunset: she ate no bread and drank no water" (10:2). After passing the entire night "groaning and weeping" (10:7), Aseneth "took all her innumerable gold and silver gods and broke them up into little pieces and threw them out of the window for the poor and needy" (10:13). Later, she took her royal dinner "and all the sacrifices for her gods and the wine-vessels for their libations; and she threw them all out of the window as food for the dogs" (10:14). Then, for seven nights and days, she remained utterly alone, without food or drink, weeping bitterly and groaning. On the eighth day, "she stretched her hands out toward the east, and her eyes looked up to the heaven" (12:1), and she expressed for the first time her plight:

> To you, O Lord . . . , will I cry:
> Deliver me from my persecutors, for to you I have fled,
> Like a child to her father and her mother.
> O Lord, stretch forth your hands over me,
> As a father who loves his children and is tenderly affectionate,
> And snatch me from the hands of the enemy. . . .
> The gods of the Egyptians whom I have abandoned and destroyed
> And their father the Devil are trying to destroy me. . . .

was told to fast (7:4). And it is no accident that the one baptizing and able members of the community fasted in solidarity with the candidate (7:4). During this period, all "the food sacrificed to idols" eaten by the candidates was being expelled, and they were prepared for eating only the pure and sacred food at the homes of "brothers and sisters" since the communion meals binding them to ancestral gods would now be forever forbidden to them. This fasting, therefore, which was propaedeutic for the biweekly practice of fasting hardly needed an expressed theology.

The fasting prior to baptism led to feasting. While the Didache gives no strict chronology as to how much time expired between baptism and the first Eucharist, one can read between the lines. If the candidate was meeting his/her "new family" for the first time at baptism, it is difficult to imagine that the newly baptized did not celebrate immediately thereafter. Given the eschatological significance of the Eucharist, it is improbable that this celebratory meal would not have been the weekly Eucharist. Without going into the details, therefore, I would propose that the Didache signals this sequence of events:

1 Community gathers in the place of baptism (many have been fasting)
2 Candidates are led in by their spiritual mentors and all grow silent
3 Mentors recite the Way of Life and Way of Death with the appropriate refrains
4 Each candidate is immersed, dried off, and reclothed in a dry tunic
5 New members are embraced and kissed (same sex only) by their new family
6 Lord's Prayer is prayed together for the first time (facing East)
7 All retire to the home where the fast-breaking Eucharist has been prepared

Testing Various Origination Hypotheses – the Placement of *Did.* 14

When contending origination hypotheses examine the peculiarities of the Didache, they necessarily act like lenses that force their users to see things quite differently. Consider, for example, an easily recognized peculiarity of the text: *Did.* 9-10 presents what the text calls "the Eucharist" (9:1) and, four chapters later, the confession of failings is described as taking place *prior to* the Eucharist (14:1). One may wonder why the compiler did not place *Did.* 14 just prior to *Did.* 9-10 and thereby retain a topical and chronological unity to his finished text. Jean-Paul Audet takes this problem up as follows:

> Save me, O Lord, deserted as I am,
> For my father and mother denied me,
> Because I destroyed and shattered their gods;
> And now I am an orphan and deserted,
> And I have no other hope save in you, O Lord
> (12:8f, 11; grammar corrected).

This prayer vividly portrays the distress of a convert abandoned by her parents and defenseless against the gods whom she has betrayed. Aseneth's fasting and weeping, consequently, portray the force of the terrors associated with her conversion. One might expect that many gentiles embracing the Way of Life were similarly situated.

The author returns to the subject [in *Did.* 14] not because he is a bad writer, or because he had, oddly enough, forgotten something, or because he is compiling his materials at random, or because someone else had created a subsequent interpolation of 14:1-3, but simply because experience has demonstrated, in the meantime, the inadequacy of the instructions in 9-10.[36]

Audet's unwarranted assumption here is that the Didache was composed in writing. The author comes back with a fresh idea, the confession of failings, but there is no blank space prior to the eucharistic section to place it. Hence, he was forced to put it where he left off writing the last time (i.e., after 13:7).

Kurt Niederwimmer, for his part, imagined that the compiler of the Didache was "a respected and influential bishop" who "quotes existing, sometimes archaic rules and seeks both to preserve what has been inherited and at the same time to accommodate that heritage to his own time [turn of the second century]."[37] Niederwimmer was uneasy with the hypothesis of Rordorf[38] to the effect that *Did.* 14 was added later by a second compiler. He was also put off by Audet's thesis that the original writer returned to his document at a later time in order to supplement what he had written earlier. Rather, Niederwimmer tried to discern the internal logic ordering the text. Here is what he found: "in chaps. 11-13, the Didachist had, in a sense, looked outward (toward the arriving guests of the community), in chaps. 14-15 he looks inward (at the relationships within the community itself)."[39] Thus, according to Niederwimmer, the eucharistic prayers (9-10) came early because they were grouped with the prayer section (8:1-10:7); the confession of failings comes later because it is grouped in the "internal relationships" section (14-15). Beyond this grouping of materials, Niederwimmer did not look for or expect to find any reason why one grouping should come before or after another. In a word, given the lenses used by Niederwimmer, he did not see nor hear any sequential plan in the Didache.

Georg Schöllgen supplies us with an origination hypothesis much different from that of Niederwimmer. For him, the author "simply provides an authoritative regulation on controversial points."[40] Thus, *Did.* 9-10 responds to the problem of having "an aberrant or insufficient" or "no fixed formula"[41] for the Eucharist. *Did.* 14, on the other hand, is directed toward resolving the author's concern for "the purity" of those eating the eucharistic meal.[42] Two topics; two places. Seemingly the author takes up controversial points in the idiosyncratic order that they occur to him. The origination hypothesis of Schöllgen does not lead him to anticipate finding any progression or ordering of topics beyond this. Schöllgen is neither surprised nor disappointed that no order exists. His theory teaches him how to look and what to look for. Schöllgen, not

---

[36] Audet, *La Didachè*, 460. Here and elsewhere, I have translated the French into English.
[37] Niederwimmer, *The Didache*, 228.
[38] Rordorf-Tuilier, *La doctrine des douze apôtres* (1978) 49-50 and 2nd ed.(1998) 226-228.
[39] Niederwimmer, *The Didache*, 199.
[40] Schöllgen, "The Didache as a Church Order," 63.
[41] *Ibid.*, 50.
[42] *Ibid.*, 59.

surprisingly, embraces an origination hypothesis that is entirely blind to any ordering or chronology of the topics.

My own origination hypothesis, on the contrary, leads me to anticipate a closely worked out progression of topics that follows the ordering of training and the experiences given to new members. Thus my hypothesis leads me to look for something which, for the moment, is hidden within the clues of the narrative:

> Under ordinary circumstances, the Didache informs us that a confession of failings would have taken place by way of preparing the members of offer "a pure sacrifice" (14:1). The candidate preparing for baptism is informed of this confession near the end of his/her training (4:14). When one encounters the eucharistic prayers (9f), however, this confession of failings is curiously omitted. So I am puzzled. I strain at the seeming "misplacement" of things. But I am urged on by the discovery that every part of the Way of Life follows an orderly progression. I am also urged on by the discovery that the abstention from food sacrificed to idols was not included in the Way of Life because it would have been chronologically out of place there. Could it be then that there is a reason why the confession of failings does not show up prior to the eucharistic prayers?
>
> My surmise, due to my origination hypothesis, is that this omission of the confession of failings is deliberate and signals what everyone knew – namely that the order of events within the Didache follows the order whereby a candidate comes to experience these events. Thus, if my surmise is correct, the eucharist in the Didache must represent "the first eucharist" and the omission of the confession of failings hints at the fact that this public confession was suppressed whenever new candidates were baptized just prior to the eucharist. Many practical and pastoral reasons could be put forward to sustain suppressing a public confession of failings at "the first eucharist." Foremost among them would be the fittingness of joyfully welcoming the new "brothers" and "sisters" who had just been baptized without confronting them with a recital of the failings of permanent members...[43]

For the moment, the question is not whether my origination hypothesis is correct or whether I have supplied probable reasons for suppressing the confession of failings at "the first Eucharist." What is important is to notice how my origination hypothesis forces one to probe the text more deeply in order to find out just how far the evidence supplied by the text can be understood to support the explanatory matrix being tested. The origination hypothesis of Schöllgen expects an unorganized movement from topic to topic. Even Niederwimmer only expects the grouping of topics. Audet, for his part, sees the confession of failings as operative prior to every Eucharist, but the absence of blank space on the page prevents him from giving it its rightful place. None of these three expects to find, therefore, a hidden logic that guides the narrator from topic to topic from beginning to end.

---

[43] Freely adapted from the original in Milavec, *The Didache*, 238-39.

The Independence of the Didache from Matthew's gospel

Elsewhere I have offered a detailed examination of the method and the results for determining how one can demonstrate the independence of the Didache from the written gospel of Matthew.[44] For our purposes here, however, let it suffice to consider briefly the case just considered.

Both the Didache and Matthew had to deal with backsliders and with misbehaving members. To accomplish this, the Didache prescribes confessing personal transgressions before the weekly Eucharist (14:1) and the shunning of members unwilling to amend their lives (15:3). Matthew's gospel, meanwhile, endorses quite a different procedure. The injured party takes the initiative to resolve a grievance in three well-defined stages: first, privately, then with the help of a few witnesses, and finally with the force of the entire community (Matt 18:15-18). At each stage, the misbehaving member is invited to acknowledge his/her failing and make amends. Only the one who persistently refuses ends up being shunned. In Matthew's community, this procedure is seemingly normative, since Jesus is heard to endorse it in his own words. Had the framers of the Didache known of this saying of Jesus (either by reading Matthew's gospel or experiencing Matthew's community),[45] it would be difficult to understand why they

---

[44] "Synoptic Tradition in the Didache Revisited." This article is also available at www.Didache.info. In part, my study concludes:

> When parallel texts are listed or even compared side by side, a plausible case can always be made for dependence upon Matthew's gospel. More recently, however, more rigorous criteria have been developed in order to establish dependence. Jefford and Tuckett, for example, make the point that verbal agreement, in and of itself, cannot establish literary dependence since, in every case, one has to consider the possibility that the agreement present is due to both the Didache and Matthew having access to a common Jesus tradition. Thus, to establish dependence, one has to explore, even in cases of close or exact verbal agreement, to what degree the contexts and meanings overlap. Furthermore, one has to explore to what degree shared issues (fasting, praying, almsgiving, correcting, shunning) are defined and resolved along parallel lines. When these investigations were undertaken, however, they progressively revealed areas of wholesale divergence between Matthew and the Didache. In the end, consequently, this present study concludes that Matthew's gospel and the Didache reveal two religious systems that grew up independent of each other. While they occasionally made use of common sources in defining their way of life, each community shaped these sources in accordance with their own distinctive ends. Hence, in the end, even their common heritage directs attention to their diversity.

[45] The mandate to "reprove each other . . . as you have it in the good news" (15:3) cannot be used to confirm reliance upon a known gospel. When the Didache itself uses the term εὐαγγέλιον ("gospel"), it refers, first and foremost, to the "good news of God" preached by Jesus (as in Mark 1:14; Rom 1:1, 15:16; 2 Cor 2:7; 1 Thess 2:2, 9; 1 Pet 4:17). Thus, in each of the four places wherein the "good news" (εὐαγγέλιον) is mentioned as a source (8:2; 11:3; 15:3, 4), there is nothing to suggest that this term refers to a book or "a gospel." One has to wait until the mid-second century before the term "gospel" takes on the extended meaning of referring to written texts (Koester, *Ancient Christian Gospels,* 1-48 and Kelber, *The Oral and the Written Gospel,* 144-148).

Despite this, "most scholars agree" that the term "good news" found in the Didache "refers to some written gospel" (Van de Sandt-Flusser, *The Didache,* 352). When examined closely, however, "nothing in the context of these references indicate the presence of materials which were derived from any known gospel in writing" (50, n. 135). Van de Sandt thus surmises that the term "gospel" within the Didache can be "best understood as a reference to oral or written collections of sayings" (50, n. 135). Niederwimmer notes further that these

would not have made use of it. As it is, they had to stretch and strain Mal 1:11 to support the seemingly novel practice of using the Eucharist as a gate for reconciliation: "Everyone having a conflict with his companion, do not let him come together with you [for the Eucharist] until they be reconciled, in order that your sacrifice not be defiled" (14:2). Alternately, instead of cited Mal 1:11 to support this practice, it could be argued that the framers of the Didache could have made easy use of Matt 5:23 due to its ready-made juxtapositioning of reconciliation and sacrifice.[46] But they didn't! It becomes very difficult, therefore, to imagine that the framers of the Didache were aware of either Matthew's gospel or of those Matthean traditions that guided the practice of Matthean communities.[47]

Brief Considerations Respecting the Date and Provenance of the Didache

The date and provenance of the Didache has been heavily dominated by the question of the sources used in its composition. Adolph von Harnack, in his 1884 commentary, wrote, "One must say without hesitation that it is the author of the Didache who used the Epistle of Barnabas and not the reverse."[48] Von Harnack, accordingly, dated the Didache between C.E. 135 and 165 and fixed the place of origin as Egypt since *Barn.* was thought to have been composed there. It wasn't until 1945 that E.J. Goodspeed,[49] aided by the Latin versions of *Barn.* that had no Two-Way section, finally put to rest the assumption that the Didache depended upon Barnabas.

---

sayings did not pertain to "the Christological kerygma" or "the epiphany, death, and resurrection of Jesus for our sake" (*The Didache,* 50) but to a set of practical rules known to members of the Didache communities. For details, see Milavec, *The Didache,* 720-723.

[46] One cannot help but notice that Matt 5:23-24 makes an appeal to reconciliation in which the offending party takes the initiative – very much unlike Matt 18:15-18. Furthermore, since it is unclear whether Matthew's community would have celebrated the Eucharist as "a sacrifice," it cannot be supposed that 5:23-24 ever served to define their eucharistic discipline. Within the context of the Didache, however, even a chance visitor familiar with 5:23-24 would have called the attention of the community to a saying of Jesus that authorized their eucharistic practice. The absence of 5:23-24 in the Didache, consequently, presses one to surmise not only that the framers of the Didache were unaware of Matthew's gospel but that prophets/visitors from Matthew's community never had the occasion to experience the Eucharist within a Didache community.

[47] When it comes to reproving misbehaving members "not in anger but in peace" (*Did.* 15:3), Van de Sandt finds "a marked affinity with Qumran [1QS 5:24-25] concepts" (*The Didache,* 353). Thus, when it comes to identifying the "good news" (*Did.* 15:3) source for this practice, he surmises that this source must have been comparable to 1QS and "at variance with our present gospel of Matthew" (352). Van de Sandt expands this argument in the paper included in this volume.

[48] Von Harnack, *Die Lehre der zwölf Apostel,* 82.

[49] E. J. Goodspeed published a landmark article in which he was troubled by the Latin versions of Barnabas which had no Two-Way section. Goodspeed argued that "early Christian literature usually grew not by partition and reduction, but by combination and expansion," and, from this, it can be deduced that the oldest version of *Barn.* must have been prepared without any Two-Way section ("The Didache, Barnabas and the Doctrina," 228).

Once the Epistle of Barnabas was no longer considered as the source for the writer of the Didache, a fresh impetus was given to the question of which, if any, of the known gospels were used by the framers of the Didache. It is telling that, in 1958, Audet devoted forty-two pages to the Barnabas-dependence issue and only twenty pages to the gospel-dependence issue.[50] When examined closely, Audet concluded that even the so-called "evangelical addition" of *Did.* 1:3b-5 cannot be explained as coming either from Matthew or from Luke.[51] Audet's enduring accomplishment was to demonstrate that the Didache can be best understood when it is interpreted within a Jewish horizon of understanding more or less independent of what one finds in the gospels. Accordingly, in the end, Audet was persuaded that the manifest Jewish character[52] of the Didache pointed to a completion date prior to C.E. 70 in a milieu (Antioch) *that did not yet have a written gospel.*[53]

Audet's enduring accomplishment was to demonstrate that the Didache can be best understood when it is interpreted within a Jewish horizon of understanding. Following the observations of Jacob Neusner in *Why No Gospels in Talmudic Judaism?*,[54] one can further understand how the halachic character of the Didache emerges within Judaism while the gospel form did not. It remains very problematic, therefore, to imagine that the framers of the Didache would have used or relied upon either a written or oral gospel. When one combines this with the recognition that the Didache communities defined their response to backsliders and misbehaving members (to take just the single example considered above) without any awareness of the Jesus traditions and the practice of Matthew's community, it becomes increasingly certain that Matthew's gospel and the Didache reveal two religious systems that grew up independent of each other. Niederwimmer, a champion of redaction criticism, likewise came to this same conclusion: "The Didache lives in an entirely different linguistic universe, and that is true not only of its sources but of its redactor as well."[55]

Following upon this, Court's surmise that "the Didache stands in the tradition of St. Matthew's Gospel,"[56] Draper's surmise that "the Didache is the community rule of the Matthean community,"[57] and Massaux's surmise that the Didache was created "as a catechetical résumé of the first evangelist"[58] cannot stand up to close examination. The gospel of Matthew and the Didache, point after point, evoke two religious systems addressing common problems in divergent ways. Once the venue for Matthew's gospel

---

[50] Audet, *La Didachè*, 121-163 (Barnabas independence) and 166-186 (gospel independence).

[51] Audet, *La Didachè*, 186.

[52] In effect, it is not just the Jewish character of the Didache as such but the early form of its Christology (#5e, #5m), ecclesiology (#9d, #9f), and eschatology (#10m, #10r) that argue in favor of an even earlier date of around 50 C.E.

[53] Audet, *La Didachè*, 192. 210.

[54] Neusner, *Why No Gospels in Talmudic Judaism?*

[55] Niederwimmer, *The Didache*, 48.

[56] Court, "The Didache," 112.

[57] Draper, "Torah and Troublesome Apostles,," 372. Draper continues to uphold this position in his paper included in this volume.

[58] Massaux, *Influence de l'Évangile* (1986), 604-646; esp. 644.

is settled upon, therefore, one can know, with a high degree of certainty, that the Didache would not have originated there.[59]

Should Didache scholars come to accept this position, the way would be open for an early dating of the Didache and for its interpretation as a well-integrated and self-contained religious system that should be allowed to speak for itself. One has only to consider how studies devoted to the Letter to the Hebrews, the gospel of Thomas, and the Q-gospel have flourished due to the fact that they have been allowed to stand alone. If the Didache were accorded the same treatment, a new era of Didache studies would thus lie open before us.

Conclusion

The brief time available does not allow me to further elaborate my origination hypothesis or to press forward its repercussions for the dating of the Didache. Stepping back, however, I will be content if I leave you with enough specific instances of how I came to discover that the Didache is a unified production that conceals within its oral logic a hidden key that marvelously accounts for the progression of topics from beginning to end. With what I have provided, you can go on to make further discoveries by yourself. Being scholars, we always like to have the thrill of making discoveries for ourselves rather than simply being told. Then, when you read my thousand-page volume, you will have the prospect of seeing just how far you were able to anticipate, and, in many instances, even to outdo my own.[60]

In closing, I would say that the Didache has a special relevance within our modern society.[61] Any community that cannot artfully and effectively pass on its cherished way of life as a program for divine wisdom and graced existence cannot long endure. Any way of life that cannot be clearly specified, exhibited, and differentiated from the alternative modes operative within the surrounding culture is doomed to growing insignificance and to gradual assimilation. Faced with these harsh realities, the Didache unfolds the training program calculated to irreversibly alter the habits of perception and standards of judgment of novices coming out of a pagan life style.[62] The content

---

[59] The same thing holds true for the Pauline communities as well. Here again, one discovers that the authentic Pauline letters and the Didache, point after point, evoke two religious systems addressing common problems in divergent ways.

Jefford, in this volume, argues that the Antioch community had sufficient diversity to include Ignatius (a champion of Paul), Matthew's gospel, and the Didache. As soon as such a mix got down to practical matters such as celebrating a Eucharist, the diversity among them would prove insurmountable.

[60] My commentary, needless to say, does not just settle with establishing the unity of the Didache, it goes on to milk every line of the document in order to recover all we can know about the faith, hope, and life of those communities that existentially committed themselves to the Way of Life. Such a reconstruction becomes possible because the unity of the Didache has been established as pointing back to living communities fixed in space and time. As long as the Didache was viewed as a collage of materials, it necessarily represented multiple points of view held by different persons/groups separated by place and time.

[61] For further reflections on the spirituality of the Didache and its relevance for addressing pressing problems within our contemporary society, see Milavec, *The Didache*, 842-909.

[62] For further details, see Milavec, *To Empower as Jesus Did*, 177-240.

and the modality of this process of human transformation can be gleaned from the verbal clues conveyed within the text itself. Once this is established, then it becomes possible to combine linguistic, historical, and sociological tools to recover the faith, hope, and life of those communities that existentially committed themselves to living the Way of Life. This is the way of scholarship. This is the way of life.

III Two Documents from the Same
    Jewish-Christian Milieu?

Chapter Five

The Sermon on the Mount and the Two Ways Teaching of the Didache

Kari Syreeni

University of Uppsala (Sweden)

A comparison between the Sermon on the Mount (Matt 5–7) and the Two Ways section in *Did.* 1–6 is rewarding on several counts, but especially on the premise that both of these early Christian collections of moral teachings stand in a historical continuum in terms of time, geographical location and religio-cultural context. With a number of scholars, I am inclined to think this is the case.[1] In principle, we should then be able to deepen comparative observations by (re)constructing possible trajectories and changing *Sitze im Leben*.[2]

However, the comparative and the tradition-historical tasks are severed by the obvious differences between these two collections of moral teachings. Apart from the *sectio evangelica* (*Did.* 1:3b–2:1) and the mention of two ways in Matt 7:13–14, there is little that immediately ties the texts together. The paraenetic-catechetic forms stand apart: here we have a section with the sapiential τέκνον address and a list of vices, there a series of beatitudes and antitheses coupled with similes and prophetic warnings. The composition history of the collections is divergent. In *Did.* 1–6, an earlier Greek *Vorlage* has been expanded into the first section of what appears to be a church manual. In Matthew, a Q sequence introducing Jesus' moral teaching has been substantially amplified and systematised to form the first of the "great" discourses of a new gospel. To be sure, there is more in common, but first we must follow the two paths separately. Assuming that the final form of the Didache is later than Matthew and presupposes it (rather than simply uses or quotes it), I start with the former.

---

[1] See Jefford, *The Didache in Context*, esp. the contributions of Kloppenborg, Patterson and Jefford; Draper, "The Didache in Modern Research," 1–42; Van de Sandt-Flusser, *The Didache*, 48–52. Huub van de Sandt and David Flusser (*Ibid.*, 48–49) speak of "(a)n ever-growing consensus emerging in recent scholarship" that the Didache was composed by the turn of the first century, and of "(a)n increasing number of authors" attributing the text to Syria-Palestine. The alleged "new consensus" date seems somewhat optimistic, but since more cautious scholars, such as Vielhauer (opting for the beginning of the second century), are included as witnesses, perhaps I too may be counted in, though I am quite comfortable with the older majority view that the Didache in its final form is an early or mid-second century document. Even in this case, its import for New Testament scholars is immense. Cf. Barnard, *Studies in the Apostolic Fathers*, 99 n. 2: "In any event the Didache is not a late hole-in-the-corner production which can safely be ignored in reconstructing the history and teaching of the primitive Church. I believe that the document dates from the period A.D. 100–130 and depends on the Matthaean stream of the Gospel tradition."
[2] Cf. my article, "Separation and Identity," 539–41.

The Composition History of *Did.* 1–6

The Didache is a composite work consisting of three or four major parts. It opens with the Two Ways teaching (Chaps. 1–6), continues with cultic prescriptions (Chaps. 7–10) and a church order (Chaps. 11–15), and ends with a short eschatological section (Chap. 16). The overarching plan seems to allow two different interpretations. A "progressive" interpretation would stress the tripartite sequence of pre-baptismal basic teaching, life and worship in the community, and the eschatological goal. The Didache would basically outline moral stages in the Christian way of life from beginning to fulfilment. As to literary genre, the paraenetic and catechetic aspects of the document are then seen as dominant. Composition-historically, the Two Ways section, possibly together with Chap. 16, would be the starting-point of the literary evolution. By contrast, a "centric" interpretation would regard Chaps. 7–15 as the core of the writing, while the opening and concluding sections would be seen as framing elements. As to genre, the document would be labelled as a manual of discipline or a church order. Composition-historically, the main interest then lies with the development of ritual, liturgy and ministry.

It seems, however, that the Didache is really a purposeful blend of genres. The catechetic and the church order elements obviously had separate lines of development until the Didachist united them, with equal stress on both.[3] The Two Ways teaching is addressed directly to those in need of moral guidance. Its tone is largely catechetic, especially in the two inserted major blocks (the evangelical section and the τέκνον section), with some systematising elements (typically, the summarising "first" and "second" in 1:2). Similarly, the apocalyptic ending starts with second person plural imperatives and prohibitions, and the whole chapter is paraenetically attuned with minor catechetical systematising devices (the three eschatological "signs" in 16:6, the definition of the resurrection doctrine with scriptural proof in 16:7). Such paraenetic-catechetic traits cannot be ignored in assessing the literary genre of the Didache. At the same time, it is clear that the transition from the Two Ways section to the cultic section with the topical "handbook" formula, Περὶ δὲ τοῦ βαπτίσματος and the practical instruction οὕτω βαπτίσατε (7:1), mark a change of style. More important, the addressees change, which becomes explicit with the redactional remark, ταῦτα πάντα προειπόντες.

---

[3] Van de Sandt and Flusser, *The Didache*, 32. 339–340, propose that *Did.* 1–6 and 7 go together because of baptism, while *Did.* 7–15 (without Chaps. 11–13) might reflect "an ancient scheme" which is also present in 1 Tim 2:1–3:13. The latter suggestion is to be doubted, but clearly important steps towards a topically arranged and paraenetically motivated "church order" are taken within the epistolary genre. The topical marker περὶ δε + gen. is used in Pauline letters to introduce matters of church discipline, the Deutero-Paulines contain household codes and requirements for ministry. The Didachist's combination of sayings material and church order topics is rather original, however. Below, an attempt is made to interpret this combination as a development within the instructional (paraenetic-catechetic) "gospel" form (Q, Matthew's great discourses).

The handbook style of the central parts of the document is communicatively one level above the catechesis/paraenesis of the outer parts, but the preservation of the direct speech mode in the frames need not be due to redactional clumsiness. Rather it may reflect a hesitation to subordinate the direct admonition to indirect speech given through a mediating instance. Even in the central sections, the addressees are not "office holders" or a special group, but the community as a whole. There seems to be a tendency to preserve an *undifferentiated* view of the community as a corporate entity with dual roles: as those who give *and* receive teaching, baptise *and* have been baptised. The community is set both under the teaching, as its hearer and doer, and as its guardian or authorised transmitter. This dual perspective is, to some extent, captured in the *longer inscription*,[4] which stresses the continuity with apostolic proclamation and the Lord's teaching. This purported historical continuum embraces the members of the community in a chain of tradition from teacher to disciple, or from a spiritual father to his children. Ultimately it goes back to the great Master: "My child, you shall be mindful day and night of the one who speaks to you the word of God. You shall honor him as the Lord, for at the source of discourse on lordship the Lord is there (*Did.* 4:1)."[5] The formulation of the longer title seems inspired by the final commissioning in Matthew (28:18–20),[6] which I think is also the "gospel" referred to in *Did.* 8:2; 11:3; 15:3, 4.

The Didachist obviously took the material in Chaps. 1–6 as *pre-baptismal catechesis;* προειπόντες hardly implies just a recitation in the baptismal liturgy.[7] There is no reason to question this *Sitz im Leben,* but a one-to-one correspondence between *Did.* 1–6 and the community's pre-baptismal teaching need not be assumed. Georg Schöllgen has pointed out that the central part of the Didache is a highly selective church order. It does not attempt to expose all the existing rules and practices, but rather clarifies some particular contested issues.[8] This may well hold true for the pre-baptismal teaching, too. The Two Ways scheme offers a plausible general structure for preparatory teaching, which may have included other topics besides those present in *Did.* 1–6. As end-expectation was still a live issue and was referred to in the community's

---

[4] The scribe of the Jerusalem manuscript clearly regarded the first, short form as the title and the second, longer form as belonging to the tractate itself; see Van de Sandt-Flusser, *The Didache,* 21. In my opinion, the chances are that the long title was attached to the document at an earlier stage. It is probably not the title given by the Didachist. The document does not appeal to the authority of the (twelve) apostles even where it might be expected to do that (11:3–6), as Vielhauer, *Geschichte der urchristlichen Literatur,* 724, notes. It may, however, be an early and in fact the first title attached to the document. While it should not be used as a *Leseanweisung* that informs about the Didachist's purpose (rightly Niederwimmer, *Die Didache,* 82), I think that the title is a plausible interpretation of some aspects of the original purpose.

[5] My English quotations come from Cody, "The Didache: An English Translation," 3–14.

[6] Note Matthew's stress on the identity/continuity of Jesus' teaching and its transmission by the apostles, the close connection between teaching and baptising, and the mention of the gentiles.

[7] Rightly Schöllgen, "The Didache as a Church Order," 46 n. 7. Van de Sandt-Flusser, *The Didache,* think the instruction "may well have been part and parcel of the baptismal liturgy" (280) but concede that "the later lines of demarcation between catechetical instruction and liturgical celebration were not drawn so sharply in the first century" (281).

[8] Schöllgen, "The Didache as Church Order," 43–45. 63–64. However, some of the conclusions he draws go too far in the direction of literary unity. The notion of selectiveness does not remove all tensions in the text.

eucharistic prayers (9:4; 10:5–6), it is conceivable that the eschatological hope was one topic in the initial teaching. It is unlikely, however, that the whole of Chap. 16 formed a literary unity with the Two Ways section before the redaction of the document. The eschatological endings in the letter of Barnabas (*Barn.* 21) and in the Apostolic Church Order (ACO 14) do not give sufficient proof for this. The last sentence that with certainty stood in the Two Ways tractate known to the Didachist is *Doctr./Did.* 6:1. It is possible, but uncertain, that the Doctrina Apostolorum, in its first epilogue (*Doctr.* 6:4–5), renders the sapiential ending[9] that was in the Didachist's source.[10]

To test the assumption that the Two Ways section of the Didache takes up especially those issues of initial teaching that needed clarification or particular attention, we may consider the latest *inserted* block in 1:3b–2:1[11] and the *appended* verses 6:2–3,[12] which likely represent the interests of the final composition of the Didache. The first-mentioned block, the evangelical section, is in my opinion dependent on Matthew (and possibly Luke).[13] The section makes sense as an "updating" of traditional material

---

[9] However, this ending, too, has an eschatological – and undoubtedly Christian – perspective *(spea tua, peruenies ad coronam)*.

[10] Thus Niederwimmer, *Die Didache,* 152–53 (he calls *Doctr.* 6:4–5 the *first* epilogue and the secondary doxology in *Doctr.* 6:6 the *second* epilogue). Van de Sandt-Flusser, *The Didache,* also assume that *Doctr.* 6:4–5 is the original conclusion of the Jewish Two Ways tractate (pp. 119–120; p. 128 with a translation into Greek), but they consider *Did.* 6:2–3 to be a pre-Didachist supplement (pp. 238–270). The separation of the eschatological section from the earliest Greek form of the Two Ways tractate would be rather unproblematic, were it not for the parallelism between *Did.* 16:1–2 and *Barn.* 4:9–10 (the only obvious parallel between the documents apart from the Two Ways section; but the context of *Barn.* suggests proximity to the Two Ways tradition). While I am not quite convinced that this connection can be explained (away) as being due to a common oral tradition (thus Vielhauer, *Geschichte der urchristlichen Literatur,* 731–33), the parallel surely does not indicate that the Didache is dependent on *Barn.* (rightly Niederwimmer, *Die Didache,* 259).

[11] The evangelical section was likely inserted at the time when, or just shortly before, the earlier Two Ways tractate was incorporated in the Didache as a whole, since it is absent in both *Doctr.* and *Barn.* while being attested in the two direct textual witnesses of the Didache (the Jerusalem manuscript discovered by Bryennios and the two Oxyrhynchus fragments containing *Did.* 1:3c–4a and 2:7b–3:2) as well as in the Apostolic Constitutions and (as it seems) in the Didascalia Apostolorum. See Van de Sandt-Flusser, *The Didache,* 40–41, where other opinions are also recorded; e.g., Wengst was so certain it is a later interpolation that he transferred it to a footnote in his Didache text. One might add that according to Layton, "The Sources, Date and Transmission," 343–83, either a pre- or a post-Didachist interpolation is to be preferred, while the remaining hypothesis, an insertion by the Didachist, "is no doubt the least attractive (though it is the simplest)" (381). But as Niederwimmer, *Die Didache,* 94, points out, the notion of perfection (1:4) recurs in 6:2 (cf. 16:2), and the phrase κατὰ τὴν ἐντολήν (1:5) and the quotation formula in 1:6 are typical of the Didachist's redaction.

[12] Van de Sandt-Flusser, *The Didache,* 238–70, argue at length that 6:2–3 is a pre-Didachist, Jewish-Christian addition to the Jewish Two Ways tractate. The addition is said to originate with a Jewish-Christian group marked by a strict Torah observance, while the Didachist was a gentile Christian who could only include the verses by virtue of a drastic reinterpretation. See also Flusser, "Paul's Jewish-Christian Opponents," 195–211. However, I rather concur with those scholars who regard *Did.* 6:2–3 as integral to the Didachist's theological posture.

[13] See Tuckett, "Synoptic Tradition in the Didache," 92–128, esp. from p. 110 on. I do not agree with all details, but Tuckett's analysis is methodologically sound and well informed in matters of synoptic redaction criticism. The strength of the analysis lies first and foremost in the recognition of Matthaean and Lukan *redactional* elements in *Did.* 1:3–5a. However, the most salient Lukan feature in *Did.* 1:3 (ποία . . . χάρις) might perhaps be explained without Luke, because Sir 12:1–2 (note ἔσται χάρις, v.1) may be one source of inspiration in the evangelical section (particularly at *Did.* 1:6).

in order to bring in some Christian specifics. The initiates learn a superior way of life that exceeds the common ethic of the surrounding society.[14] Interestingly, the boundaries to paganism (cf. τὰ ἔθνη in 1:3) rather than to Judaism (the "hypocrites") are stressed. In the added conclusion to the Two Ways, 6:2–3, the Didachist employs the handbook style for the first time (Περὶ δὲ τῆς βρώσεως). In this case, too, the converts from paganism are of special concern. The warning against eating food offered to idols is vital, because the baptised members participated in the community's common meals, where this observance was followed.

The uniformly designed τέκνον section in 3:1–6 is an *earlier insertion* not found in *Barn.* The section as it stands seems a (Jewish) Christian adaptation of a Jewish sapiential tradition. It makes good sense as pre-baptismal catechesis stressing the renunciation of all evil, especially pagan practices (3:4; soothsaying, astrology etc. lead to idolatry). The urgency to resist temptations before they lead to fatal deeds recalls the general idea of the first four Matthaean antitheses (Matt 5:21–37), but a literary dependency cannot be assumed. The recurring, pregnant predicates γεννᾶται/γεννῶνται in the conclusion of each warning (vv. 2, 3, 4, 5)[15] cohere with the τέκνον μου vocatives in the opening parts and enhance the baptismal undercurrent of the teaching.[16]

To what extent the rest[17] of *Did.* 1–5 betrays (Jewish) Christian reworking is more debatable, and partly dependent on how one reconstructs the precise stemma of the Greek Two Ways teaching. The majority view is that the archetype used by *Barn.* is the most archaic version, while the Doctrina/Didache branch is secondary both in regard

---

[14] An instructive point of comparison is the baptismal treatise in the Ps.-Clementine Homilies XI, 25–33, which may come from the Jewish-Christian source *Kerygmata Petrou* (around 200 C.E.); thus Strecker, "Die Kerygmata Petrou," 69.78–80. The early date and the source hypothesis are uncertain, however; see Jones, "The Pseudo-Clementines," 18, referring to the studies of Rius-Camps and Wehnert. At 32,1, parallel material from Matt 5:21–22; 5:27–28; 5:43–44 is used to substantiate the necessity of doing "more" (τὸ πλεῖον) and "better" works (κρεῖττον ποιεῖν) than those who live in error and only know the present age (32,2). Here, as in the Didache, the antithetical formula is absent. For the text, see Rehm-Irmscher-Paschke, *Die Pseudoklementinen* 1, 169–70.

[15] See the lucid exposition in Niederwimmer, *Die Didache,* 125–26. However, Niederwimmer misses the baptismal connection in the Didache's rhetoric of birth and comments: "Γεννᾶσθαι insinuiert die gleichen psychologischen Erwägungen wie das ὁδηγεῖν in der ersten Warnung" (126). Consequently, he proposes simply "das jüdische Lehrhaus" as the original *Sitz im Leben* of the τέκνον section (125).

[16] I agree with Van de Sandt-Flusser, *The Didache,* 171, who suggest that the pericope initially only included the ὁδηγεῖν pattern, which can be traced to a Jewish tradition. Of early Christian parallels, the letter of James comes closest to the ethos of *Did.* 3 (including the *anawim* section in *Did.* 3:7–10). The "birthing" language in connection with sins in Jas 1:15 seems, in light of 1:18, a contrasting allusion to baptism, so that an implicit two-ways scheme is present (the way of sin leads to death, the way of life through the implanted divine word leads to perfection). A contrasting baptismal allusion seems implied in *Did.* 3:1–6 as well, though it may be superficial and hardly carries all the theological implications of James. The Didache's understanding of baptism may resemble that of Matthew, which is quite non-Pauline; see Luomanen, *Entering the Kingdom of Heaven,* 204–209 (p. 209: "baptism is first of all an act of commitment to the full observance of God's will").

[17] The Way of Death section is absent from ACO and the Epitome but is surely a part of the earliest reconstructable Greek Two Ways tractate. The omission is due to the use of the eleven apostles as transmitters of the teaching, and is possibly grounded in a theological consideration (the missing twelfth apostle, the betrayer, signals the Way of Death).

with the additional material discussed above and in its more systematic presentation of the love commandments as the core of the law. Van de Sandt and Flusser, however, argue extensively for the priority – and the Jewishness – of the latter textual tradition.[18] I remain unconvinced and would regard *Barn.* in these respects as the most rudimentary form of the Greek Two Ways tractate. There is no obvious reason why the author of *Barn.* should have distorted the well-structured teaching on the commandments in Didache/Doctrina 1:1–3a + 2:2–7. Following Niederwimmer's lead, Van de Sandt and Flusser take the nearly identical epistolary greetings (Χαίρετε κτλ.) in *Barn.* 1:1 and in the proem of the Apostolic Church Order, together with the parallelling eschatological endings in *Barn.* 21:2–8* (ἐρωτῶ κτλ.) and ACO 14:1–3 (ἐρωτῶμεν κτλ.), as indication that the Two Ways version underlying these documents had a secondary epistolary framing with eschatological admonitions.[19] If so, the epistolary frame and genre were retained in *Barn.*, while the ancestor of ACO/ Epitome[20] developed it into a speech of the eleven apostles. However, this theory creates several problems that can be avoided by assuming that the compiler of ACO was familiar with *Barn.*[21] On the other hand, even though *Barn.*'s general literary shape (no interpolated sections; less systematic structure) and many details (the two angels, "the Black One," etc.) must be archaic, its eschatological tenor need not tradition-historically antecede the more sapiential[22] Doctrina/Didache branch. There are traces in the treatise of the Two Spirits in the Manual of Discipline (1QS 3:13–4:26) of a pre-Essene Two Ways instruction that contains the same main parts as we have in *Did.* (and *Barn.*), namely a theological introduction, a list of righteous deeds, a list of immoral deeds, and a concluding (hortatory) statement.[23] This general outline has nothing inherently eschatological about it.

The net result, however, is not necessarily that the Doctrina/Didache version instead of Barnabas gives the best approximation of the wording of the original Greek Two Ways tractate. It may also be that *both* textual branches are equally remote from it, but in different respects. This would also imply that the underlying Jewish original is one step farther away from us, and that its reconstruction must remain very conjectural. In all cases, both the Barnabas and the Didache renderings of the Two Ways are Christian products and there is no guarantee that their immediate *Vorlagen* were purely Jewish documents. The caution articulated by M. de Jonge concerning the Jewish original of the Testaments of the Twelve Patriarchs is a good point of comparison: the safest perspective is to see the *T. 12 Patr.* as Christian literary products and

---

[18] Van de Sandt-Flusser, *The Didache,* 70–80.

[19] *Ibid.* Niederwimmer's solution (*Die Didache,* 59–63) is basically the same, even though he does not stress that this assumption implies that the *Vorlage* of *Barn.* was framed as an epistle. However, the letter form seems integral to *Barn.*'s literary character and purpose; see Hvalvik, *The Struggle for Scripture,* 71–108.

[20] However, the Epitome lacks a parallel to both *Barn.* 1:1 and 21.

[21] See Prostmeier, *Der Barnabasbrief,* 106–111, esp. nn. 75 and 80–83.

[22] It is common to speak of a "dualistic" and a "non-dualistic" Two Ways tradition. I would think that all this tradition is "dualistic" by definition, but can be so cosmologically/eschatologically (two angels, two ages, two places), anthropologically (two dispositions or inclinations), and/or ethically (two types of behaviour). The terms "apocalyptic" and "sapiential" refer to mainly literary characteristics, but in the latter case the ethical aspect is more dominant.

[23] Van de Sandt-Flusser, *The Didache,* 147–55.

to observe the "continuity in ethical thought between Hellenistic-Jewish and Early Christian circles."[24] I think the same applies to the Didache's Two Ways tractate, at least insofar as we refrain from the painstaking reconstruction of the ancestor behind *both* the *Doctr./Did and* the Barnabas versions.

What makes de Jonge's caution especially pertinent to the present discussion is, besides the presence of an elaborate Two Ways/Dispositions treatise in the Testament of Asher (1:3–6:6),[25] the fact that the *T. 12 Patr.* are among the principal witnesses of combining the commandments to love God (Deut 6:5) and the neighbour (Lev 19:18) as well as the Golden Rule, as we have in *Doctr./Did.* 1:2. I am inclined to see Jewish-Christian adaptation already at *Did.* 1:2. While I do think that a Jewish Two Ways tractate is very likely behind the Didache and Barnabas, I will not attempt a reconstruction here.[26] Nor is it possible to discuss here the early Jewish tradition-his-

[24] De Jonge, "The Two Great Commandments," 374; cf. Hollander-De Jonge, *The Testaments of the Twelve Patriarchs*, 83–85. For another recent warning, see Kraft, "Setting the Stage," 387: "What shall I do with the *'Testaments of the 12 Patriarchs'?*" I can try to divide and conquer, exercising my source-critical as well as text-critical arguments on this complex body of materials, but I'm still left with relatively late and quite popular texts of Christian provenance, with little guarantee that significant adjustment and enhancement has not taken place in Christian hands." For a traditional, optimistic view, see Ulrichsen, *Die Grundschrift*, 315–16 (only scattered Christian interpolations in the eschatological sections and practically none in the paraenesis).

[25] This is a sophisticated theological (or quasi-philosophical) treatise applying a Two Ways/Spirits/Dispositions *scheme*, rather than a Two Ways catechism; however, the scheme is used as a large-scale structuring principle, cf. Hollander-De Jonge, *The Testaments of the Twelve Patriarchs*, 338–339.43. The introduction initially mentions the "two ways" that God has given to the sons of men, but proceeds to define these as "two dispositions, two kinds of action, two modes of living, and two goals" (1:3). The overarching metaphors are those of the two "ways" and "dispositions" (1:5). The basic tenet of the treatise is that though good and evil appear to be mixed, in the last analysis every work and person is either wholly good or wholly bad, depending on the soul's ultimate disposition.

[26] Wengst's reconstruction in *Tradition und Theologie des Barnabasbriefes*, 65–66, follows *Barn.* closely and need not be more remote from the *Vorlage* than is the very different *Doctr./Did.* type of the reconstruction in Van de Sandt-Flusser, *The Didache*, 123–28. I take just one example to highlight the difficulties with reconstruction. On the face of it, it might seem that the parallels at *Barn.* 19:9–10/ ACO 12:1 with Epitome 9/ *Doctr.* and *Did.* 4:1 provide a simple test for deciding on the relative originality of the principal versions. See the synopsis in Niederwimmer, *Die Didache*, 60; Van de Sandt-Flusser, *The Didache*, 76. The differences are clear, but both versions make sense in their present contexts. While *Barn.* urges the addressees to think of *the day of judgment* "day and night," the *Doctr./Did.* version admonishes the disciple to be mindful of *the teacher* "day and night." The most elaborate ACO version sides with the latter but includes other features that parallel the wording of *Barn.*; this version has the appearance of conflation and amplification (as a result, reverence to the teacher is expressed three times). Which reference is original? Here is a rare case where Wengst opts for the Didache version. But does the theme of judgment really interrupt the line of thought in *Barn.* (thus Van de Sandt-Flusser, *The Didache*, 77)? The notion of judgment in *Barn.* 19:10 motivates one's keen work for the community: "Thou shalt *remember the day of judgment* day and night, and thou shalt seek each day the society of the saints, either labouring by speech, and going out to exhort, and striving to *save souls* by the word, or working with thine hands *for the ransom of thy sins*" (Trans. Lake in Loeb's edition; emphases mine). The last sentence of *Barn.* 4:10 makes as good sense as the parallel *Did.* 4:6, where the reference is to almsgiving. Oddly, while the Didache lacks the words (ἀγαπήσεις) ὡς κόρην τοῦ ὀφθαλ-μοῦ σου in *Barn.* 19:9, Barnabas in turn lacks the phrase (τιμήσεις δὲ αὐτὸν) ὡς κύριον in the same sentence. *Barn.*'s nice OT idiom might explain the emergence of the Didache's (Christianised) formulation, but it is also possible that *Barn.*'s formulation (τὸν λόγον) κυρίου in the same verse reveals knowledge

tory of the Two Ways scheme and topics.[27] Instead, I shift the direction of composition analysis and discuss the tendencies in the "downstream" history leading back to the final Didache version of the Two Ways.

Tendencies in the Pre-Didachist and the Didachist's Adoption of the Two Ways Tradition

In an analysis of the moral exhortation in *Did.* 1–5, John S. Kloppenborg[28] discerns three features that are typical of the Two Ways recension of the Didache/Doctrina: 1) the assimilation of the list of prohibitions in 2:2–7 into the second register of the decalogue; 2) the programmatic use of Lev 19:18 in the framework of Chapters 2–3; and 3) the insertion of the so-called τέκνον section.[29] Kloppenborg's discussion is very helpful, not least because of its side-glances to Matthew, but some of his conclusions need testing and further tendencies are seen as we come to the final redaction of the Didache.

The first two tendencies go together with the emphasis on the double love commandment in *Did.* 1:2, which Kloppenborg recognises may reflect a Christian tradition.[30] The juxtaposition of the commandments of Deut 6:5 and Lev 19:18 together with the numerical ordering "first-second" is found only in Christian sources, notably Mark 12:30–31 and Matt 22:37–39.[31] The Golden Rule, in a negative form (πάντα δὲ ὅσα ἐὰν θελήσῃς μὴ γίνεσθαί σοι κτλ.) that might, but need not, suggest familiarity with a positive formulation (such as Matt 7:12a) is also adduced.[32] *Barn.*

of the Didache's wording (τὸν λόγον) τοῦ θεοῦ. On the whole, *Did.* 4:1–4 addresses the catechumens, stressing their loyalty to the teachers and the community, and leads to the teaching concerning almsgiving and the sharing of property (4:5–8), apparently a moot issue in the Didache's community (cf. *Did.* 1:5–6 in the evangelical section). Barnabas addresses those who are teaching and working in the community, and the practical problems with almsgiving are not his concern. Both versions may be reworking a source that only contained a series of terse exhortations.

[27] Tradition-historically, there is much worth considering in the lineage given by Van de Sandt-Flusser, *The Didache* (e.g., the pre-Essene Hassidic origins, pp. 147–55; growing emphasis on the Way of Life and the influence of the *Derekh Erets* tradition, pp. 172–80). That Jesus belonged to the Hassidim (182) is unlikely, however.

[28] Kloppenborg, "The Transformation of Moral Exhortation," 88–109.

[29] *Ibid.*, 99.

[30] *Ibid.*, 98, referring to Niederwimmer and Giet. See also Tuckett, "Synoptic Tradition in the Didache," 106–107.

[31] The examples in Kloppenborg, "The Transformation of Moral Exhortation," 98 n. 41, indicate that outside the New Testament passages the double love commandment is most conspicuous in *T. 12 Patr.*, being in fact a mannerism there (for more examples, see De Jonge, "The Two Great Commandments"). The idea of the two registers of the law, however, is well attested in (Hellenistic) Judaism, notably in Philo and Josephus and at least *in nuce* since the time of Ben Sirach (cf. Sir 17:14).

[32] Regarding the Golden Rule in *Did.* 1:2b, Kloppenborg does not assume dependence on Matt 7:12b, while Tuckett, referring to Butler, thinks that knowledge of Matthew's finished gospel is the simplest solution. I agree that the peculiar formulation of the Golden Rule in *Did.* 1:2b (with a postponed μή) *might* be explained from Matthew's πάντα οὖν ὅσα ἐὰν θέλητε κτλ.; at least it does not rule out the possibility of Matthaean influence. However, the fact remains that, as the Didache has a negative formulation, the redactor was familiar with a non-Matthaean wording.

19:2 lacks this three-part condensation of the commandments, but in its stead there is a three-part admonition to love, fear and praise God.[33] Kloppenborg recognises in the *Doctr./Did.* version a "Torahizing" of the Two Ways. The prohibitions of 2:2–7 list murder, adultery, theft (omitted in the Doctrina), covetousness, and false witness – all from the second register of the ten commandments – whereas Barnabas (19:4,6) has only adultery and covetousness. Moreover, the syntactical peculiarities (the repetitive use of οὐ with the second person singular future indicative, coupled with the asyndetic structure of the string of prohibitions) imitate the LXX rendering of the decalogue in Exod 20 and Deut 5. The list of vices in *Doctr./Did.* 5 is longer than the parallel in *Barn.* 20, containing additions derived from the ten commandments (fornications, thefts, false witnesses), and is structured more in accordance with the decalogue. While the reference to the decalogue is clear, many of the prohibitions in *Did.* 2:2–5:2 go beyond the decalogue, such as pederasty, abortion, and child exposure, and are typical of the Hellenistic Jewish elaboration of the Torah. Kloppenborg further observes that the Christian Two Ways tradition is not involved in Hellenistic Jewish apologetics: it does not argue *to* the Torah, but *from* it, taking its authority as self-evident.[34] Like the letter of James, the *Doctr./Did.* Two Ways teaching employs Lev 19:18 together with other material from the Holiness Code (e.g., the prohibition of partiality, προσωπολημψία) in its ethical concentration of the Torah.[35]

Kloppenborg also seems right in interpreting the pre-Didachist version, including the τέκνον section, as implying the fundamental *validity* and *unity* of the law. This understanding of the law differs somewhat from the rabbinic prophylactic idea of "building a fence" around the Torah (*m.Abot* 1:1), and from the rigoristic rhetoric in Matthew's antitheses, according to which anger *is* murder and lust *is* adultery. Kloppenborg refers to the Testament of Asher and the letter of James as the closest parallels to the pre-Didachist conception of the law.[36] In fact these two texts differ from each other.[37] In stressing the unity of the law as an ethical code, the core of which is the

---

[33] It is difficult to say whether the tripartite formula in *Barn.* is traditional or the author's creation. In view of, e.g., Sir 7:30–31, a Jewish origin would seem quite natural. However, the author seems elsewhere fond of triadic compositions, and the aorist λυτρωσάμενον suggests a post-baptismal paraenetic setting (Prostmeier, *Der Barnabasbrief*, 537–38, notes that the aorist refers to baptism and ". . . auf ein Heilsgeschehen *zurückblickt*, das Gott gewirkt hat").

[34] Kloppenborg, " The Transformation of Moral Exhortation," 99–102.

[35] *Ibid.*, 102–104.

[36] *Ibid.*, 107.

[37] The polemical (or apologetical) tone of *T. Ash.* should not be dismissed. The edge is directed at the "two-faced" who consider the "single-faced" to be sinners (4:1), whereas in fact they themselves serve evil desires (3:2), imitate the spirits of error and join in the struggle against mankind (6:2; a secondary addition according to Hollander and De Jonge, *The Testaments of the Twelve Patriarchs*, 353). By contrast, the single-faced person imitates the Lord (4:3). Such persons seem wild and unclean, but actually they are clean (4:5). The peculiar distinction between "swines" or "hares" (2:9) and "stags" or "hinds" (4:5) suggests that some who seemingly keep the law are hypocrites, while seeming sinners may be doing what the true law of the Lord requires. I am not confident that this reasoning honestly reckons with the unity of the Jewish law. It may reflect a *Christian assimilation* of the Torah and the Lord's/Christ's commandments. This can be assumed for the letter of James, too, but there the polemic seems to be against gentile Christians who do not keep the law. James represents a genuine Jewish-Christian stance, even if "the perfect law of liberty" (Jas 1:25) is not precisely the Torah. See Syreeni, "James and the Pauline Legacy," 418–21.

decalogue and the principle of neighbourly love, the pre-Didachist Two Ways teaching stands closer to the ethos of James. But precisely for this reason it is unwarranted to conclude that the *Doctr./Did.* tradition "has not yet taken the step that Matthew did to make Lev 19:18 into an interpretive principle."[38] Already James assumes a Christian assimilation of the Torah and the "perfect law of liberty" (1:25) as manifested through "our Lord Jesus of glory" (2:1). The "royal law" of Lev 19:18, which the Christians are to fulfil according to Jas (2:8), is then an interpretative – *assimilating*, though not consciously *selective* – principle.

At the same time, the pre-Didachist Two Ways teaching is not necessarily the "precedent" that "eventually" leads to Matthew's concept of the law.[39] The τέκνον section shows that the pre-Didachist concern for the Christian understanding of the law did not need to take a Matthaean turn, but could be articulated in terms of a subtle baptismal allusion: keeping to the new Way of Life (beginning from the baptismal "birth") involves avoiding apparently minor sins that belong in the opposite way and ultimately "give birth" to mortal sins. The evangelical section shows that the Didachist's community did without the antithetical rhetoric of Matt 5:17–48. To be sure, *Did.* 1:3–4 postulates a great difference between the Christian ethos and that of the outsiders, an antagonism which is simultaneously a "more than" relation, and the Christian ethos is expressed as the ideal of perfection (καὶ ἔσῃ τέλειος, 1:4). All this is present in Matt 5:21–48, as is the first bulk of material in the evangelical section, but Matthew's antithetical formula and scriptural quotations are absent. The Didachist avoids any contrast between the Mosaic law and the dominical teaching. While the *social* antagonism with the allegedly "hypocritical" Judaism is strong, the basic moral values remain the same and the Christian understanding of the law is expressed in terms of continuity.[40]

The Didachist's redaction shows a tension between the high *ideal* of perfection and the more modest *practical* requirements. The evangelical section ends with a warning not to receive alms without need (1:5) and with the quotation, "Let your charitable gift sweat in your hands until you know to whom you are giving it" (1:6).[41] This seems a drastic reinterpretation, if not denial of the exhortation to give to anyone who asks (1:5). However, if we assume that the community was trying to practice the ethos of generous giving, the tension shows that the practical consequences were realised and a counterbalancing maxim was called for. According to many interpreters, the practical motivation of the ideal of enemy love lacks persuasiveness: "Just love those who hate you *and you will not have any enemy*" (1:3). However, this statement hardly rests

---

[38] Kloppenborg, "The Transformation of Moral Exhortation," 104.

[39] Cf. *Ibid.,* 109.

[40] As a result I am not convinced by the argument in Van de Sandt-Flusser, *The Didache,* 241, that *Did.* 6:2–3 cannot come from the redactor who in 8:1–2 "exhibits an apparent hostility against Judaism."

[41] The scriptural reference is notoriously obscure, see Niederwimmer, *Die Didache,* 111–14. If Sir 12:1 was the source of its inspiration from the beginning (which I think is fairly possible), then *Did.* 1:5b–6 may be understood as a scriptural "correction" of the indiscriminating attitude recommended in the earlier part of the evangelical section. The ethos of Sir 12 differs clearly from that of Q 6:27–36 and Matt 5:38–48; cf. Zerbe, *Non-Retaliation in Early Jewish and New Testament Texts,* 39–44.

on calculations about the enemy's reaction to unexpected kindness,[42] rather it is an encouraging promise of God's assistance.[43] The remark, "If someone takes away from you what is yours, do not claim it back *since you cannot do so anyway*" (1:4), need not be taken as an instance of confused biblical (Lukan) exegesis;[44] it may well be a realistic observation, to be compared with Matthew's down-to-earth wisdom, "Let the day's own trouble be sufficient for the day" (Matt 6:34).

In *Did.* 6:2, we meet the same practical and realistic attitude: "If you can bear the entire yoke of the Lord, you will be perfect, but if you cannot, do what you can." The "yoke of the Lord" recalls Matt 11:28–30, where the Jewish imagery of the Torah as a (light) yoke is applied to the Christian understanding of the law.[45] *Did.* 6:2–3 is only more explicit in stating the practical, indispensable purity requirement for entering and staying in the community, viz., abstaining from idol food. This compromise was widely acknowledged in late first-century and second-century communities and allowed a *modus vivendi* for Jewish and gentile Christians.[46]

From the Inaugural Speech Q 6:20b–49 to the Sermon on the Mount

As we now move to the composition history of Matt 5–7, the main redactional stages from the final form of the Sermon on the Mount to the underlying speech Q 6:20b–49 are relatively clear, provided that we accept the synoptic two-source theory. In fact, the very structure of Matthew's gospel gives evidence for this theory. The literary constituents of the new gospel – a continuous narrative with embedded, thematically

---

[42] Niederwimmer, *Die Didache*, 103, paraphrases: "Wer seinen Feind beharrlich liebt, paralysiert schliesslich dessen Aggression. Liebe zerstört die Feindschaft!"

[43] Cf. *T. Jos.* 18:2: "If anyone wants to do evil to you, do well to him and pray for him, and you will be released by the Lord from all evil."

[44] Tuckett, "Synoptic Tradition in the Didache," 126–27, suggests that the Didache's comment reflects the incongruity in the Lukan text.

[45] Van de Sandt-Flusser, *The Didache*, 240, point out that the "yoke of the Lord" in *Did.* 6:2 is not said to be a *nova lex Christi*. However, if the Didache's conception of the law stresses continuity, this observation is no argument against a reference to the yoke of Christ. Luomanen, *Entering the Kingdom of Heaven*, 117, concludes that the "light yoke" in Matt 11:29 designates Jesus' new interpretation of the law; the "heavy laden" are those who are burdened by the Pharisaic interpretation of the law (cf. Matt 23:4; note φορτίον here and in 11:30). Draper, "Torah and the Troublesome Apostles," 357, argues that the "yoke of the Lord" in the Didache "refers to the Torah, *as maintained and interpreted in the Christian community*" (emphasis added). Thus, both Matt 11:28–30 and *Did.* 6:2–3 basically *assimilate* the Torah and its Christian understanding.

[46] It is quite unlikely that the Didache expects that the (gentile) converts who initially keep the minimum law end up with fulfilling the whole Torah (including circumcision). *Did.* 16:2 would then imply that those who have not taken on the whole yoke of the law before the final judgment will not benefit from their partial obedience. Thus, e.g., Draper, "Torah and the Troublesome Apostles," 359: "In other words, the Didache allows the proselyte flexibility about the timetable, but at the end of the day, it is required of him/her that he/she become a full Jew in order to attain salvation." But how can uncircumcised "second class Christians" (358) qualify as Christians at all if they will not be saved "at the end of the day?" How does this "flexible" strategy comply with Draper's reference to the rabbinic proselyte tractate (*Gerim*), where "the proselyte is *first* introduced into the disadvantages of the Torah" (p. 362, emphasis added)?

grouped discourses – were suggested by the two principal sources, Mark and Q. The redactor also coined two sets of formulaic expressions to indicate the dual yet unified nature of the document: the five καὶ ἐγένετο expressions to mark the shift back to the main narrative after each of the five great discourses, and the two ἀπὸ τότε markers (4:17; 16:21) to call attention to the decisive turning points in the narrative plot.[47] By means of these formal hints the evangelist makes clear that the whole gospel includes *the story of Jesus* – his origin, ministry and passion – as well as the authoritative *teaching of Jesus*. Thus both Matthew and the Didachist combined different sources into a new comprehensive document, where the literary properties of the main sources were purposefully preserved: Matthew created a narrative-and-discourse gospel, the Didachist produced a paraenetic manual of instruction.

The Sermon on the Mount is the first of Matthew's formally marked great discourses, and it may have a representative (*pars pro toto*) function as the quintessence of "all that I have commanded you" (28:19).[48] The placing of the Sermon after Jesus' baptism and testing and the calling of the first disciples, as well as the presence of the crowds (the would-be disciples),[49] give the Sermon an air of baptismal teaching, and in the reaction of the crowds (7:28–29, borrowed from Mark 1:22) Jesus' inaugural speech is described as the authoritative teaching (διδαχή). However, while much of its material was probably used in pre-baptismal and elementary teaching, and the gospel as a whole shows traces of a catechetical and liturgical *Sitz im Leben*,[50] the Sermon is as much a literary entity and a part of Matthew's overall (discourse *and* narrative) plot as it is a teaching unit for practical purposes.

There is considerable agreement in Q research that Luke's Sermon on the Plain (Luke / Q 6:20b–49), with the exception of the woes, reproduces Jesus' inaugural speech in the sayings gospel. This speech is the compositional basis of Matthew's sermon and can be divided into a programmatic statement 6:20b–23 (the beatitudes), admonitions 6:27–35 (love of enemies, non-retaliation), further admonitions 6:36, 37–38 (mercy, not judging, generosity), warnings to teachers 6:39–45 (blind leaders, disciple and teacher, speck in the eye), and a conclusion 6:46, 47–49 ("Lord, Lord", parable of the builders).[51] The general appearance of the Q speech is sapiential, however in an unconventional, subversive way (cf. the macarisms) and with an eschatological perspective (cf. the concluding parable). In its literary context, the inaugural sermon is in the middle of the first thematic block of material dealing with John and Jesus (Q 3:7–9, 16–17; 4:1–13; 6:20b–49; 7:1–10, 18–35). By and large, the Sayings gospel Q seems to comprise four major sections or topical groupings: John and Jesus

---

[47] For Matthew's structure and literary plan, see Syreeni, *The Making of the Sermon on the Mount*, 75–131.

[48] *Ibid.*, 100–102.

[49] The narrative function of the crowds is complex but includes the notion of would-be disciples; cf. Syreeni, *The Making of the Sermon on the Mount*, 122–24.

[50] Hultgren, "Liturgy and Literature," 659–73.

[51] For the contents of the Q speech, see Syreeni, *The Making of the Sermon on the Mount*, 132–39. For its rhetorical structure, see Kloppenborg, *Excavating Q*, 155–56; consult also Kloppenborg's earlier exposition of the Q sermon in *The Formation of Q*, 171–90.

(Inaugural Discourse), Jesus and his Disciples (Mission Discourse), Jesus and his Opponents (Controversy Discourse), and the Last Things (Eschatological Discourse).[52]

The composition history of Q is a hotly debated issue and cannot be discussed here more fully.[53] However, in spite of the recent development of Q research, I do not feel compelled to revise the main conclusion reached in my 1987 thesis concerning Q 6:20b–49. The Q speech is a composite, containing several originally independent sayings and clusters of sayings, as well as secondary interpretative elements (e.g., the fourth beatitude and its sequel, vv. 22–23) and transitional links (e.g., v. 46 to introduce the concluding parable). At the same time, the inaugural sermon shows such proximity to the overarching themes of the "John and Jesus" section that it is doubtful that the speech with all its main parts came into being before the section was formed.[54] Moreover, Q 6:(46,) 47–49 obviously has the entire sayings gospel in view. The inaugural sermon owes its structure to a comprehensive and late (or final) redaction of Q, and reflects the concerns and the self-understanding of an established group of early Christian communities: the beatitudes define the people of God and the blessings they receive; the teaching on enemy love shows its behavior toward outsiders; the next set of admonitions discusses the community's internal affairs; and the eschatological conclusion reminds all readers and hearers of the necessity of doing what the Teacher says (in that very document), lest one miss the promised reward.

The paraenetic-catechetic logic of the inaugural speech follows *in miniature* the "first things first, last things last" pattern visible in the whole Q composition, Matthew's great discourses and the Didache. The "first things" include initial and basic issues of discipleship (Inaugural Discourse / Sermon on the Mount / Two Ways), the "last things" involve eschatology (the eschatological discourses in each text). Certainly this is a very general and intrinsic structuring principle, showing much variation especially in the central sections. In the Q sermon the central parts expound moral and behavioural principles toward outsiders (love of enemies, non-retaliation) and within the community (not judging, following the good teacher). In the whole of Q, the inner life of the community is not as elaborate a thematic principle as it is in Matthew's third and fourth discourses (Chaps. 13 and 18) and especially in *Did.* 7–15. Instead, the central Q sections deal with the community's external relations (Mission Discourse;

---

[52] See Kloppenborg, *The Formation of Q*, 90–92. According to Kirk, *The Composition of the Sayings Source*, 289–403, each of the four topical sections (macro-compositions) shows a carefully designed centric structure (ring composition) with one central saying. In the inaugural discourse, the central saying would be Q 6:40: "A disciple is not above his teacher, but everyone, when well trained, will be like his teacher." However, the details of the Q text are too uncertain to allow such refined reconstructions. Kirk assumes that the first macro-composition in Q contained an account of the baptism of Jesus; but this is debatable, and if the baptism scene is excluded, the symmetry of the "John and Jesus" section is partially lost. If Q 6:40 is about John and Jesus, as Kirk would have it, the saying contradicts the main idea of the section (John proclaims the mightier "coming one," Q 3:16 – and even he who is least in the kingdom of God is greater than John, Q 7:28).

[53] For research history, see Kirk, *The Composition of the Sayings Source*, 1–64. I have problems with the influential stratification model advanced by Kloppenborg (see, e.g., his "The Sayings Gospel Q," 1–66). However, the problems are not necessarily solved by Kirk's critique of the *Kleinliteratur* model and by his synchronic approach, which in fact is suggestive of a two-stage model (from "speeches" to "macro-compositions").

[54] Syreeni, *The Making of the Sermon on the Mount*, 147–53.

Controversy Discourse), while Matthew's great discourses are halfway between Q's more external and the Didache's decidedly inner-community focus.[55]

The amount of material in Matthew 5–7 added to the Q speech is so impressive that the question arises whether Matthew's redaction is understandable without previous catechetic collections besides the Q sermon.[56] While an enlarged, written Q^{mt} version of the inaugural speech is an unnecessary hypothesis, the Matthaean masterpiece of redaction was aided by other developments. Much of the additional material may be oral expansions of the Q speech or its sayings clusters; e.g., the macarisms in the opening of the Q speech were probably amplified in Matthew's community (into a series of seven?). Further sayings come from Q outside of the inaugural sermon. The Lord's Prayer (6:9–13; Q 11:2–4) was obviously an important liturgical text and a catechetic centre of gravity around which other Q and special material was gathered in the community's teaching.[57] Matthew used parts of this teaching in the frames of the Lord's Prayer (6:7–8, 14–15) and added other topics from the same catechetic context in his Sermon a little later (6:25–34; 7:7–11).[58] Another significant block was Q 16:16–18, which contributed to the redaction of Matt 5:17–20 and the following antitheses (cf. 5:32 and Q 16:18).[59] However, it is unlikely that the ecclesiastical special material consisted solely of oral expansions of Q. The instructions on almsgiving, prayer and fasting in 6:2–6, 16–18 are clearly independent of Q, showing typically Jewish-Christian concerns and a relatively late polemical *Sitz im Leben* after the community's break with the synagogue.[60] The so-called primary antitheses in 5:21–30, 33–37 have similar concerns and polemical side-glances. When Matthew transformed Q 6:27–36 into an antithetical form (5:38–48), the tone became even sharper. The final antitheses arrive at the point of breaking with the already tense rhetoric of "fulfilment" (5:17) and "exceeding righteousness" (5:20), and push it toward a sheer antithesis.[61]

Despite the added material, the Sermon on the Mount has preserved the main structure of the Q speech. The beatitudes define the nature, task and privileges of the people of God, and the concluding parable stresses the importance of hearing and doing the words of Jesus, the only Teacher (cf. 23:8). Matthew's only large-scale

---

[55] Like Q, Matthew has a mission discourse, but the controversy speech, Chap. 23, is used as a "preamble" to the eschatological parables, Chaps. 24–25.

[56] For the following, see Syreeni, *The Making of the Sermon on the Mount*, 160–65.

[57] *Ibid.*, 171–73. See also my article, "A Single Eye," 98–103.

[58] Syreeni, *The Making of the Sermon on the Mount*, 172–73.

[59] Ibid., 190–196. See also Luomanen, *Entering the Kingdom of Heaven*, 70–80. In addition to Matt 5:17, 18, 32 / Q 16:16–18, Luomanen observes the parallelism between Matt 5:19, 20 and Q 7:28, 26.

[60] Syreeni, "Separation and Identity," 537–38.

[61] The much-debated issue of the meaning of the antitheses cannot be discussed here at length. Suffice it to note that any interpretation that neglects the *difference* between the primary and the last two antitheses fails to recognise the dynamic of the redaction. The programme of "fulfilment" and "doing more" (5:17–20) seems to be Matthew's main thrust, but the application of the antithetical pattern in 5:38–48 (necessitating the formation of the problematic scriptural "quotation" in v. 43) pushed the already tense logic still further. For the ambiguities in Matthew's theological programme in 5:17–20, see Luomanen, *Entering the Kingdom of Heaven*, 86–91. He argues convincingly that the tense rhetoric serves the purpose of *legitimation*. Obviously, the Didache community was not in need of such a theological (christological) legitimation for its interpretation of the law.

transposition of material within the inaugural discourse is the relocation of the Golden Rule (7:12a; cf. Q 6:31), now formulated more pregnantly and interpreted as the core of "the law and the prophets" (7:12b), hence equal to the love commandments (cf. 22:40). Through this reformulation, transposition and theological equation, and by means of the formal *inclusio* 5:17–7:12, the Golden Rule functions as a summary of Jesus' teaching in the central section of the Sermon on the Mount.[62] Matthew did with the Golden Rule analogously to what a pre-Didachist redactor must have done with the quotation Lev 19:18, which in an earlier *Vorlage* was embedded in a series of ethical instructions (cf. *Barn.* 19:5) and was then elevated as a summary of the Way of Life, together with Deut 6:5 and the Golden Rule.

One may ask whether Matthew's compositional move was just an individual redactor's innovation or rather reflects a scribal tradition in the community, where not only the love commandments were juxtaposed (as in Mark) but also the Golden Rule was equated with these (and possibly epitomised as "the law and the prophets"). Such a catechetic tradition would explain how it occurred to Matthew in the first place to use the Golden Rule as an interpretative principle. A mere reading of the Q sermon did not readily suggest it.[63] Of course, it cannot be excluded that the Golden Rule in its prominent Matthaean location and formulation is the redactor's literary achievement with a powerful *Wirkungsgeschichte*, beginning as early as *Doctr./Did.* 1:2a. However, it is also quite conceivable that the catechetic triad suggested by Matt 22:36–40 + 7:12 and explicated in *Doctr./Did.* 1:2a points to a common tradition. Van de Sandt and Flusser assume the latter case and hypothesise further that Matthew knew some form of the Two Ways tradition, which included a parallel to the Didache's τέκνον section and the Golden Rule (as well as the love commandments). They see traces of this tradition in 5:17–48 and 7:12, 13–14.[64] In addition, they believe that the Matthaean macarisms (5:3–12), the piety instructions (6:1–18) and the prohibitions concerning wealth, judgment of others and perverted zeal (6:19–7:6) might have appeared in this catechetical source.[65] The appeal of this hypothesis rests on two considerations. First, it is likely that Matt 7:13–14 makes use of a Q logion (cf. Luke 13:23–24) which only had the narrow "door" (or "gate"). Thus the motif of the two ways is a redactional feature.[66] Matthew's introduction of the motif asks for an explanation, all the more so as the

---

[62] Syreeni, *The Making of the Sermon on the Mount*, 158–160.173–180. Matthew's complex redaction suggests that the hermeneutical and ethical key role of the Golden Rule hardly originates with Jesus. Whether or not Jesus referred to this maxim is impossible to tell; cf. Alexander, "Jesus and the Golden Rule," 382: "The evidence that Hillel quoted the Rule is shaky in the extreme ... There are better grounds for believing that Jesus quoted the Rule, but his positive formulation of it is not so innovative as has often been claimed."

[63] This possibility was not discussed in my 1987 thesis.

[64] Van de Sandt-Flusser, *The Didache*, 225–34.

[65] *Ibid.*, 230. The fluidity of this hypothesis is noteworthy: "Because the present evidence is insufficient, however, we have no real way of telling whether the Two Ways items conflated with the underlying framework of the Sermon merely in the final stage of the editing of the gospel, or whether the fusion was a long-lasting process ... It would be even more conjectural to restore the form itself of the Two Ways version which guided Matthew in systematizing his material for the gospel ... After all, the genre of catechesis is fundamentally open to transformation, revision, and emendation of individual parts."

[66] Luz, *Das Evangelium nach Matthäus*, 395–97; Kloppenborg, *The Formation of Q*, 223–24.

metaphor of "way" seems unproductive after the carefully formed *inclusio* 5:17–7:12, where "gate" – suggestive of entrance, cf. εἰσέρχεσθαι, 5:20; 7:13 – is the appropriate metaphor. Second, the presence of special material in Matthew's sermon would seem easier to explain if it came from one fixed (literary or oral) catechetic context.

However, the conjectural "two-ways source" is too amorphous to provide a basis for explaining Matthew's redaction. There is simply too little common material to connect the special Matthaean elements in the Sermon on the Mount with the content of the pre-Didache Two Ways teaching.[67] Since most of the inserted material comes from other Q sections or represents oral expansions of the Q sermon, it can hardly be said that Matthew or his tradition conflated the Q sermon with a "two-ways source." We are not necessarily left with more than Luz's modest proposal that Matthew and his community were familiar with the *motif* (or "thought", "topos", "style") of the two ways.[68] Certainly, if both the two-ways motif and the use of the Golden Rule to explicate the love commandments rest on a catechetic tradition common to Matthew and the Didache, we do have a two-ways *scheme*, which could be filled with a variety of further material; but we cannot tell whether and in what manner this was done in Matthew's community. To the degree that the literary composition of Matt 5–7 reflects an attempt to provide a model for the community's teaching for converts, it appears not to introduce, but rather to replace a Two Ways catechesis – which, however, it failed to do in the Didache community.

Conclusion: From Matthew to the Didache

This analysis has confirmed important tradition-historical links between Matthew and the Didache. Matthew's community was familiar with the two-ways motif and may have applied it as a catechetic scheme. There are traces of a common scribal tradition. The seemingly very different literary products, a gospel and a church manual, share a similar intrinsic paraenetic-catechetic logic. Both texts breathe the presence of Jewish-Christian traditions and an openness to gentile converts. Both combine a rhetoric of perfection with practical concerns and a relatively lenient application. Still, the paucity of common material in the Sermon on the Mount and *Did.* 1–6 is undeniable, and the theological postures are not identical.

---

[67] Suggs, "The Christian Two Ways Tradition," rightly pointed out that more than the metaphor of two "paths" is required to establish a connection, and that "not even the proximity of the Golden Rule (7:12) is enough to make the case entirely convincing" (63). The few thematic connections between the antitheses and *Did.* 3:1–6 (anger–murder; lust–adultery) do not make the case substantially stronger.

[68] Luz, *Das Evangelium nach Matthäus*, 397: "Es lässt sich wahrscheinlich sogar zeigen, dass in der mt Gemeinde der Gedanke der beiden Wege bekannt gewesen ist . . . Da die Didache aus einer Mt geprägten Gemeinde stammt, können wir vermuten, dass Mt das aus Q stammende Wort vom engen Tor durch einen in seiner eigenen Gemeinde geläufigen paränetischen Topos erweitert hat. Seine Redaktion wäre dann durchaus 'traditionell'! Er hat den ihm literarisch vorgegeben Q-Text im Stil der seiner Gemeinde vertrauten Paränese erweitert."

All things considered, it is unlikely that Matthew's gospel and the Didache were written in the same community approximately at the same time.[69] When the Didachist compiled his work and included the evangelical section in the Two Ways teaching, a generation or more had passed since the issue of Matthew's "double gospel," which was soon acknowledged and used in the Didache community. The Didachist is explicit about the authoritative voice (ἐκέλευσεν) of the Lord "in his gospel" (8:2), and refers to the δόγμα τοῦ εὐαγγελίου (11:3) as a valid norm.

In this light, it is remarkable that the Didache community *continued* to use the Two Ways catechesis long after Matthew's text and the Sermon on the Mount were available. Even in the "updated" version of the catechesis the Christian specifics are vague. There is no suggestion of a new law of Christ as opposite to the Torah, no christologically motivated fulfilment theology. Matthew's *theological* antagonism with Judaism is avoided, and the perspective of the admonitions in *Did.* 1–6 remains Jewish in that the warnings often concern pagan sins. Yet the document is quite clear – much clearer than Matthew – about the *real-life* differences between the community's worship and the practice of the "hypocrites" (8:1–3). It mentions the "Sunday of the Lord" as the day of assembly (14:1) and speaks for an advanced church structure (15:1).[70] All this indicates a long, surprisingly smooth movement from a Torah-observant, Christ-believing congregation with prophets and teachers toward a "catholic", Jewish and gentile Christian church with bishops and deacons.

[69] This is not to deny the possibility of temporal overlap and interchange between Matthew's and the Didache's traditions or sources. However, the emergence of a written gospel may have affected the Didache community in a profound way; cf. Draper, "Social Ambiguity," 307.

[70] Note the careful persuasive strategy: the bishops and deacons should not be disregarded, "for they too perform the functions of prophets and teachers for you" (15:1) and are "honourable men" like the prophets and teachers (15:2). The new hierarchic order is presented as the continuation of charismatic leadership, which ultimately flows from the Teacher's authority (Matt 23:8; *Did.* 4:1).

Chapter Six

The Use of the Synoptics or Q in *Did.* 1:3b-2:1

John S. Kloppenborg

University of Toronto (Canada)

Since its publication in 1883[1] the Didache has been at the centre of controversies on a number of topics, including its relationship to the Epistle of Barnabas, its use of the "two ways" motif, the history and development of eucharistic practices, the relation of apostles and prophets in *Did.* 11:3-12; 13:1-7 to the *episkopoi* and *diakonoi* of *Did.* 15:1-2, and the relation of the Didache to the Synoptic Gospels.

On the latter topic almost every conceivable relationship has been asserted: (a) that the Didache is principally or exclusively dependent on the final written forms of Matthew and Luke;[2] (b) that the Didachist had no direct knowledge of the text of Matthew but knew Matthaean sayings through their oral usage in his community;[3] (c) that Matthew used the Didache;[4] (d) that the Didache is independent of the final form of the Synoptic Gospels and derives instead from oral pre-synoptic tradition in whole[5]

---

[1] Bryennios, Διδαχὴ τῶν δώδεκα ἀποστόλων. The manuscript, found in the Monastery of the Holy Sepulchre ("Jerusalem Monastery") in Constantinople, is dated June 11, 1056 C.E.

[2] Massaux, *Influence de l'évangile*, 604–46; Butler, "The Literary Relations," 265–83; "The Two Way," 27–38; Vokes, *The Riddle of the Didache*, 92–119; Johnson, "A Subsidiary Motive," 112; Richardson, "The Teaching of the Twelve Apostles," 163. 165–166; Layton, "The Sources, Date and Transmission," 343–83 (for 1:3—2:1 only); Barnard, "The Dead Sea Scrolls," 99 n. 2; Schweizer, *Matthäus,* 141 n. 12. 164–65; Tuckett, "Synoptic Tradition in the Didache," 197–230; Wengst, *Didache (Apostellehre)*, 19. 24–31.

[3] Aono, *Die Entwicklung,* 164–89; for 1:3–2:1 Aono posits dependence on a "collection of dominical sayings" based mainly on Matthew but influenced by Luke (p. 189).

[4] Garrow, *The Gospel*.

[5] Audet, *La Didachè*, 166–86; Rordorf, "Does the Didache Contain?," 394–423.

or in part;[6] (e) that the Didachist used Q, or a source resembling Q;[7] and (f) that the Didache depends on some other collection of sayings of Jesus.[8]

While earlier scholarship tended to favour to the view that the Didache drew on the Synoptic Gospels, either Matthew alone or Matthew and Luke, the tide has turned recently and decisively, such that most recent monographic and commentary treatments of the Didache conclude that the Didache is independent of the Synoptics. In 1978 Rordorf and Tuilier concluded that the Didache "ne cite aucun texte néo-testamentaire," reiterating that conclusion in their second (1998) edition: "la *Didachè* ne dépend pas des évangiles que nous possédons et qu'elle remonte en conséquence à une époque ancienne."[9]

Kurt Niederwimmer argues that if there is any influence of the New Testament, it is only at the level of the redactor of the Didache. The Two Ways documents (*Did.* 1:1-2; 2:2–6:1), the liturgical section (7:1–10:7), the church order (11:1–15:4), and probably the apocalypse (16:3-8) display no dependence on the New Testament at all.[10] But Niederwimmer concludes that even the christianizing insertion in *Did.* 1:3–2:1 depends not on Matthew and Luke but on either oral tradition or "(perhaps better)... an apocryphal sayings collection."[11] The most recent monographic study of the Didache by Huub van de Sandt and David Flusser argues that Didache 16 "reveals no dependence on either Mark or Matthew... but rather represent a tradition upon which Matthew drew." *Did.* 1:3–2:1 "preserve[s] a Jesus tradition independently of the gospels of Matthew and Luke."[12]

---

[6] Kirsopp Lake, writing in Bartlet-Lake, *The New Testament*, argued that one could not distinguish between use of Matthew and use of pre-Synoptic tradition in the Two Ways section or in *Did.* 7–15 even if the Didache "corresponds closely to what is found in our Synoptics, particularly Matthew, and is alluded to under the phrase τὸ εὐαγγέλιον, which apparently means the Message itself rather than any special record" (30). For Didache 16, Lake noted the close resemblance to Matthew but concluded that these "cannot be said to prove its [the Didache's] author's knowledge of our Matthew, as distinct from the tradition lying behind it, which may well have been that of the region in which the *Didache* itself was compiled" (33). On *Did.* 1:3b-2:1 Lake was similarly undecided (35–36). For argument for the Didache's use of pre-Synoptic tradition, see Koester, *Synoptische Überlieferung*, 159–241; Kloppenborg, "Didache 16,6–8," 54–67.

[7] Glover, "The Didache's Quotations," 12–29; "Patristic Quotations," 234–51. This view was already anticipated by Streeter, *The Four Gospels*, 511, on *Did.* 16:1 and Luke 12:35-38, which Streeter argued derived from Q. "If our hypothesis that Q was the original gospel of the church of Antioch be correct, and if the *Didache* was composed in Syria, for some years after Matthew was written certain sayings would still be remembered in their Q form." In general, however, Streeter accepted Matthaean influence on Q.

[8] Drews, "Untersuchungen zur Didache," 53–79; Lake, in Bartlet-Lake, *The New Testament*, 30–6; Tuilier, "La Didachè et le problème," 110–30 posits a "collection de *logia* du Seigneur en araméen" which was in turn the source of "l'Évangile du Seigneur en grec (source Q)," the immediate source of the Didache. Koester, *Synoptische Überlieferung*, 238–40, by contrast, argued *Did.* 1:3-2:1 represented a *Herrnwortsammlung* which drew on the written forms of Matthew and Luke. Similarly Aono, *Die Entwicklung*, 189.

[9] Rordorf-Tuilier, *La Doctrine des douze apôtres*, 91. 232.

[10] Niederwimmer, *The Didache*, 48–51. Niederwimmer expresses some hesitations about this conclusion in regard to the apocalypse (16:3-8) (p. 48, n. 39).

[11] Niederwimmer, *The Didache*, 76. 80.

[12] Van de Sandt-Flusser, *The Didache*, 39. 48.

The issue of the possible influence of written gospels on the Didache cannot be divorced from the composition history of the document, which is clearly a complex one. Comparison of the Didache with the Epistle of Barnabas, the Doctrina Apostolorum, Canons of the Holy Apostles (or Apostolic Church Order),[13] the Epitome of the Canons of the Holy Apostles[14] and Apostolic Constitutions indicates, first, that the Didache and the Apostolic Constitutions (Book VII)[15] are closely related, so close indeed that the latter appears to have copied the entire Didache, including the so-called *sectio evangelica* (*Did.* 1:3b–2:1). Second, the Doctrina, which otherwise agrees closely with *Did.* 1:1-3a; 2:2–5:2 (Doctrina 1:1–5:2), lacks the *sectio evangelica* and 6:2-3.[16] This encourages the conclusions (a) that the Doctrina and the Two Ways section of the Didache are siblings, and (b) that the *sectio evangelica* represents an interpolation into the Didache's Two Ways. The interpolation of 1:3b–2:1 into the Two Ways section has made necessary the addition of δευτέρα δὲ ἐντολὴ τῆς διδαχῆς in *Did.* 2:1 to serve as a transition to the original Two Ways document.[17]

Third, the Canons of the Holy Apostles 4:1–13:4 (or Apostolic Church Order, hereafter the *Canons*) agrees with much of the Didache/Doctrina up to *Did.* 4:8 but omit Didache/Doctrina 4:9–14 as well as the entire Way of Death (Didache/Doctrina 5:1-2).[18] The Epitome is similar, lacking the entire Way of Death, though it does preserve the conclusion to the Way of Life (*Did.* 4:9-14).[19] Fourth, the *Canons* and the Epitome display some parallels to Barnabas in material that is completely lacking in the

---

[13] Schermann, *Die allgemeine Kirchenordnung.*

[14] Edited by Schermann, *Eine Elfapostelmoral.*

[15] Funk, *Didascalia.*

[16] Parallels to *Did.* 6:2-3 are lacking in both the Doctrina and the *Canons*. According to Stuiber ("Das ganze Joch des Herrn," 323–29), 6:2-3 is a "jüdischen Nachtrag zur jüdischen Zweiweglehre" at home in a Diaspora synagogue and written with gentiles in view. But Rordorf-Tuilier (*La Doctrine des douze apôtres*, 32) point out that τέλειος ἔση of 6:2 has the strongest connections with the language of 1:3b–2:1 (ἔση τέλειος, 1:4) and argue that the phrase ὅλον τὸν ζυγὸν τοῦ κυρίου "doit être celui du Seigneur Jésus" (ibid.). Moreover, they adduce a late second century sermon, *De centesima, de sexagesima, de tricesima* as a parallel to the content: "si potes quidem, fili, omnia praecepta domini facere, eris consummatus; sin autem, uel duo praecepta, amare dominum ex totis praecordiis et similem tibi quasi te ipsum" (58:10-13; see Daniélou, "Le traité de centesima," 171-81). *Did.* 6:2-3 is also regarded as an insertion of the final redactor by Niederwimmer, *The Didache*, 121–23.

[17] See, *inter alii*, Niederwimmer, *The Didache*, 68–8; Jefford, *The Sayings of Jesus*, 53; Van de Sandt-Flusser, *The Didache*, 40–1.

[18] There is a partial parallel between *Did.* 4:13, οὐ μὴ ἐγκαταλίπης ἐντολὰς κυρίου, φυλάξεις δὲ ἃ παρέλαβες, μήτε προστιθεὶς μήτε ἀφαιρῶν and *Canons* 14:3, ἑαυτῶν γίνεσθε νομοθέται, ἑαυτῶν γίνεσθε σύμβουλοι ἀγαθοί, θεοδίδακτοι· φυλάξεις ἃ παρέλαβες μήτε προσθεὶς μήτε ὑφαιρῶν. The first portion of this is paralleled by *Barn.* 21:4: ἑαυτῶν γίνεσθε νομοθέται ἀγαθοί, ἑαυτῶν μένετε σύμβουλοι πιστοί, ἄρατε ἐξ ὑμῶν πᾶσαν ὑπόκρισιν, which has led Niederwimmer (*The Didache*, 32) to suggest that "something from the epilogue to the tractate, which is absent in the *Didache*, could be concealed in 14:3a."

[19] Schermann, *Eine Elfapostelmoral*, 16–18.

Didache/Doctrina,[20] suggesting that the relationship between the *Canons* and Barnabas is not mediated by the Didache/Doctrina. Finally, the version of the Two Ways in the Didache/Doctrina differs from that in Barnabas in three important respects. First, the Didache/Doctrina has assimilated the rather chaotic list of admonitions in *Barn.* 19:4-6 to the second register of the Decalogue (*Did.* 2:2-7). Second, Lev 19:18 ([ἀγαπήσεις] τὸν πλησίον σου ὡς σεαυτόν), quoted later in Barnabas (2:5), is relocated and used in *Did.* 1:2 and Doctrina 1:2 to frame Chaps. 2-3. And finally, the Didache and Doctrina have inserted the so-called τέκνον section (3:1-6), missing in Barnabas, even though the latter has parallels with materials in the immediate vicinity of this section (2:2-7; 3:7–4:14).[21] In those three respects, Barnabas appears to be more primitive than the Didache/Doctrina, though Barnabas is hardly the direct ancestor of the Didache.

The available data suggest three basic forms of the Two Ways document, one used by Barnabas and displaying rather loose topical organization (α), a second expanded form with more topical organization (β) used independently by the Didache and the Greek original of the Doctrina (δ), and a slightly attenuated version (γ), closely paralleling β but missing the Way of Death and sharing a few elements with α.[22]

1 Methodological Considerations

In surveying the discussion of the Didache's relationship to the Synoptics over the past century and a quarter, what is striking is that critics could compare the Didache to precisely the same set of Synoptic texts and arrive at diametrically opposed judgments. Thus Paul Sabatier took the lack of exact agreement between the Didache and the Synoptics as an indication that it used none of the Synoptics and indeed was composed *prior* to the Synoptics.[23] Jean-Paul Audet ventured that if the Didachist knew Matthew and Luke, one might surmise that he would have used one as a base text and incorporate the odd detail from the other. But as it stands "il est impossible

---

[20] *Barn.* 1:1: χαίρετε, υἱοὶ καὶ θυγατέρες, ἐν ὀνόματι κυρίου τοῦ ἀγαπήσαντος ἡμᾶς; *Canons* 1:1: χαίρετε υἱοὶ καὶ θυγατέρες ἐν ὀνόματι κυρίου 'Ιησοῦ Χριστοῦ.

Barn. 19:2: δοξάσεις τόν σε λυτρωσάμενον ἐκ θανάτου· *Canons* 4:2: δοξάσεις τόν σε λυτρωσάμενον ἐκ θανάτου.

Barn. 19:9–10: ἀγαπήσεις ὡς κόρην τοῦ ὀφθαλμοῦ σου πάντα τὸν λαλοῦντά σοι τὸν λόγον κυρίου. 10 μνησθήσῃ ἡμέραν κρίσεως νυκτὸς καὶ ἡμέρας; *Canons* 12:1: τέκνον, τὸν λαλοῦντά σοι τὸν λόγον τοῦ θεοῦ καὶ παραίτιόν σοι γινόμενον τῆς ζωῆς καὶ δόντα σοι τὴν ἐν κυρίῳ σφραγῖδα ἀγαπήσεις ὡς κόρην τοῦ ὀφθαλμοῦ σου, μνησθήσῃ δὲ αὐτοῦ νύκτα καὶ ἡμέραν, τιμήσεις αὐτὸν ὡς τὸν κύριον (cf. *Did.* 4:1a: τέκνον μου, τοῦ λαλοῦντός σοι τὸν λόγον τοῦ θεοῦ μνησθήσῃ νυκτὸς καὶ ἡμέρας, τιμήσεις δὲ αὐτὸν ὡς κύριον).

Moreover *Barn.* 21:2–4, 6a (lacking in the Didache/Doctrina) finds close parallels in *Canons* 14:1–3.

[21] See Kloppenborg, "The Transformation," 99, 104–8; Van de Sandt, "*Didache* 3:1–6," 21–41.

[22] Similarly, Giet, *L'énigme de la Didachè*, 71; Niederwimmer, *The Didache*, 40. Barnard ("The Dead Sea Scrolls," 107) proposes a similar stemma, but (following Goodspeed) places the Greek original of the Doctrina as the direct source of Barnabas and the Didache.

[23] Sabatier, *ΔΙΔΑΧΗ ΤΩΝ ΙΒ' ΑΠΟΣΤΟΛΩΝ*, 150–65.

Figure 1

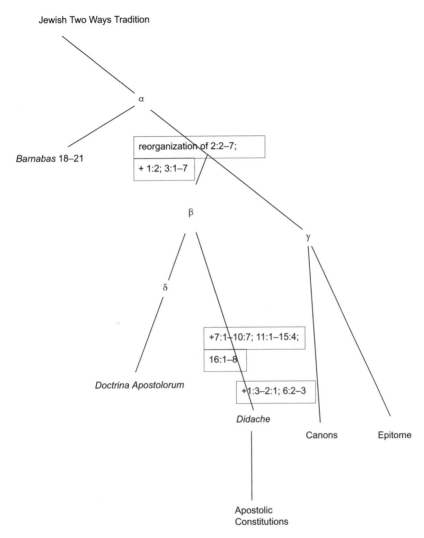

Jewish Two Ways Tradition

α

Barnabas 18–21

reorganization of 2:2–7;
+ 1:2; 3:1–7

β

γ

δ

+7:1–10:7; 11:1–15:4;
16:1–8

Doctrina Apostolorum

+1:3–2:1; 6:2–3

Didache

Canons   Epitome

Apostolic
Constitutions

d'imaginer comment [the author of 1:3–2:1] aurait pu travailler sur *Mt.* et *Lk.* pour arriver à son texte."[24] But F.E. Vokes, examining precisely the same words and phrases could assert that "mere reminiscence of New Testament thought and language" was sufficient evidence of knowledge and dependence on the New Testament in written form.[25] J.A. Robinson even went so far as to claim that the Didachist *deliberately* used inexact quotations to disguise the fact that he had used the gospels in order to give his work the marks of authority and apostolic authorship.[26]

[24] Audet, *La Didachè*, 185.
[25] Vokes, *The Riddle of the Didache*, 93.
[26] Robinson, *Barnabas, Hermas and the Didache*, 81–82.

Assessment of the significance of *differences* between the Didache and the Synoptics is the key problem. Three preliminary methodological comments are in order here. First, much of the earlier work done on the relationship between the Didache and the Synoptics tacitly assumed that the texts of the Synoptic Gospels were essentially stable from the time of their compilation, so that verbatim agreement of the Didache with, say, Matthew meant dependence on Matthew and disagreement meant either that the Didache was independent of Matthew or that it quoted Matthew from memory. But as Helmut Koester has argued, there is good reason to think that during the second century C.E. the text of the Synoptic Gospels was quite unstable. Koester solves some of the "minor agreements" by proposing that the text of Mark used by Matthew and Luke differed in significant respects from the third century text of Mark known from $\mathfrak{P}^{45}$ and its successors. Moreover, 2 Clement and Justin's *Apology* evidence extensive harmonizations of Matthew and Luke.

> With respect to Matthew and Luke, there is no guarantee that the archetypes of the manuscript tradition are identical with the original text of each Gospel. The harmonizations of these two Gospels demonstrate that their text was not sacrosanct and that alterations could be expected, even if they were not always as radical as in the case of Marcion's revision of Luke, the *Secret Gospel's* revision of Mark, and Justin's construction of a harmony.[27]

The fluidity of the texts of the Synoptics, the near-complete lack of manuscripts of the Synoptic Gospels before the fourth quarter of the second century, and the reality of harmonization and cross-fertilization of readings should caution us against relying too much on the notion of *the* text of Matthew, Mark, or Luke, as if we were in a position to reconstruct a determinate text for each of the gospels as they came of the pens of their editors. Not only is it impossible to bridge with certainty the century of transmission between the composition of the Synoptics and their first manuscript attestation, but also the very notion of *the* text of a gospel is a fiction encouraged by modern models of publication.[28] Ancient composition likely occurred in successive stages,[29] and we know of ancient authors who produced several diverging versions of their own works. There is no good reason to believe that Matthew, for example, existed in a single form even in Matthew's day: given its complex relationship to Mark, Q and its other sources, there is nothing improbable about the existence of multiple drafts and given the vagaries of ancient scribal practices, it is likely that multiple copies existed, each with at least copyists errors and probably with other variations too. Consequently, determining the relationship between "Matthew" and the Didache will necessarily be clouded by uncertainties since we cannot be sure to which "Matthew" the Didache might be comparable.

---

[27] Koester, "The Text of the Synoptic Gospels," 37. I am grateful to Arthur Bellinzoni for bringing this article to my attention.

[28] Kloppenborg, *Excavating Q,* 109.

[29] Downing, "Word-Processing in the Ancient World," 29–48.

Willy Rordorf has raised a second methodological consideration. He argues that divergences between the Didache and Matthew must be assessed in the context of the general tendencies of transmission and redaction. For example, he noted that while the form of the rhetorical question in *Did.* 1:3b (οὐχὶ καὶ τὰ ἔθνη τοῦτο ποιοῦσιν;) is close to that of Matt 5:47 (οὐχὶ καὶ οἱ ἐθνικοὶ τὸ αὐτὸ ποιοῦσιν;), the transmissional tendency of this verse is clearly *away* from the mention of the gentiles. Later textual tradition of Matthew substitutes οἱ τελῶναι, assimilating Matt 5:47 to 5:46;[30] Luke introduces οἱ ἁμαρτωλοί in place of ἐθνικοί; and Justin Martyr substitutes οἱ πόρνοι. Rordorf concludes:

> Cela signifie que la tradition textuelle de la *Didachè* plonge ici ses racines dans un milieu proche de l'*Evangile de Matthieu*, sans pour autant dépendre directement de ce dernier. En d'autres termes: le texte de la *Didachè* est ici porte-parole d'une tradition judéo-chrétienne indépendante.[31]

Jonathan Draper draws out the implication of Rordorf's observation even more clearly. Given the well-known tendency of textual transmission toward harmonization with the Synoptics,

> divergence in the *Didache* with regard to the Jesus tradition in the Synoptics Gospels must be held to be specially significant and indicative of an independent witness, unless it can be demonstrated that a later redactor would have had a motive in altering the form of the text.[32]

Huub van de Sandt has recently made a similar point: Since the Bryennios manuscript (H) is an eleventh century manuscript, "one may thus expect that, in the intervening ten centuries, the temptation to harmonize discordant parallels must have been intensified since copyists became increasingly familiar with the written gospels."[33]

C. M. Tuckett objects that Draper's principle is applicable to the phenomenon of quotations but not to free allusions. That is, since the Didache does not, with four exceptions,[34] signal its intention to *quote* anything, "it is inappropriate to judge the Didache's use of synoptic tradition as if it were a case of explicit quotation and to expect exact agreement between the quoted version and the source used."[35] This is similar to the point made eighty years ago by Vokes, who urged that the Didachist's technique was, like Hermas' technique, "very allusive" and hence we ought not expect to find "explicit or exact quotations."[36]

---

[30] 𝕽 W Θ *al* syᵖ (cf. Matt 5:46: οὐχὶ καὶ οἱ τελῶναι).

[31] Rordorf, "Le problème de la transmission," 503.

[32] Draper, "The Jesus Tradition in the *Didache*," 75.

[33] Van de Sandt-Flusser, *The Didache*, 42.

[34] The exceptions are *Did.* 1:6 (ἀλλὰ καὶ περὶ τούτου δὲ εἴρηται); 8:2 (μηδὲ προσεύχεσθε ὡς οἱ ὑποκριταί, ἀλλ' ὡς ἐκέλευσεν ὁ κύριος ἐν τῷ εὐαγγελίῳ αὐτοῦ); 9:5 (καὶ γὰρ περὶ τούτου εἴρηκεν ὁ κύριος); and 16:7 (οὐ πάντων δέ, ἀλλ' ὡς ἐρρέθη).

[35] Tuckett, "Synoptic Tradition in the Didache," 199.

[36] Vokes, *The Riddle of the Didache*, 93.

Tuckett's general point is well taken but begs the question, since irrespective of whether the Didachist uses a quotation formula or not, one does know *a priori* whether the Didachist's technique of usage is "allusive" or not. What can be controlled to some extent is the textual history of the Didache and this, as Audet has shown, provides evidence of gradual harmonization of the eleventh century text published by Bryennios (H) with the Synoptics.

For example, at *Did.* 1:3b H has ἐὰν ἀγαπᾶτε τοὺς ἀγαπῶντας ὑμᾶς in agreement with Luke 6:32, but the parallel text in the (dependent) Apostolic Constitutions reads ἐὰν φιλῆτε τοὺς φιλοῦντας ὑμᾶς. The same phenomenon is seen at 1:3c where both the fourth century parchment fragment of the Didache (*POxy* XV 1782) and the Apostolic Constitutions read ὑμεῖς δὲ φιλεῖτε τοὺς μισοῦντας ὑμας and against H's ὑμεῖς δὲ ἀγαπᾶτε τοὺς μισοῦντας ὑμᾶς.[37] In both instances it seems a reasonable conclusion that the text of H has been assimilated to the wording of the Synoptic Gospels. Likewise *POxy* XV 1782 has τοῦτο at *Did.* 1:3c, in agreement with the Apostolic Constitutions against H (which has τὸ αὐτό, agreeing with Matthew and Luke). What is significant is that at the very few points where one can control the manuscript tradition of the Didache before the eleventh century by reference to the two leaves of *POxy* XV 1782 (containing *Did.* 1:3c-4a, 2:7b, and 3:1-2a), there are eight points where *POxy* XV 1782 differs from H and two (both in 1:3b) where the *POxy* version is *less* assimilated to the Synoptics than H. Thus whatever the Didachist's citation technique might be, it seems a defensible thesis that the H-text is the product of harmonization and that earlier forms of the Didache were *less* like their Synoptic counterparts than now appears in H. In the face of the textual data, Tuckett's objection does not meet or refute Draper's original point about difference.

One cannot, of course, generalize from two instances to the conclusion that the "original" Didache was consistently dissimilar to its synoptic parallels. On the other hand, the likelihood of assimilation also means that one cannot safely generalize from a few cases of convergence with the Synoptics to a theory of dependence. But can we move beyond the mere observation of divergence and convergence to a more secure ground for discussion the relation of the Didache to Matthew and Luke?

This brings me to the third point. Tuckett has insisted, rightly in my view, that the best measure of whether the Didache is dependent upon the Synoptics is not convergence or divergence in general, but the presence or absence in the Didache of elements that owe their existence to the *redactional activities* of the Synoptic evangelists.[38] Mere convergence in wording is not a sufficient test, for unless it can be shown that the Didache has taken over redactional elements of the Synoptics, it is not possible to distinguish the Didache's use of the Synoptics from its use of common tradition. Should the Didache betray elements of Synoptic redaction, there would still remain the question of whether the Didachist used written versions of the Synoptics or quoted and conflated them as they were used orally in the Didachist's community.[39]

---

[37] Audet, *La Didachè*, 53–54; Niederwimmer, *The Didache*, 22–23.

[38] Tuckett, "Synoptic Tradition in the Didache," 199. 217. This point has been made earlier by others, including this author ("Didache 16,6–8," 57).

[39] The oral/aural nature of ancient culture also makes it difficult to rule out complex possibilities, such as the Didache simultaneously being influenced by oral performances of the finished forms of the Synoptic Gospels, and by 'pre-synoptic' forms that were still in circulation.

I am generally of the conviction that for most of the Didache, it cannot be shown that the author used the final forms of the Synoptic Gospels, even though many of its formulations approximate Matthew's. In the case of *Did.* 16:3-8 I have argued that there are good grounds for supposing that the Didache used pre-synoptic apocalyptic tradition that Matthew also used, fusing it with Mark 13.[40] This judgment now seems to have been endorsed by Rordorf, Niederwimmer, and Van de Sandt.[41] Rather than revisit those arguments, I shall examine the section of the Didache where the strongest argument for knowledge of the Synoptics (Matthew and Luke) can be made, the *sectio evangelica*, *Did.* 1:3b–2:1.

2   Didache 1:3b–2:1 and the Synoptic Gospels

By most accountings, *Did.* 1:3b–2:1 is one of the latest additions to the Didache. It is the only obviously "Christian" portion of the Two Ways section; it interrupts the flow between 1:2-3a and 2:2; and a parallel to it is lacking in the Doctrina Apostolorum. Its relationship to the Synoptics has been controverted. A century ago Lake offered four possibilities, each in his view as likely as the next: (a) *Did.* 1:3b–2:1 might represent a blending of Matthaean and Lukan texts; (b) it may depend on another Greek source related to the *Logia* source (i.e., Q); (c) it may come from oral (pre-synoptic) tradition; or (d) from an early gospel harmony.[42] Contemporary representatives of each of these views can still be found.

Because this section appears to represent a late addition to the Didache, it is possible that it displays a *different* relationship to the Synoptics than does the Didache in general. This indeed was the view of the influential study by Koester:[43] while the Didache in general did not know the written gospels, this section betrayed knowledge of the final forms of Matthew and Luke, whose sayings it had conflated and expanded. When I first addressed this problem some twenty-five years ago, I found Koester's conclusion convincing.[44] A redactional analysis of Matt 5:38-48 and Luke 6:27-36 led to the conclusion, for example, that *Did.* 1:4 reflected Matthew's redactional addition of the saying about conscription (Matt 5:41) and Luke's redactional inversion of the order of χίτων-ἱμάτιον in the saying about giving up one's cloak.[45] This conclusion had consequences both for understanding the relationship of 1:3b–2:1 to the rest of the Didache and for the dating of insertion of the *sectio evangelica*. As Koester observed, the Didachist elsewhere employed Jesus' sayings in a relatively straightforward fashion, refraining from modifying or expanding them. In 1:3b–2:1, however, the Jesus tradition had been reworked considerably and Jesus' sayings were expanded by means of Jewish

---

[40] Kloppenborg, "Didache 16,6–8."

[41] Rordorf, "Does the Didache Contain?," 412–9; Niederwimmer, *The Didache*, 48 n. 39. 207–13 (with some hesitations); Van de Sandt-Flusser, *The Didache*, 39: "Did. 16 reveals no dependence upon either Mark or Matthew as we know it but rather represents a tradition upon which Matthew drew. It is likely, therefore, that both Matthew and the Did. 16 are grafted upon a common early collection of apocalyptic materials."

[42] Lake, in Bartlet-Lake, *The New Testament*, 35–36.

[43] Koester, *Synoptische Überlieferung*, 238–39.

[44] Kloppenborg, "The Sayings of Jesus in the Didache," 205–206.

[45] *Ibid.*, 198–99.

or Jewish-Christian paranetic material also used by Hermas (*Mand.* 2:4-6).[46] Because of the marked differences in citation technique between *Did.* 1:3b–2:1 and the rest of the Didache, Koester argued that it was well to distinguish between the editor of *Did.* 1:3b–2:1 and the compiler of the Didache. The editor was responsible for the rather complex manipulations visible in 1:3b–2:1, while the compiler appears simply to have incorporated into his work the already-completed *Logiensammlung*, more or less without alteration.[47] This sayings collection cannot have arisen much earlier than the second century, that is, the point at which Matthew and Luke were in general circulation. But Koester did not want to date this collection later than the first half of the second century, arguing that "the style in which [conflation] occurs, where the sections of the Gospels that are reproduced are not set off from other Jewish materials [i.e., *Did.* 1:5b-6] indicates a relatively early time when the gospels had not yet achieved a status as 'Scripture'."[48] This conclusion, however, seems problematic, for it assumes that the more Jesus-sayings achieved an authoritative status, the greater would be the tendency to distinguish them from "Jewish" materials. The saying in 1:6, however, is quoted as authoritative (ἀλλὰ καὶ περὶ τούτου δὲ εἴρηται) and even though its exact origin remains rather unclear,[49] it was widely used in early Christian paraenesis and quoted by Latin authors as if it were scripture, as Niederwimmer has shown.[50] Hence, it seems to me doubtful that even a later editor would necessarily have distinguished the Jesus-sayings in 1:3b-5a from the equally authoritative sayings in 1:5b-6.

Koester's student, Bentley Layton, put 1:3b–2:1 after 150 C.E., since he argued not only that the compiler knew the final forms of the Synoptics but also quoted Hermas *Mand.* 2:4-6, whose composition could not be placed any earlier than mid-century.[51] In my earlier work on the Didache, I also placed the interpolation of 1:3b–2:1 about 150 C.E., not on the supposition that the interpolator knew Hermas (which is doubtful), but because the first datable instances of conflations of Synoptic texts seems to come from the time of Justin Martyr and Tatian.[52]

---

[46] Hermas, *Mand.* 2:4-6: πᾶσιν δίδου· πᾶσιν γὰρ ὁ θεὸς δίδοσθαι θέλει ἐκ τῶν ἰδίων δωρημάτων. 5 οἱ οὖν λαμβάνοντες ἀποδώσουσιν λόγον τῷ θεῷ, διατί ἔλαβον καὶ εἰς τί· οἱ μὲν λαμβάνοντες θλιβόμενοι οὐ δικασθήσονται, οἱ δὲ ἐν ὑποκρίσει λαμβάνοντες τίσουσιν δίκην. 6 ὁ οὖν διδοὺς ἀθῷός ἐστιν. The Doctrina contains a partial parallel to Did. 1:5 in 4:8: omnibus enim dominus dare vult de donis suis, "the Lord wishes to give to all from his gifts."

[47] Koester, *Synoptische Überlieferung*, 239.

[48] *Ibid.*, 239.

[49] P. W. Skehan, "Didache 1,6 and Sirach 12,1," 533–36 suggests Sir 12:1 as the source: ἐὰν εὖ ποιῇς, γνῶθι τίνι ποιεῖς, καὶ ἔσται χάρις τοῖς ἀγαθοῖς σου, "If you do a benefaction, know the person to whom you give it and you will have credit for your good deeds."

[50] Niederwimmer, *The Didache*, 84–85, citing Augustine, *Enarr. in Ps.* 102:12 (CCSL 40, 1462); *Enarr in Ps.* 103; *Sermo* 3:10 (CCSL 40, 1509); *Enarr. in Ps.* 146:17 (CCSL 40, 2135); Cassiodorus, *Expositiones in Psalterium* 40 (PL 70, 295D); *Expositiones in Psalterium* 103 (PL 70, 733B); Gregory the Great, *Regula Pastoralis* 3:20 (PL 77, 84CD), etc.

[51] Layton, "The Sources, Date and Transmission," 378–82 entertains two possibilities: either (a) the compiler of the Didache, sometime after 150 C.E., interpolated 1:3b–2:1 into the 'Two Ways' document and that shortly thereafter the Christianized 'Two Ways' and other materials were collected into what now appears as the Didache; or (b) 1:3b–2:1 was interpolated into a first edition of the Didache that included the 'Two Ways' document and chs. 6–16, sometime after 150 C.E.

[52] Kloppenborg, "The Sayings of Jesus in the Didache," 205–206. On Justin's use of the Synoptics, see Bellinzoni, *Sayings of Jesus.*

114

With the publication of the *Critical Edition of Q* there is opportunity to revisit the question of the use of Matthew and Luke by *Did.* 1:3b–2:1.[53] While the *Critical Edition* should hardly be taken as the definitive reconstruction of Q, it does provide a benchmark and useful point of reference. Moreover, the reconstruction of Q 6:27–35 was effected without reference to *Did.* 1:3b–2:1 or to any suppositions about a direct literary relationship between Q and the Didache. Hence the reconstruction of Q in the *Critical Edition* is not skewed from the beginning to favour a theory of the dependence of the Didache on Q.

Rordorf, who argued that this section of the Didache preserved Jesus tradition independent of the final form of the Synoptics hesitated to explore the question of the relationship of this independent tradition to Q because, he averred, the "question of the sayings-source Q is so controversial among New Testament scholars that I do not intend to burn my fingers on this hot potato" and because he doubted that it was possible to reconstruct Q.[54] Jonathan Draper suggests that this section "draws on material found also in the collection of sayings which is often referred to as the source 'Q' in Matthew and Luke" but nevertheless argues against Tuckett "that we do not possess 'Q' and even its existence in written form is questionable."[55] Niederwimmer argues that *Did.* 1:3b–2:1 depends on "an apocryphal sayings collection" without raising the issue of its relationship to Q.[56]

But the question cannot be so easily avoided, regardless of whether it might seem rash to reconstruct Q or not, or whether fingers get burned. For Ockham's razor suggests that it is gratuitous to posit the existence of an apocryphal sayings collection unrelated to Q that just happens, like Q, to combine parallels to Q 6:27-28 (*Did.* 1:3b), Q 6:32-35 (*Did.* 1:3c), Q 6:29-30 (*Did.* 1:4-5), and Q 12:58-59 (*Did.* 1:5c). We have no indication in other sources of the early Jesus movement that these particular sayings were combined in any other catena or cluster.

Individual Jesus sayings which appear in Q are, of course, also found in *1 Clem.* 13:2 (|| Q 6:36-38),[57] *1 Clem.* 46:8 (|| Mark 9:42; Q 17:1-2),[58] *2 Clem.* 3:2 (|| Q 12:8),[59] *2 Clem.* 6:1 (||Q 16:13),[60] *2 Clem.* 13:4a (|| Q 6:32, 27),[61] *2 Clem.* 4:2, 5 (||

---

[53] Robinson-Hoffmann-Kloppenborg, *The Critical Edition of Q; The Sayings Gospel Q; Die Logienquelle Q; El Documento Q.*

[54] Rordorf, "Does the Didache Contain?," 411–12.

[55] Draper, "The Jesus Tradition in the Didache," 79. 75.

[56] Niederwimmer, *The Didache,* 76. 80.

[57] *1 Clem.* 13:2: ἐλεᾶτε, ἵνα ἐλεηθῆτε· ἀφίετε, ἵνα ἀφεθῇ ὑμῖν· ὡς ποιεῖτε, οὕτω ποιηθήσεται ὑμῖν· ὡς δίδοτε, οὕτως δοθήσεται ὑμῖν· ὡς κρίνετε, οὕτως κριθήσεσθε· ὡς χρηστεύεσθε, οὕτως χρηστευθήσεται ὑμῖν· ᾧ μέτρῳ μετρεῖτε, ἐν αὐτῷ μετρηθήσεται ὑμῖν.

[58] *1 Clem.* 46:8: οὐαὶ τῷ ἀνθρώπῳ ἐκείνῳ· καλὸν ἦν αὐτῷ, εἰ μὴ ἐγεννήθη, ἢ ἕνα τῶν ἐκλεκτῶν μου σκανδαλίσαι· κρεῖττον ἦν αὐτῷ περιτεθῆναι μύλον καὶ καταποντισθῆναι εἰς τὴν θάλασσαν, ἢ ἕνα τῶν ἐκλεκτῶν μου διαστρέψαι.

[59] *2 Clem.* 3:2: τὸν ὁμολογήσαντά με ἐνώπιον τῶν ἀνθρώπων, ὁμολογήσω αὐτὸν ἐνώπιον τοῦ πατρός μου.

[60] *2 Clem.* 6:1: οὐδεὶς οἰκέτης δύναται δυσὶ κυρίοις δουλεύειν· ἐὰν ἡμεῖς θέλωμεν καὶ θεῷ δουλεύειν καὶ μαμωνᾷ, ἀσύμφορον ἡμῖν ἐστίν.

[61] *2 Clem.* 13:4a: οὐ χάρις ὑμῖν, εἰ ἀγαπᾶτε τοὺς ἀγαπῶντας ὑμᾶς, ἀλλὰ χάρις ὑμῖν, εἰ ἀγαπᾶτε τοὺς ἐχθροὺς καὶ τοὺς μισοῦντας ὑμᾶς.

Matt 7:21-23), *2 Clem.* 5:2-4 (|| Q 10:3; 12:4-5), Polycarp, *Phil.* 2:3 (|| Q 6:37-38; Q 6:20b), 12:3 (|| Matt 5:44, 48), and in the gospel of Thomas. But what one finds there is either the citation of a *single* saying also found in Q, or several sayings which are *combined differently* from the way in which they are combined in Q.[62] Thomas has three of Q's makarisms (*Gos. Thom.* 54, 68-69a, 69b) but they are not combined into the anaphoric cluster in which they are found in Q 6:20-23; Thomas has a saying on anxiety (*Gos. Thom.* 36 / *POxy* 655 || Q 12:22-28), but it is not combined with the parable of the Rich Fool (Q 12:16-21), which appears in a difference context in Thomas (Gos. Thom. 63). The only early source of which I am aware that combines Q 6:27-28, Q 6:32-35, Q/Matt 5:41, and Q 6:29-30 is Justin *Apol.* 15:9-14; 16:1-2; but Bellinzoni appears to have demonstrated that Justin has either harmonized Matthew and Luke himself or drawn on an earlier harmonizing source.[63]

This would appear to leave us with only a few viable options: either (a) *Did.* 1:3b–2:1 used and harmonized Matthew and Luke, or (b) it used Q in its near "final form," or (c) it employed a sub-collection of Q (say, Q 6:20–49) that was later incorporated into the Sayings Gospel.[64] Tuckett entertains a fourth possibility, that the Didache might depend on an expanded version of Q that existed prior to Matthew or Luke's use of Q, i.e., Q^{Mt} or Q^{Lk}. One could also imagine that Q^{Mt}, say, continued to be used and expanded long after the compilation of Matthew and that the Didache used this rather than Matthew. Of course it becomes more and more precarious to suppose a connection between the Didache and a sub-collection of Q or a secondary expansion of Q that is already twice- or thrice removed from the literary sources from which Q is reconstructed. A final possibility, advanced by Alan Garrow, is that Matthew knew and used *Did.* 1:3b–2:1, a possibility which on the Two Document hypothesis would also entail Q knowing the Didache.[65]

In what follows, I will examine the sayings of Jesus in *Did.* 1:3b-5 and argue that, while there is not convincing evidence of dependence on the Synoptics (at least Luke) in all instances, there is sufficient indication of knowledge of the redactional interventions of Luke in 1:4-5 to warrant the conclusion that the compiler knew Luke and either Matthew or Q.

---

[62] E.g., *Gos. Thom.* 33 || Q 12:3 + 11:33; *Gos. Thom.* 34-36 || Q 6:39 + 11:21-22 + 12:22; *Gos. Thom.* 44-47 || Q 12:10 + 6:43-45 + 7:28 + 16:13; *Gos. Thom.* 54-55 || Q 6:20b + 14:26.

[63] Bellinzoni, *Sayings of Jesus*, 76–86.

[64] I do not presuppose for the purposes of this paper the stratigraphical analysis offered in Kloppenborg, *The Formation of Q*, but merely wish to point out that many recent critical analyses of Q have argued for the existence of sub-collections in Q: Sato, *Q und Prophetie*; Allison, *The Jesus Tradition in Q*; Jacobson, *The First Gospel*; Bergemann, *Q auf dem Prüfstand* and others.

[65] Garrow himself does not subscribe to the Two Document Hypothesis and thinks rather that Matthew used Luke.

Draper comments that the form of the admonition to bless and pray for one's enemies "cannot realistically be viewed as a harmony of the Gospels."[66] The closest parallel to the admonition to pray for enemies indeed is neither Matthew nor Luke, but *POxy* X 1224, which otherwise displays no evidence of dependence on the Synoptics and seems to be the fragment of a non-canonical gospel or visionary account. That *POxy* X 1224 is not a fragment of the Didache or of Justin's *Apology*, which also quotes the admonition in the same form (15:9), is indicated by the continuation of the saying in *POxy* X 1224: κ]αὶ π[ρ]οσεύχεσθε ὑπὲρ [τῶν ἐχθ]ρῶν ὑμῶν· ὁ γὰρ μὴ ὢν [κατὰ ὑμ]ῶν ὑπὲρ ὑμῶν ἐστιν. [ὁ σήμερον ὢ]ν μακράν, αὔριον [ἐγγὺς ὑμῶν γ]ενήσεται, καὶ ἐν [.....]. τοῦ ἀντιδίκου... "And pray for your enemies; for the one who is not [against yo]u is for you. [The one] far away [today], tomorrow will be [near you] and in [...] the advers[ary]."[67] What is noteworthy about the version in *POxy* X 1224, however, is that the logic of the admonition resembles that of *Did.* 1:3: *POxy* X 1224 buttresses its admonition to pray with the claim that such a prayer will ultimately bring the enemy near; and *Did.* 1:3 expressly concludes that the result (or purpose?) of loving those who hate is to win them over (καὶ οὐχ ἕξετε ἐχθρόν). This is not the logic of Luke, Matthew or Q, nor indeed is it the conclusion which Justin draws from his citations.[68] The logic of the textualizations of the admonition in the Didache and *POxy* X 1224 is pragmatic, quite distinct from the claims of Q (and its successor documents) that by loving one's enemies one thereby emulates divine action and thus can claim to be υἱοὶ τοῦ πατρὸς ὑμῶν.

That the Didache employs the admonitions in 1:3b to different effect than the admonitions of Q 6:27-28 does not, of course, prove that the Didache is independent of Q or its successor documents, Matthew and Luke. It might only mean that the admonition to pray for enemies is no longer used to create an in-group identity by claiming attitudes congruous with those of God, but came to be deployed as a strategy for dealing with an unfriendly world. The Testaments of the Twelve Patriarchs, with which the Didache has other affinities, in fact imagine the possibility of befriending

---

[66] Draper, "The Jesus Tradition in the Didache," 83; Tuilier, "La Didachè et le problème," argues that Matthew and Luke are closer to one another than they are to the Didache, "mais ils dépendent également de la même source que cette dernière, une partie de la tradition manuscrite ancienne de Matthieu ..." (112).

[67] Restoration: Grenfell and Hunt. Lührmann, *Fragmente apokryph gewordener Evangelien*, 176–77 restores the last two lines as [οἱ ἀπέστησα]ν μακράν, αὔριον [ἡ ὥρα αὐτῶν γ]ενήσεται following Jer 2:5 τάδε λέγει κύριος· τί εὔροσαν οἱ πατέρες ὑμῶν ἐν ἐμοὶ πλημμέλημα, ὅτι ἀπέστησαν μακρὰν ἀπ' ἐμοῦ καὶ ἐπορεύθησαν ὀπίσω τῶν ματαίων καὶ ἐματαιώθησαν and Josh 11:6 καὶ εἶπεν κύριος πρὸς Ἰησοῦν· μὴ φοβηθῇς ἀπὸ προσώπου αὐτῶν, ὅτι αὔριον ταύτην τὴν ὥραν ἐγὼ παραδίδωμι τετροπωμένους αὐτοὺς ἐναντίον τοῦ Ισραηλ· τοὺς ἵππους αὐτῶν νευροκοπήσεις καὶ τὰ ἅρματα αὐτῶν κατακαύσεις ἐν πυρί.

[68] Justin *Apol.* 15:13 καὶ γίνεσθε δὲ χρηστοὶ καὶ οἰκτίρμονες, ὡς καὶ ὁ πατὴρ ὑμῶν χρηστός ἐστι καὶ οἰκτίρμων, καὶ τὸν ἥλιον αὐτοῦ ἀνατέλλει ἐπὶ ἁμαρτωλοὺς καὶ δικαίους καὶ πονηρούς.

Figure 2: Didache 1:3b

Did 1:3b	Q 6:27-28	Matt 5:44	Luke 6:27-28
		ἐγὼ δὲ λέγω ὑμῖν,	Ἀλλὰ ὑμῖν λέγω τοῖς ἀκούουσιν,
εὐλογεῖτε τοὺς καταραμένους ὑμῖν[1] καὶ προσεύχεσθε ὑπὲρ τῶν ἐχθρῶν ὑμῶν,	ἀγαπᾶτε τοὺς ἐχθροὺς ὑμῶν ▯ ▯ [[καὶ]] προσεύχεσθε	ἀγαπᾶτε τοὺς ἐχθροὺς ὑμῶν,[2] καὶ προσεύχεσθε	ἀγαπᾶτε τοὺς ἐχθροὺς ὑμῶν, καλῶς ποιεῖτε τοῖς μισοῦσιν ὑμᾶς, εὐλογεῖτε τοὺς καταρωμένους ὑμᾶς, προσεύχεσθε
νηστεύετε δὲ ὑπὲρ τῶν διωκόντων ὑμᾶς·	ὑπὲρ τῶν [[διωκ]]όντων ὑμᾶς.	ὑπὲρ τῶν διωκόντων ὑμᾶς,	περὶ τῶν ἐπηρεαζόντων ὑμᾶς.

POxy 1224 2.r.i: κ]αὶ π[ρ]οσεύχεσθε ὑπὲρ [τῶν ἐχθ]ρῶν ὑμῶν.

Rom 12:14: εὐλογεῖτε τοὺς διώκοντας [ὑμᾶς], εὐλογεῖτε καὶ μὴ καταρᾶσθε.

Ignatius, *Pol.* 2:1: καλοὺς μαθητὰς ἐὰν φιλῇς, χάρις σοι οὐκ ἔστιν· μᾶλλον τοὺς λοιμοτέρους ἐν πραΰτητι ὑπότασσε. οὐ πᾶν τραῦμα τῇ αὐτῇ ἐμπλάστρῳ θεραπεύεται. τοὺς παροξυσμοὺς παῦε.

Polycarp, *Phil.* 12:3: orate etiam pro regibus… atque pro persequentibus et odientibus vos et pro inimicis crucis, ut fructus vester manifestus sit in omnibus, ut sitis in illo perfecti.

Justin, *Apol.* 15:9: περὶ δὲ στέργειν ἅπαντας ταῦτα ἐδίδαξεν· εἰ ἀγαπᾶτε τοὺς ἀγαπῶντας ὑμᾶς, τί καινὸν ποιεῖτε καὶ γὰρ οἱ πόρνοι τοῦτο ποιοῦσιν. ἐγὼ δὲ ὑμῖν λέγω· εὔχεσθε ὑπὲρ τῶν ἐχθρῶν ὑμῶν καὶ ἀγαπᾶτε τοὺς μισοῦντας ὑμᾶς καὶ εὐλογεῖτε τοὺς καταρωμένους ὑμῖν καὶ εὔχεσθε ὑπὲρ τῶν ἐπηρεαζόντων ὑμᾶς.

Justin *Dial.* 133:6: εὔχεσθε καὶ ὑπὲρ τῶν ἐχθρῶν καὶ ἀγαπᾶν τοὺς μισοῦντας καὶ εὐλογεῖν τοὺς καταρωμένους.

2 Clem. 13:4: ὅταν γὰρ ἀκούσωσιν παρ᾽ ἡμῶν, ὅτι λέγει ὁ θεός· οὐ χάρις ὑμῖν, εἰ ἀγαπᾶτε τοὺς ἀγαπῶντας ὑμᾶς, ἀλλὰ χάρις ὑμῖν, εἰ ἀγαπᾶτε τοὺς ἐχθροὺς καὶ τοὺς μισοῦντας ὑμᾶς.

Didascalia (Syriac) 1 (Corpus scriptorum christianorum orientalium 401,14; 402,12): And again he says in the gospel: Love those who hate you and pray for those who curse you, and you shall have no enemy.

Didascalia (Latin: 2,28-31): nam iterum in evangelio dicit: diligite odientes vos et orate pro maledicentibus vos et inimicum nullum habebetis.

1. *CA* ὑμᾶς.
2. Matt 5:44: ἐγὼ δὲ λέγω ὑμῖν, ἀγαπᾶτε τοὺς ἐχθροὺς ὑμῶν, εὐλογεῖτε τοὺς καταρωμένους ὑμῶν (1071 *l* 866 *l* 1066 cop^pt geo; Clem Eusebius^1/2 Tert). καλῶς ποιεῖτε τοῖς μισοῦσιν ὑμᾶς; D* L W Δ Θ φ 28 33 157 565 579 597 700 892 1006 1010 1241 1243 1292 1342 1424 1505 arm eth geo slav it^d f h syr^h.(pal) cop^mg Matt 5:45: καὶ προσεύχεσθε ὑπὲρ τῶν ἐπηρεαζόντων ὑμᾶς (1241 *l* 253 *l* 547 *l* 563 *l* 858 *l* 1223 geo; Theophilus (Clement) Origen^1/6) καὶ διωκόντων ὑμᾶς; D* L (W 1505) Δ Θ φ

an enemy through displays of mercy and prayer.[69] On the other hand, it must be said that the Didache betrays no knowledge or influence of the particular use to which Q and its successor documents have put the admonition to bless and pray for enemies.[70]

Some scholars invoke the triadic structure of *Did.* 1:3b as a sign of secondary development of the Synoptics. Matthew's structure is binary (love/pray), while Luke has a double-binary structure (love/do good; bless/pray). The IQP (International Q Project)'s reconstruction of Q accepts the minimal agreement of Matthew with Luke (love/pray) but it is less certain about other two Lukan verbs, excluding both, but only at a {C} level of probability. This grade reflected the fact that grounds for thinking that Luke added εὐλογεῖτε τοὺς καταρωμένους ὑμᾶς were not strong, especially when it could not be shown that Luke regularly elaborated parallelism,[71] and when there is evidence from Rom 12:14 of an admonition to bless persecutors. As Tuckett grants,

> [t]he strongest argument for the activity of LkR[edaction] concerns the uses of καλῶς ποιεῖτε. This links with the use of ἀγαθοποιεῖν later in this context in Luke, and this is widely regarded as LkR. But it is just this phrase of Lk 6,27f. which does *not* have a parallel in *Did.* 1,3.[72]

Layton argued that the triadic structure of *Did.* 1:3b represented a "deliberate 'improvement' of the Lukan text, which has three members but no climax."[73] But this argument, aside from its oversight of the fourth Lukan verb, is weak and subjective. Layton detects a rhetorical climax in the Didache's progression from "those who curse you" to "your enemies" to "those who persecute you;" but Luke's careful balancing of each half of the double binary (enemies/those who hate; those who curse/those who abuse), while clearly different in tone, is an instance of αὔξησις or *amplificatio*.[74] Thus *Did.* 1:3b and Luke 6:27-28 represent two *different* rhetorical figures, but it is difficult to argue that one is an improvement of the other.

Clayton Jefford draws attention to a similar triad in the next Matthaean pericope, Matt 6:1-18, which mentions almsgiving, prayer, and fasting.[75] Tuckett likewise asserts that "a reference to fasting, secondarily added to an injunction to prayer, would not be

---

[69] *T. Benj.* 5:1-4: Ἐὰν ἔχητε ἀγαθὴν διάνοιαν, τέκνα, καὶ οἱ πονηροὶ ἄνθρωποι εἰρηνεύσωσιν ὑμῖν, καὶ οἱ ἄσωτοι αἰδεσθέντες ὑμᾶς ἐπιστρέψουσιν εἰς ἀγαθόν, καὶ οἱ πλεονέκται οὐ μόνον ἀποστήσονται τοῦ πάθους, ἀλλὰ καὶ τὰ τῆς πλεονεξίας δώσουσι τοῖς θλιβομένοις. 5:2 Ἐὰν ἦτε ἀγαθοποιοῦντες, καὶ τὰ ἀκάθαρτα πνεύματα φεύξεται ἀφ' ὑμῶν, καὶ αὐτὰ τὰ θηρία φεύξεται ἀφ' ὑμῶν φοβηθέντες. 5:3 ὅπου γὰρ ἔνι φόβος ἀγαθῶν ἔργων εἰς διάνοιαν, τὸ σκότος ἀποδιδράσκει αὐτοῦ. 5:4 ἐὰν γὰρ ὑβρίσῃ τις ἄνδρα ὅσιον, μετανοεῖ· ἐλεεῖ γὰρ ὁ ὅσιος τὸν λοίδωρον, καὶ σιωπᾷ. *T. Jos.* 18:2: καὶ ἐὰν θέλῃ τις κακοποιῆσαι ὑμᾶς, ὑμεῖς τῇ ἀγαθοποιίᾳ εὔχεσθε ὑπὲρ αὐτοῦ· καὶ ἀπὸ παντὸς κακοῦ λυτρωθήσεσθε διὰ Κυρίου.

[70] See in general, Stendahl, "Hate, Non-Retaliation and Love," 343-55.

[71] See Cadbury, *The Style and Literary Method*, 85; Jeremias, *Die Sprache des Lukasevangeliums*, 140.

[72] Tuckett, "Synoptic Tradition in the Didache," 218 citing Van Unnik, "Die Motivierung der Feindesliebe," 284-300.

[73] Layton, "The Sources, Date and Transmission," 353.

[74] See Mees, "Die Bedeutung der Sentenzen," 55-76.

[75] Jefford, *The Sayings of Jesus*, 43-46.

unexpected in a later development of the tradition."[76] But whether or not the triadic structure of *Did.* 1:3b is secondary or not, the key issue is whether the expansion has been motivated by Matthew. And as Rordorf rightly observes, Matthew's triad in 6:1-18 begins not with "blessing" but with "almsgiving."[77] Tuckett offers another argument, that the Didache betrays knowledge of both parts of Luke 6:27, "*love* your enemies" and "do good to *those who hate you*" in *Did.* 1:3c "love those who hate you."[78] This argument, however, works better in English than in Greek, for this is precisely the point at which H differs from the earlier *POxy* XV 1782, which has φιλεῖτε rather than ἀγαπᾶτε, thus diminishing the convergence with Luke 6:27.

The only other possible indications of the Didache's use of the Synoptics is its use of ὑπὲρ τῶν διωκόντων ὑμᾶς and τοὺς καταρωμένους ὑμῖν. Tuckett urges that ἐπηρεαζόντων ὑμᾶς (Luke) represents Q here,[79] and it should be noted that the original decision of the IQP was against Matthew's διωκόντων and in favour of Luke's ἐπηρεαζόντων.[80] This decision was reversed in the *Critical Edition*, which printed ὑπὲρ τῶν [[διωκόντων]] ὑμᾶς but only with a {C} level of probability.[81] Given the uncertainties concerning the reconstruction of Q, it is not possible to decide whether *Did.* 1:3b is related. Hence we still lack clear evidence of the Didache's use of Luke (or Matthew).

The Didache does have εὐλογεῖτε τοὺς καταρωμένους ὑμῖν in agreement with Luke 6:27. Tuckett seems to regard this phrase as a candidate for Q, while observing that some manuscripts of Matthew add the phrase.[82] The International Q Project

---

[76] Tuckett, "Synoptic Tradition in the Didache," 219.

[77] Rordorf, "The Jesus Tradition in the Didache," 401.

[78] Tuckett, "Synoptic Tradition in the Didache," 218.

[79] Tuckett (*Ibid.*, 219) quotes 1 Pet 3:16, which uses the word in a similar context: ἀλλὰ μετὰ πραΰτητος καὶ φόβου, συνείδησιν ἔχοντες ἀγαθήν, ἵνα ἐν ᾧ καταλαλεῖσθε καταισχυνθῶσιν οἱ ἐπηρεάζοντες ὑμῶν τὴν ἀγαθὴν ἐν Χριστῷ ἀναστροφήν.

[80] Moreland-Robinson, "The International Q Project," 496. R. Conrad Douglas, who prepared the database, and Sean Carruth and Ronald Piper who responded to it, all proposed a conjectural emendation: ὑπὲρ τῶν [[<μισόντωνων>]] ὑμᾶς, but this was eventually rejected by the IQP, following Paul Hoffmann's argument, in favour of Luke's ἐπηρεαζόντων ὑμᾶς "or undecided."

IQP Sigla: μισόντωνων: reconstruction with a {A} or {B} rating; [[μισόντωνων]]: reconstruction with a {C} rating; [[()]]: exclusion of a Matthaean element with a {C} rating; [[[]]]: exclusion of a Lukan element with a {C} rating; [[<μισόντωνων>]]: conjectural reading.

[81] Paul Hoffmann's responsum (15 vii 1993): "Das mt διώκω läßt sich für Q nicht ausschließen, da QR auch in 11,49 die Verfolgerungssituation der Boten thematisiert und der Terminus auch in 6,22b schon verwendet worden sein kann (!). Gegen διώκω = Q spricht allerdings, daß die in Q folgenden Sprüche keinen Bezug zu einer solchen Verfolgerungssituation erkennen lassen (anders 12,2ff. nach 11,49-51). Ist die Einfügung des Motivs das Werk einer oder der späteren QR? Oder ist für Q eine unspezifischere Formulierung vorauszusetzen?"

[82] Matt 5:44: ἐγὼ δὲ λέγω ὑμῖν, ἀγαπᾶτε τοὺς ἐχθροὺς ὑμῶν, εὐλογεῖτε τοὺς καταρωμένους ὑμᾶς (1071 *l* 866 *l* 1066 cop^pt geo; Clem Eusebius ^1/2 Tert). καλῶς ποιεῖτε τοῖς μισοῦσιν ὑμᾶς: D^c L W Δ Θ φ 28 33 157 565 579 597 700 892 1006 1010 1241 1243 1292 1342 1424 1505 arm eth geo slav it^c d ^f h syr^h.(pal) cop^mg. Matt 5:45: καὶ προσεύχεσθε ὑπὲρ τῶν ἐπηρεαζόντων ὑμᾶς (1241 *l* 253 *l* 547 *l* 563 *l* 858 *l* 1223 geo; Theophilus (Clement) Origen^1/6) καὶ διωκόντων ὑμᾶς: D^c L (W 1505) Δ Θ φ 28 (33 1342 *l* 524) 180 565 579 700 892 1006 1010 1071 1243 1292 1424 it^(a) (b) c (d) f (h) syr^(p) h (pal) arm eth geo slav; (Eusebius) Basil (Gregory-Nysa).

excluded the phrase from Q, but only with a {C} rating, because nothing in the phrase was obviously Lukan and the stylistic arguments for Luke's addition were hardly compelling. Hence for *Did.* 1:3b there is no strong indication of use of the redactional text of either Matthew or Luke.

2.2 *Did. 1:3c / Q 6:32-35*

I have already indicated that the text of H has been assimilated to the Synoptic Gospels in course of transmission at two points. *POxy* XV 1782 (supported by the Apostolic Constitutions) reads φιλεῖτε τοὺς μισοῦντας ὑμᾶς where H has ἀγαπᾶτε, and the same shift is suggested by the Apostolic Constitutions for the first phrase of 1:3c (where the reading of *POxy* XV 1782 is not extant). Since the Apostolic Constitutions otherwise harmonize their readings with the Synoptics, the disagreement is striking. Tuckett points out that ἀγαπᾶν and φιλεῖν are synonyms and that the Apostolic Constitutions treats them as such. He offers, rather weakly, that the "author of the Didache [may have] wanted to avoid having three uses of ἀγαπάω very close together" and so changed his source's ἀγαπᾶν το φιλεῖν.[83] This seems like special pleading; both Luke and Justin also has three iterations of ἀγαπᾶν and neither felt the need to avoid repetition.

Supporters of the independence of the Didache make much of its use of τὰ ἔθνη, regarding it as "tactless" in a work ostensibly directed at gentiles and a sure mark of the Jewish-Christian character of the Didache.[84] For our purposes, however, not much can be made of the Didache's usage, since it is not an instance of the Didache's appropriation of redactional Matthaean vocabulary (who uses ἐθνικοί), for Matthew likely merely reproduces Q here. One simply cannot know whether *Did.* 1:3c here reflects Matthew, Q, or some pre- or post-Q recension of the saying.

The only possible instance of the Didache's appropriation of a redactional element is its agreement with Luke's ποία ὑμῖν χάρις against Matthew's [= Q?] τίνα μισθὸν ἔχετε. This is hardly strong evidence, since as Tuckett admits, χάρις, while Lukan, normally has the sense of "divine favour" rather than "thanks" as it does here.[85] Nevertheless, the IQP gave Van Unnik's argument concerning the Lukan nature of χάρις considerable weight, for the Lukan term appears to belong to the word field of Hellenistic reciprocity that Luke introduces in 6:33 (καὶ γὰρ ἐὰν ἀγαθοποιῆτε τοὺς ἀγαθοποιοῦντας ὑμᾶς, ποία χάρις ἐστίν;) and 6:35 (ὅτι αὐτὸς χρηστός ἐστιν ἐπὶ τοὺς ἀχαρίστους καὶ πονηρούς).[86] Moreover, Luke's use of μισθός

---

[83] Tuckett, "Synoptic Tradition in the Didache," 222.

[84] Glover, "The Didache's Quotations," 14; Rordorf, "Le problème de la transmission," 502–503; cf. Draper, "The Jesus Tradition in the Didache," 82.

[85] Tuckett, "Synoptic Tradition in the Didache," 223 citing Wrege, *Die Überlieferungsgeschichte*, 224–25. Luke 17:9 uses χάριν ἔχειν in the same sense of 'thanks'.

[86] Van Unnik, "Die Motivierung der Feindesliebe," 295: "In diesem Gedankenkomplex hat auch das Wort χάρις seine feste Stelle, wie in den oben angeführten Texten [Ps-Aristotle, *Rhet. ad Alex.* 1446; Xenophon, *Mem.* II, 2, 1-2; Thucydides II, 40, 4] reichlich belegt ist." Tuckett ("Synoptic Tradition in the Didache," 223) concurs that χάρις is Lukan and thus *Did.* 1:3c betrays knowledge of Lukan redaction.

Figure 3: Didache 1:3c

Didache 1:3c	Q 6:32-35	Matt 5:45-47	Luke 6:32-35
ποία γὰρ χάρις, ἐὰν φιλῆτε τοὺς φιλοῦντας[1] ὑμᾶς;	32 ε[ἰ[ι].. ἀγαπ[[ᾶ]]τε τοὺς ἀγαπῶντας ὑμᾶς, τίνα μισθὸν ἔχετε; οὐχὶ καὶ οἱ τελῶναι τὸ αὐτὸ ποιοῦσιν;	46 ἐὰν γὰρ ἀγαπήσητε τοὺς ἀγαπῶντας ὑμᾶς, τίνα μισθὸν ἔχετε; οὐχὶ καὶ οἱ τελῶναι τὸ αὐτὸ ποιοῦσιν;	32 καὶ εἰ ἀγαπᾶτε τοὺς ἀγαπῶντας ὑμᾶς, ποία ὑμῖν χάρις ἐστίν; καὶ γὰρ οἱ ἁμαρτωλοὶ τοὺς ἀγαπῶντας αὐτοὺς ἀγαπῶσιν. 33 καὶ [γὰρ] ἐὰν ἀγαθοποιῆτε τοὺς ἀγαθοποιοῦντας ὑμᾶς, ποία ὑμῖν χάρις ἐστίν; καὶ οἱ ἁμαρτωλοὶ τὸ αὐτὸ ποιοῦσιν.
οὐχὶ καὶ τὰ ἔθνη τοῦτο[2] ποιοῦσιν;	34 καὶ ἐὰν [[δανίσητε παρ᾽ ὧν ἐλπίζετε λαβεῖν, τί<να μισθὸν ἔχε>τε]] οὐχὶ καὶ [[οἱ ἐθνικοὶ]] τὸ αὐτὸ ποιοῦσιν;	47 καὶ ἐὰν ἀσπάσησθε τοὺς ἀδελφοὺς ὑμῶν μόνον, τί περισσὸν ποιεῖτε; οὐχὶ καὶ οἱ ἐθνικοὶ τὸ αὐτὸ ποιοῦσιν;	34 καὶ ἐὰν δανίσητε παρ᾽ ὧν ἐλπίζετε λαβεῖν, ποία ὑμῖν χάρις ἐστίν; καὶ ἁμαρτωλοὶ ἁμαρτωλοῖς δανίζουσιν ἵνα ἀπολάβωσιν τὰ ἴσα. 35 πλὴν ἀγαπᾶτε τοὺς ἐχθροὺς ὑμῶν καὶ ἀγαθοποιεῖτε καὶ δανίζετε μηδὲν ἀπελπίζοντες· καὶ ἔσται ὁ μισθὸς ὑμῶν πολύς,
ὑμεῖς δὲ φιλεῖτε[3] τοὺς μισοῦντας ὑμᾶς,	35 (ὅπως γένησθε) υἱοὶ τοῦ πατρὸς ὑμῶν, ὅτι τὸν ἥλιον αὐτοῦ ἀνατέλλει ἐπὶ πονηροὺς καὶ ἀγαθοὺς καὶ βρέχει ἐπὶ δικαίους καὶ ἀδίκους.	45 ὅπως γένησθε υἱοὶ τοῦ πατρὸς ὑμῶν τοῦ ἐν οὐρανοῖς, ὅτι τὸν ἥλιον αὐτοῦ ἀνατέλλει ἐπὶ πονηροὺς καὶ ἀγαθοὺς καὶ βρέχει ἐπὶ δικαίους καὶ ἀδίκους.	καὶ ἔσεσθε υἱοὶ ὑψίστου,
καὶ οὐχ ἕξετε ἐχθρόν.			ὅτι αὐτὸς χρηστός ἐστιν ἐπὶ τοὺς ἀχαρίστους καὶ πονηρούς.

Justin, Apol. 15:9: περὶ δὲ στέργειν ἅπαντας ταῦτα ἐδίδαξεν· εἰ ἀγαπᾶτε τοὺς ἀγαπῶντας ὑμᾶς, τί καινὸν ποιεῖτε; καὶ γὰρ οἱ πόρνοι τοῦτο ποιοῦσιν. ἐγὼ δὲ ὑμῖν λέγω· εὔχεσθε ὑπὲρ τῶν ἐχθρῶν ὑμῶν καὶ ἀγαπᾶτε τοὺς μισοῦντας ὑμᾶς καὶ εὐλογεῖτε τοὺς καταρωμένους ὑμῖν καὶ εὔχεσθε ὑπὲρ τῶν ἐπηρεαζόντων ὑμᾶς.

1. CA: φιλῆτε τοὺς φιλοῦντας; H: ἀγαπᾶτε τοὺς ἀγαπῶντας.
2. POxy CA: H: τὸ αὐτό.
3. Text: POxy, CA; H: ἀγαπᾶτε.

in 6:35 is perhaps a reminiscence of the term in Q. In one of its rare conjectural emendations, the IQP proposed ⟦τί<να μισθὸν ἔχε>τε⟧, avoiding Matthew's more clearly redactional τί περισσὸν ποιεῖτε, and replicating the earlier phrase used by Matt 5:45. The implication of these considerations for our question is that the Didache appears to betray knowledge of Lukan redaction, although again the case is not overwhelming.

There is, however, another consideration. As I have already indicated, the Didache's rhetoric is controlled by a pragmatic concern to win over the opponent by means of blessing, prayer and fasting. This stands in sharp contrast to the rhetoric of Q and its successors, for whom love, blessing, and prayer are demonstrative, designed to distinguish the ethos of the Jesus movement from others. In Matthew and probably in Q the purpose (ὅπως γένησθε) of the countercultural behavior is demonstrative, to act in congruity with God, whose benefactions rise above the distinctions of the just and the wicked. Luke's point is only slightly different, concluding with two result clauses, καὶ ἔσται ὁ μισθὸς ὑμῶν πολύς, καὶ ἔσεσθε υἱοὶ ὑψίστου.... Luke's argument resembles that of 1 Pet 2:11-20 which, as Van Unnik has shown,[87] engages Hellenistic reciprocity ethics and encourages well-doing (ἀγαθοποιεῖν) as a strategy for achieving divine approbation (1 Pet 2:12) and human recognition of superior moral achievement (1 Pet 2:12, 20). In both the Q /Matthaean and the Lukan forms of the argument it makes sense to pose the rhetorical question, "what credit/reward do you have if you do the ordinary?" (cf. 1 Pet 2:19, 20), since the point is to encourage behaviour which is sharply dissimilar from ordinary behavior and which can be said to be congruous with the Divine. The Didache's pragmatic argument, however, requires no such appeal, since the point of the admonitions to bless, pray and fast is neither to achieve human or divine approbation nor to demonstrate superior "God like" virtue, but to win over the enemy. The motive clause (ποία γὰρ χάρις ... ποιοῦσιν;) is thus otiose, which is probably why the initial admonition must be resumed with ὑμεῖς δὲ φιλεῖτε before stating the intended result, καὶ οὐχ ἕξετε ἐχθρόν. What this implies is that the Didache has taken over from its source the rhetorical question, ποία γὰρ χάρις ἐὰν φιλῆτε τοὺς φιλοῦντας ὑμᾶς, but has not in fact been able to incorporate it effectively into its own rhetoric.[88] Since Matthew, Luke, and Q all have a similar question, we are left not knowing which of these to identify as the source, even though the use of χάρις seems to favour dependence on Luke.

As with *Did.* 1:3b, the evidence of the Didache's use of the Synoptic Gospels is ambiguous. The Didache's inclusion of the rhetorical question "what credit is it..." is a good indication that it is quoting something. The use of ἔθνη is consistent with the Didache's use of either Q or Matthew; and the presence of ποία γὰρ χάρις might signal knowledge of Luke. But this pericope provides no purchase for a firm decision.

---

[87] Van Unnik, "Die Motivierung der Feindesliebe;" "The Teaching of Good Works," 92–110.
[88] Similarly, Tuckett, "Synoptic Tradition in the Didache," 224: "the author of this section of the Didache seems to presuppose Luke's version here in a way that goes beyond simply using the word χάρις: he takes over the Lukan rhetorical question, but fails to see its significance and hence betrays the secondary nature of his own text."

2.3 Did. 1:4 / Q 6:29-30

It is only in this pericope that we find convincing evidence of the Didache's use of the Synoptic Gospels though not all elements point in this direction. The Didache's admonition against retaliation agrees with Matthew against Luke (and Q?) in referring expressly to striking the *right* cheek, evidently a grave insult (*m.B.Qam.* 8:6).[89] Yet Tuckett allows the possibility that this might have belonged to Q or to Q[Mt] since it would be difficult to prove that Matthew added it.[90]

Defenders of the independence of the Didache usually point to the phrase διδόναι ῥάπισμα as an archaism vis à vis Matthew's ῥαπίζειν.[91] Indeed the form is attested in the John 18:22 (ἔδωκεν ῥάπισμα τῷ 'Ιησοῦ).[92] In this case Matthew probably reproduced Q and hence there is no way to distinguish between affinities with Matthew and affinities with Q. The phrase καὶ ἔση τέλειος might be taken as an instance of Matthaean redaction (see Matt 5:48), though the fact that the phrase also occurs redactionally in the Didache (6:2: εἰ μὲν γὰρ δύνασαι βαστάσαι ὅλον τὸν ζυγὸν τοῦ κυρίου, τέλειος ἔση) should caution us against too quickly inferring dependence on Matthew. Rordorf argues that this is merely a feature of the Didachist's redaction that suggests proximity to Matthew's world but not dependence on Matthew.[93]

The command to submit to corvée, found only in Matthew, might at first glance clinch the case for the Didache's dependence on Matthew. Tuckett makes two important points: first, that since the Didache otherwise is indifferent to the problem of contact with Roman troups, *Did.* 1:4c is "almost certainly due to the writer's use of his tradition." Second, he argues that it is unlikely that the command came from Q: "the examples of non-retaliation in Lk 6,29f. constitute a reasonably neatly balanced pair of couplets; the presence of Mt 5,41 makes for five examples and this seems rather overloaded." Yet he concedes that one might also suppose that an original trio of admonitions (striking the cheek, surrendering a surety, submitting to corvée) were subsequently expanded by the two sayings on giving (6:30).[94] Jefford and Rordorf plead that Matt 5:41 was in Q[Mt].[95] Such an expedient may no longer be necessary if, following the IQP, Matt 5:41 is placed in Q. It has been long argued that Luke's motive for excising such a saying, had he seen it, is patent if he lived in a senatorial province such as Asia or Achaia, where forced labour was not a reality because no legions were stationed there. Thus while one can agree with Tuckett's first point, the presence of the saying on corvée does not help in distinguishing between Matthew or Q as the Didache's source.

---

[89] *m. B.Qam.* 8:6: "R. Judah in the name of R. Jose the Galilean says that [he has to pay him] a maneh; if he smacked him [on the face] he has to pay him two hundred zuz; [if he did it] with the back of his hand he has to pay him four hundred zuz."

[90] Tuckett, "Synoptic Tradition in the Didache," 225.

[91] Rordorf-Tuilier, *La Doctrine des douze apôtres*, 85; Rordorf, "Does the Didache Contain?," 404.

[92] It is sometimes asserted that the idiom appears in Isa 50:6 LXX as well, but the Septuagint has διδόναι + acc. εἰς ῥάπισμα, 'to present [a body part] to a blow.'

[93] Rordorf, "Does the Didache Contain?," 405.

[94] Tuckett, "Synoptic Tradition in the Didache," 226–27.

[95] Jefford, *The Sayings of Jesus*, 47; Rordorf, "Does the Didache Contain?," 405.

Figure 4: Didache 1:4

Did 1:4	Q 6:29-30	Matt 5:39-42	Luke 6:29-30
4 ἀπέχου τῶν σαρκικῶν καὶ σωματικῶν ἐπιθυμιῶν·		39 ἐγὼ δὲ λέγω ὑμῖν μὴ ἀντιστῆναι τῷ πονηρῷ· ἀλλ᾽	
ἐὰν τίς σοι δῷ ῥάπισμα εἰς τὴν δεξιὰν σιαγόνα, στρέψον αὐτῷ καὶ τὴν ἄλλην,	29 [[ὅστις]] σε [[ῥαπίζει]] εἰς τὴν σιαγόνα [[0]] στρέψον [[αὐτῷ]] καὶ τὴν ἄλλην,	ὅστις σε ῥαπίζει εἰς τὴν δεξιὰν σιαγόνα [σου], στρέψον αὐτῷ καὶ τὴν ἄλλην·	29 τῷ τύπτοντί σε ἐπὶ τὴν σιαγόνα πάρεχε καὶ τὴν ἄλλην,
καὶ ἔσῃ τέλειος·			
ἐὰν ἀγγαρεύσῃ σέ τις μίλιον ἕν, ὕπαγε μετ᾽ αὐτοῦ δύο·	41 [[καὶ ὅστις σε ἀγγαρεύσει μίλιον ἕν, ὕπαγε μετ᾽ αὐτοῦ δύο.]]	41 καὶ ὅστις σε ἀγγαρεύσει μίλιον ἕν, ὕπαγε μετ᾽ αὐτοῦ δύο.	
ἐὰν ἄρῃ τις τὸ ἱμάτιόν σου,	29 καὶ [[τῷ θέλοντί σοι κριθῆναι καὶ]] τὸ χιτῶνά σου [[λαβεῖν]], ἄφες αὐτῷ]] καὶ τὸ ἱμάτιον.	40 καὶ τῷ θέλοντί σοι κριθῆναι καὶ τὸν χιτῶνά σου λαβεῖν, ἄφες αὐτῷ καὶ τὸ ἱμάτιον·	καὶ ἀπὸ τοῦ αἴροντός σου τὸ ἱμάτιον
δὸς αὐτῷ καὶ τὸν χιτῶνα·			καὶ τὸν χιτῶνα μὴ κωλύσῃς.
ἐὰν λάβῃ τις ἀπὸ τὸ σόν,[1]	30 τῷ αἰτοῦντί σε δός, καὶ [[ἀπὸ]] [[τοῦ δανιζο<μένου> τὰ]] σ[[ά]] μὴ ἀπ[[αίτει]].	42 τῷ αἰτοῦντί σε δός, καὶ τὸν θέλοντα ἀπὸ σοῦ δανίσασθαι μὴ ἀποστραφῇς.	παντὶ αἰτοῦντί σε δίδου, καὶ ἀπὸ τοῦ αἴροντος τὰ σὰ
μὴ ἀπαίτει· οὐδὲ γὰρ δύνασαι.			μὴ ἀπαίτει.

1. CA τὰ σά

125

The case for the dependence of *Did.* 1:3b–2:1 on the Synoptics comes down to the final two admonitions, concerning robbery and free giving. The Didache's formulation agrees with Luke against Matthew in imagining the scene as a robbery, where the ἱμάτιον is first stolen and then the χίτων is offered. Matthew, as is well known, treats the scene as a forensic one where Matthew presupposes the prohibition of Exod 22:25-26 concerning the seizing of a creditor's ἱμάτιον as a surety against a loan.[96] Matthew (and Q) counsel against insisting even on the protection afforded by the Torah. When a surety is demanded, even the ἱμάτιον can be given. The next sayings in Q and Matthew, Q/Matt 5:41 on corvée and Q 6:30 on lending without expectation of return, all concern the situation of Roman Palestine where draft animals could be requisitioned and where spirals of indebtedness led to seizure and expropriation of lands and possessions.[97] That Luke had seen the reference to borrowing in Q 6:30 is indicated by the fact that he mentions lending in his summarizing statement in v. 35 (καὶ δανίζετε μηδὲν ἀπελπίζοντες). Luke's reconceptualization of Q's (= Matthew's) scenario of the seizure of a surety as a robbery and his omission of the saying on corvée probably reflects Luke's somewhat more well-to-do audience, less troubled by the threats of debt, corvée and expropriation. Instead Luke nurtures an ethos of benefaction and almsgiving (12:33-34; contrast Q 12:33-34; Luke 14:7-14). The threat to such persons is not expropriation or corvée but robbery (Luke 12:33-34, 39-40). But this leaves Luke with somewhat odd advice: While he transformed Q's saying on sureties into an admonition to acquiesce to robbery, he took over almost unchanged from Q the imperative to "give to all who ask" adding, not to demand back from the one who takes your possessions. The context for Luke is still that of a robbery. It is this notion that has been taken over by the Didache, which also imagines a robbery. The Didache's use of μὴ ἀπαίτει, drawn from Luke 6:30, is otiose since presumably if one were in a position to take back from a robber, one would not have been robbed in the first place. Sensing this tension, the Didachist adds, rather lamely, the puzzling phrase οὐδὲ γὰρ δύνασαι, "for you are not able [to take it back]," thus making a virtue of necessity!

The key point here is that the Didache's rather odd formulation depends logically on Luke's reformulation of Q. What is awkward about this explanation is that it requires imagining that the Didache is following Q or Matthew in 1:4bc but then prefers Luke's robbery scene over Q/Matt's lawsuit. This probably implies that the compiler of *Did.* 1:3a–2:1 is not looking at the text of the gospels (or Q), but rather harmonizing from memory.

The situation here is rather like that in the preceding section, where the Didache took over a Lukan phrase, ποία χάρις, that did not fully suit his own editorial interests. For in *Did.* 1:4-6 the stress falls on generous but careful giving. According to 1:5-6 giving is in accordance with God's wishes (πᾶσι γὰρ θέλει δίδοσθαι ὁ πατὴρ ἐκ τῶν ἰδίων χαρισμάτων) and it is a sign of blessedness (μακάριος ὁ διδοὺς κατὰ τὴν ἐντολήν). But it must be done with deliberation lest alms go to persons

---

[96] See Neufeld, "Self-Help in Ancient Hebrew Law," 291–98.

[97] See Goodman, "The First Jewish Revolt," 417–27; Kloppenborg, *Excavating Q*, 254–55; Freyne, "Geography, Politics, and Economics of Galilee," 75–121.

undeserving. But what the Didachist has borrowed from Luke – the robbery scene and his attempt to make sense of it – illustrates neither point.

The compiler of 1:3–2:1 evidently composed the collection of sayings with two principles in view: the interpretation of the love of enemies admonition as a pragmatic strategy of conflict reduction (1:3), and the encouragement of reciprocity within the Jesus group, but a reciprocity that was guarded against abuse. The citation technique adopted here is perhaps freer than that seen in other sections of the Didache, but it is nonetheless still relatively wooden, and it is precisely this woodenness that creates two argumentative difficulties. In both cases, the difficulty comes from Luke's modification of Q, and thus seems to provide prima facie evidence of the compiler's knowledge of the final form of the Synoptics.

2.4 Did. 1:5 / Q 12:58-59

The compiler of *Did.* 1:3b-2:1, more successfully than Luke, has handled the injunction παντὶ τῷ αἰτοῦντί σε δίδου καὶ μὴ ἀπαίτει, by formulating it as a *separate* admonition, syntactically distinct from the three preceding ἐάν τις statements. That *Did.* 1:5 has taken over an existing admonition (including Luke's παντὶ) is shown by the fact that the apparently unconditional injunction to free giving, along with its warrant (πᾶσι γὰρ θέλει δίδοσθαι ὁ πατὴρ ἐκ τῶν ἰδίων χαρισμάτων) is immediately qualified, not only from the standpoint of the receiver, but from that of the giver (1:6). The agreement with Luke's παντὶ and δίδου, both normally attributed to Lukan redaction, seems to signal the Didache's knowledge of Luke.

Turning to the final parallel, the agreement between Matthew and Luke makes it a relatively simple matter to reconstruct Q for the final verse (12:59). The only real disagreement concerns the choice of κοδράντης (Matt) or λεπτόν (Luke). The IQP has, with the majority of critics, opted for Matthew's *quadrans*, principally because Luke at 21:2 has also eliminated κοδράντης in favour of Mark's λεπτόν (12:42).[98] Here the Didache agrees with both Matthew and Q, except in its use of μέχρις οὗ in place of Q's ἕως construction. It should be noted that the Didache's formulation seems to represent a standard formula concerning arrest and imprisonment as *coertio* for debt repayment.[99]

In *Did.* 1:5 the only indication of knowledge of Matthew comes not from the vocabulary of the saying, since Matthew apparently has simply reproduced Q, but from the placement of the saying on repayment. Matthew apparently transferred Q 12:58-59 from its location as a warning concluding a series of eschatological admonitions (Q 12:49, 51-53, 54-56) to his antithesis on anger (Matt 5:21). The Didache's use of the saying on repayment in the same general context as the sayings on non-retaliation (‖ Matt 5:39-42) and love of enemies (‖ Matt 5:44-47) might be seen as an indication of knowledge of Matthew's location of the saying (Matt 5:26), though it must be

---

[98] Garsky-Heil-Hieke-Amon, *Q 12:49–59*, 412–13.
[99] E.g. *P.Monach.* III, 52,16-17: μέχρι τοῦ τὴν ἀπόδοσίν [μ]οι αὐτὸν ποήσασθαι, 'until he makes repayment to me;' *UPZ* 1.124.23-24: μέχρι τοῦ τὰ δίκ[α]ια αὐτὸν ποῆσαι. See Llewelyn, *New Documents*, 59–61.

Figure 5: Didache 1:5

Did 1:5	Q 6:30; 12:58-59	Matt 5:42; 5:25-26	Luke 6:30; 12:58-59
5 **πάντὶ[1] τῷ αἰτοῦντί σε δίδου** **καὶ μὴ ἀπαίτει·** πᾶσι γὰρ θέλει δίδοσθαι ὁ πατὴρ ἐκ τῶν ἰδίων χαρισμάτων.	30 **τῷ αἰτοῦντί σε δός,** **καὶ [[ἀπὸ]] [[τοῦ δανιζο<μένου> τὰ]] σ[[ά]] μὴ ἀπ[[αίτει]].**	42 **τῷ αἰτοῦντί σε δός,** καὶ τὸν θέλοντα ἀπὸ σοῦ δανίσασθαι **μὴ ἀποστραφῆς.**	**παντὶ αἰτοῦντί σε δίδου,** καὶ ἀπὸ τοῦ αἴροντος τὰ σὰ **μὴ ἀπαίτει.**
μακάριος ὁ διδοὺς κατὰ τὴν ἐντολήν· ἀθῷος γάρ ἐστιν. οὐαὶ τῷ λαμβάνοντι· εἰ μὲν γὰρ χρείαν ἔχων λαμβάνει τις, ἀθῷος ἔσται. ὁ δὲ μὴ χρείαν ἔχων δώσει δίκην, ἱνατί ἔλαβε καὶ εἰς τί·			
ἐν συνοχῇ δὲ γενόμενος ἐξετασθήσεται περὶ ὧν ἔπραξε,	12:58 [[ἕως ὅτου]] .. μετὰ τοῦ ἀντιδίκου σου ἐν τῇ ὁδῷ, δὸς ἐργασίαν ἀπαλλάχθαι ἀπ᾽ αὐτοῦ, μήποτέ σε παραδῷ [[<ὁ ἀντίδικος>]] τῷ κρίτῃ καὶ ὁ κρίτης τῷ ὑπηρέτῃ]] σε β[[α]]λ[[εῖ]] εἰς φυλακήν.	5:25 ἴσθι εὐνοῶν τῷ ἀντιδίκῳ σου ταχὺ ἕως ὅτου εἶ μετ᾽ αὐτοῦ ἐν τῇ ὁδῷ, μήποτέ σε παραδῷ ὁ ἀντίδικος τῷ κριτῇ, καὶ ὁ κριτὴς τῷ ὑπηρέτῃ, καὶ εἰς φυλακὴν βληθήσῃ·	12:58 ὡς γὰρ ὑπάγεις μετὰ τοῦ ἀντιδίκου σου ἐπ᾽ ἄρχοντα, ἐν τῇ ὁδῷ δὸς ἐργασίαν ἀπαλλάχθαι ἀπ᾽ αὐτοῦ, μήποτε κατασύρῃ σε πρὸς τὸν κρίτην, καὶ ὁ κρίτης σε παραδώσει τῷ πράκτορι, καὶ ὁ πράκτωρ σε βαλεῖ εἰς φυλακήν.
καὶ οὐκ ἐξελεύσεται ἐκεῖθεν, μέχρις οὗ ἀποδῷ τὸν ἔσχατον κοδράντην.	12:59 λέγω σοι, οὐ μὴ ἐξέλθῃς ἐκεῖθεν, ἕως τὸν ἔσχατον [[κοδράντην]] ἀποδῷς.	26 ἀμὴν λέγω σοι, οὐ μὴ ἐξέλθῃς ἐκεῖθεν ἕως ἂν ἀποδῷς τὸν ἔσχατον κοδράντην.	12:59 λέγω σοι, οὐ μὴ ἐξέλθῃς ἐκεῖθεν, ἕως καὶ τὸν ἔσχατον λεπτὸν ἀποδῷς.

1 *CA* omit πάντι.

said that the Didache's deployment of the saying betrays none of the particulars of Matthew's antithesis on anger.[100]

3   Conclusion

To conclude: In *Did.* 1:3b, no grounds could be found by which to distinguish the Didache's use of Matthew or Luke from its possible use of Q, since the Didache differs significantly from each of these, and because the reconstruction of Q is here quite problematic. For *Did.* 1:3c there is a weak indication of knowledge of Luke's ποία χάρις ὑμῖν, a clause which, in the literary contexts of Q, Matthew and Luke, makes perfect sense, but which is otiose in the Didache. In *Did.* 1:4, however, we have better evidence of the Didache's knowledge of Luke's redaction of Q in the reconceiving of Matthew's scene, about borrowing and sureties as a scene about robbery. *Did.* 1:5 provides no strong grounds for distinguishing the Didache's use of Q from its use of Matthew.

What this suggests is that the compiler of *Did.* 1:3b–2:1 knew Luke. But did he know Matthew? I see no way to distinguish Matthew from Q in this respect, since where the Didache agrees with Matthew, Matthew is simply adapting Q. It is worth observing that the Didache lacks the obvious elements of Matthew's formulation of the antitheses – the antithetical formulation, the contrast with teachings from the Torah, and the ἐγὼ δὲ λέγω ὑμῖν formula which highlights Jesus' authority as an interpreter of Torah. Thus we might imagine that the Didache here used not Matthew but Q (or Q^Mt), but was also aware of distinctively Lukan transformations of Q.

As indicated above, the resolution of this question has bearing on the dating of the *sectio evangelica* in relation to the rest of the Didache. Comparison of the Didache with other versions of the Two Ways tradition makes it clear that *Did.* 1:3b–2:1 is an insertion into the christianized Two Ways tradition. This insertion cannot have occurred much before the early to mid-second century, when Luke's gospel was in circulation. My suspicion is that the harmonization of Luke with Q (or Matthew) was not a literary operation, but rather occurred in oral performance.

---

[100] Massaux, *Influence de l'évangile*, 613.

Chapter Seven

The Halakhic Evidence of Didache 8 and Matthew 6 and the Didache Community's Relationship to Judaism

Peter J. Tomson

Faculty of Protestant Theology in Brussels (Belgium)

> It was not dogma but law that was apt to produce lasting schisms in Judaism. It was not theological differences that created the Karaite schism in the eighth century but differences of opinion about matters of law, and one may confidently assert that so long as Jewish-Christianity was not distinct from the bulk of the people in its attitude to the Law, it was regarded as a normal part of it in spite of its peculiar dogmas. Accordingly, for the correct understanding of the circle in which the fragments that here engage our attention originated, the Halakah contained in them is much more important than their theological position. (L. Ginzberg, *An Unknown Jewish Sect*, 105)

Louis Ginzberg, who wrote these words, was a great scholar of what he called "Jewish Law and Lore."[1] He produced four volumes of dense Hebrew commentary on the Palestinian Talmud Berakhot; he edited the Geniza textual variants to the Palestinian Talmud; he compiled the ever-reprinted collection work of aggada, *The Legends of the Jews*; and he began his career with an innovating study on *Aggada in the Church Fathers*.[2] The above quotation is taken from the study on the Damascus Document that he originally published in 1922: *Eine unbekannte jüdische Sekte*. In this ground-breaking work he analysed both the halakha and the theology of the underlying "Jewish sect" that by then was still very unknown.[3] Ginzberg was, therefore, well placed to pass judgment on the particular importance of halakha for the historiography of ancient Judaism in its various subspecies, an ability he made explicit in his essay, "The Significance of the Halachah for Jewish History."[4]

This last title well sums up a major interest of the following paper, in particular since indeed we appear to be dealing with documents of some other ancient "Jewish sect." We shall focus on chapters in the Didache and the gospel of Matthew that reflect halakhot clearly identifiable in relation to the Pharisaic-rabbinic tradition. We shall then ask what communities are to be supposed behind both texts and, in line with the present volume, whether the Didache community has kept identifying with Jewish

---

[1] See the volume of his studies, *Jewish Law and Lore*.

[2] *A Commentary on the Palestinian Talmud*; *Yerushalmi fragments from the Genizah*; *The Legends of the Jews*; *Die Haggada bei den Kirchenvätern*.

[3] On the halakha in CD, cf. Hempel, *The Laws of the Damascus Document*; see my review evaluating its socio-historical relevance, in *Journal for the Study of Judaism* 34(2003)327-29.

[4] Originally delivered in Hebrew at the Hebrew University of Jerusalem in 1929-1930, in *Jewish Law and Lore*, 77-126.

tradition or not. We shall see that other than halakhic evidence must also come in if we want to answer that question. But first let me sketch some preliminaries.

1 Halakha in the Didache

a. There is a broad consensus among scholars that the traditions on which the Didache draws must be located in Jewish and Judaeo-Christian surroundings.[5] This is sufficiently shown by the Two Ways Tractate that was wholesale integrated in the document, and whose relatedness to Jewish documents and traditions has been extensively demonstrated in the new book by Huub van de Sandt and David Flusser. It can also be seen from the many semitisms and from the closeness to the synoptic tradition.[6] In view of the Jewish beginnings of Christianity, the likely inference is that the Didache community consisted primarily of Jews.

b. The word *halakha* is not Hebrew but Aramaic (*halakh*, *halkha*). It ultimately seems to derive from Akkadian *ilku* or *alku* and means "rule" or "tax".[7] In rabbinic usage it denotes either a single law or the prevailing law, while in modern rabbinic studies the word also came to denote, in the singular, the genre of rabbinic law as distinct from the genre of aggada. For some time it was then thought possible to speak of *the* Halakha meaning rabbinic law, but this has changed since the halakha in the Damascus Document and especially that in the Qumran scrolls began to be studied. Nowadays it is used for the legal elements in such Jewish texts as the scrolls, rabbinic literature, or the writings of Philo and Josephus.[8] There is no reason why we should not expect to find halakha in a Christian text drawing on Jewish sources.

c. The study of the halakha contained in the Didache was initiated by Gedalyahu Alon, a brilliant rabbinic scholar and historian of Judaism who taught at the Hebrew University till his early death in 1950. His study, "The Halakha in the Teaching of the Twelve Apostles," appeared in *Tarbiz* in 1939-40, was reprinted in his collected studies of 1958,[9] and appeared in English in 1996.[10] Basing himself on the critical analysis

---

[5] See Van de Sandt-Flusser, *The Didache*; Draper, *The Didache in Modern Research*; Niederwimmer, *Die Didache*; Rordorf-Tuilier, *La doctrine des douze apôtres*; Audet, *La Didachè*.

[6] See esp. Niederwimmer, *Ibid.*, 64-78.

[7] Lieberman, *Hellenism in Jewish Palestine*, 83 n. 3 cites the land tax called הלכא in an Aramaic papyrus from the ancient Persian banking house of Murashu (see Driver, *Aramaic Documents*, 31). Referring to the same surroundings, Frye, *The Heritage of Persia*, 113f mentions old Persian *harâka*, a land tax. This lines up with the tax called הלך in (Aramaic) Ezra 4:13, 20; 7:24, which Koehler-Baumgartner, *Lexicon*, s.v., associate with old Persian *harâka*, which in turn would derive from Akkadian *ilku / alku / allûku / alâku*. This last connection is rejected by Driver, *Aramaic Documents*, 70, but confirmed by the cuneiform study on the Murashu archives by Stolper, *Management and Politics*, 50: "taxes are summarized by the term *ilku*, service," and p. 60 n. 46, "Babylonian *ilku* is rendered by Aramaic *hlk'* [הלכא]."

[8] E.g. Belkin, *The Alexandrian Halakah*; Goldenberg, *Halakhah in Josephus and in Tannaitic Literature*.

[9] Alon, "Ha-halakha."

[10] Alon, "The Halachah." Unfortunately the translation is replete with error to the extent of making many passages incomprehensible; cf. below nn. 17 and 18.

of the Didache by leading Christian scholars, Alon proceeded to elucidate a series of halakhot contained both in the Two Ways tractate and in the ensuing "Christian" chapters. His focus was on the development of Pharisaic-rabbinic halakha, using the Didache as an early, independent source, just as he did using Pseudo-Barnabas in a follow-up study which as yet is only available in Hebrew.[11] Needless to say, he had no idea of what the Qumran scrolls were soon to reveal.

d. Halakha is not just legal literature but corresponds to practical life and thus to social reality.[12] For one thing, this implies both change and variety. As in any legal system, there is an interval both at the beginning, i.e. at the point where change in practical conduct is codified into formulated law, and at the end, where formulated law goes out of use. The scope of these initial and terminal intervals varies and depends on many factors both from within and from outside. Likewise, the degree of inner variety is subject to change, due to external and internal factors. The multiformity of modern Judaism in democratic societies has many reminiscences of the Second Temple period, and in spite of major differences the function of halakha is analogous. One's identity as a Jew towards the inside and the outside is largely defined by the degree and type of one's observance. In the second place, therefore, the halakha constitutes a *social grid*, and that is why the study of halakha is such an important instrument for the history of Judaism. This includes sects and break-away groups. Ginzberg offers a helpful formulation, if we may paraphrase him: "For the correct understanding of the [community] in which the [texts] that here engage our attention originated, the [halakha] contained in them is much more important than their theological position."

e. It is also clear that our text in its extant form addresses gentile Christians. This is not so much because the longer, second title in the Jerusalem MS ends with the phrase "to the gentiles," for there are good grounds to doubt its primary character, along with that of the two titles as such.[13] More decisively, *Did.* 6:2-3 reminds the reader of "the yoke of the Lord" and of the prohibition to consume "idol offerings" in a way that would make little sense for Jews, but all the more so for gentiles joining the community.[14] The question what this meant for the position of the community vis-à-vis Judaism can not be answered off-hand. Pre-70 synagogues could harbour any number of "God-fearing" gentiles, and this situation could well have persisted in post-70 (Judaeo-) Christian circles. Conversely, rising tensions between Jews and non-Jews could have caused the Didache community to break away from Jewish tradition in times of social crisis.

f. Alon isolated a series of early halakhot in the text of the Didache, ranging from the areas of abortion and infanticide, magic, and slavery in the Jewish "Two Ways" part, to prayer, fasting, immersion or baptism, and priestly offerings in the "Christian" part.

---

[11] "Ha-halakha ba-Iggeret Bar-Nava."

[12] Cf. the theoretical observations in Tomson, *Paul and the Jewish Law*, 19-30.

[13] Niederwimmer, *Die Didache*, 80f; Van de Sandt-Flusser, *The Didache*, 85-87.

[14] For analyses of this passage see Van de Sandt-Flusser, *The Didache*, 238-70; Flusser, "Paul's Jewish-Christian Opponents," 195-211 (1996); Draper, "A continuing enigma: the 'Yoke of the Lord,'" 106-23.

The halakhot concerning baptism (*Did.* 7:2-3) well demonstrate both the specific aim of Alon's investigation and the scope of his expertise. The obvious parallel of the graded qualifications of baptismal water to the enumeration in Mishna Miqwaot, Chap. 1, is mentioned by most commentaries nowadays,[15] but it is not by Alon. This may well be because its basic archaism seems obvious already from the Mishna, involving as it does a dispute on details between the schools of Shammai and Hillel. The antiquity of this halakha, we may add, is confirmed by terminology also found in Qumran evidence.[16] Instead Alon unearthed two more subtle halakhot, i.e., the permission in constrained circumstances to pour on a quantity of water instead of immersing,[17] and to use hot water.[18] Both of these halakhot appear only in later rabbinic literature but are first documented by the Didache, which reflects the interest of Alon's study.

g. Another preliminary concerns the widely recognised ties between the Didache and Matthew. Probably the most decisive element, because of its halakhic implications, is among those that concern us here in particular, i.e. the Lord's Prayer in its two practically identical versions.[19] Furthermore there is the proverb of which the Didache says "the Lord pronounced" it and that is also found in Matthew: "Do not give the holy to the dogs" (*Did.* 9:5; Matt 7:6). Another saying, the one about the "blasphemy of the Spirit," appears in divergent forms to the extent of betraying a basic relationship not through a common written source but an oral tradition.[20] It is also obvious that both texts have gone through an extended process of editing. The most likely possibility seems to be that the Didache and Matthew reached their fixed form in about the same period, when at least for a stretch of time their authors had shared the same community traditions. The two chapters under discussion here may help us further pinpointing the whereabouts of the communities involved.

[15] Audet, *La Didachè*, 200, 359f perceives here, incorrectly I think, the work of the interpolator reflecting subsequent development of the rite; he sees no link with *m.Miqw.* Similarly Van de Sandt-Flusser, *The Didache*, 281-283, though noting the link, read a process of softening of the primitive Christian austerity of baptising in "living water." More likely, Niederwimmer, *Die Didache*, 163 supposes that the graded qualification of immersion water was adopted wholesale from Jewish tradition, only to be watered down (if that is the word) in subsequent gentile Christian tradition; cf. Tertullian, *De Bapt.* 4:3; *Trad. Apost.* 21 (= Botte, *La Tradition Apostolique*, 80).

[16] See schools dispute in *m.Miqw.* 1:5. For terminology see *m.Miqw.* 1 and CD 10:11-13 (text 4Q270 frag. 6 col. iv:20), which involves immersion in a גבא, "rock cavity" – paralleling מי גבאות in the Mishna chapter – and in a מרעיל, which must mean a volume measure. Lieberman, *Greek in Jewish Palestine*, 135 n. 151 pointed out that מרעיל (or מרחיל) does appear in rabbinic literature and denotes a "big hamper" measuring 40 *se'ah* (480 litres) – exactly the measure stipulated in *m.Miqw.* 1:7!

[17] Paralleled in *b.Ber.* 22a (not 22,1 as indicated in the translation [above n10] p. 190; also it involves *Ben Azzai*, not the inexistent "Rabbi Azai").

[18] Missed by the translator, *ibid.*, 190, who renders ולענין החמין (referring to *Did.* 7:2-3, not 6:2-3 as indicated) as "and as far as the *Hachamim* is concerned." It is probably not "still water" as supposed by Van de Sandt-Flusser, *The Didache*, 282-83, following Niederwimmer, *Die Didache*, 162 n. 20 and others, but, as the earlier opinion had it, hot water from a bath house, as in the passage in *b.Hul.* 105a which they cite; cf. *b.Šabb.* 40a; *b.Pesah.* 8b, חמי טבריא.

[19] For a comparison of the versions see Luz, *Das Evangelium nach Matthäus* 1, 334; Niederwimmer, *Die Didache*, 168-73.

[20] *Did.* 11:7; Matt 12:31. See Tomson, *'If this be from Heaven...'*, 385-86.

h. Finally, we must pay attention to some literary aspects of *Did.* 8 and Matt 6. As observed by the commentators, *Did.* 8 reads much like a later insertion into the "book of ritual" which runs from Chaps. 7 through 10.[21] The fast before baptism having been mentioned, there follows a polemical section against the fasting practice of the "hypocrites" as also against their way of praying. Adding to the contrast, we can also observe that unlike the sections preceding and following, the two injunctions given here are not introduced with the casuistic technical formula περὶ δέ...[22] The topics of "fasting" and "prayer" are proverbially linked, and this represents one level on which *Did.* 8 is connected with Matthew. Matt 6:1-18 is a carefully constructed pericope dealing with alms, prayer and fasting, in which verses 7-15 stands out as a separate section or insert containing the Lord's prayer.[23] Another level of linkage is the near-identity of the Lord's Prayer versions just mentioned, as also the polemical demarcation over against the "hypocrites", the precise nature of whom remains to be investigated.

2   *Did.* 8:1 – Halakha concerning Fasting

> Let your fasting not be in communion with the hypocrites, for they are fasting on the second and fifth day from the sabbath; but you must fast on the fourth day and the preparation day.

Fasting must not be done on Monday and Thursday but on Wednesday and Friday. This ruling has an obvious halakhic import. Before trying to establish who are the "hypocrites", we must therefore inquire about the halakhic background of the custom.[24] Alon refers us to an earlier study,[25] where, citing a range of rabbinic and Patristic sources, he established that Monday and Thursday were the days fit for fasting according to the tradition of the rabbis or – as Epiphanius says – of the Pharisees.[26] The reason is not the one thought up by Billerbeck,[27] i.e. that these days were equally remote from each other and from the sabbath. Rather, these were the market days in the Palestinian villages, on which also the Torah was read out and court sessions were held, occasions

---

[21] Rordorf-Tuilier, *La doctrine des douze apôtres*, 36 consider it an "insertion (qui) interrompt la suite logique de la partie liturgique." Niederwimmer, *Die Didache*, 165: "Exkurs," "Zusatz" similar to *Did.* 7:4. Draper, "Christian Self-Definition," 226-27 thinks the abrupt opposition to the "hypocrites" constitutes a "hiatus" and postulates this section is "from a different context." In the Ethiopic version it comes after 11:3-13.

[22] *Did.* 6:3, on food; 7:1, on baptism; 9:1, on the Eucharist; 11:3, on apostles and prophets. On the formula see Mitchell, "Concerning *PERI DE*," 229-56; the Qumran equivalent must be added, see Tomson, "Paul's Jewish Background," 263-64.

[23] Luz, *Das Evangelium nach Matthäus* 1, 320-23. The ἐθνικοί in Matt 6:7 contrasts with the ὑποκριταί of vv. 2, 5, 16; see below.

[24] *Pace* Van de Sandt-Flusser, *The Didache*, 292 who go with the major commentaries in pre-determining it concerns "pious Jews" in general (exceptionally, Rordorf-Tuilier, *La doctrine des douze apôtres*, 36-37 think Judaisers are meant), only then to address the halakha involved.

[25] "Le-yishuva shel baraita ahat," 120-27. See also Safrai, "Religion in everyday life," 816.

[26] Epiphanius, Panarion II, 15, 1.

[27] Strack-Billerbeck, *Kommentar zum Neuen Testament* 2, 242, n. 2.

which facilitated the prayer gatherings connected with fasting. This situation must have prevailed till the fall of Beitar in 135 CE, but in any case the custom of fasting on those days remained intact after that date. It is important to note the community aspect inherent in the issue of fast days.

The Didache's exclusive opting for Wednesday and Friday seems to indicate its community parted company with the tradition of Pharisees and rabbis, and we shall have to ask why. For the moment we must ask another question: why Wednesday and Friday to start with?[28] Alon does not help us here, understandably, for it is only the Qumran discoveries that have provided us with convincing material for comparison. Many Didache commentaries duly note Annie Jaubert's theory about the 364 day solar calendar based on the book of Jubilees, following which all festival days fall on *Sunday, Wednesday* or *Friday*, and never on a sabbath, as dinstinct from the Pharisaic luni-solar calendar which allows festivals to fall on a sabbath. The celebrations on Sunday are extremely important in this context but transcend the limits of this study.[29] However, my impression is that the force of the evidence is often underestimated.

The use of the Jubilee calendar at Qumran is well-established by now. The famous "halakhic letter," 4QMMT, even seems to have begun with an extensive mapping out of the 364 day calendar.[30] That this was a burning issue is eloquently evident from the complaint in the Habakkuk Pesher about the "Wicked Priest" from Jerusalem who came to punish the sectarians precisely on the Day of Atonement according to their calendar.[31] It is important, however, that we know of yet another group that differed with the Pharisees on the calendar. Rabbinic literature preserves a series of calendar disputes with the Sadducees, notably with the high-priestly House of Boethus. They involve similar clashes such as the Boethusians placing stones on palm branches left in the temple in order to prevent the people from swaying them on the next day of Tabernacles because that was a sabbath.[32] The implication is that the Sadducees shared the Qumranite concern to safeguard the sabbath from coinciding with festival days and most likely adhered to some similar type of calendar.[33] On the other hand it is most important to note that both Josephus and rabbinic literature stress that the Sadducees could not maintain their own ritual tradition in the temple but had to follow the Pharisaic one that enjoyed the support of the majority of the people; incidentally, this included Josephus himself.[34]

---

[28] Audet, *La Didachè*, 368-69 notes Jaubert's theory yet correctly indicates that the exclusive choice for the alternative calendar must have other grounds; cf. Van de Sandt-Flusser, *The Didache,* 293 and references *ibid.*, n. 76. For the theory see Jaubert, *La date de la Cène*, 13-75.

[29] For the importance of Sunday, see Jaubert, *ibid.*, 60-62. It is to be noted that Jaubert reckons with calendar forms mediating between the solar and the luni-solar systems and hypothetically associates these with the earliest Christian tradition.

[30] 4QMMT beginning, ושלמה השנה שלוש מאת וש[שים וארבעה] יום..., "And the year is complete, three hundred and sixty-four days" (= 4Q394 3 - 7 I:1-3), see García Martínez-Tigchelaar, *The Dead Sea Scrolls* 2, 790-91; cf. 4Q326 and 4Q327, *ibid.*, 698-701. For evaluation see e.g. VanderKam, "The Calendar," 179-94.

[31] 1QpHab 10:2-8.

[32] *t.Sukkah* 3:1 ; *b.Sukkah* 43b ; *y.Sukkah* 4, 24b = *y.Šebu.* 1, 33b.

[33] Cf. Baumgarten, "Halakhic Polemics," 390-99.

[34] See Tomson, "Les systèmes de halakha," 189-220.

Now if we recall the words of Ginzberg quoted at the beginning, it will be clear that a serious schism must have existed between the Pharisees – apparently backed by the majority of the people – over against the Qumran Essenes and the Sadducees, the divisive issue being the calendar. Certainly there were other such issues, as we have it explicitly in the same halakhic letter, where the Qumran covenanters said of themselves in relation to purity rules: "We have segregated ourselves from the majority of the people."[35] This allows us provisionally to place the Didache's stance on the map of first-century Judaism. Taking in the information that fast days were fixed on days when people used to gather together, it is by all means possible for a non-Pharisaic movement to consider the preferred festival days of the Jubilees calendar eligible for fast days. This insight justifies the supposition that the Didache's preference for Wednesday and Friday harks back to some ancient tradition, possibly somehow relating to the 364 day solar calendar. It does not yet explain why the Didachist opted for an *exclusive opposition* to Pharisaic-rabbinic tradition.

3 *Did.* 8:2-3 – Halakha concerning Prayer

And do not pray as the hypocrites do, but as the Lord commanded in his gospel, pray as follows: Our Father who art in heaven (...). Thrice daily must you pray thus.

First some more literary analysis. The link with the gospel of Matthew is particularly close here. First, before giving the prayer text almost identical to Matt 6:9-13, the Didachist says this is "as the Lord commanded in his gospel."[36] Second, the actual prayer in both passages is preceded by the identical words: οὕτως προσεύχεσθε [ὑμεῖς]. In both cases, the emphasis is put on the exact and almost identical prayer wording that follows. There is also a subtle difference: whereas the Didache contrasts the Lord's Prayer to that of the "hypocrites", Matt 6:7 puts it in opposition to the prayer of the "gentiles". The fact that the Vaticanus and some other mss. replace Matthew's ἐθνικοί with ὑποκριταί is revealing, however. It is not just a secondary adaptation to the oppositional function of the "hypocrites" in the pericope (Matt 6:2, 5, 16). It is also in line with the tendency of Matthew more than other gospels to use "hypocrite" as an invective for adversaries, notably the Pharisees.[37] As to prayer, the stance taken by the Didache and by Matthew over against the "hypocrites" is particularly close. We have no evidence for a similar conclusion as to fast days, but we would not be surprised to run into it one day.

---

[35] 4Q397 frgs 14-21 line 7, [...ם]העל מרוב פרשנו ש[ודעים יודעים ואתם], García Martínez-Tigchelaar, *The Dead Sea Scrolls* 2, 800-801.

[36] Meaning Jesus' teaching rather than a written gospel; cf. discussion in Van de Sandt-Flusser, *The Didache*, 49-50.

[37] Mark 1x, Luke 3x, Matt 13x. Against Pharisees: Matt 15:7 = Mark 7:6; Matt 22:18; 23:13, 15, 23, 25, 27, 29.

Now let us study the halakha involved. In the first place it involves the ancient custom to pray three times a day, which appears already in Dan 6:11 and is presupposed in the Mishna discussion about the exact hours of prayer: "The morning prayer (is said) till mid day, R. Yehuda says: till the fourth hour; the *minha* prayer...; the evening prayer..."[38] The next question is which prayer is to be said. Two paragraphs on, we read in the Mishna:

> Rabban Gamliel says: One must pray the eighteen berakhot every day. R. Yoshua says: a summary of the eighteen (מעין שמונה עשרה). R. Akiva says: When prayer is fluent in his mouth, he must pray the eighteen, if not, a summary of the eighteen. R. Eliezer says: He who makes his prayer fixed, his prayer is no supplication. (*m.Ber.* 4:3-4)

A series of rabbinic reports portray Rabban Gamliel as the harsh and domineering ruler of the rabbis of the later Yavne generation.[39] This portrait differs distinctly not only from his peace-loving predecessor, Rabban Yohanan ben Zakkai, but also from the Pharisee Gamaliel mentioned in Acts 5:34 and 22:3 who quite probably was our Gamliel's grandfather and whose leniency in religious matters is reminiscent of their common ancestor, Hillel. Indeed, Shmuel Safrai has shown that in a number of halakhot Gamliel the Younger departed from the tradition of the school of Hillel he was supposed to represent and taught according to the school of Shammai.[40] Incidentally, R. Yoshua was the outstanding representative of Hillelite teaching in the Yavne generation as opposed to his Shammaite colleague, R. Eliezer, while R. Akiva, having studied with both, undeniably developed the tradition of Hillelite thought.[41]

Given this information, the opposition to Gamliel's opinion voiced by his three colleagues is striking. Eliezer's objection is singular in nature and seems to oppose any regularisation of prayer. Yoshua and Akiva, for their part, clearly oppose making "the 18 benedictions" a compulsory prayer three times a day for everyone or, as Akiva puts it tellingly, for everyone including those who do not know how to pray. Instead they only want to impose "a short prayer summarising the eighteen" (תפלה קצרה מעין שמונה עשרה) on the community, i.e. a brief prayer roughly following the same outline.[42]

None of these rabbis, however, object to the custom *per se* of saying a prayer three times a day. Their discussion was about the institution of *an obligatory thrice-daily community prayer*. That is what was at stake in Gamliel's proposal, for, as Shmuel Safrai and Ezra Fleischer have shown, a similar institution did not yet exist in Second

---

[38] *m.Ber.* 4:1; cf. *t.Ber.* 3:1-3. See Alon, "Ha-halakha," 284-286 / "The Halakah," 179-81.

[39] For a description of the episode see Tomson, "The wars against Rome," 8-12.

[40] See Safrai, "The Decision according to the School of Hillel," 35-40 / 396-401.

[41] See Epstein, *Introduction to Tannaitic Literature*, 59-84; Safrai, "Halakha," 185-207.

[42] Following the expression of R. Yoshua, *m.Ber.* 4:4 (version ms Kaufmann and Yerushalmi); cf. the explicit later definitions of Rav and Shmuel in *b.Ber.* 29a, who (especially Rav) follow the outline of "the 18."

Temple Judaism.[43] Subsequently, the opposition to the proposal must have faded away in rabbinic circles, so that it could become one of the many decrees (*takkanot*) for which the regime of Rabban Gamliel is known.[44]

This late first century rabbinic discussion illuminates our passages from the Didache and Matthew. Apparently all, the Didachist included, agreed on prayer three times a day; Matthew's evangelist is silent on this point but may well have joined in. What they differed about is *which* prayer. Gamliel's 18 benedictions are too difficult for an obligatory prayer incumbent on all, not only Yoshua, Akiva but also the Didachist and Matthew would maintain. Only for the alternative "short prayer similar to the eighteen," the latter would propose the one used in their own community, a prayer that in outline and content was not unlike the ones quoted in rabbinic literature,[45] i.e. the Lord's Prayer. The rather surprising emergence of Jesus' prayer among ancient Jewish prayers is confirmed by the brief report in Luke 11:1-4 that Jesus taught it to his disciples "as John (the Baptist) also taught his disciples."[46]

The evidence of the halakha on prayer enables us to conclude that both the Didache and Matthew maintained an alternative Jewish tradition over against the one put forward by the "hypocrites". As did the Didache in the case of fast days, moreover, they did so in an exclusive way. Our texts do not offer a means of knowing what made them take such a stance.

4 The Schism with the "Hypocrites" – and Beyond

Explanations which fail to take in the strong Judaeo-Christian colouring of both Matthew and the Didache do not get to the heart of the matter. It is unsatisfactory to speak, as do Van de Sandt and Flusser, of the Didache community "irreversabl(y) (...) moving away from its Jewish roots."[47] At the level of the halakha we have studied, we are facing a rupture between distinct but related Jewish communities. Looking from a distance, we can safely conclude that the Judaism of the Yavne generation offered much less room for diversity than pre-70 Judaism. This conclusion is confirmed and specified if we take in other information.

---

[43] Safrai, "Gathering in the Synagogues," 7–15, as different from the opinion of Alon, *The Jews in the Talmudic Age* 1, 266f; Fleischer, "On the Beginnings," 397-441. This insight must be added to the exposition in Van de Sandt-Flusser, *The Didache*, 294.

[44] On the takkanot, see Alon, *The Jews in the Talmudic Age* 1, 253-87.

[45] Cf. the short prayers quoted *m.Ber.* 4:2 (Nehunya); *m.Ber.* 4:4 (Yoshua); *t.Ber.* 3:7 = *b.Ber.* 29b (Eliezer, Yose [probably not Yoshua as in *b.Ber.* 29b], Elazar bar Tsadok, and 'others'). Cf. also Shmuel's more formalised "summary of the 18" that went down in tradition, *b.Ber.* 29b.

[46] Cf. the excellent remarks on the Lord's Prayer by Luz, *Das Evangelium nach Matthäus* 1, 332-353, notably the quotes from Grotius and Wettstein (339 n. 48).

[47] Van de Sandt-Flusser, *The Didache*, 295-96, also saying, "It is the Jewish Prayer ritual which is rejected here and it seems that this message is directed first of all at Christian converts of gentile provenance." Cf. Audet's sadness, *La Didachè*, 397 bottom. Contrast Draper, "Christian Self-Definition," 233; I largely agree with Draper's study, while adding the Jubilees calendar and the decrees of Rabban Gamliel.

We already noted Matthew's use of the word "hypocrites" to indicate the Pharisees. This is particularly the case in Matt 23, the sustained attack against "Scribes and Pharisees, you hypocrites." When compared with Mark and Luke, it is immediately clear that Matthew has inserted this address into the discussions Jesus has with Jewish leaders on the Temple square. In other words, where Mark and Luke have the "upper priests and scribes (and the elders)" for Jesus' mortal enemies, Matthew adds the Pharisees.[48] Another feature typical of Matthew is the prohibition pronounced by Jesus "to have yourselves called *rabbi*" (Matt 23:8). As I have observed in another study, this contrasts with the disciples' own usage as testified in Mark and John and seems to refer to another innovation issued under Rabban Gamliel's regime, i.e. "rabbi" as a title for ordained Torah teachers.[49] We thus find cumulative evidence that Matthew's community experienced a head-on collision with this regime. The same is clearly true of the Didache community, given the halakhic evidence on fasting and prayer. In view of the near-identity of the prayer text they propound in an analogous polemical context, it is most likely that at this stage Didache and Matthew represented one and the same community.

Reassessing the evidence, I concluded in the same study that the best explanation for such observations is that indeed the rabbinic reports about Rabban Gamliel's rephrasing of the Birkat Ha-Minim, the "benediction of the heretics," correspond to the community ban referred to three times in the gospel of John (9:22; 12:42; 16:2).[50] Apart from Gamliel's ambition, this state of affairs becomes understandable from the social upheavals brought about by the war against Rome. Though it is true that Matthew's gospel and the Didache contain no traces of the decree, their stubborn resistance to a dominant Pharisaic regime makes it very hard not to think of the impact of Gamliel's decree.

On the other hand, two important Christian documents from the same period, Luke-Acts and 1 Clement, while being equally open to Judaeo-Christian influence, do not show a similar enmity to the Pharisees. The likely conclusion is that Gamliel's community ban against Christians at first was followed only in areas such as Palestine and Asia Minor, where Didache and Matthew are usually located, but not in others. In this connection the Roman background of 1 Clement and possibly of Luke-Acts is most interesting.[51]

This causes us once again to come back to Ginzberg, who said that it was "matters of law" that created schisms like that of the Karaites. Judging from our case, we must enlarge the perspective and add that it was a geo-political process of change that provoked a divisive halakhic development, and this constituted the schism between rabbinic Jews and Judaeo-Christians. Put differently, the rupture in the halakha corresponded to the socio-religious schism triggered by the war. Where many synagogues in Palestine and Syria in their prayers now placed Christians outside the community as *minim*, the Christian communities of Didache and Matthew henceforth prayed and fasted exclu-

[48] See Tomson, '*If this be from Heaven...*', 267-76.
[49] Tomson, "The wars against Rome," 13.
[50] *Ibid.* 14-18.
[51] *Ibid.* 20-21.

sively according to non-Pharisaic rites. It is probable that it was at this point that the polemically charged rules on the times for fasting and prayer (*Did.* 8) found their way into the "book of ritual" contained in *Did.* 7-10.

The rupture most likely was followed by a period of further schisms, notably in Judaeo-Christian and mixed Jewish-gentile churches. We noted the presence of non-Jews in the Didache community; obviously this was true of the Matthean one as well. Part of the Judaeo-Christians must now have gone separate ways of their own, while others went along with the gentile Churches in their opposition to Judaism. The extant gospel of Matthew must have travelled with the second group and undergone a final redaction that expresses a general distancing over against the Jews. Main passages are the ones stating that "the children of the Kingdom will be thrown out" as opposed to the gentiles coming from East and West (Matt 8:12); that the Kingdom will be taken from "the chief priests and the Pharisees" and given to another "people" (21:43-45); and that "the chief priests and Pharisees" convince Pilate to put a guard on the tomb and when Jesus' corpse has disappeared, spread the rumour "among Jews" that his disciples have stolen it (27:62-66; 28:11-15).[52]

As far as I can see, however, similar passages are not to be found in the Didache. The only identifiable references are the distancing remarks vis-à-vis the halakha of the "hypocrites" that we have also found in Matthew and that most probably reflect the schism with Gamliel's rabbinic Judaism. One possibility is that the Didache simply is an earlier text than the extant Matthew. Another one is that while indeed Matthew underwent its final, anti-Jewish redaction, the Didache community still remained within the boundaries of tradition to form a surviving specimen of non-Pharisaic, non-rabbinic Judaism. This could still have included non-Jewish members who, much like the God-fearers before 70, bore as much of "the yoke of the Lord" as they could.

Ultimately, the Didache passed into the Apostolic gentile churches and for a couple of centuries enjoyed near-canonical status.[53] We do not have sufficient information to decide whether this excluded the continued existence of a Judaeo-Christian Didache community with a number of non-Jewish members.

---

[52] For this aspect of Matthew, see Stanton, *A Gospel for a New People*, 113–68; Strecker, *Der Weg der Gerechtigkeit*, 15–85 (3rd ed.); Luz, "Das Matthäusevangelium und die Perspektive," 233-48; Id., "Antijudaismus im Matthäusevangelium," 310-27; Tomson, *'If this be from Heaven...'*, 380-91.

[53] Cf. elaborate data in Niederwimmer, *Die Didache*, 15-33.

Chapter Eight

Didache 9-10: A Litmus Test for the Research on Early Christian Liturgy Eucharist

Gerard Rouwhorst

Catholic Theological University of Utrecht (The Netherlands)

Since the discovery of the Didache at the end of the nineteenth century, the liturgical parts of this document, the Chapters 6 to 10, have met with very divergent reactions among liturgical historians. These reactions range from a strong fascination to a profound embarrassment. On the one hand, a large number of scholars has considered those liturgical sections of the Didache an important source of information for the reconstruction of the development of early Christian rituals. They occupy a key position in numerous monographs and articles dealing with topics related to these rituals. On the other hand, the discovery made by Archbishop Bryennios has also caused embarrassment in the relatively small world of liturgical historians and continues doing so, even to the present day. Many a liturgical scholar has had great difficulty in reconciling the data derived from the liturgical chapters of the Didache with their own overall picture of the emergence and earliest development of Christian liturgy.

It may be observed that the embarrassment has decreased considerably in the course of the twentieth century and especially during the last few decades. This certainly holds true for the publications dealing with Chapters 6 to 8. While reading the articles collected by Clayton Jefford[1] and Jonathan Draper[2] as well as the recent monograph written by Huub van de Sandt and the late David Flusser,[3] one finds, for instance, a relatively large consensus regarding issues related to the administration of baptism, especially concerning the antiquity of the varying baptismal formulas and the relationship with Jewish proselyte baptism.[4] Incidentally, this consensus is reflected in monographs and handbooks on the history of Christian baptism.[5] This also pertains to Chapter 8 mentioning the custom of thrice praying the Our Father,[6] although the precise historical relationship with Jewish traditions of daily prayer, especially the Amidah, continues to raise some questions, since the origin and the antiquity of this

---

[1] Jefford, *The Didache in Context.*

[2] Draper, *The Didache in Modern Research.*

[3] Van de Sandt-Flusser, *The Didache.*

[4] Cf., for instance, Rordorf, "Baptism according to the Didache;" Mitchell, "Baptism in the Didache;" Van de Sandt-Flusser, *The Didache,* 272-291. Cf. also Draper, "The Didache in Modern Research," 24-26.

[5] See especially Benoit, *Le baptême chrétien,* 5-33; Nocent, "Christian Initiation," 12; Johnson, *The Rites of Christian Initiation,* 1-32.

[6] Cf., for instance, Van de Sandt-Flusser, *The Didache,* 293-296. See also Niederwimmer, *Die Didache,* 167-173.

prayer and its daily recitation, still remains difficult to establish and is a matter of debate.[7] Still, it seems to me that things are more complicated with regard to Chapters 9 and 10 which contain texts and rubrics for a ritual meal called Eucharist and, by the way, belong to the most difficult and debated parts of the Didache. Judging by some important recent publications one cannot but conclude that, to the present day, no general agreement has yet been reached concerning many aspects of these intriguing chapters. It will suffice here to compare the editions and monographs of Klaus Wengst,[8] Kurt Niederwimmer[9] and Van de Sandt/Flusser[10] on this point. These scholars have rather different views on such important issues as the character of the celebration concerned and the sources which are used. In this regard, one may also point to the prolific book the German New Testament scholar Matthias Klinghardt has devoted to the "sociology and liturgy of early Christian meal celebrations" which attempts to explain the emergence of early Christian communal meals, including the so-called "Eucharist", from the perspective of the Hellenistic "symposium-tradition" and argues that *Did.* 9-10 fits in this mould as well.[11] While trying to substantiate this approach, he calls into question numerous generally accepted ideas about the Jewish origin of the prayer traditions encountered in the Didache and thereby challenges the consensus regarding the interpretation of both chapters, assuming that at least some sort of global consensus exists.

From recent overviews of the available literature,[12] it soon appears that considerable disagreements exist with regard to three main issues: a) The shape and the content of the ritual meal, the "Eucharist", underlying the extant text of the Didache which is commonly assumed to be the work of a redactor who made use of older sources; b) The development of the chapters prior to their final redaction or compilation, especially the antiquity of the sources employed and the milieu, Jewish or Christian, from which they were derived. c) The place of the rituals underlying the final stage of the Didache as well as the sources in the overall development of the Eucharist and other ritual meals in early Christianity. One of the first questions that will arise here is how the "Eucharist" of the Didache as well as that of the underlying ritual traditions used by its redactor relate to data derived from the New Testament, especially the institution narratives and their different versions, for instance that of Matthew. No less important is the question as to how the Eucharist of the Didache and its sources should be situated in the development of the Eucharist and the ritual meals in the period after the New Testament, especially in the second and third century. Without doubt, this third issue is the most difficult and also the most debated one. It is here that the opinions of the scholars are divided most clearly and sharply. It is here as

---

[7] See for this complicated and debated question: Reif, *Judaism and Hebrew Prayer*, 84-85 and Langer, "The 'Amidah as Formative Rabbinic Prayer."

[8] Wengst, *Didache (Apostellehre)*, 43-57.

[9] Niederwimmer, *Die Didache*, 173-209.

[10] Van de Sandt-Flusser, *The Didache*, 296-329.

[11] Klinghardt, *Gemeinschaftsmahl und Mahlgemeinschaft*, 375-492.

[12] See, besides the publications mentioned in footnotes 8-10, the overview of the most relevant publications and hypotheses given by Draper, "The Didache in Modern Research," 26-31.

well that it becomes most apparent what Andrew McGowan has pointedly called the "litmus test character of the Didache for the presuppositions of any modern theory of order in early Christian meals."[13] Scholars dealing with this aspect betray most clearly the limitations or the possibilities of their methodological approach as well as all sorts of theological and ideological hidden agendas. Therefore, I have decided to focus on this intriguing and controversial issue. However, it cannot be discussed in isolation from the first two questions we will therefore have to address first.

1 The Celebration underlying the Extant Text

When it comes to reconstructing and trying to understand the "Eucharist" of the Didache encountered in the extant text of the Didache, we are immediately faced with a crucial preliminary question concerning the Didache as a whole, but which is particularly pertinent with regard to Chapters 9 and 10. What is the "nature" of the Didache? Should it be considered a more or less comprehensive church order which gives us a relatively complete insight into some (of the most important) aspects of the life of the church? More specifically with regard to the rituals, does the redactor present us with a relatively complete description of liturgical rituals, in this case, the "Eucharist"? Or is it a rather "selective" church order which does not aim for comprehensiveness at all, but limits itself to dealing *ad hoc* with some burning issues of the day. As is known, Georg Schöllgen has defended the latter position and, on this basis, he has warned against the tendency of some scholars to draw argumentative conclusions from what is *not* mentioned in the text of the Didache.[14] The position one takes with regard to this question may have far-reaching implications for the interpretation of the Didache as a whole, but more, in particular, for that of Chapters 9 and 10. In fact, one of the most controversial issues here is precisely whether these chapters present us with a more or less complete picture of the Eucharist or whether essential parts of the celebration are not alluded to by the redactor/author because, in his eyes, they needed no special comment. While a large – and it may be added, increasing – group of scholars base their conclusions on the text as it is transmitted by the manuscript, another group is convinced that indeed some essential parts of the ritual presupposed remain unmentioned for one reason or another and, more importantly, they make suggestions as to how the gaps in the description of the ritual should be filled.

Here we should mention in the first place different theories which assume that the prayers of thanksgiving transmitted by the Didache belong to a so-called agape or a "breaking of the bread" which was followed by a "Eucharist" or a "major Eucharist," the latter not explicitly being mentioned but being alluded to by the invitation to "come" (ἐρχέσθω) which is found in 10:6.[15]

---

[13] McGowan, *Ascetic Eucharists*, 21.

[14] Schöllgen, "Die Didache als Kirchenordnung."

[15] See for an overview of the different theories: Niederwimmer, *Die Didache*, 177-178; Draper, "The Didache in Modern Research," 28-30. Most of the scholars concerned employ the terms "agape" and "Eucharist". J.-P. Audet, however, uses the indications "breaking of the bread" – which includes a full meal – and "major Eucharist" (see Audet, *La Didachè*, 410-424).

A completely different attempt to fill the so-called lacunae in the description of the ritual meal is made by Matthias Klinghardt in his aforementioned book. His interpretation of *Did.* 9-10 cannot be understood independently from his view on the emergence and development of early Christian Eucharist in general. According to him, the roots of this celebration are to be primarily looked for in the Hellenistic symposium, a communal banquet which, at the beginning of the Common Era, was very common among all kinds of associations and guilds, both pagan and Jewish, and was also adopted by early Christianity (and, of course, further developed in a specifically Christian way, on the basis of the gospel traditions). One of the most striking characteristics of this type of symposium was that the meal, a supper, was followed by a "symposium" in the proper sense, that is a drinking party consisting of a "paean", that is a hymn sung in unison, libations, speeches, singing and so on.[16]

Klinghardt argues that this symposium-pattern underlies the structure of the ritual meal described in *Did.* 9-10. The prayer of thanksgiving of Chap. 10 which comes after the meal is compared by him with the paean at the beginning of the "symposium" and the short formulas of verse 6 are interpreted as rubrical allusions to Christian hymns that were sung at the end of the Christian symposium.[17] Finally, the prayer of thanksgiving over the "good smell" (10:8), transmitted by the Coptic version, but lacking in the Manuscript of Jerusalem (H), is considered as belonging to the original core of the text. Klinghardt argues that the origins of this prayer are to be equally looked for in the Hellenistic symposium in which the use of scented oil or incense was customary.[18] On the other hand, the relevance of the parallelism between the prayers of Chaps. 9 and 10 and Jewish blessings and thanksgivings (such as the Birkat Ha-Mazon) is strongly toned down by Klinghardt. He does not deny that the thanksgivings of the Didache have been influenced by Jewish prayer texts, but he emphatically points to the differences which exist between the two categories of texts. He, moreover, stresses the fact that, in the period of the Didache, the form and the content of the Jewish berakhot with which the thanksgivings of the Didache are mostly compared, had not yet been standardised. All this leads Klinghardt to reject a direct *literary* dependence of the prayers of the Didache from written Jewish prayer texts.[19]

What conclusions can be deduced from all this? While looking at the different theories presented, it seems to me that a double risk is looming here. The first is the one signalled by Schöllgen. It consists of categorically excluding the possibility that the "Eucharist" of the Didache includes elements which are not mentioned in the text. However, to be honest, it seems to me that this temptation is a minor one in comparison with the second one which consists of filling in assumed gaps on the basis of our own presumptions about what early Christian Eucharists might have looked like. This is most obvious for the hypothesis of the "Eucharist" or the "major Eucharist" following the prayer of thanksgiving of Chapter 10. This theory is mainly based on a disputable interpretation of the word ἐρχέσθω, the primary meaning of which is to "come" and not to "approach" (to communion).[20] What is perhaps even more important, is that

[16] Klinghardt, *Gemeinschaftsmahl und Mahlgemeinschaft*, 98-129.

[17] *Ibid.*, 387-405. 478-479.

[18] *Ibid.*, 465-476. 484-487.

[19] *Ibid.*, 407-427.

[20] Cf., for instance, Van de Sandt-Flusser, *The Didache*, 301-302.

it depends on a problematic and outdated view on the origins and the development of the early Christian Eucharist. I will develop this question further on, in the third and last part of this paper, and therefore limit myself here to some short remarks.

In fact, one of the main reasons why the scholars concerned hypothesise the existence of a "real Eucharist" – taken for granted without being mentioned – is that they miss some elements considered by them essential to the celebration of the (early Christian) Eucharist. What strikes them first and foremost is the lack of any reference to the institution narrative, but they are also puzzled by the fact that any explicit reference to the Last Supper or the death of Christ is missing.[21] This argument, however, can no longer be considered convincing. In fact, the Didache is definitely not the only Christian source in which these elements are lacking.[22] It will suffice here to mention the eucharistic celebrations described in the Apocryphal Acts of the Apostles[23] and the fifth Mystagogic Catechesis of Cyrillus of Jerusalem. Furthermore, it should be emphasised that the institution narrative is missing in some Eastern anaphoras, in particular that of Addai and Mari and in the oldest core of the Egyptian anaphora of Marc. Incidentally, the idea that an institution narrative was an essential part of the eucharistic prayer from the first or second century onwards has recently been further undermined by the debate about the antiquity and origins of what was for long considered to be the oldest source containing a fully developed institution narrative, namely the Apostolic Tradition. Until recently it was commonly assumed that this document was of Roman provenance and dated back to the beginning of the second century. This view, then, is severely questioned now by several scholars who reckon with the possibility that the document as a whole is of a later date (end of the third or even first half of the fourth century) or that it consists of several strands which possibly arise from different historical periods.[24] This may be used as a further objection against traditional views on the development of the Eucharist which assume the presence of an institution narrative from a very early period onwards. On the other hand, Klinghardt's attempt to fit Chapters 9 and 10 in the mould of the symposium-pattern seems speculative to me as well. Both theories have in common that they give the impression of stretching the ritual Didache until it fits specific, preconceived views on the Eucharist, not unlike the way Procrustus dealt with guests he considered to be too short.

I would like to add that the structure of the ritual which we obtain if we uphold the data provided by the Didache, without further additions or subtractions, has nothing illogical in itself. Quite the contrary, it is a pattern which, in its broad outlines, doubtless

---

[21] See, for instance, Niederwimmer, *Die Didache*, 176. See also Rordorf, "Die Mahlgebete in der Didache," 233vv.

[22] Cf. for instance Rouwhorst, "La célébration de l'Eucharistie" (1993), 101-106.

[23] Cf. also Rouwhorst, "La célébration de l'Eucharistie" (1990), 51-77; Messner, "Zur Eucharistie in den Thomasakten," 493-513.

[24] Cf. especially Metzger, "Enquêtes," 7-36; Markschies, "Wer schrieb die sogenannte *Traditio Apostolica?*," 1-74; Id., "Neue Forschungen," 583-598; Bradshaw, "The Problems of a New Edition," 613-622; Bradshaw-Johnson-Philips, *The Apostolic Tradition*, 1-17; Stewart-Sykes, *Hippolytus*, 11-51. For that matter, in so far as these authors have more specific ideas about the date, composition and origin of this source, these appear to differ considerably.

was current in the Jewish environment in which the Didache must have originated. In addition, it may be remarked that, apart from the question of the institution narrative, the ritual pattern of the Didache fits in strikingly with some other New Testament passages which relate to early Christian meals. One of the most remarkable features of the Eucharist of the Didache is the much discussed bread-cup order: contrary to the institution narratives, the thanksgiving over the cup precedes the thanksgiving over the bread. Several scholars, however, have rightly noted that the same order recurs in the tenth chapter of Paul's first letter to the Corinthians and in the short version of the institution narrative as preserved in the famous Codex Bezae.[25] I have elsewhere argued that both passages might reflect an early Christian liturgical practice parallel to that of the Didache.[26] Finally, I would like to add that the ritual meal as it appears from Chapters 9 and 10 – without further additions – remarkably matches the sociological character of the community of the Didache. Several scholars, amongst others Jonathan Draper, have pointed out that that community was characterised by strong group boundaries, whereas the internal social and hierarchical organisation, the grid, to use the terminology of Mary Douglas,[27] is very weak.[28] The Didache betrays a strong awareness of exclusiveness and holiness of the community which goes together with rather undefined internal boundaries and, in particular, an unclear and precarious position of leadership. The ritual of the Eucharist as it emerges from an unbiased reading of Chaps. 9 and 10 fits in wonderfully with such a strong group-low grid community. The exclusiveness and holiness of the community appear first of all from the fact that the meal, i.e. the Eucharist, is strictly reserved for members who have been purified by baptism. These characteristics become all the more striking since no clear distinction is made between what we would tend to call a "normal" meal and the Eucharist. In other words, it is not just participation in a special, sacred meal which is forbidden for those who are not members of the holy community – as will become normal in later centuries –, but any form of commensality, of eating and drinking with Christians.[29] On the other hand the division of the tasks and roles between the members of the holy community themselves is rather vague and diffuse. This emerges from the fact that prophets are allowed to give thanks as much as they like (10:7).

---

[25] Cf. Van de Sandt-Flusser, *The Didache*, 305-309; Rouwhorst, "La célébration de l'Eucharistie" (1993), 96-101. See for the parallellism and the relationship between the Didache and 1 Cor 10:16-17 also Mazza, "L'eucaristia di «1 Cor 10, 16-17»," 77-109.

[26] Rouwhorst, "La célébration de l'Eucharistie" (1993) 96vv.

[27] See esp. her seminal study *Natural Symbols. Explorations in Cosmology.* New ed. New York 1982.

[28] Cf. esp. Draper, "Social Ambiguity," 285-294.

[29] It may be remarked in this regard that the idea that partaking in (ordinary) meals was bound by purity rules and was reserved for people considered "pure" was widespread in (early) Judaism, especially among Pharisees and Essenes. See, for instance, Dunn, "The Incident at Antioch," 3-57. However, what distinguishes the Didache from Jewish sources containing rules for table fellowship is that the decisive criterion for admission is baptism. See also Mitchell, "Baptism in the Didache," 226-255.

2 The Sources Used

The ritual of the extant text thus having been established, the next equally much debated question which arises is that of the sources used by the redactor (taking for granted that he did, as is commonly assumed). It will not be possible to address here all the issues related to these questions. I will limit myself to three important aspects which are of particular relevance for the theme of my paper: a) the degree of dependence on Jewish prayers and b) the degree to which those Jewish prayers were Christianised and c) the provenance of the Christian elements, i.e. the milieu in which they may have originated.

First, it has been observed since long that a close relationship exists between the prayers of both Chaps. 9 and 10 and a number of Jewish (Hebrew) prayer texts known from later Jewish sources.[30] The similarities of the thanksgiving over the cup of wine and the bread with the wine- and bread-berakhot are undeniable. The same holds for the affinity which exists between the prayer of thanksgiving of Chap. 10 and the Jewish Birkat Ha-Mazon. Finally, it is beyond dispute that 9:4 and 10:5 must somehow be related to Jewish petitions for the gathering of Israel from the Diaspora as known from the tenth benediction of the Amidah and the Musaph-prayer for Yom Kippur. All these facts can only be accounted for by postulating some sort of dependence of the passages of the Didache on Jewish prayers.

However, the prayers of the Didache do not only show similarities with the Jewish prayer texts known from later sources. There are some remarkable differences to be noted as well. These differences do not only concern the fact that some themes mentioned are obviously of Christian origin (Jesus who is the servant (παῖς) of God and the church gathered from the four winds or from the ends of the world into the kingdom; cf. 9:4 and 10:5). The prayers of the Didache also contain some other peculiarities which are lacking in the Hebrew prayers. To begin with, the Didache appears to have a specific predilection for the verb "to give thanks" (εὐχαριστεῖν) over against "bless" (εὐλογεῖν).[31] In this connection, attention has been also called upon the fact that in 10:2-3 the order of the first two strophes of the Birkat Ha-Mazon has been changed: the prayer which is related to the thanksgiving for the land (Birkat Ha-Arets) precedes the one that is obviously derived from the blessing of the food (Birkat Ha-Zan).[32] Further, compared with the Hebrew texts of a later date, the prayers of the Didache betray a "spiritualising" tendency. Tellingly, in 10:3 God is thanked for the (material) food and drink he gave to human beings for enjoyment, but the text emphatically adds that God graced us with spiritual food and drink through Jesus. This expression obviously refers to the spiritual values mentioned in the same verse as well as in 10:2: "knowledge", "belief", "(eternal) life" (cf. 9:3) and "immortality".

Various solutions have been proposed by scholars to account for these deviations from the Jewish sources. Globally speaking, two major tendencies may be discerned

---

[30] Cf., for instance, Rordorf-Tuilier, *La doctrine des douze apôtres*, 175-181; Wengst, *Didache (Apostellehre)*, 47-53; Van de Sandt-Flusser, *The Didache*, 310-313.

[31] Cf., for instance, Talley, "From Berakah to Eucharistia," 115-137.

[32] *Ibid.* See also Van de Sandt-Flusser, *The Didache*, 314-316.

here. On the one hand, several scholars are inclined to consider the deviations the result of a conscious Christianising. An interesting example of this tendency is provided by the fact that the prevalence of the aspect of thanksgiving, instead of the "blessing", is sometimes ascribed to Christian influences.[33] On the other hand, one may perceive a tendency to reduce the impact of the process of Christianising to a minimum. Thus, in the wake of Martin Dibelius,[34] several scholars postulate the existence of an Hellenistic version of the Jewish prayers which would have been used as a source by the Christian author/redactor of the Didache. This intermediate Greek version serves in particular to explain the so-called spiritualising tendency which, so it is argued, would not have been due to directly Christian influences, but would have been taken over by a (gentile) Christian redactor from that Hellenistic Jewish version.

In my view, serious objections can be raised against both of these approaches. To start with the hypothesis of Dibelius, two German words which occur most frequently in his essay, are "Annahme" (assumption) and "Voraussetzung" (presupposition) and one cannot be struck by his abundant use of verbal forms expressing mere probability and uncertainty. Still more importantly, Dibelius does not succeed in substantiating his argument by a reference to any version of a Hellenistic Jewish prayer text available in a source that has come down to us.[35] The only sources which he adduces are passages from the works of Philo and Josephus which indisputably contain the same themes and represent the same "spiritualising" tendencies as the prayers of thanksgiving of the Didache, but are not part of prayer texts. A similar critical observation may be made with regard to the idea that the preference for "thanksgiving" instead of "blessing" is due to Christian influence. This hypothesis is difficult to substantiate by solid arguments and, therefore, remains rather speculative.

However, the major problem I have with both these approaches is not caused by their speculative character. Even more questionable is the fact that they are based on a very questionable premise, namely the assumption that in the period when the Didache came into existence, Jewish liturgical traditions and, more specifically, prayer texts had already obtained fixed forms and, moreover, had been written down. During the last few decades, this supposition has proved more and more untenable and, on this specific point, I wholeheartedly agree with Klinghardt. Two facts have to be mentioned in this regard. First, the process of standardisation of liturgical texts and rites in the period after the destruction of the temple has been much more gradual and slower than has often been believed. More in particular, one should be wary about uncritically projecting liturgical traditions described by later, especially rabbinic sources on to the period prior to the destruction of the Second Temple. Second, in the period prior to the reorganization and standardization by the rabbis an enormous multiformity and variety of liturgical customs must have existed with respect to liturgical traditions.[36]

---

[33] So Talley, "From Berakah to Eucharistia."

[34] Cf. Dibelius, "Die Mahl-Gebete der Didache," 32-41/ 117-27.

[35] Cf. also Niederwimmer, Die Didache, 187: "... Die Hypothese von Dibelius ist durch nichts erwiesen ... ."

[36] See especially Bradshaw, The Search, 1-29; Id., "Parallels between Early Jewish and Christian Prayers," 21-36; Reif, Judaism and Hebrew Prayer, 53-87.

The possibilities for improvisation must have been considerable and, still more importantly, it is most probable that prayer texts had not been written down, but were transmitted by oral tradition. This must also have held for the development of Jewish prayer forms. It is very questionable whether the first Christians were already familiar with the traditional forms of the short berakhot as we find them in later rabbinic sources. It is much more likely that this euchological genre was still in development and that the process of standardization of that formula, especially the opening, had not yet come to an end, but, on the contrary, had just started.[37]

What does this mean for the sources underlying the prayers of *Did.* 9 and 10? How to demarcate the Jewish and the Christian elements in the prayers, assuming that such a procedure is legitimate, at least to some extent. Which elements may be attributed to pre-Christian traditions and which may be the result of a reworking by a Christian author?

All things considered, two major conclusions seem to emerge. First, one should be very cautious about making too much out of the prevalence of the "thanksgiving". It is very well possible that, in this respect, the Didache simply reflects a certain stage in the development of Jewish prayer traditions in which certain ancient forms of what would later become the typically rabbinic berakha coexisted with forms which began by forms derived from the verb "hodah", such as we find them in the Qumran scrolls.[38] Second, the postulate of a Jewish Hellenistic intermediary, as formulated by Dibelius and others, may best be abandoned. Needless to say, the last-mentioned conclusion has important implications for the interpretation of the "thanksgivings" of the Didache. It follows that, as far as their content is concerned, the part taken by the specifically Christian element may have been considerably larger than Dibelius has believed. Most probably, the Christianisation will not have been reduced to some additions mentioning Jesus, the servant and the church. The introduction of other characteristic themes, such as "life", "knowledge", the "vine", the "dwelling of the Name" may equally have been the result of this process. In this connection, it may be recalled that Johannes Betz has already called attention to the fact that these themes also occur in the gospel of John, for instance in the sixth chapter.[39] One cannot exclude the possibility that the Christian author who reworked the Jewish prayer traditions, was somehow affiliated to circles in which the traditions which eventually would result in the fourth gospel, were developing.

3 The Place of *Did.* 9-10 in the Overall Development of the Early Christian Eucharist

If we accept the reconstruction of the development of the ritual meal underlying *Did.* 9-10 proposed in the preceding section, the question finally arises how we should

---

[37] Cf. Heinemann, *Prayer in the Talmud*. See also Rouwhorst, "Identität durch Gebet," 45-52.
[38] See, in particular, the Hodayoth (cf. García Martínez-Tigchelaar, *The Dead Sea Scrolls*, 147-203, esp. 163 ff. Cf. also Van de Sandt-Flusser, *The Didache*, 320vv).
[39] See Betz, "The Eucharist in the Didache," 244-75.

situate it in the overall history of the Eucharist, and more in general, ritual meal traditions in early Christianity.

While examining the numerous publications which have been devoted to the chapters concerned, one will discover that very diverging theories have been developed in answering this question. To conclude my contribution, I will review those theories and briefly consider their pros and cons. For the sake of clarity, I will emphasise that here I will discuss no more certain views which marginalize the chapters by considering the meal concerned as a non-eucharistic agape or by ascribing to the Didache a fairly late date (second half of the second century).[40] Nor will I repeat the remarks I have made about the hypothesis according to which Chapters 9 and 10 would constitute an introduction to a "real Eucharist" or would refer to some parts of an early Christian symposium.

Before examining the various theories, I would like to point out that two principal issues are at stake here. On the one hand, the view one adopts with regard to the place of the Eucharist of the Didache crucially depends on the dating of the sources used by the redactor as well as that of the final stage of the document. On the other hand, it is inextricably connected with one's ideas about the overall development of ritual meals in early Christianity. I have touched upon this issue already before. Yet there is one specific question related to it which I have not yet mentioned. That is the relationship between the institution narratives and the liturgical practice, more specifically the ritual meals of the first generations of Christians. The crucial question here is whether these narratives are seen as exclusively "historical" reports about the last meal of Jesus and his disciples or whether they are believed to relate in one way or another to the ritual meals of early Christians. As for the last-mentioned alternative for which the majority of the scholars appear to opt, one may distinguish two variants. On the one hand, one may maintain, at least to a certain degree, the historical character of the institution narratives and, in addition, argue that the Christians modelled their own ritual meals held regularly, for instance once a week, on the pattern of the meal described in this narrative.[41] On the other hand, several scholars tend to deny or to strongly relativize the historical character of the institution narratives, while at the same time ascribing them a (primarily) etiological function: according to them, these narratives were created or even invented to legitimise the ritual meal practices of the first Christians.[42] In a way, the latter view is diametrically opposed to the former, but it has at least one thing in common with the "historical" interpretation mentioned: to fulfil its etiological function it has to be assumed that the meal described had roughly the same structure and content as the early Christian meals because otherwise the supposedly foundational narrative would miss the mark. Here now arises a serious problem as has already been noticed before.

[40] Cf. for the (English and more especially Anglican) scholars defending such a late date: Draper, "The Didache in Modern Research," 10-11.

[41] This position is defended in Jeremias' classical work *Die Abendmahlsworte Jesu.*

[42] Thus, for instance, De Jonge, "The Early History of the Lord's Supper," 217-20.

Every scholar taking part in this discussion, will be obliged to clarify his position with regard to these two key questions. Theoretically, four combinations are possible. In practice, only three of them play a decisive role in the debate.

1. Some scholars hold the view that the institution narratives of the gospel reflect a liturgical practice which was widespread in early Christianity and they combine it with a very early dating of the sources used by the redactor of the Didache. In that case, the ritual described or alluded to in these sources can be accounted for as a very archaic form of Eucharist which was older than the celebration underlying the institution narrative. The ritual pattern emerging from those sources would have soon been superseded by a celebration based on the model of the Last Supper. This appears to be the position of, for instance Johannes Betz[43] and Enrico Mazza[44] and equally of some New Testament exegetes who distinguish two traditions in the New Testament institution narratives, the oldest one being highly eschatological and the more recent one focussed on the commemoration of the death of Jesus or on the sacramental interpretation of bread and wine (the Didache may then be appealed to as a testimony to the oldest eschatological stratum of the institution narratives).[45] The question that then immediately arises is how we should account for the fact that the redactor of the Didache has preserved this archaic type of Eucharist which was outdated in his time. Some scholars, at least Johannes Betz, argue that in fact the redactor did not preserve that archaic celebration, but that he has transformed it into an agape-celebration.[46] However, as I have tried to demonstrate in the first part of my lecture, the agape-thesis in whatever form it may be presented, does not match an objective reading of the text as transmitted by the final redaction.

2. A second solution is provided by some sort of theory of the dual origins of the Eucharist. The most comprehensive version of this theory is doubtless the one elaborated by Hans Lietzmann.[47] The most essential characteristic of his well-known hypothesis is that, for a rather long period, two types of Eucharist existed side by side in early Christianity, albeit in different communities and geographical areas. One of those traditions was based on Paul's interpretation of the death of Christ. It is reflected in the various institution narratives and its principal focus was on the remembrance of the death of Christ. The other had its roots in the table-fellowship of the historical Jesus and was continued in the meals with the risen Lord. The crown witness of this meal-tradition, called the "breaking-of-bread," is precisely the Didache.[48] In this hypothesis, the redactor of the Didache ceases to

---

[43] Betz, "The Eucharist in the Didache."

[44] Mazza, "Didaché IX-X." Cf. also Cullmann, *Urchristentum und Gottesdienst*, 21-23 (though Cullmann does not explicitly deal with the question of the dating of the Didache).

[45] Cf. for an overview of the different hypotheses and solutions developed by New Testament scholars: Feneberg, *Christliche Passafeier und Abendmahl*, 60-70.

[46] Betz, "The Eucharist in the Didache," 251.274-275.

[47] Lietzmann, *Messe und Herrenmahl*.

[48] Cf. *Ibid.*, 230-238 / 188-194.

be an isolated and somewhat strange conservative. In fact, he is a representative of a practice which eventually would be superseded by the "Pauline" type of Eucharist. But the type of Eucharist he transmitted was far from exceptional in early Christianity. Many Christian communities were familiar with it and we still find traces of it in the various apocryphal Acts of the Apostles and in the Egyptian Euchologion of Serapion.[49]

3. There is a third possibility of explaining the difference between the structure of the Last Supper as presented by the institution narratives on the one hand and the early Christian Eucharist. This third solution which recently appeared to have found an increasing number of proponents is to deny that the institution narratives reflect an early Christian meal practice.[50] Naturally it is not denied that, at a certain moment, the first Christians started modelling their Eucharist after the pattern of the Last Supper, but it is argued that they started doing so only very gradually. The imitation of the Last Supper is viewed as a long process which eventually came to a close in the third and fourth century when a version of the institution narrative was incorporated in the eucharistic prayer. In this hypothesis, the reconstruction of the development of the eucharist can no longer be based on indications derived from the institution narratives. First and foremost, one has to draw upon sources which directly refer or allude to early Christian meal practice. These are basically the texts which Lietzmann held to belong to the "breaking-of-bread" tradition and the Didache holds a key position among these sources.

While overlooking these three solutions, I think that, in the present state of the research, the third one is the most plausible. It does not oblige us to postulate an extremely early date of the prayers of thanksgiving of the Didache, prior to the emergence of the oldest versions of the institution narrative, as for instance Mazza does. Neither do we need to consider the redactor of the Didache as a somewhat extravagant conservative who had antiquarian ideas about the liturgy. Further, it is not necessary to hypothesise that the liturgical traditions of the communities of the Didache were radically different from those of more Hellenised or Paulinian churches. Finally, this view matches best the profoundly altered picture we have of the development of the Eucharist in the second and third century.

On the other hand, some unanswered questions remain. In particular, the precise relationship between the institution narratives and early Christian liturgical practice remains enigmatic. First of all, it may be asked with what purpose the institution narratives were transmitted, assuming that it was not merely in order to preserve historical information about the last meal Jesus had held with his disciples. In case one would deny the basically historical character of the narratives, the question would even rise why they were composed or "invented" at all. It is interesting to notice in this regard that A. McGowan and P. Bradshaw have advanced the hypothesis that these texts for long

---

[49] Cf. *Ibid.*, 256-263 / 209-215.
[50] See in particular McGowan, "Is there a Liturgical Text ...?," 73-87. Cf. also Bradshaw, "Parallels between Early Jewish and Christian Prayers," 31-32.

fulfilled a catechetical rather than a liturgical function in early Christianity.[51] However, if one would accept that hypothesis, it would be difficult to imagine that the catechesis in question would not relate in one way or the other to liturgical practice, apart from the fact that most probably it was less easy to make a distinction between catechesis and liturgy than it is in modern church communities. Moreover, the institution narratives contain several elements which might be best accounted for by assuming a liturgical background.[52] The question arises at least how we should otherwise account for the fact that two versions of the institution narratives (1 Corinthians 11 and the long version of Luke) contain the command to "do this in memory of Me"?

Elsewhere, I have tried to answer these questions by arguing that at least on one specific occasion there may have been a closer connection between the Eucharist on the one hand and the institution narratives on the other hand, namely during the yearly Quartodeciman Passover. What the narratives and the yearly celebration of Passover had in common was a strong focus on the commemoration of the death of the Lord and, in addition, the Christian feast was concluded by a ritual meal. Whether this means that the institution narratives were recited during the Christian Passover or not, perhaps as part of the Passion Narrative, must remain a matter of speculation, although I consider it to be an attractive hypothesis. Anyhow, the institution narratives of the Synoptic Gospels appear pre-eminently apt to serve as etiological stories tracing the origins of the yearly Passover celebration back to the initiative of Jesus,[53] whereas they hardly seem appropriate to fulfil that same foundational function with regard to the Eucharist of the Didache and of several other early Christian meal traditions which do not focus on the commemoration of the death of Christ.

I will conclude with some brief remark about the relationship between the Didache and Matthew, the central theme of this symposium, which I was asked to pay special attention to. In fact, I have tried to do so, but, regretfully, I must admit that the conclusion to which I have arrived regarding this question, is a rather negative one. I am aware that there are striking similarities between practically all the chapters of the Didache and Matthew, but Chapter 9 and 10 appear to be an exception. In fact, the features which these chapters have in common with Matthew are very reduced in number. The ritual pattern of the meal underlying the sources as well as the final stage does not specifically recall the gospel of Matthew, but rather the Acts of the Apostles, the gospel of Luke and, possibly, Paul's first Letter to the Corinthians, Chapter 10 and of course the aforementioned Jewish berakhot. As for their content, the prayers of thanksgiving definitely have a number of elements in common with the Jewish

[51] *Ibid.*

[52] See Jeremias, *Die Abendmahlsworte Jesu,* 100-118; Pesch, *Das Abendmahl und Jesu Todesverständnis.*

[53] Obviously this remark does not pertain to the Quartodeciman celebration of the Christians of Asia, as for instance attested by Melito of Sardis (cf. for instance Stewart-Sykes, *The Lamb's High Feast*). As a matter of fact, the Asian Quartodeciman tradition was in a special way related to Johannine tradition, whereas precisely in the fourth gospel an institution narrative is lacking. However, it is very probable that in the first century C.E. the phenomenon of Quartodecimanism was not limited to Asia (cf. Rouwhorst, "The Quartodeciman Passover," 157-160) and, in addition, that the Asian type of Quartodecimanism was not the only one known at that period.

berakhot which is referred to in almost all relevant publications. If this content does relate to any of the canonical gospels, it is that of John (no matter how this fact should be best accounted for). As for the gospel of Matthew, as far as I can see, Chaps. 9 and 10 have only two elements in common with this gospel, namely a rather striking proximity to Jewish tradition – which is characteristic of all the chapters for that matter – and the saying of *Did.* 9:5 which is either a quotation of Matthew 7:6 or – what seems more likely to both Huub van de Sandt[54] and many others, including myself – represents a very interesting variant of this saying.

I realise that this basically negative conclusion may sound deceiving. However, with regard to the aim of this conference which it is to clarify the relationship between the Didache and Matthew, it may have a certain relevance. If it cannot be denied that many passages of this source bear a clear resemblance whatsoever to the first gospel, the fact that this does not hold for some parts, is interesting enough and, anyway, should not remain unnoticed.

[54] See Van de Sandt, "Do not give what is holy," 223-246.

Chapter Nine

Les charismatiques itinérants dans la Didachè et dans l'Évangile de Matthieu

André Tuilier

Bibliothèque de la Sorbonne (Directeur honoraire), Paris (France)

Comparer la situation des charismatiques chrétiens itinérants dans l'Évangile de Matthieu et dans la Didachè est important pour apprécier correctement les deux textes et approfondir les origines du christianisme lui-même. En situant respectivement ces deux textes à leur époque, cette comparaison permettra de les dater en connaissance de cause en fournissant des repères utiles à cet égard. Encore faut-il préciser ce que sont ces charismatiques itinérants qui caractérisent la mission chrétienne dans l'Église primitive.

1 Les charismatiques itinérants dans la Didachè

À vrai dire, en dehors des apôtres, ces charismatiques n'apparaissent pas toujours explicitement comme tels dans l'Évangile de Matthieu. C'est la Didachè qui révèle leur existence dans cette mission. Elle est claire à ce sujet lorsqu'elle évoque des apôtres, des prophètes et des docteurs.[1] Tous sont considérés comme des ministres qualifiés de l'Évangile, qui visitent les communautés primitives pour leur annoncer la Bonne Nouvelle et les instruire du message chrétien. Les apôtres occupent la première place. Ils doivent être reçus comme le Seigneur dont ils sont les envoyés, et c'est pourquoi la Didachè les assimile implicitement au collège apostolique, puisque les deux titres successifs de l'ouvrage font référence aux douze disciples qui figurent dans l'Évangile de Matthieu (Matt 10:15).[2] Doit-on considérer que les apôtres cités au ch. 11 de la Dida-

---

[1] *Did.* 10:13. cf. 1 Cor 12:28-29: Καὶ οὓς μὲν ἔθετο ὁ θεὸς ἐν τῇ ἐκκλησίᾳ πρῶτον ἀποστόλους, δεύτερον προφήτας, τρίτον διδασκάλους, telles sont les trois fonctions ecclésiastiques de caractère charismatique que Paul cite pour l'Église de Corinthe. C'est après avoir placé ces trois fonctions sur le même rang que l'Apôtre évoque les charismes personnels qui sont introduits par l'adverbe ἔπειτα. Sur les ministères dans la Didachè, voir notamment Niederwimmer, "Zur Entwicklungsgeschichte des Wanderradikalismus," 145-167; De Halleux, "Les ministères dans la Didachè," 5-29; Schöllgen, "Wandernde oder sesshafte Lehrer?," 19-26; Ysebaert, *Die Amtsterminologie im Neuen Testament*; Rordorf-Tuilier, *La Doctrine des douze apôtres*, 51-63. 226-29; Van de Sandt-Flusser, *The Didache*, 330-364.

chè appartenaient tous à ce collège? Le texte ne permet pas d'être catégorique à ce sujet, et nous reviendrons ultérieurement sur le problème qu'il pose à la critique moderne. Mais, étant donné que les apôtres sont considérés par le didachiste comme les envoyés du Seigneur,[3] ils jouissent d'une situation particulière dans les communautés qu'ils visitent. Ils sont peu nombreux d'ailleurs et, s'ils sont des imposteurs ou s'ils résident plus de trois jours au même endroit (11:5), l'auteur les assimile aux faux prophètes qui sont fréquemment cités dans le texte lui-même.[4] L'apostolat est donc assimilé au prophétisme parmi les charismes de l'Église primitive. Annoncer l'Évangile, c'est aussi annoncer le retour et la présence du Christ parmi les hommes.

C'est pourquoi les prophètes jouent un rôle important dans la Didachè, qui leur réserve une place de choix entre les apôtres et les docteurs.[5] Ils doivent être respectés par les chrétientés qu'ils visitent, parler sous l'inspiration de l'Esprit et avoir les façons de vivre du Seigneur (11:7-8). À l'instar des apôtres, leur enseignement doit être également prouvé par leur conduite (11:8). Tout prophète qui n'agit pas conformément à la mission qu'on attend de lui est un faux prophète. Il ne devra pas être écouté, s'il demande de l'argent aux fidèles (11:12). Qu'on ne le juge pas cependant, si sa quête a pour but de soulager ceux qui sont dans le besoin *(ibid.)*.

Mais si les apôtres occupent une place éminente dans les communautés chrétiennes qu'ils visitent, les prophètes y jouent un rôle majeur parce qu'ils sont vraisemblablement plus nombreux qu'eux et qu'ils essaient de s'y établir dès que les Églises sont stables.[6] Ils peuvent recevoir les prémices du pressoir et de l'aire et des bœufs et des brebis.[7] Ils sont même considérés comme les grands prêtres de cette communauté, et l'information permet de supposer vraisemblablement qu'ils présidaient à ce titre

---

[2] Ces douze disciples qui sont exclusivement appelés apôtres, quand Matthieu les énumère comme tels en présentant le collège apostolique: Καὶ προσκαλεσάμενος τοὺς δώδεκα μαθητὰς αὐτοῦ ἔδωκεν αὐτοῖς ἐξουσίαν πνευμάτων ἀκαθάρτων ὥστε ἐκβάλλειν αὐτά, καὶ θεραπεύειν πᾶσαν νόσον καὶ πᾶσαν μαλακίαν. Τῶν δὲ δώδεκα ἀποστόλων τὰ ὀνόματα ἐστιν ταῦτα... Τούτους τοὺς δώδεκα ἀπέστειλεν ὁ Ἰησοῦς... On relèvera ici la distinction entre les substantifs μαθητάς et ἀποστόλων, qui désignent les mêmes hommes dans des situations différentes. Ces derniers sont des disciples avant d'être des apôtres et d'être envoyés en mission comme tels par le Christ. Voir plus loin. Le substantif ἀπόστολος a un sens très précis dans le Nouveau Testament. C'est ainsi que l'auteur de l'Épître aux Hébreux, 3:1, appelle Jésus lui-même apôtre et grand prêtre, ἀπόστολον καὶ ἀρχιερέα.

[3] *Did.* 11:4: Que tout apôtre qui vient chez vous soit reçu comme le Seigneur!

[4] *Did.* 11:5, 6, 8, 9, 10; 16:3. Sur les faux prophètes dans la Didachè, voir Milavec, "Distinguishing True and False prophets," 117-136.

[5] *Did.* 11:3 les place sur le même plan que les apôtres: «Pour les apôtres et les prophètes..., agissez de cette manière».

[6] La tendance qu'ont les prophètes itinérants de s'établir dans les Églises où ils s'arrêtent pour un temps plus ou moins long est attesté par *Did.* 13:1: «Mais, tout vrai prophète, qui veut s'établir chez vous, mérite sa nourriture». Cf. Matt 10:10, et note 11. Tout en attestant cette tendance propre à l'époque de la Didachè (voir plus loin), ce verset révèle que les prophètes étaient le plus souvent au départ des charismatiques itinérants. Cf. Rordorf-Tuilier, *La Doctrine des douze apôtres*, 72. 226-29 et Van de Sandt-Flusser, *The Didache*, 330-64, qui sont moins affirmatifs à cet égard.

[7] *Did.* 11:13. La pratique ne signifie naturellement pas que tous les prophètes étaient établis d'une manière permanente dans les communautés chrétiennes. Mais la plupart étaient au départ des itinérants, notamment à l'époque où la majorité des Églises n'avaient pas de structure fixe. Ce sont la croissance et la dynamique propres aux communautés locales qui provoqueront le déclin et la disparition par étapes des ministères itinérants. Van de Sandt-Flusser, *ibid.*, ont raison d'affirmer la persistance de ces ministères itinérants au delà du 1er siècle.

l'Eucharistie. Cette pratique est confirmée par le ch. 15, qui affirme que les évêques et les diacres célèbrent la même liturgie que les prophètes et les docteurs.[8]

La présidence de cette célébration était effectivement propre au charisme prophétique, puisque l'Eucharistie annonce le retour du Christ, comme le précise le ch. 10:6 : *Maranatha*.[9] C'est ainsi que le texte peut dire, au ch. 11:11, que le prophète agit en vue du mystère de l'Église dans le monde et qu'on ne peut le contraindre d'enseigner ce qu'il fait notamment en assurant cette présidence et en exerçant son ministère charismatique. Les autres interprétations qui ont été données de la phrase «tout prophète éprouvé, vrai, qui agit en vue du mystère de l'Église dans le monde, mais qui n'enseigne pas de faire tout ce qu'il fait lui-même, ne sera pas jugé chez vous» (11:11), ne se situent pas dans la perspective eucharistique de l'initiation chrétienne et sont par conséquent dénuées de sens.[10] Cependant ce mystère est insondable et incommunicable à beaucoup d'égards. Tel est aussi le sens de la phrase en question. Par conséquent, comme nous le constaterons plus loin, les prophètes de la Didachè ne sont pas différents de ceux de l'Ancien Testament dans l'exercice de leur fonction charismatique (*ibid.*). Mais, à l'opposé de ces derniers qui annonçaient le Rédempteur, ils ont pour mission de prêcher son retour.

Pour leur part, les docteurs, qui s'établissent aussi peu à peu dans les Églises,[11] apparaissent être les collaborateurs des prophètes, comme les diacres le sont des évêques – ou des presbytres épiscopes – de la chrétienté primitive.[12] La comparaison est importante

---

[8] *Did.* 13:3 et *Did.* 15:1.Pour justifier le rapprochement que nous opérons entre le ch. 13:3 et le ch. 15:1-2, il faut effectivement admettre que, si la Didachè est faite de plusieurs sources différentes, le texte, tel qu'il nous a été transmis par le manuscrit de Jérusalem, est l'œuvre entière du même auteur. Dans leur première édition de la Didachè (1978), Rordorf-Tuilier avaient dit que les ch. 14 et 15 avaient été joints à ce texte postérieurement au travail du didachiste (93-94). Mais ils ont reconnu dans leur seconde édition de l'ouvrage que « la tension apparente qui existe entre les ch.14-15 et les autres ne permet pas de contester l'unité de la Didachè » (*Ibid.*, 227). C'est pourquoi on peut vraisemblablement rapprocher le ch. 13 du ch. 15:1-2, pour soutenir le parallélisme qui existe entre les prophètes et les épiscopes d'une part, les docteurs et les diacres d'autre part (voir plus loin). Ce parallélisme ressort du texte lui-même. Quant au terme «office» que Rordorf-Tuilier utilisent (193) pour traduire le substantif λειτουργίαν du ch. 15:1, il a en français une acception religieuse et civile qui répond parfaitement au double sens que le mot possède en grec.

[9] Cf. I Cor 16:23 qui exprime la même espérance eschatologique à la fin de la lettre. Cf. Milavec, "Distinguishing True and False prophets" pour les prophètes et l'Eucharistie.

[10] Pour la bibliographie de ces interprétations, voir Van de Sandt-Flusser, *The Didache*, p. 345, note 47.

[11] Immédiatement après le verset 13:1 que nous avons cité note 6, le didachiste affirme (13:2): « De la même manière, le vrai docteur mérite, lui aussi, comme l'ouvrier sa nourriture ». En se complétant, les deux textes révèlent que, venant de l'extérieur, les docteurs cherchent comme les prophètes à s'installer dans les Églises à l'époque de la Didachè. Cf. Matt 10:10, qui applique également aux apôtres en mission l'expression ὁ ἐργάτης τῆς τροφῆς αὐτοῦ (cf. Luc 10:7). On notera que la Didachè emploie justement cette expression au sujet des διδάσκαλοι, comme le veut la tradition juive. On sait effectivement que les rabbis avaient le droit de vivre des dons de leurs disciples dans certaines conditions (cf. 1 Cor 9:14-18 ; 2 Cor 11:7-11 et 1 Tim 5:18). Cette tradition rabbinique est parfaitement commentée par Van de Sandt-Flusser, *The Didache*, 345.

[12] *Did.* 15:1-2. Dans l'Église primitive, les docteurs sont d'abord, semble-t-il, des catéchistes, dont l'enseignement n'a pas la profondeur et l'autorité de celui des prophètes qui les précèdent dans la hiérarchie de l'époque. C'est pourquoi on peut croire que leur enseignement s'adressait de préférence à des néophytes, baptisés ou non, qui n'avaient pas la maturité suffisante pour saisir tous les degrés de l'initiation chrétienne. Le témoignage de la Lettre Festale 39 de saint Athanase (voir plus loin) sur l'usage de la Didachè conçue comme manuel d'enseignement des catéchumènes est significatif à cet égard. Au reste, la Didachè ne s'appesantit pas sur la fonction des διδάσκαλοι, parce que ces enseignants ne peuvent être des docteurs au sens strict. Ils sont avant tout des διδάσκοντες (11:1-2).

pour saisir le rôle des charismatiques itinérants répartis entre les apôtres, les prophètes et les docteurs. Sans que cet ordre hiérarchique ait toujours été très strict dans des communautés en pleine évolution, les docteurs étaient plus particulièrement chargés d'enseigner les principes de l'Évangile aux néophytes, baptisés ou non. Mais cette mission, était également le fait de tous les charismatiques itinérants du christianisme primitif, quels qu'en fussent la nature et le degré. La Didachè est claire à cet égard, puisqu'elle introduit de cette manière les chapitres consacrés aux apôtres, aux prophètes et aux docteurs: «Si quelqu'un vient pour vous enseigner tout ce qui a été dit précédemment,» [c'est-à-dire les Deux Voies et la pratique liturgique] « recevez-le» (11:1).[13]

Cet enseignement était donc la tâche essentielle de ce christianisme et de ses charismatiques. À cet égard, l'Église se situe dans la perspective de la tradition synagogale du judaïsme post-exilique, où l'enseignement religieux et moral joue un rôle fondamental dans la culture juive. C'est cette préoccupation qui ressort des deux titres successifs de la Didachè: «Doctrine des Douze apôtres» ou «Doctrine du Seigneur (enseignée) aux nations par les Douze apôtres.»[14]

C'est aussi de cette manière que l'ouvrage se situe dans le prolongement des deux derniers versets de l'Évangile de saint Matthieu, qui rapportent en ces termes le testament du Christ à ses disciples : «Allez donc, de toutes les nations, faites des disciples, les baptisant au nom du Père et du Fils et du Saint Esprit, leur apprenant à garder tout ce que je vous ai prescrit.»[15]

C'est apparemment cette conclusion de l'Évangile de Matthieu à laquelle répond le titre long de l'ouvrage, en affirmant que celui-ci contient l'enseignement des douze apôtres aux nations. Autrement dit, il existe un lien étroit entre ce titre et la mission que le Christ a confiée à ses disciples auprès des nations dans cet évangile.

2   L'Évangile de Matthieu et les charismatiques

Mais, si la Didachè se situe dans l'accomplissement de la mission prévue par le texte évangélique, celui-ci appartient nécessairement à l'époque antérieure à cet accomplissement. C'est pourquoi les noms des charismatiques itinérants qui apparaissent dans la Didachè n'existent pas dans l'Évangile de Matthieu, ou tout au moins n'ont pas le même sens dans cet évangile. Dans saint Matthieu, le substantif προφήτης s'applique avant tout aux prophètes de l'Ancien Testament et à Jean Baptiste, qui est consi-

---

[13] *Did.* 11:1. Dans la mesure où ce verset introduit justement les chapitres sur les apôtres, les prophètes et les docteurs, Neymeyr, *Die christlichen Lehrer*, 139-55; Schöllgen, "Wandernde oder sesshafte Lehrer?;" et Van de Sandt-Flusser, *The Didache*, 342-43, se sont posés la question de l'existence des docteurs itinérants. On peut de fait croire que ces derniers n'apparaissent qu'après une certaine période et qu'au départ les apôtres et les prophètes constituent seuls la hiérachie missionnaire de l'Église. Mais G. Schöllgen, *ibid.*, a répondu négativement à cette question. Voir Rordorf-Tuilier, *La Doctrine des douze apôtres*, 54.

[14] Sur les deux titres de la Didachè, voir Rordorf-Tuilier, *ibid.*, 13-17.

[15] Matt 28:19-20: πορεύθεντες οὖν μαθητεύσατε πάντα τὰ ἔθνη βαπτίζοντες αὐτούς..., διδάσκοντες αὐτοὺς τηρεῖν πάντα ὅσα ἐνετειλάμην ὑμῖν. Les verbes μαθητεύω et διδάσκω, qui apparaissent ensemble dans ce passage, soulignent tout particulièrement le caractère initiatique de l'enseignement du Christ. μαθητεύω a un sens prégnant à cet égard; cf. Matt 13:52 et Actes 14:21. Cf. Rordorf-Tuilier, *Ibid.*, 15-17, et Van de Sandt-Flusser, *The Didache*, 84-85 et 343, note 41.

déré comme le plus grand et le dernier d'entre eux (Matt 11:10, cf. 14:5). Même si le Christ est également appelé προφήτης par la foule et par ses admirateurs, Il refuse ostensiblement de prendre ce titre à son compte en dénonçant les faux prophètes.[16] Il n'a pas besoin d'être reconnu comme tel, puisqu'il accomplit lui-même les prophéties de l'Ancien Testament et de Jean Baptiste sur sa mission. En revanche, la situation sera tout à fait différente à l'époque apostolique à laquelle appartient la Didachè. À cette époque, les prophètes ont de nouveau leur raison d'être pour annoncer le retour du Christ et entretenir cette espérance, qui était celle de la primitive Église dans une perspective eschatologique immédiate. Ils sont d'ailleurs prévus par le Christ dans les invectives qu'Il prononce contre les Pharisiens avant sa passion : «Voici que j'envoie vers vous, leur dit-il, des prophètes, des sages et des scribes. Vous en tuerez et mettrez en croix, vous en flagellerez dans vos synagogues et vous les pourchasserez de ville en ville» (Matt 23:34).

Le verbe ἀποστέλλω, qui est employé par le Christ à cet endroit, confirme d'ailleurs que la différence qui existe entre les prophètes de la Didachè et ceux de l'Évangile de Matthieu s'applique également aux apôtres, qui seront exclusivement considérés comme tels après la mort et la résurrection du Christ. C'est pourquoi le substantif ἀπόστολοι est utilisé d'une manière exceptionnelle pour désigner les Douze dans cet évangile, qui appelle couramment ces derniers les disciples (μαθηταί) du Seigneur.[17] Ce terme convient parfaitement aux Douze pendant la vie de Jésus. Si le Christ ne peut s'appeler lui-même prophète pour les raisons que nous venons d'évoquer, Il est en revanche considéré par Matthieu comme le Maître par excellence de ceux qui le suivent. Au reste, fidèles ou hostiles à sa mission, les interlocuteurs de Jésus s'adressent à Lui en l'appelant à leur tour διδάσκαλος ou Rabbi.[18] Qu'il soit grec ou araméen, le substantif Maître a un sens fort dans la tradition juive et dans la tradition hellénistique, où il désignait le chef d'une école philosophique ou d'une secte religieuse qui était reconnu comme tel.[19] Ce chef avait nécessairement des disciples auxquels il enseignait sa doctrine et c'est pourquoi les futurs apôtres sont appelés μαθηταί pendant la vie de Jésus. C'est exclusivement après la Résurrection du Christ et après avoir reçu le Saint-Esprit qu'ils seront effectivement des apôtres (ἀπόστολοι) envoyés en mission par le Seigneur.

[16] Matt 7:15: Προσέχετε ἀπὸ τῶν ψευδοπροφητῶν. Le Christ refuse implicitement le titre de prophète au moment où Pierre reconnaît en Lui le Fils de Dieu, Matt 16:17. Quant aux foules, elles reconnaissaient notamment Jésus – ὁ προφήτης Ἰησοῦς – comme un prophète le jour des Rameaux, Matt 21:11. Cf. Matt 21:46: εἰς προφήτην αὐτὸν εἶχον. Cf. note 4.

[17] Voir note 2.

[18] Le terme διδάσκαλος attribué à Jésus est fréquent chez saint Matthieu. Il est utilisé par dérision quand les Pharisiens et les Sadducéens s'adressent au Christ (Matt 12:38; 19:16; 22:16, 24, 36). Pour l'équivalent sémitique ῥαββί, voir Matt 23:7-8. Les termes διδάσκαλος ou ῥαββί ont une connotation si forte que Jésus défend à ses apôtres de les revendiquer pour eux (Matt 23:8).

[19] Si le substantif διδάσκαλος désignait à l'origine l'enseignement du grammairien dans l'Antiquité classique, il est appliqué à partir de l'époque hellénistique et de l'époque romaine aux chefs d'école philosophique ou de secte religieuse. Pour les Juifs, où l'enseignement synagogal constituait le fondement de l'éducation intellectuelle, religieuse et morale à tous les degrés du savoir, le titre διδάσκαλος ou ῥαββί atteste la maîtrise du savoir qu'un scribe a pu obtenir dans son enseignement et dans l'interprétation des textes. Mais beaucoup revendiquaient ce titre sans le mériter ; cf. Matt 23:7. C'est pourquoi on peut croire que le terme διδάσκαλος n'a pas nécessairement dans la Didachè l'acception magistrale qu'il avait dans le judaïsme officiel du temps. Sur le sens de ce terme, voir Van de Sandt-Flusser, *The Didachè*, 340-41.

En attendant, ces apôtres sont exclusivement des disciples à l'écoute de la parole et de l'enseignement du Maître. Le caractère initiatique de cet enseignement est clairement attesté par les deux degrés qui lui sont propres et qui sont exprimés par le Christ en ces termes : «À vous,» [dit-il à ses disciples] «il a été donné de connaître le mystère du royaume des cieux, mais aux autres pas... c'est pourquoi je parle en paraboles.»[20] Tel est le caractère initiatique de la doctrine chrétienne, qui s'adresse en paraboles à la multitude et qui réserve le sens caché de ces paraboles et la quintessence de cette doctrine à un petit nombre de disciples.

On comprend dès lors comment le terme ἀπόστολος ne pouvait s'appliquer aux apôtres qu'après une série d'épreuves qui devaient leur permettre de mériter le titre d'envoyé du Seigneur. Très rapidement d'ailleurs, ce terme dépassera le cercle des onze disciples qui avaient survécu comme tels après la trahison de Judas et la mort du Maître. Le choix de Matthias pour remplacer Judas[21] et l'appel personnel de Paul à l'apostolat étendront bientôt l'acception du substantif ἀπόστολος, en incluant avec les Onze d'autres personnalités qui n'avaient pas été les proches disciples du Seigneur pendant sa vie terrestre, et qui étaient progressivement envoyées en mission par ces derniers et par Paul pour les remplacer et fonder à leur tour des communautés chrétiennes.

Tels seront Timothée, Tite ou Clément de Rome par exemple.[22] Alors que les apôtres avaient disparu ou étaient dispersés aux extrémités de la terre dans la seconde moitié du Iᵉʳ siècle, ces disciples de la seconde génération chrétienne étaient – comme le dit Clément de Rome lui-même (I, 44:3) – des personnalités éminentes, qui se substitueront peu à peu aux membres du collège apostolique pour continuer la mission des Douze et de Paul. Ce sont principalement eux qui figurent dans la Didachè sous le terme ἀπόστολος, sans que ce terme exclue naturellement dans le livre les Douze ou même saint Paul.[23]

---

[20] Matt 13:11-13; cf. Luc 8:10, qui développe ce passage en le commentant.

[21] Actes 1:22-26. On sait que les apôtres cherchaient un témoin du Seigneur ressuscité pour remplacer Judas, et que Matthias fut élu à ce titre. Il avait été mis en concurrence avec un certain Joseph Barsabas. D'après Papias de Hiérapolis cité par Eusèbe de Césarée, *Histoire ecclésiastique* III, 39, 9-10 (Migne, *PG* 20, 300 A, et Bardy, *Eusèbe de Césarée: Histoire ecclésiastique* 1, 155), ce Joseph Barsabas avait été sauvé par la grâce du Seigneur du poison mortel qu'il avait bu.

[22] D'après Actes 1:22 notamment, on a pu croire qu'il fallait avoir été disciple du Seigneur pendant sa vie terrestre et témoin de sa Résurrection pour mériter le nom d'apôtre. Mais, puisque le substantif ἀπόστολος signifie étymologiquement l'envoyé de quelqu'un, il a pu désigner dans la seconde génération chrétienne ceux qui avaient reçu une mission des apôtres auprès des communautés chrétiennes pour aider ces apôtres et les remplacer en exerçant les fonctions que les Douze et Paul accomplissaient auprès des Églises, qu'ils avaient fondées. Le fait apparaît clairement dans 1 Tim 1:3 et dans Tite 1:5. Quant à Clément de Rome, les deux épîtres qui lui sont attribuées ont été insérées jusqu'au IVᵉ siècle dans le canon du Nouveau Testament, parce qu'elles avaient une autorité équivalente à celle d'un apôtre. Enfin, on sait aussi que Barnabé, le compagnon de saint Paul, fut aussi considéré comme un apôtre par Actes 14:14 et par la tradition ecclésiastique ancienne, parce qu'il a été envoyé en mission par l'Esprit Saint et par l'Église. Cf. Rordorf-Tuilier, *La Doctrine des douze apôtres*, 58-59; Van de Sandt-Flusser, *The Didache*, 343.

[23] Mais les Douze et saint Paul avaient disparu pour la plupart à l'époque de la rédaction de la Didachè. Quant aux soixante-dix disciples évoqués par Luc 10:1-12 dans un récit qui démarque celui de saint Matthieu, 10:6-16, ils ont pu devenir de véritables apôtres après la Résurrection du Christ. Mais Luc, *ibid.*, ne permet pas de croire qu'ils ont été nécessairement des envoyés du Seigneur après sa Résurrection.

Quant aux docteurs, ils n'apparaissent pas non plus dans l'Évangile de saint Matthieu, avec le sens sous lequel ils sont compris dans la Didachè. Mais si le terme διδάσκαλος désigne exclusivement dans cet Évangile le Maître par excellence, c'est-à-dire le Christ, il n'en est pas moins vrai que le verbe διδάσκω, dont ce terme est issu, s'applique chez saint Matthieu à la fonction enseignante, qui était propre à la tradition synagogale et qui apparaît encore dans la Didachè. Certains emplois sont significatifs à cet égard. Pendant sa mission en Galilée, Jésus enseignait dans les synagogues en dehors des discours qu'il adressait aux foules et à ses disciples, et il enseignera notamment dans la synagogue de Nazareth.[24] Plus tard, il enseignera dans le temple de Jérusalem (Matt 21:23) et la pratique confirme son magistère de docteur et de Rabbi aux yeux de tous. Même si les διδάσκαλοι de la Didachè n'ont pas ce magistère, leur rôle n'en révèle pas moins la persistance de cette pratique synagogale dans la pédagogie catéchétique de l'Église primitive. Ce rôle ne cessera pas de croître à l'époque apostolique. Les διδάσκαλοι susciteront notamment le moment venu les hérésies gnostiques et ils seront notamment à l'origine du διδασκαλεῖον alexandrin, qui sera créé au IIᵉ siècle pour combattre ces hérésies.[25] Au reste, en assimilant les διδάσκαλοι itinérants aux diacres de la hiérarchie sédentaire dans le christianisme primitif, le ch. 15 de la Didachè se situe dans une perspective d'avenir. Le diaconat devait effectivement tenir une place de choix pour l'enseignement des catéchumènes dans l'Église ancienne.[26]

Il est clair dès lors que la comparaison entre le premier Évangile et la Didachè, au regard des charismatiques itinérants de la primitive Église, situe la rédaction de cette dernière dans la période intermédiaire qui sépare la mission apostolique des Douze et de Paul, des premiers temps de l'épiscopat monarchique en Orient. A cette époque, les apôtres, les prophètes et les docteurs, qui constituaient la structure fondamentale de la communauté charismatique des origines,[27] sont en voie de disparition comme tels. Ils n'ont souvent plus qu'une mission adventice et, comme l'atteste la Didachè,

[24] Matt 9:35 et 13:54. Cf. Rengstorf, "διδάσκω, διδάσκαλος, νομοδιδάσκαλος, κτλ.," 138-68.

[25] Si l'on en croit Eusèbe de Césarée, *Hist. eccl.* V, 10, 1-4 (*PG* 20, 453 C - 456 B, et Bardy, *Eusèbe de Césarée: Histoire ecclésiastique 2*, 39-40), ce διδασκαλεῖον sera dirigé à cette époque par saint Pantène, avant d'être illustré par Clément d'Alexandrie et Origène. Mais il va sans dire que les responsables successifs de ce διδασκαλεῖον seront de vrais docteurs qui dispenseront un enseignement savant à la différence des διδάσκαλοι de l'Église naissante.

[26] D'après les *Constitutions apostoliques* VIII, 32, 2, ce sont les diacres qui présentaient les candidats au baptême à l'évêque et au presbyterium. Ce faisant, ils devaient témoigner que ces candidats étaient aptes, en donnant toutes les informations nécessaires à leur sujet. Ils participaient donc à la formation des catéchumènes, et c'est précisément ce qu'attestera entre autres le *De catechizandis rudibus* que saint Augustin adressera au diacre Deo Gratias de l'Église de Carthage. Naturellement, les prêtres pouvaient participer à cette catéchèse, comme le révèlent les *Huit catéchèses baptismales* prononcées par saint Jean Chrysostome, lorsqu'il était prêtre à Antioche (éd. Wenger, *Huit catéchèses baptismales inédites*). Mais les prêtres étaient plus particulièrement chargés comme διδάσκαλοι d'un enseignement supérieur de la théologie et de la spiritualité chrétiennes. Le fait ressort d'un examen attentif des fonctions qui leur sont réservées comme tels par les Constitutions apostoliques (éd. Metzger, *Les constitutions apostoliques*). Inversement, les diacres pouvaient parvenir dans certains cas à un enseignement supérieur de la théologie et de l'exégèse; le témoignage de saint Ephrem est significatif au IVᵉ siècle à cet égard. Il ne faut donc pas établir une séparation trop rigoureuse entre les fonctions des uns et des autres. La réalité était certainement plus complexe.

[27] 1 Cor 12:28. Voir à ce sujet note 1.

les communautés chrétiennes s'organisent peu à peu sur le plan local, en se choisissant elles-mêmes des épiscopes et des diacres, qui leur sont propres et qui n'existaient pas auparavant dans la plupart des cas (15:1-2). Ce choix est imposé par les besoins de la croissance des Églises et le dépérissement lent et progressif des charismatiques itinérants, qui ne suffisent plus aux nécessités issues de cette croissance.

Au reste, les limites, que le didachiste fixe à la présence de ces charismatiques dans les communautés chrétiennes, permettent de croire que les apôtres, les prophètes et les docteurs itinérants suscitaient à ses yeux les réserves de ces communautés, à des degrés divers.[28] L'hypothèse vient d'elle-même à l'esprit du lecteur du texte. En tout cas, pour toutes les raisons que nous venons d'évoquer, la Didachè appartient à l'époque intermédiaire que nous avons circonscrite et qui se situe aux alentours de 70-75 apr. J.-C.[29]

C'est précisément cette époque que suggèrent les rapports entre la Didachè et l'Évangile de Matthieu qui fut d'abord écrit en araméen, si l'on en croit les plus anciens témoignages patristiques depuis Papias d'Hiérapolis au début du IIe siècle.[30] Pour sa part, la Didachè ne connaît certainement pas cet Évangile dans la traduction grecque qui nous est parvenue par la tradition canonique. Les variantes qui existent entre les deux textes évangéliques – notre Évangile grec de Matthieu d'une part et l'Évangile grec du didachiste d'autre part – sont significatives à cet égard, dans le texte du Pater notamment. Mais, comme nous le préciserons plus loin, il n'en est pas moins vrai que l'Évangile grec de la Didachè est proche de notre Mathieu, sans en dépendre en ligne directe.

---

[28] *Did.* 11:13. Ces réserves sont nombreuses, et il est difficile de ne pas croire que les activités des charismatiques itinérants avaient subi des dérives et qu'il fallait les réglementer à l'époque de la Didachè. Mais il faut se méfier de toute position systématique. C'est pourquoi, on se reportera à l'exposé nuancé de Van de Sandt-Flusser, *The Didache*, 336-40, qui rapprochent justement *Did.* 11:15 de 1 Tim 3:1-13. Cf. aussi Rordorf-Tuilier, *La Doctrine des douze apôtres*, 62-63 et 228-29. Pour sa part, Niederwimmer, "Zur Entwicklungsgeschichte des Wanderradikalismus," souligne avec raison l'intégration progressive des charismatiques itinérants dans les communautés chrétiennes.

[29] Pour cette date qu'on peut fixer à la même époque par d'autres critères, voir Tuilier, "La Didachè et le problème synoptique." Cf. Rordorf-Tuilier, *La Doctrine des douze apôtres*, 232, et Van de Sandt-Flusser, *The Didache*, 48, note 128.

[30] Sur l'original araméen de l'Évangile de saint Matthieu et ses traductions en grec, le témoignage le plus caractéristique et le plus ancien est effectivement celui de Papias de Hiérapolis, cité par Eusèbe de Césarée, *Hist. eccl.* III, 39, 16 (*PG* 20, 300 C et Bardy, *Eusèbe de Césarée: Histoire ecclésiastique* 1, 157): Ματθαῖος μὲν οὖν Ἑβραΐδι διαλέκτῳ τὰ λόγια συνετάξατο, ἡρμήνευσεν δ' αὐτὰ ὡς ἦν δυνατὸς ἕκαστος. Gustave Bardy traduit le texte de cette manière: «Matthieu réunit donc en langue hébraïque les logia (de Jésus) et chacun les interpréta comme il en était capable» (157). Certes le verbe ἡρμήνευσεν peut signifier en même temps interpréter et traduire. Mais ces deux sens répondent précisément à la situation dans laquelle se trouve le texte de saint Matthieu, écrit en araméen et traduit en grec. De toute manière, l'information est celle d'un témoin digne de foi, puisque Papias avait connu la génération apostolique et qu'il avait composé un commentaire en cinq livres des paroles du Seigneur rassemblées par Matthieu; *Hist. eccl.* III, 39, 1 (*PG* 20, 296 A-B, et Bardy, *ibid.*, 153): τοῦ δὲ Παπία συγγράμματα πέντε... ἃ καὶ ἐπιγέγραπται Λογίων κυριακῶν ἐξηγήσεως. Il est clair dès lors que cet auteur du début du IIe siècle connaissait parfaitement les problèmes posés par les origines du premier évangile et sa diffusion. D'après ce qu'il dit, celui-ci était diffusé apparemment dans plusieurs versions – ou recensions – différentes en grec et en araméen à l'époque de la Didachè, et Papias utilisait une traduction qui n'est pas celle que nous lisons dans le canon du Nouveau Testament.

3   La comparaison entre la Didachè et l'Évangile de Matthieu

Quoi qu'il en soit, le déclin lent et progressif des charismatiques itinérants, qu'atteste la Didachè, pose d'une autre manière les rapports entre cette dernière et le premier Évangile. Quand on lit cet ouvrage qui a pour titre l'«Enseignement des Douze apôtres aux nations»,[31] on est frappé du caractère normatif qui lui est propre dans la primitive Église et qui le distingue de cet évangile, auquel il est lié cependant d'une manière ou d'une autre. Quels qu'ils soient, les charismatiques itinérants du premier siècle sont principalement jugés dans la Didachè sur leur conduite extérieure, et non sur l'initiation christique qui inspire cette conduite. C'est pourquoi on reconnaît mal dans cette œuvre le souffle évangélique, qui apparaît avec force dans le récit de saint Matthieu. Assurément, les premières recommandations du Christ à ses disciples dans ce récit (Matt 10:6-10) évoquent singulièrement la section évangélique de la Didachè par leur caractère normatif. Mais, soucieux de révéler la formation initiatique approfondie que les disciples recevaient de leur Maître, saint Matthieu montre comment ces derniers étaient appelés à découvrir progressivement le sens de la parole du Seigneur, par la foi, l'amour de Dieu et du prochain, la confiance dans l'Esprit divin, le renoncement à soi-même et à ses propres œuvres et l'invitation à accepter la souffrance et les épreuves qui les attendaient pour prêcher et imiter le Christ.[32]

C'est exclusivement de cette manière que les disciples du Christ peuvent remplir leur mission, et le message s'adresse à tous les charismatiques de l'Évangile, apôtres, prophètes, docteurs ou autres. Tel est le sens de la parole de Jésus qui accompagnait son enseignement par des expériences pratiques. Conformément à l'esprit et à la lettre de cet enseignement, les disciples sont invités par le Maître à chasser les démons et à accomplir des miracles à sa suite (Matt 17:16-17). C'est pourquoi, lorsqu'ils échouent dans cette mission charismatique et qu'ils demandent au Seigneur les raisons de cet échec, le Christ attribue sans hésitation celui-ci à leur manque de foi.[33] En revanche cette foi ne manquait pas à ceux que le Christ guérissait et qui peuvent être considérés à leur tour comme des témoins charismatiques de l'Évangile à cet égard.[34]

La portée de l'enseignement du Christ, fondé sur la prière et la vie intérieure, avait une valeur exemplaire pour les charismatiques itinérants de la primitive Église, et on s'étonne parfois que cet enseignement n'apparaisse pas explicitement dans la Didachè. Faut-il désormais penser qu'à l'époque de cette dernière, le souffle de la Bonne Nouvelle avait perdu sa vigueur première avec la disparition progressive de ces charismatiques, et qu'on devait exprimer ce souffle par l'enseignement des Deux Voies, qui était plus

---

[31] Voir plus haut et note 14 pour les deux titres de la Didachè.

[32] Matt 10:16 et suiv.: « Voici que je vous envoie comme des brebis au milieu des loups.» Suit la liste des épreuves qui accompagneront la mission des apôtres. Cf. *ibid.* 16:24 et 23:34.

[33] Matt 17:20. Le manque de foi des apôtres est souligné à cet endroit parce qu'il contraste avec l'épisode de la Transfiguration, qui précède immédiatement la scène (*ibid.* 17:13).

[34] Cf. notamment la foi du lépreux guéri par le Christ (Matt 8:1-4), celle du centurion dont Jésus guérit le serviteur (Matt 8:5-13), la guérison de l'hémoroïsse et de la fille d'un notable (Matt 9:18-26), la guérison de deux aveugles (Matt 9:27-31), les guérisons à Génésareth (Matt 14:34-36), la guérison de la fille de la Cananéenne (Matt 15:21-28), etc.

accessible aux fidèles que le message spirituel des Béatitudes et de l'Évangile de saint Matthieu aux disciples du Seigneur?[35]

C'est pourquoi la Didachè apparaît surtout comme le premier code de droit canonique que l'Église naissante adresse aux communautés chrétiennes de l'Orient grec. A vrai dire, en raison notamment de la disparition définitive des charismatiques itinérants au IIe siècle, ce code sera bientôt dépassé par l'essor religieux, politique et social de l'institution ecclésiastique et l'évolution rapide de la structure interne des Églises. C'est ainsi que, tout en inspirant successivement les *Canons ecclésiastiques des Saints apôtres*[36] et les *Constitutions apostoliques* qui en paraphrasent le texte,[37] la Didachè sera bientôt réservée à l'enseignement des catéchumènes en Orient. Tel est du moins ce qu'affirme au IVe siècle la 39e Lettre Festale de saint Athanase, qui présente un canon des Écritures dans l'Église ancienne.[38]

De fait, les prescriptions morales du texte s'adressaient particulièrement aux catéchumènes d'origine païenne, qui devaient surmonter les errements du paganisme à cet égard pour s'initier progressivement à la pratique des vertus chrétiennes, avant de recevoir l'onction baptismale. Cette pratique leur permettait de comprendre peu à peu la portée du message évangélique, dont ils apprenaient à pénétrer définitivement les arcanes au moment du baptême et pendant toute leur vie d'union au Christ. C'est vraisemblablement une interprétation du même ordre qu'il faut donner aux préceptes de la Didachè concernant les charismatiques itinérants. Ces préceptes reflètent pour leur part les conseils très simples qui étaient adressés aux communautés ecclésiastiques pour reconnaître l'authenticité de ces charismatiques dans la mission chrétienne, telle qu'elle est définie au ch.28:19-20 de l'Évangile de saint Matthieu.

À l'instar des Deux Voies dans le domaine qui leur est propre, les recommandations du didachiste concernant les charismatiques de l'époque apostolique étaient appelées

[35] Pour saint Matthieu, la foi exige un don total de la personne qui s'abandonne corps et âme au Christ, Matt 10:39: «Qui aura sauvé sa vie la perdra et qui perdra sa vie à cause de moi la sauvera». Cf. Matt 19:12, qui évoque ceux qui se sont faits eunuques pour le royaume des cieux. Ces paroles sont le fondement de la foi que le Christ exige de ses disciples, et qui leur permet seule de remplir leur mission apostolique et d'accomplir des miracles. Le don total exigé des disciples du Christ fait d'ailleurs l'objet d'une bonne part du ch. 10 de l'Évangile de saint Matthieu, Autrement dit, cet Évangile révèle les exigences spirituelles du ministère charismatique d'un point de vue intérieur, tandis que la Didachè exprime les manifestations de ce ministère sur le plan ecclésiastique.

[36] Pour les rapports entre la Didachè d'une part, les *Canons ecclésiastiques des Saints Apôtres* et l'*Epitome des canons des Saints Apôtres* d'autre part, voir Rordorf-Tuilier, *La Doctrine des douze apôtres*, 118-20, et Van de Sandt-Flusser, *The Didache*, 63-66.

[37] Cf. *Constitutions apostoliques*, VII, 1-32 (= Metzger, *Les constitutions apostoliques* 3, 18-65).

[38] *PG* 26, 1437 C (cf. *PG* 28, 432 B). On retiendra le titre attribué à la Didachè dans cette lettre: Διδαχὴ καλουμένη τῶν ἀποστόλων (cf. Joannou, *Discipline générale antique* 2, 71-76). Il va sans dire que le participe καλουμένη est ajouté par saint Athanase, qui entend justifier de cette manière la raison pour laquelle l'ouvrage est exclu du canon biblique. Pour sa part, Eusèbe de Césarée, *Hist. eccl.*, III, 25, 4, (*PG*, 20, 269 A, et Bardy, *Eusèbe de Césarée: Histoire ecclésiastique* 1, 134) s'exprimait dans des termes identiques en citant la Didachè parmi les livres contestés (ἀντιλεγόμενα): τῶν ἀποστόλων αἱ λεγόμεναι Διδαχαί. Van de Sandt-Flusser, *The Didache*, 86-88, se demandent cependant si le livre cité par saint Athanase dans cette lettre ne signifie pas les Deux Voies, à l'exclusion de la Didachè dans son ensemble. Mais, étant donné que le manuscrit de Jérusalem présente la Didachè avec l'Épître de Barnabé et les deux lettres de Clément de Rome aux Corinthiens, il est clair que, sous le titre de Doctrine attribuée aux apôtres, la tradition patristique désignait vraisemblablement l'ouvrage complet qui nous est parvenu sous ce titre.

à discipliner les activités de ces charismatiques, au moment même où la diffusion du texte de saint Matthieu dans le monde grec[39] permettait la pratique d'une vie chrétienne soucieuse d'éviter les dérives d'une prédication improvisée et d'un prophétisme incontrôlé. En dépit de son aspect réglementaire et de son caractère normatif – ou peut-être même à cause de cet aspect réglementaire et de ce caractère normatif – la Didachè se situe dans cette perspective et elle confirme vraisemblablement qu'elle appartient à l'époque où cet évangile se répand sous différentes versions en Orient.

Mais cette réflexion permet une conclusion de caractère général sur l'essor et le déclin des charismatiques dans la chrétienté primitive. Naturellement, ces charismatiques eurent un rôle prépondérant à l'époque où l'Évangile est principalement diffusé par des prédicateurs itinérants, apôtres ou prophètes, qui remplissaient oralement leur mission prophétique et évangélique. Cette pratique ne surprendra pas à cette époque où, sauf exception, les gens ne savaient ni lire ni écrire. Cependant, très rapidement, le besoin de fixer la tradition orale se fit sentir. Telle est l'origine des λόγια du Seigneur, rassemblés par Matthieu qui était vraisemblablement le seul membre du Collège apostolique susceptible de constituer ce recueil par écrit, puisqu'il était publicain et qu'il exerçait une profession administrative et comptable.

Pendant quelque temps, le recueil de Matthieu, écrit en araméen, fut diffusé seul dans l'Orient sémitique. Mais les besoins de la mission chrétienne auprès des populations de langue grecque dans l'Orient hellénisé entraînèrent nécessairement la traduction des *logia* du Seigneur de l'apôtre dans cette langue. Telle est l'origine de l'Évangile canonique que nous possédons sous le nom de l'Évangile de Matthieu. Cependant, comme l'indique Papias de Hiérapolis,[40] il y eut vraisemblablement à l'époque apostolique plusieurs versions grecques des *logia* du Seigneur réunis par cet apôtre. C'est pourquoi on peut dire que, sans connaître notre Évangile de Matthieu, le didachiste utilisait apparemment une traduction différente de la nôtre du texte original de Matthieu en araméen.

Au départ, ces versions concurrentes du texte original de Matthieu complétèrent la mission des charismatiques, qu'ils soient itinérants ou qu'ils soient établis dans une communauté, comme le révèlent les Actes des apôtres et les premières épîtres pauliniennes. Comme l'Évangile de Matthieu qui nous est parvenu, les λόγια du Seigneur comprenaient à la fois les paroles du Christ et le récit des miracles qui les accompagnaient, puisque le Messie doit guérir les corps et les âmes. Tel est l'Évangile du Seigneur cité explicitement par la Didachè.

Mais, grâce à son influence, cet Évangile exerce progressivement une autorité régulatrice qui se manifeste au détriment des charismatiques, et cette autorité régulatrice d'origine apostolique – sinon Matthieu lui-même – imposera plus tard la version canonique du texte grec de l'apôtre que nous possédons aujourd'hui. En tout état de cause, cette version canonique adoptée par l'Église dans son ensemble n'est vraisemblablement pas antérieure aux deux dernières décennies du premier siècle, comme on l'ad-

---

[39] Tout au moins d'un texte grec de l'Évangile de Matthieu, qui n'est pas celui qui nous est parvenu puisqu'il présentait des variantes par rapport à celui-ci (voir note 30). C'est seulement avec cette réserve que nous pouvons partager les conclusions de Van de Sandt-Flusser, *The Didache*, 48-50.

[40] Cf. Vaganay, "Matthieu," 946.

met couramment aujourd'hui.[41] En attendant, les exemplaires araméens de l'Évangile de Matthieu et les premières traductions grecques qui en ont été faites – complètes ou fragmentaires – circulaient librement en Orient, et cette diffusion était nécessairement inégale en raison des difficultés propres à la mission apostolique elle-même. C'est cette étape intermédiaire qui est attestée par la Didachè et qu'on peut situer au plus tard entre 70 et 75 apr. J.-C. Dans les premiers temps de la mission apostolique, les communautés chrétiennes se fondaient principalement sur l'accomplissement des prophéties de l'Ancien Testament pour prêcher le message du Seigneur. Désormais, le Nouveau Testament fait son apparition en imposant une catéchèse plus élaborée aux Églises. Parallèlement à l'Évangile de Marc, dont la rédaction est étroitement liée à saint Pierre et à l'Église de Rome isolée en Occident,[42] les *logia* de Matthieu exercent une primauté réelle en Orient, avant les récits évangéliques de Luc et de Jean. Les communautés orientales prennent leur essor et leur dynamique interne en retrouvant d'elles-mêmes avec ces *logia* la pratique synagogale de l'Écriture sainte, qui a désormais son plein épanouissement dans la lecture et le commentaire de la parole du Maître, telle qu'elle est rapportée par l'apôtre lui-même.[43]

On comprend dès lors comment, en dehors des facteurs sociaux qui ont précipité cette évolution, la diffusion et la traduction de l'Évangile de Matthieu ont pu favoriser également le déclin progressif des charismatiques itinérants, au profit de la hiérarchie sédentaire des Églises. Les docteurs seuls échapperont provisoirement à ce déclin. C'est que la diffusion de l'Évangile et de la littérature néotestamentaire favorisait l'essor de leur enseignement exégétique, avec les dérives gnostiques que cette fonction suscitait. On l'a dit plus haut. De toute manière, les charismatiques itinérants étaient dépassés par les développements de l'institution ecclésiastique et la prédication de l'Évangile exigeait de cette institution établie d'autres méthodes missionnaires mieux adaptées

[41] Si Matthieu n'est pas l'auteur de la traduction canonique de son Évangile, il est sûr que cette traduction est d'origine apostolique. C'est ainsi qu'une tradition attestée par plusieurs manuscrits grecs minuscules et par Théophylacte d'Ochrida, dans son commentaire de l'Évangile de Matthieu (*PG* 123, 145 C-D), attribue la traduction en question à l'apôtre Jean. Naturellement, cette tradition – ὡς λέγουσι dit Théophylacte au XIe siècle – est incertaine. Mais elle confirme l'origine apostolique de notre Matthieu grec.
[42] Avec celui de Papias de Hiérapolis cité par Eusèbe de Césarée, *Hist. eccl.*, III, 39, 15 (*PG* 20, 300 B-C, et Bardy, *Eusèbe de Césarée: Histoire ecclésiastique* 1, 156-57), les témoignages sur les origines de l'Évangile de saint Marc sont nombreux: Eusèbe, *ibid.* V, 8, 3 (*PG* 20, 449 A; Bardy, *ibid.* 2, 35); II, 15, 1-2 (*PG* 20, 172 B-173 A; Bardy, *ibid.* 1, 70-71) ; VI, 25, 5 (*PG* 20, 581 B; Bardy, *ibid.* 2, 126-27) ; III, 24, 10 (*PG* 20, 265 C-268 B; Bardy, *ibid.* 1, 131-32) ; VI, 14, 6-7 (*PG* 20, 552 B; Bardy, *ibid.* 2, 107). Et ils attestent que cet Évangile – le seul des quatre évangiles à se présenter comme tel (Marc 1:1) – a été composé à l'initiative de saint Pierre et à la requête des fidèles de celui-ci. Papias, *Hist. eccl.*, III, 39, 15, affirme d'ailleurs que Marc se distingue par sa structure littéraire des *logia* du Seigneur rassemblés par Matthieu (= Bardy, *ibid.* 1, 156-57).
[43] Puisque l'Évangile de Mathieu fut écrit et diffusé en araméen, il est clair que cet Évangile s'est d'abord répandu en Orient dans sa langue originale. C'est pourquoi saint Pantène a pu voir dans les Indes au IIe siècle un exemplaire araméen de ces *logia,* qui avait été apporté dans le pays par l'apôtre Barthélemy. Cf. Eusèbe de Césarée, *Hist. eccl.,* V, 10, 3 (*PG* 20, 456 A-B, et Bardy, *Eusèbe de Césarée: Histoire ecclésiastique* 2, 40). Mais l'information atteste également que les *logia* du Seigneur étaient au Ier siècle et au début du IIe siècle l'Évangile commun à la mission des apôtres dans tout l'Orient. Il est d'ailleurs pour l'Église ancienne l'Évangile par excellence. C'est pourquoi il est très vraisemblable que la source Q n'est pas autre chose que l'original araméen de cet Évangile. Cf. Tuilier, "La Didachè et le problème synoptique."

aux circonstances. À l'époque de la Didachè, comme le révèlent les Deux Voies, l'Église n'a pas encore totalement rompu avec le judaïsme officiel de cette époque et son caractère normatif, qui évoque la halakha. Mais cette halakha, pratiquée et prêchée par des charismatiques itinérants, apôtres ou autres,[44] suscitait nécessairement une opposition de plus en plus vive à l'autorité religieuse, sociale et cuturelle des scribes et des Pharisiens, qui étaient traités d'hypocrites par le didachiste et par saint Matthieu, et elle compromettait à terme le judaïsme, tel qu'il était conçu et vécu depuis le retour de l'exil. C'est pourquoi la Didachè et l'Évangile de Matthieu annoncent également la rupture prochaine entre ce judaïsme et les judéo-chrétiens.[45] Tel est le bilan qu'il faut tirer de la comparaison que nous avons faite entre la Didachè et le premier évangile au sujet de ces charismatiques.

[44] Sur la halakha dans le Nouveau Testament, voir Tomson, *Paul and the Jewish Halakha.*

[45] Peter J. Tomson a également montré, dans la communication qu'il a présentée au présent colloque sous le titre "The halakhic evidence of Didache 8 and Matthew 6," que le terme hypocrite désigne les Pharisiens dans les deux textes. De fait, le didachiste et l'apôtre contestent dans ces deux textes la manière dont les Pharisiens interprètent formellement la Loi juive au sujet du jeûne.

Christian itinerant charismatics in the Didache and in Matthew

ABSTRACT

A comparison between the Didache and Matthew's gospel with regard to the three classes of itinerant charismatics appearing in both writings reveals a variation in designation and meaning. The first class considered in the Didache, the apostles, should be welcomed "as the Lord" in the communities they visit, since they are the Lord's messengers. The Didache equates them implicitly with the apostolic college, since the twofold title of the document refers to the twelve apostles. The second group of charismatics are the prophets, who were more numerous than the apostles and tried to settle down in the local communities. They are valued as the high priests of the communities, and this information, in combination with the data of the 15th chapter, allows us to assert that they presided over the Eucharist. The third class are the teachers, who apparently are co-workers of the prophets. They were particularly responsible for teaching the evangelical principles to neophytes. This doesn't alter the fact, however, that according to the Didache all wandering charismatics were commissioned to teach (*Did.* 11:1), a command which is in line with the last two verses of Matthew's gospel (28:19-20).

The long title in the general heading of the Didache – mentioning the teaching of the twelve apostles to the nations – complies with the conclusion of Matthew. But if the Didache realizes the commission announced in the gospel, the latter inevitably belongs to the age preceding this development. The earlier origination of the gospel is also reflected in the different understanding of the three groups of charismatics in Matthew. The noun προφήτης is applied above all to the Old Testament prophets and to John the Baptist, whereas in subapostolic period (to which the Didache belongs) the prophets were contemporary figures who announced the return of Christ and tried to maintain this hope. Likewise, the Lord's disciples (μαθηταί) are frequently mentioned in Matthew's gospel to designate the Twelve, whereas the noun ἀπόστολος is found very rarely. Only after the death and the resurrection of Christ will this title, which very soon passed beyond the inner circle of disciples, be used. Also the teachers of the Didache do not appear in the same sense in Matthew, where the term διδάσκαλος exclusively designates the Master (Jesus).

It is thus clear that the comparison between Matthew and the Didache with respect to the itinerant charismatics of the primitive Church provides insight into the historical setting for the existence of apostles, prophets, and teachers (I Cor 12:28-29). The situation in the Didache fits the intermediate stage (70-75 C.E.) between the apostolic mission of the Twelve and the monarchical episcopacy in the East. It was the period when the leadership of local communities was in the process of being reorganized, with prophets and teachers gradually being replaced by episcopes and deacons (*Did.* 15:1-2).

A factor of significance behind the declining role of itinerant charismatic leaders in this subapostolic period is the translation and diffusion of the gospel of Matthew. The apostles, prophets and teachers had the all-important task of preaching the gospel and in so doing they made use of an Aramaic version of the *logia* (words) of the Lord collected by Matthew. For the sake of the Christian mission to the Greek-speaking peoples in the Hellenistic East, this Aramaic collection was then translated in Greek. Since this collection of *logia* of the Lord is likely to have initially circulated in various forms, the editor of the Didache, without knowing our canonical gospel of Matthew, may well have used one of these versions. This is the gospel of the Lord which is quoted explicitly in the Didache. The canonical gospel did not receive its final form until the last two decades of the first century.

The spread of Matthew's gospel has contributed to the disappearance of the itinerant charismatics in favour of an institutional hierarchy. The normative character of the Didache does not radiate the same inspiration, encouragement and incentive as does Matthew's gospel. On the contrary, the Didache is merely concerned with external behaviour. Nevertheless, the law code with regard to the itinerant charismatics is in agreement with the historical circumstances between 70 and 75 C.E. Along with the spread of Matthew's gospel in the Greek world, a set of rules was necessary in order to control the activities of the charismatics. The gospel provided measures to discipline the itinerant teachers and offered arrangements to advance a practice of Christian life without impromptu sermons and uncontrolled prophecies. As a matter of fact, the precepts in the Didache which are meant to examine the authenticity of these charismatics reflect the rules given in Matthew's gospel.

Chapter Ten

Two Windows on a Developing Jewish-Christian Reproof Practice: Matt 18:15-17 and *Did.* 15:3

Huub van de Sandt

Faculty of Theology, Tilburg University (The Netherlands)

The focus of this article is on the directive for reproof of a brother or sister, often called *correctio fraterna*. It is found in *Did.* 15:3 and in Matt 18:15-17. In Matt 18, it belongs to a selective collection of rules seeking to settle particularly controversial questions. The chapter reads much like an early church manual as it deals with situations that might have arisen in the Matthew's church such as causing others to sin (18:6-9), bringing back those who have digressed (10-14), reproving a brother (15-20), and the importance of forgiveness (21-35). We know that the Didache is also often characterized as a handbook of church morals, ritual, and discipline since it offers rules for ecclesiastical praxis. The Didache resembles later church orders in many respects.[1]

In Matt 18:15-17, the Matthean community is depicted as an organized society with its prescribed methods of church discipline. There is widespread recognition that the contents of *Did.* 15:3 closely correspond with those of Matt 18:15-17. Since explicit reference to "the gospel" is made twice (*Did.* 15:3,4), it is often assumed that the directive in the Didache draws upon Matt 18:15-17.[2]

I will discuss their interrelationship in an historical perspective. A close examination of the passages' form and context will indicate that both injunctions reflect a community's reworking of a kind of rudimentary, primitive community rule underlying Matt 18:15-17 and *Did.* 15:3. We will take the following steps. First, the two reproof passages and their contexts will be investigated and compared (sections 2 and 3). We will see that Matt 18:15-17 displays a characteristic peculiarity which distinguishes the passage from its immediate context. It has the marks of an interpolation. But what is the connection between this passage and *Did.* 15:3, which claims to be based on a

---

[1] The manual offers a glimpse of the earliest details with regard to the actual practice of the catechumenate, baptism, and the Eucharist in a specific Christian community (*Did.* 1-10). It also provides us with guidelines for the local community concerning the reception of itinerant outsiders, directives for the confession of sins and reconciliation, data about the functioning of leadership, and instructions for the reproving of a brother (*Did.* 11-15).

[2] See Drews, "Apostellehre (Didache)," 282; Massaux, *Influence de l'Évangile* (1986), 630 ("l'auteur de la Didachè s'est référé avant tout à Mt., XVIII, 15-17; ... μὴ ἐν ὀργῇ peut trouver une consonnance en Mt., V, 22."); Köhler, *Die Rezeption des Matthäusevangeliums*, 39; Goldhahn-Müller, *Die Grenze der Gemeinde*, 310; Schenk-Ziegler, *Correctio fraterna im Neuen Testament*, 296-311; esp. 310; Wengst, *Didache (Apostellehre)*, 24-32; esp. 25-26. For additional references, cf. Niederwimmer, *Die Didache*, 245, n.10.

gospel? In sections 4, 5, and 6, the examination will be extended to the act of reproach found in Jewish sources. It will become clear that the two reproof passages have a special parallel in the Manual of Discipline (1QS), a major manuscript found among the Dead Sea Scrolls. A comparison of the correspondences between 1QS 5:23b-6:1b and our reproof passages will show that Matt 18:15-17 and *Did.* 15:3 are connected collaterally, through their dependence on this or a similar Jewish ancestor. Of even greater interest to us, however, is that the modification of the Qumranic source or a similar document may represent the ethic standard of the community (-ies) in which this tradition was transmitted.

1 The Reproof Passage in Matt 18:15-17

1.1 Matthew 18

The discourse in Matt 18 is the fourth of the five major discourses in the gospel of Matthew. In the story of the blessing of the children (vv. 1-5), Matthew rewrites the Marcan account (9:33-37) and presents Jesus responding to the disciples' question about who is the greatest in the kingdom of heaven. Jesus shows them to be heading in the wrong direction and focusses on the theme of imitating children. Matt 18:6-9 moves from this child imagery to that of the "little ones," the childlike believers. One should not lead simple Christians astray so as to have them lose their faith. Jesus warns against causing these to stumble and calls for self-discipline to keep from sinning. The unit in 18:10-14 displays a concern for the community members as well. Here, the parable of the lost sheep is to illustrate the considerate and attentive attitude one has to take toward those in the community who lose the right path. The essential point is the concern for every single sheep.

The following section is Matt 18:15-20. It outlines the procedure to be adopted when a fellow believer digresses from the norms of the community. The offender is given three chances to settle the issue. If a brother has sinned against another, the offended party should reprove his brother in private and discuss the issue in such a way as to lead him to accept his fault. If this first admonishment fails, the wronged individual should take along two witnesses according to Jewish law (Deut 19:15). If this second effort likewise does not bring about a satisfactory resolution, the matter is to be brought before the whole community. When the offender remains recalcitrant and refuses to listen to the "church", he should be treated like a "gentile and tax-collector," meaning that the associations with the sinner are broken off. He is declared to be outside the limits of the community. Verses 18-20, though in contrast to the immediately preceding text addressing the audience in the second person plural, continue the section with some proverbial statements by Jesus that ground the jurisdiction of the church in these matters. The decision of the community after the three-step legal process is immediately ratified in heaven.[3] The authority of a Christian community

---

[3] Duling, "Matthew 18:15-17," 18.

whose members are in spiritual harmony is underscored. When two or three are gathered in Jesus' name, the community's prayer will become Jesus' prayer[4] and God will answer its united concern.

In 18:21-22, the focus is on the need for unlimited forgiveness. Jesus' saying about forgiving one's brother "seventy times seven" links up with the ideas of compassion and reconciliation in the parable of the lost sheep (vv. 10-14). An aggrieved brother must forgive an offending person repeatedly. The significance of this message is illustrated in the concluding parable of the unforgiving servant (18:23-35), highlighting with some severity that mercy should be a high priority.

1.2 Matt 18:15-20: An addition to the Q Source

The reproof section starts in Matt 18:15 with a saying that, in the parallel text, Luke 17:3, occurs immediately after the statement about the millstone punishment to be undergone by one who causes others to fall into sin. The millstone saying (Luke 17:1-2) is found in Matthew, too, though in a preceding position (Matt 18:6-7) and in reverse order. The facts thus seem to indicate that a close literary contact exists between Matthew and Luke[5] and most critics believe that the corresponding sayings originated in the common Q source. Two further considerations are important in this respect. Focussing on Matt 18:15-20, one not only establishes that both gospels have, in broad outlines, the same sequence (Matt 18:6-7, 15, 21-22 = Luke 17:1-2, 3, 4), but that they display striking verbal similarities (including Matt 18:6 // Luke 17:2; Matt 18:15a // Luke 17:3a and Matt 18:22 // Luke 17:4) as well. It is widely accepted that the original wording has been better preserved in Luke 17:3-4 than in Matthew.[6] The latter has separated the sayings about fraternal (and sororal) correction (Luke 17:3 = 18:15a) and forgiveness (Luke 17:4 = 18:21-22) in order to develop these themes by providing materials not found in Luke.

The materials added to the Q tradition and central to this contribution are found in Matt 18:15-20. They provide us with disciplinary measures which are repeatedly introduced with the same grammatical construction ἐάν and the aorist subjunctive. The conditional sentences are typical of casuistic law as they describe various situations which might arise. Since this pattern occurs eight times in vv 15-20, it characterizes the unit as a whole.[7] Another point to be noted in these added materials is the allusion in Matt 18:15-17 to Lev 19:17. The affinity between the reproof texts in Matthew and Leviticus becomes obvious when we establish that three words in the LXX version, the verbs ἐλέγχω ('to correct'), ἁμαρτάνω ('to sin'), and the noun ἀδελφός ('brother'), reappear in Matt 18:15. In Lev 19:17, reproof is not a punishment or sanction but a sign of brotherhood: "You shall not hate your brother (τὸν ἀδελφόν) in your heart,

---

[4] Davies-Allison, *A Critical and Exegetical Commentary* 2, 787-89.
[5] Thompson, *Matthew's Advice to a Divided Community*, 230-37; Duling, "Matthew 18:15-17," 6-7; Catchpole, "Reproof and Reconciliation in the Q community," 79-90.
[6] See, e.g., Bultmann, *Die Geschichte der synoptischen Tradition*, 151; Trilling, *Das wahre Israel*, 114; Strecker, *Der Weg der Gerechtigkeit*, 222; Hummel, *Die Auseinandersetzung*, 58; Gundry, *Matthew*, 367-71; see also Pesch, "Die sogenannte Gemeindeordnung," 226-27.
[7] Thompson, *Matthew's Advice to a Divided Community*, 176 and 186.

but you shall surely reproach (ἐλεγμῷ ἐλέγξεις) your neighbour, lest you bear sin (ἁμαρτίαν) because of him." The verb ἐλέγχω (Luke 17:3: ἐπιτιμάω), occurring twice in the Synoptics, is a Matthean hapax. In the LXX, it stands most often for the hif'il of יכח, "to reprove, expose, uncover, demonstrate the mistake or guilt of another."[8]

1.3 The Idiosyncrasy of Matthew 18:15-17

The verses 15-17 are relevant in other respects as well. Separated from their context, these verses contain a halakhic rule for how to respond to a personal offence committed by a fellow-believer:[9]

> 15. If your brother sins against you,[10] go and correct (ἔλεγξον) him, between you and him alone. If he listens to you, you have gained your brother. 16. But if he does not listen, take one or two others along with you, that every word may be confirmed by the evidence of two or three witnesses. 17. If he refuses to listen to them, tell it to the church; and if he refuses to listen even to the church, let him be to you as a gentile and a tax-collector.

A closer examination indicates that this section has preserved and reworked a carefully arranged tradition which at one time existed as a separate unit. The idiosyncrasy of this unit compared to its context is easily noticed. First, there is the judicial prominence which does not seem to flow naturally from Lev 19:17.[11] The judicial style of our passage is underscored by the reference to witnesses who may be called by the prosecution to appear before a larger judicial group of the "church" in order to testify that the sinner has been reluctant so far to recognize the criticism of his sinfulness.[12] The quotation

---

[8] The Hebrew text of Lev 19:17 requires reproof of one's neighbour by the double verb יכח (infinitive absolute followed by the finite verb: הוכח תוכיח) which in the LXX is rendered by ἐλεγμῷ ἐλέγξεις.

[9] Cf. Trilling, *Das wahre Israel*, 117.

[10] The wording εἰς σέ ("against you") in Matt 18:15 may be an early interpolation as Sinaiticus and Vaticanus do not have it. Indeed, many modern commentators deny their authenticity as it might derive from εἰς ἐμέ in v. 21 or could have crept in from Luke 17:4. We believe that the omission of εἰς σέ is deliberate (see also Bover, "Si peccaverit in te frater tuus ... Mt 18,15," 195-98; Davies-Allison, *A Critical and Exegetical Commentary* 2, 782; Luz, *Das Evangelium nach Matthäus* 3, 38, n. 1; 43; Gundry, *Matthew*, 367; Duling, "Matthew 18:15-17," 10). Its absence from some manuscripts can be explained as an assimilation to Luke 17:3. The wording may also have been deleted as the result of a wish to apply the administering of reproof to sin in general. Furthermore, it would suit the immediate context better. If a brother has sinned against another, the offended party should first seek reconciliation in private. We suggest, then, that Matthew wrote the phraseology εἰς σέ, a reading which implies personal injustices specifically committed against a Christian brother. For a critical discussion of the text, see also Metzger, *A Textual Commentary*, 45.

[11] In itself, Lev 19:17 has a moral and not a forensic character. In contrast to legal ordinances, moral and ethical norms, like the avoidance of enmity and hatred, cannot be enforced by sanctions of the courts. The legal character in the interpretation in Matt 18:15-17 probably derives from an understanding of Lev 19:17 in its wider context, specifically, in the light of Lev 19:15, a verse which is about "doing no injustice in judgment" and "in righteousness shall you judge your neighbour."

[12] Thompson, *Matthew's Advice to a Divided Community*, 182.

from Deut 19:15 in Matt 18:16 ("every word ... three witnesses") also shows that witnessing is understood here as a legal act.[13] Matt 18:15-17 has the mark of a forensic procedure which includes expulsion.

Second, the wording "as a gentile and tax-collector" in 18:17b, referring to the punishment of expulsion, stands out from the Matthean gospel as a whole with respect to its pejorative tone. The gist of the expression applies neither to the life of Jesus nor to the gospel of Matthew. It is improbable, to say the least, that the historical Jesus, who extended the possibility of conversion to the toll-collectors and sinners, would have used this phraseology in such a context.[14] With regard to Matthew, the expression appears to contradict the favourable attitude toward pagans and tax-collectors displayed throughout Matthew's gospel.[15] Matthew portrays Jesus as associating with outcast toll-collectors (9:10-13; 11:19). Since such a consideration is not implied in v. 17b at all, however, it is unlikely that we are dealing here with words pronounced by Jesus or created by Matthew.

The passage thus has certain features typifying it as a legal unit with a casuistic style: a requirement of witnesses, a quotation from Deut 19:15 referring to formal prosecution terminology, and a threat of expulsion. Both the incongruity of the passage with its immediate context and its absence from the Q source strongly suggest that it is an interpolation from an independent source. That is to say that Matthew may have preserved a tradition here stemming from an early stage in the history of his community. But where did these materials come from? The expression "like a gentile and a tax-collector," implying the impurity of outsiders, suggests a Jewish environment.[16] It contained an halakhic rule about reproof as a judicial process involving reproof alone, reproof before witnesses, and bringing the case before the full assembly.

---

[13] Schenk-Ziegler, *Correctio fraterna im Neuen Testament*, 305-306; Stendahl, *The School of St. Matthew*, 138-39.

[14] Cf. Luz, *Das Evangelium nach Matthäus* 3, 40 and n. 17; Schenk-Ziegler, *Correctio fraterna im Neuen Testament*, 298-99; Sanders, *Jesus and Judaism*, 261; see also Giesen, "Zum Problem der Exkommunikation," 193-95.

[15] Thompson, *Matthew's Advice to a Divided Community*, 185 and n. 39; Forkman, *The Limits of the Religious Community*, 125; see also Stanton, *A Gospel for a New People*, 46-47.

[16] The particular stipulation in Matt 18:15-17 may yield some additional information about the nature of the pre-Matthean source. First, the agreement between Matthew 18:15 and Lev 19:17 (LXX) with respect to the verb ἐλέγχω, and the verbal similarity of the quotation in v. 16b to Deut 19:15 (LXX) seem to indicate that the tradition was drawn up in Greek from the outset. This may be corroborated by the un-Matthean wording μεταξύ ("between"), and μόνος ("alone") in Matt 18:15. Finally, the use of the term ἐκκλησία for the local assembly in v. 17a appears to be unaffected by the later meaning of the term in 16:18 referring to a community which is not narrowed down to time or space (cf. Forkman, *The Limits of the Religious Community*, 125; Catchpole, "Reproof and Reconciliation," 80-81; see also the contribution of Wim Weren in this volume [p. 58, n. 20]). Matthew may thus have incorporated at this point in his gospel an independent reproof tradition in its final form (cf. Goldhahn-Müller, *Die Grenze der Gemeinde*, 171-72; Forkman, *The Limits of the Religious Community*, 129) which originated in a Jewish or Jewish-Christian congregation in a Greek-speaking part of the early Mediterranean world (see Forkman, *The Limits of the Religious Community*, 125.128-29; Goldhahn-Müller, *Die Grenze der Gemeinde*, 172; Sand, *Das Evangelium nach Matthäus*, 371; Grundmann, *Das Evangelium nach Matthäus*, 419).

2 A Comparison between the Reproof Passages in Matt 18:15-17 and *Did.* 15:3

Did. 11-15 comprises guidelines for good order and church discipline. While Chapters 11-13 are concerned with the attitude of the local Didache community towards outsiders who visit the community, Chaps. 14-15 focus on the circumstances within the community itself. The successive topics seem to be loosely strung together.

In *Did.* 14, the Eucharist is understood as a sacrifice and anyone who neglects to confess his or her transgressions prior to the Eucharist on the "Sunday of the Lord" can not be considered as offering the "pure sacrifice" which the Lord requires. The succeeding passage gives some information about bishops and deacons (15:1-2). The community members are advised to select for themselves bishops and deacons who are qualified for their offices. It reveals that they were elected from local community members and, in addition to the more general qualification of being "worthy of the Lord," it mentions the most important prerequisites for these offices. They are to be honest, unassuming, and not greedy.

What follows next is the "reproof of a brother," implying a friendly confrontation of someone with an error he or she has committed:

> Correct (ἐλέγχετε) one another not in anger but in peace, as you have it [written] in the gospel; and let no one speak to anyone who wrongs another – let him not hear [a word] from you[17] – until he has repented.

If the errant brother (or sister), despite this correction, continues to wrong his fellow believer, the members of the community are prohibited from further relating to him until he repents (15:3).[18] At the end of the text (*Did.* 15:4), the members of the community are called upon to conduct themselves in accordance with the requirements of the gospel. The verse has the features of a concluding comment; the prayers are for those who are still unwilling to listen after previous efforts to achieve reconciliation (cf. *Did.* 2:7), while the almsgiving might be considered a penance for the remission of sins (cf. *Did.* 4:6).[19]

Comparing the reproof passage in *Did.* 15:3 with the one in Matt 18:15-17, one establishes that these passages are very different, as the first one displays a striking

---

[17] Because the shift in subject makes this translation somewhat problematic, the rendering of Giet (*L'Énigme de la Didachè*, 244) may be correct: "ni de votre part ne lui prête l'oreille," that is, "let no one on your part listen to him." Giet – probably in imitation of Nautin ("Notes critiques," 119) – does not take the ἀστοχῶν ("offender") but the μηδείς ("no one"), which is also the subject of λαλείτω ("speak"), to be the subject of ἀκουέτω ("hear"). See Rordorf-Tuilier, *La Doctrine des douze Apôtres*, 79, n. 2.

[18] The verb ἀστοχέω means "to miss the goal, to fall away." In *Did.* 15, it is used in a specific sense: ἀστοχέω κατὰ ἑτέρου must mean "to fall short, to sin against another" and here it refers to a person who errs by sinning against another person.

We consider 15:3b to make up the logical sequence of 15:3a rather than as an isolated part of the verse. This means that the verb form tense is a Present Continuous, implying "the one who persists in sin." The directive applies to those who do not admit their fault but stubbornly continue sinning notwithstanding brotherly correction; see Knopf, *Die Lehre der zwölf Apostel*, 38; Niederwimmer, *Die Didache*, 245-46.

[19] Goldhahn-Müller, *Die Grenze der Gemeinde*, 310-11. See also Niederwimmer, *Die Didache*, 246.

concern for charity toward the offender. Whereas Matthew emphasizes reproof as a necessary part of the legal process, every legal connotation is missing in *Did.* 15:3. The Didache does not have reproof taking place in front of witnesses who may eventually give evidence of the sinner's disobedience. On the contrary, *Did.* 15:3 does not mention witnesses at all! The act of reproving is marked by brotherly love. Moreover, in Matthew, a rigidly official procedure is found which emphasizes the possibility of permanent expulsion without any indication that the offender can be received back again in the community.[20] The Didache, however, envisages expulsion as a pedagogical injunction and limits the duration to the moment of repentance.

At first glance, it would thus seem that, despite certain links between the passages in Matthew and the Didache (both dealing with reproof), the parallel material does not display much resemblance. In order to evaluate this phenomenon correctly, however, one must differentiate between Matt 18:15-17 as a separate passage and as part of the whole of Matt 18. Admittedly, Matt 18:15-17 probably has preserved a carefully arranged tradition which at one time existed as a separate unit. However, the evangelist may have incorporated this unit precisely at this very position in his gospel for a special purpose. The forensic process passage is set within a literary context of humility (vv. 1-5), responsibility (6-9), individual loving care (110-14), forgiveness, and mercy (21-35). Matthew surrounds the traditional segment on fraternal correction with material promoting a spirit of generosity and unbounded merciful love.

In view of the pastoral context, the Matthean reproof passage acquires a different meaning. The general drift of the passage changes. The Matthean setting suggests an extension of the function of the witnesses. At variance with the statement in Deut 19:15, the witnesses in Matthew apparently attempt to convince their fellow disciple by exposing his guilt in such a way as to persuade him of his sin. They try to substantiate the truth of the reprover's evidence and add greater weight to his arguments so as to help the offended party in winning over his brother. A similar situation is found with respect to the expulsion topic. Indeed, when the rule is taken at face value, it is the expulsion which is emphasized. However, by inserting the passage after the parable of the shepherd's concern for the one sheep going astray (110-14) and directly before the parable of the unforgiving servant (23-35), Matthew stresses the eagerness which a disciple is to display in pursuit of a brother who has sinned. The effort to save the offender has replaced excommunication.[21]

The conventional forensic procedure underlying Matt 18:15-17 has been commuted by Matthew. Instead of presenting regulations dealing with a juridical process of excommunication, the passage now emphasizes a threefold attempt at restoration to harmony and friendship. In the light of the wider context of Matt 18, the regulation in Matt 18:15-17 displays an essential correspondence with the reproof

---

[20] "There is nothing to indicate that he can be received back again;" cf. Forkman, *The Limits of the Religious Community*, 129. See also Goldhahn-Müller, *Die Grenze der Gemeinde*, 181; Schenk-Ziegler, *Correctio fraterna im Neuen Testament*, 298.

[21] For these transformations, see Thompson, *Matthew's Advice to a Divided Community*, 182-83 and 187. See also Forkman, *The Limits of the Religious Community*, 129-30 and Schenk-Ziegler, *Correctio fraterna im Neuen Testament*, 307-10.

passage in *Did.* 15:3. The act of reproach in Matt 18:15-17 has the same purpose as the one in *Did.* 15:3, that is, to gain a brother by having him listen to the evidence of his culpability and admit his sin.

3 Comparable Reproof Passages in the Qumran Scrolls

In addition to Matt 18:15-17 and *Did.* 15:3, the act of reproach is also found elsewhere in the Jewish cultural world. It has a counterpart in two parallel passages, found in Sir 19:13-17 and in the Testament of Gad 6:1-7. Both writings emphasize caution and care in reproaching an offender and display fraternal features. They envisage the process of reproaching in a friendly and warm-hearted way only[22] as their concern is first of all with the maintenance of peace and the achievement of reconciliation.

The rebuke in the separate unit of Matt 18:15-17 can be compared with the forensic procedure developed uniquely by the Qumran community and, to a certain extent, with the rabbinic requirement of "warning", the התראה. Both the rabbinic institution of *hatra'ah* and the Qumranic law of rebuke were intended for prosecuting transgressors. In each case, the procedure served the purpose of preventing violations resulting from one's ignorance of the severity of an offence and its punishment. However, there are also crucial differences between the rabbinic *hatra'ah* and the Qumranic reproof. Firstly, in rabbinic documents, Lev 19:17 is never quoted as support for the duty of witnesses to warn the culprit. While in Qumran, the legal rule of reproof is linked to Lev 19:17-18, the rabbinic law of *hatra'ah* is inferred from a metaphorical explanation of Lev 20:17, that is, an instruction teaching a man to be conscious of the consequences of his wrongdoing before transgressing. Secondly, this indicates that, according to rabbinic sources, the *hatra'ah* was always to be performed before a person transgressed. No one might be tried for an offence without having been warned. In Qumran, however, the reproof occurred after the committing of a crime and a person was liable for conviction after a recurrence of a similar transgression. This procedure brings us to the third difference, i.e., the requirement that the sectarians kept written records as a proof that a transgressor had been forewarned. At any time, one had to be in a position to find out if the reproof had taken place for a previous violation of the same law. At least two analogous crimes were required for conviction. According to rabbinic law, however, the warning had to take place orally before the very same offence for which a person could be tried.[23]

---

[22] Cf. Kugel, "On Hidden Hatred," 47-52. 57-59; Catchpole, "Reproof and Reconciliation," 82-84; Schenk-Ziegler, *Correctio fraterna im Neuen Testament*, 101-107. 166-75.

[23] See Schiffman, "Reproof as a Requisite for Punishment," 97-98 (this article [pp. 89-109] was published in an almost identical version as "Reproof as a Requisite for Punishment in the Law of the Dead Sea Scrolls," 59-74); Weinfeld, *The Organizational Pattern*, 74-76 (Weinfeld, however, disagrees with Schiffman as to the purpose of the rabbinic *hatra'ah* and the Qumranic reproof); Jackson, "*Testes singulares*," 175-76 and n. 6.

The whole forensic course of proceedings connected with reproof which probably lies buried in the text of Matt 18:15-17 was developed exclusively by the Qumran community. It was not part of the legal system in the rest of Palestine. The major passages in the Qumranic writings include the Community Rule or Manual of Discipline (1QS) 5:25-26 and the Damascus Document (CD) 9:2-8, 16-23. These texts, like those in Sir 19:13-17 and *T. Gad*, all reflect the principle set out in Lev 19:17.[24]

3.1 CD 9:2-8

The Damascus Document presents reproof as part of the judicial procedure in CD 9:2-8 and 16-23. When the law has been violated, the person to do the reproaching is required to notify the offender at once of his transgression before charging him formally with the offence.[25] Reproof in front of witnesses, it is stated in CD 9:2-8, was a legal requirement to be carried out prior to the judicial decision:

> 2 And as to that which he said, "you shall not take vengeance nor keep a grudge against the sons of your people," (Lev. 19:18a) anyone of those who enter
>
> 3 the covenant who brings a charge against his neighbour without reproof before witnesses (יביא על רעהו דבר אשר לא בהוכח לפני עדים),
>
> 4 but brings it in his burning wrath or tells it to his elders to put him to shame, is taking vengeance and bearing a grudge.
>
> 5 It is written only, "He takes vengeance against his adversaries and keeps a grudge against his enemies." (Nah 1:2)
>
> 6 If he was silent from day to day (מיום ליום) and in his burning wrath charged him with a capital offence,
>
> 7 his iniquity is upon him, for he did not fulfill the ordinance of God which says to him, "You shall surely
>
> 8 reprove (הוכח תוכיח) your neighbour so that you do not bear sin because of him." (Lev 19:17b-c)[26] ...

The text in the lines above attempts to explain the meaning of Lev 19:18a and 19:17b-c. One must reproach one's fellow before bringing the case before the offender's "elders". Lev 19:18a ("you shall not take vengeance or bear any grudge") is interpreted in the following way: every member of the Covenant who accuses his neighbour without rebuking him before witnesses but, instead, is motivated by anger or by the aspiration to defame him among the members of the sect, he is one who takes vengeance and is bearing a grudge. Cases may not be brought to the "elders" if the transgressor has not been reproved. On the

---

[24] Additional interesting reproof passages with the hif'il of יכח – but less relevant to our investigation - are found in CD 7:1-3; 20:4-8; 1QS 9:16-18.

[25] The reproacher himself, however, need not be the victim here; Kugel, "On Hidden Hatred," 58; Duling, "Matthew 18:15-17," 16.

[26] For the original text and English translation, see Charlesworth, *The Dead Sea Scrolls* 2, 42-43.

other hand, when a person who ought to immediately reprove an offender is silent and saves his hatred up from day to day (cf. also Num 30:15), that is, when he accumulates his rancour for the day when he is angry, the offender's crime is blamed on the one who neglected to reprove him on the spot. This is the reason why Nah 1:2 is quoted, since only God may take vengeance and bear a grudge. Anyone who fails to reprove his neighbour but piles up the offences will "bear sin because of him" (Lev 19:17b-c).[27]

3.2 CD 9:16-23

Whereas the passage in CD 9:2-8 is preoccupied with a member of the community intending to accuse an offending fellow member, another passage in the same document (CD 9:16-23) deals with the duty of witnesses to reprove:

16 ... Any trespass committed by
17 a man against the Torah, which is witnessed by his neighbour – he being but one – if it is a capital matter, he shall report it
18 before his eyes with reproof (בהוכיח) to the Examiner (למבקר). And the Examiner shall write it down with his hand until he does it
19 again before one who again reports it to the Examiner. If he is again caught in the presence of
20 one, his judgment is complete. And if they are two and they testify about
21 different things, the man shall only be separated from the purity, provided they are
22 reliable. And on the day when a man sees it, he shall make it known to the Examiner. And concerning property they shall receive two
23 reliable witnesses, while one is sufficient to separate (him from) the purity.
...[28]

Reproving is again a necessary part of the legal process. At variance with CD 9:2-8, however, in which the "elders" are the instance before whom the reproof is brought, here it is the "Examiner" (or the "Overseer") in whose presence the process must take place. An individual member, as Lev 19:17 (cf. the verb כי) is understood here, has to report to the Examiner in the presence of the offender any violation of the Torah he sees even if he is the only witness. The passage assumes that three witnesses are required for the purposes of prosecution in capital cases and two in financial matters (Deut 17:6; 19:15). The text, however, facilitates eventual conviction. Successive occurrences of the same offence committed by the same person and witnessed by one single witness on each occasion, could be combined to constitute grounds for conviction.[29]

---

[27] Forkman, *The Limits of the Religious Community*, 48-49; Schiffman, "Reproof as a Requisite for Punishment" (1983), 93-94; Kugel, "On Hidden Hatred," 53-54; see also Schenk-Ziegler, *Correctio fraterna im Neuen Testament*, 143-47; Carmody, "Matt 18:15-17," 142-50.

[28] For the original text and English translation, see Charlesworth, *The Dead Sea Scrolls* 2, 44-45.

[29] Levine, "Damascus Document IX, 17-22," 196; Schiffman, "The Qumran Law of Testimony;" Id., "The Law of Testimony," 73-76; Jackson, "*Testes singulares*," 172-201. See also Hempel, *The Laws of the Damascus Document*, 93-100.

3.3 1QS 5:20b–6:1b

The situation in 1QS 5:23b-25 seems to resemble that of *T. Gad* 6:1-5. It is important to first quote the passage within its immediate context:

20 ... And therefore he shall enter into the covenant in order to act according to all these statutes for the Community (which is) a holy Congregation. And they shall examine

21 their spirits within the Community, between (each) man and his neighbour according to his insight and his works in the Torah, under the authority of the Sons of Aaron who dedicate themselves within the Community to establish

22 his covenant and to observe all his statutes which he commanded to do, and upon the authority of the multitude of Israel who dedicate themselves to return to his covenant through the Community.

23 They shall register them in the rule, each before his companion, according to his insight and his works. They shall all obey one another; the lower one (in rank obeying) the higher one (in rank). In order to examine

24 their spirit and their works year after year, so as to elevate each according to his insight and the perfection of his way, or to keep him back according to his perversion. They shall admonish (להוכיח)

25 one another in t[ru]th, humility, and merciful love (באֿ[מת] וענוה ואהבת חסד) to another. – *vacat* – He must not speak to his fellow with anger or with a snarl,

26 or with a [stiff] neck [or in a jealous] spirit of wickedness. And he must not hate him [in the fores]k[in] of his heart, for he shall admonish him (יוכיחנו) on the (very same) day (ביום)[30] lest

6:1 he bear iniquity because of him. And also let no man *accuse his companion* before the Many (לפני הרבים) *without a reproof before witnesses.* ...
אל יביא איש על רעהו דבר לפני הרבים אשר לוא בתוכחת)
לפני עדים)[31]

The above lines form part of the section envisaging the organisation of community life (1QS - Columns 5-7). It is worth noting that the wording "And therefore he shall enter into the covenant in order to act according to all these statutes"[32] in 5:20b introduces the passage while the heading in 6:1c suggests the beginning of a new section (6:1c-8a) offering regulations which are quite different from the previous material.[33] The section we are concerned with (1QS 5:20b-6:1b) deals with the admission of new

---

[30] In the Hebrew document, some letters have been erased after the word ביום.

[31] For the original text and English translation, see Charlesworth, *The Dead Sea Scrolls* 1, 24-27.

[32] For arguments, see Metso, *The Textual Development*, 129.

[33] "The regulations in this passage" (1c-8a) "appear to be directed at members of the Essene movement who lived, not at Qumran, but amongst their fellow Jews;" cf. Knibb, *The Qumran Community*, 115. See also Metso, *The Textual Development*, 115-16.

members, the annual examination of all members, and the reproof of fellow members. The way in which reproach is administered in 1QS 5:20b-6:1b is important for our investigation. More will be said about this in the next section.

4 The Reproof Passages in 1QS 5:23b-6:1b and Matt 18:15-17

According to 1QS 5:20b-23a, persons aspiring to membership are to be examined by the whole community. The procedures described in this division are closely connected with those found elsewhere in 1QS.[34] The remaining lines of the section, 5:23b-6:1b, are especially instructive. The passage appears to be divided in two separate parts. The lines 24b-25a are closely linked to 23c-24a, which describe the annual inspection of the position of each member of the community's complex hierarchic system. The statements are linked grammatically by the third person plural. The reproach is to be administered "in truth, and humility and merciful love." Interestingly, in the middle of line 25, the scribe of 1QS left a space, and made a mark in the margin as a paragraph sign. This is also the point at which the third person plural changes into the singular. Some commentators suspect, therefore, that the passage in 5:25b-6:1 forms an interpolation, but since some parts do occur in the versions of the manuscripts S[b.d] (= 4Q256 and 4Q258, respectively),[35] this is not likely. These features may, however, indicate a distinct break in the literary pattern and leave us with a basic division of the passage.

The substance of the second part (5:25b-6:1) enlarges on the exegesis of the biblical reproof passage in CD 9:2-8. The lines 5:26b-6:1a present a free quotation of Lev 19:17: "And he must not hate him [in the fores]k[in] of his heart, for he shall admonish him on the (very same) day lest he bear iniquity because of him." The subsequent exegesis of this quotation in 1QS 6:1b requiring the presence of witnesses apparently presupposes the legal clarification of Lev 19:17 given in CD 9:2-8. This consideration is corroborated by the verbatim agreement of 1QS 6:1b - highlighted here by the use of italic type - with CD 9:3. Moreover, the insertion of the expression "on the (very same) day" (ביום) in the free quotation of Lev 19:17 also reflects the explanation of the verse in CD 9:2-8: the reproacher is not free to keep silent if any hostility or "burning wrath" remains in his heart, but "he shall admonish him on the (very same) day lest he bear iniquity because of him." The reproof must be done as soon as possible and a grudge must not be held overnight. In 1QS as well as in CD, reproof is associated with keeping the accuser from hating the offender.[36]

In CD and 1QS, the reproaching of one's fellow seems to be presented as a preliminary step in the judicial process: in 1QS, one must reproach one's fellow before bringing the case before "the Many" (הרבים, a technical term referring to the full

---

[34] 1QS 5:7-20a and 6:13b-23. In the latter passage, the access of new members to the community is dealt with in even more detail; cf. Metso, *The Textual Development*, 129-30; Knibb, *The Qumran Community*, 113-14.

[35] Cf. Metso, *The Textual Development*, 115 and n. 25.

[36] Schiffman, "Reproof as a Requisite for Punishment" (1983), 93-94; Kugel, "On Hidden Hatred," 52-54; Schenk-Ziegler, *Correctio fraterna im Neuen Testament*, 130-34; Carmody, Matt 18:15-17," 146-48.

members of the community), and, in the CD passage, before bringing the matter to the offender's "elders" or the "Examiner". The statements in 1QS 6:1; CD 9:3-4 and 17-19 show that reproof in front of witnesses is required when carrying out a legal action. Instead of reproving a fellow privately, it must be part of a formal procedure in the presence of witnesses. In general, reproof had a juridical character in Qumran.[37]

It is doubtful, however, whether 1QS shows the same extent of legality as do the two passages in the Damascus Document. If the passage 5:23b-6:1b is divided structurally into two separate parts – as is shown above –, we can establish that the first part reveals a particular concern for the offender.[38] Even if it belongs to a forensic procedure which must be executed in accordance with specific legal norms, it has no judicial air to it. Reproof in the first part (5:23b-25b) seems to belong to the private sphere of relationships where the precepts are formulated in terms of warm encouragement.

In 1QS 5:23b-25, reproof does not function within the judicial framework of a violation of the law of Moses but serves as part of the annual examination and classification of the Qumran members. Each year, the community is to convene in a special session to examine the spiritual qualities and actions even of full members so as to re-allot their positions in the community. Interestingly, the annual mustering is mentioned for the first time in 1QS 2:19b-25, and that at the ceremony of the so-called Entry into the Covenant. The priests, holding the first place in the administrative structure, marched in first. After these, the Levites followed and finally "all the people" entered (2:21). Once every year, each man's position and status within each of these groups was determined, in order, on the basis of his spiritual character (knowledge) and his deeds.[39]

The transgressions evaluated on this annual occasion probably included not only violations of biblical law but offences against community regulations. There is evidence that only offences which were morally undesirable – but not considered punishable by society in general – were actually referred to under these circumstances. In this respect, the text in 4Q477 is of importance, a manuscript recording the names of several members of the community who were rebuked for specific sins. In addition to the personal names of offenders, however, the text has also preserved a list of offences. All recorded wrongdoings are morally objectionable transgressions rather than criminal acts.[40]

---

[37] García Martínez, "La Represión fraterna," 23-40 = ET: "Brotherly Rebuke," 221-32; Schiffman, "Reproof as a Requisite for Punishment" (1983), 94-96.

[38] Similar fraternal and ethical features of reproof are found in Ben Sira, *T. Gad* and some New Testament books (cf. Kugel, "On Hidden Hatred," 47-52). See also Forkman, *The Limits of the Religious Community*, 47-48; Carmody, "Matt 18:15-17," 147.

[39] Knibb, *The Qumran Community*, 89; Schiffman, *The Halakhah at Qumran*, 66-67; Wernberg-Møller, *The Manual of Discipline*, 98. For the ceremony of entering the Covenant, see Dimant, "Qumran Sectarian Literature," 500.

[40] According to Esther Eshel, the following sins are referred to in 4Q477: "Doing evil, being short-tempered, being haughty in spirit, loving one's relatives and therefore failing to rebuke them, disturbing the spirit of the חד, and choosing a good life;" cf. "4Q477: The Rebukes by the Overseer," 121. And see Reed, "Genre, Setting and Title of 4Q477," 147-48; Nitzan, "The Laws of Reproof in 4QBerakhot (4Q286-290)," 153-54. And cf. also Schenk-Ziegler, *Correctio fraterna im Neuen Testament*, 157-58.

It is in the context of the setback in status due to disloyalty to the community's moral instruction in the preceding year that the notion of reproof occurs in 1QS 5:23b-25b.[41] The verb להוכיח ('to reprove, expose, uncover, demonstrate the mistake or guilt') in line 24 conceivably prepares for the second part (5:25b-6:1) of the unit to proceed to the comment on Lev 19:17-18. While in CD 9:2-8, 16-23, the process of reproving occurs in two stages, in 1QS, the member at fault has three chances to have the problem solved. The members are apparently stimulated to solve their difficulties between themselves and they should appeal to the legal system when this fails.

In conclusion, the following points seem relevant. The evidence shows the distinct passage in Matt 18:15-17 to be reminiscent of Qumran. Since the judicial scenario of reproach was developed uniquely by the sect, the Matthean tradition must have been influenced by (a document from) Qumran or a similar community. Second, the particular relationship with 1QS 5:23b-6:1b has become evident. In 1QS (as well as in Matt), the first act of the reproach is to take place privately (in the form of a moral exhortation) between the two contenders alone[42] whereas, in CD, the presence of witnesses is vital for reproving from the very first step. Reproof in 1QS 5:23b-6:1b, like in Matthew, involves a three-step process: in private (5:23-26 = Matt 18:15),[43] before witnesses (6:1b = Matt 18:16), and before the many (6:1b = Matt 18:17).[44]

[41] Carmody, "Matt 18:15-17," 147-49 and Knibb, *The Qumran Community*, 114.

[42] Cf. Weinfeld, *The Organizational Pattern*, 38-41 and 75; Licht, *The Rule Scroll*, 137; Knibb, *The Qumran Community*, 115.

[43] It is not contended here that the private or fraternal reproof generally precludes prosecution for offences. In this case, it precedes the forensic one. A similar procedure may be found, however, in the Laws of Reproof in 4QBerakot 1-11. This text was tentatively reconstructed by Bilhah Nitzan on the basis of 4QBer[a] frag. 20, 4QBer[c] frag. 1 and 1QBer[a] frag. 13-14 ("The Laws of Reproof," 158-63). The fragments are copies from the beginning of the first century C.E. of an annual covenantal ceremony (see also Nitzan, "4QBerakhot[a-e] (4Q286-290)," 487-506). The hypothetical text runs as follows:

1   ... [each man should reprove his fellow in truth, in proper meekness and in] upright [purpos]e
2   [in the Community of God. And whoever] erred while returning [to the truth], he will reprove him (יוכיחנו) [according to] their [commandments] and will have mercy
3   [upon him if he si]ns. And [each man] will not bear a grudge [against his fellow from one day] to [the nex]t. [He will] not
4   [hate him in his heart and so will incur] n[o guilt because of him. And whatever is revealed to the me]n of the Community
5   [he will teach him with] his [com]passionate [love], and with the spirit [of humility he will remove him from deeds of] dece[i]t
6   [The Overseer of the Many will di]scipline him in all [their rules, rooting out his deeds]
7   [from all iniquity while re]proving him (בה[ו]כיחו) in the presence of wi[tnesses. ...] ...

The lines 1-4a (1-5) are very similar to the reproof with humility and gentleness in 1QS 5:24b-25 and have all the marks of a private reproach preceding the more formal one. B. Nitzan, who favours the whole process of reproof as a forensic procedure, admits that one could "distinguish between the fraternal reproof performed privately and its formal feature performed by the Overseer. However", she continues, "these are not two separate features, as the formal education mentioned here could not have been performed unless the one who has reproved his fellow, explaining his sin to him in private, had informed the Overseer of the case in the presence of witnesses." If we take the text at face value, however, it does not support this view.

[44] 1QS 6:1 suggests two stages in the process, one before witnesses and the other before the assembly of the full members of the community (*pace* García Martínez, "La Represión fraterna," 31, n. 23 = ET: "Brotherly Rebuke," 267, n. 355): "Note Vermes' excellent idiomatic rendering: 'Let no man accuse his companion before the Congregation without having first admonished him in the presence of witnesses;'" cf. Charlesworth, *The Dead Sea Scrolls* 1, 27, n. 135.

5   The Reproof Passages in 1QS 5:23b-6:1b and *Did.* 15:3

While reproving represents a formal procedure in Matt 18:15-17, it is a matter of mutual concern in the Didache. Admittedly, Matthew surrounds his legal directives with material promoting a spirit of unbounded merciful love and forgiveness. However in *Did.* 15:3, it is the instruction itself which displays an intense preoccupation with the spirit in which reproof is undertaken:

> Correct one another not in anger but in peace, as you have it [written] in the gospel (ὡς ἔχετε ἐν τῷ εὐαγγελίῳ); and let no one speak to anyone who wrongs another – let him not hear [a word] from you – until he has repented.

The expression ὡς ἔχετε ἐν τῷ εὐαγγελίῳ ("as you have it in the gospel") appeals to "the gospel" in order to support the contents of the first statement (*Did.* 15:3a). The remainder of 15:3, however, does not refer to a "gospel" and appears to be peculiar to the Didache itself, that is, a person who, in spite of the congregation's correction, continues to wrong his brother has to be excluded from the community until he repents.

The wording "as you have it in the gospel" may refer to some written gospel, but it is difficult to determine whether the text alludes to a canonical or apocryphal gospel. It could also direct attention to Jesus' teaching that may have circulated orally. The same clause "as you have it in the gospel" is found in 15:4 with the added wording "of our Lord." But the content of the reference appears to be most explicit in 15:3a: "Correct one another not in anger but in peace, as you have it in the gospel." Thus, the directive to correct one another not in an hostile way but with a respectful attitude is something that can be read or heard in the "gospel". The evidence is almost completely against the hypothesis that the composer of the Didache took the reproof materials from Matt 5:23 or 18:15-17.[45] The injunction in *Did.* 15:3a only faintly reflects some materials of that gospel, as it varies from Matt 5:23, which forbids wrath in general without referring to fraternal correction. We have seen already that the verse does not show any likeness in substance to the separate unit in Matt 18:15-17.

It might be appropriate, therefore, to suggest that Matthew was not used as a source for *Did.* 15:3a. Instead, "the gospel" which is referred to may be a source which shows a marked correspondence with 1QS 5:24b-25. While the series of reproof regulations in Matthew begins with a description of the concrete case of a brother who has sinned (conditional clause), the regulation in *Did.* 15:3 starts with a general rule. The same holds true for the Manual of Discipline. The phrase "Correct one another" (ἐλέγχετε δὲ ἀλλήλους) in *Did.* 15:3a may even be a verbal translation of its counterpart "They shall admonish one another" (להוכיח איש את רעהו) in 1QS 5:24b-25. Moreover, in both cases, the focus is on the circumstances in which mutual correction is to take place, as it says

---

[45] See also the general argument in the contribution of Aaron Milavec (pp. 80-81), included in this volume.

They shall admonish (להוכיח) one another in t[ru]th, humility, and merciful love (בא[מת] וענוה ואהבת חסד) to another. He must not speak to his fellow with anger (באף) or with a snarl, ... (1QS 5:24b-25).

The opposition brought up here is the same as the one found in *Did.* 15:3a, i.e., the attendant conditions should not be conflict, rage, or agitation (ἐν ὀργῇ // באף) but harmony and friendliness (ἐν εἰρήνῃ // בא[מת] וענוה ואהבת חסד).[46]

A final consideration with regard to the composition of *Did.* 14 and 15 is crucial in our examination in order to determine the interrelationship between *Did.* 15:3 and 1QS 5:23b-6:1b. *Did.* 14 and 15 discuss themes of internal community life but it is difficult to find in this collection of directives any comprehensive order. They seem loosely related. A closer look at the themes within these chapters, however, shows that they appear in the same sequence in that part of the Manual of Discipline which focusses on the organisation of community life: *Did.* 14 // 1QS 5:10b-20; *Did.* 15:1-2 // 1QS 5:(20b-23a),[47] 23b-24a and *Did.* 15:3 // 1QS 5:24b-25. The correspondence of *Did.* 15:3 with 1QS 5:24b-25 was substantiated above. Both passages – emphasizing fraternal correction in a spirit of generosity, friendliness, and compassion – show similarity in that they are almost identical verbally and present an analogous contrastive structure. In order to understand why the topic of reproof in *Did.* 15:3 is preceded by the subject of selecting bishops and deacons worthy of the Lord in 15:1-2, it is useful to consider the arrangement of the topics in 1QS 5:20b-25.

It was established above that the reproof directive in 1QS 5:23b-24a was accommodated to the assigning of individuals' position within the community's ranking system. According to 1QS 5:20b-23a, new members were tested and classified on their admission into the community. Each member was obligated to abide by the directions of any person of higher rank. Once a year, as is recounted in 5:23b-24a, the full members of the Qumran community were inspected closely and graded according to a strict order. In this approach, the relevant trespasses were first of all violations of community discipline rather than sins against the law. Some who showed perfect

---

[46] Cf. Audet, *La Didachè*, 180 and Schenk-Ziegler, *Correctio fraterna im Neuen Testament*, 126-58; esp. 130-32; Van de Sandt-Flusser, *The Didache*, 352. A more distant parallel is found in *T. Gad* 6:3: "Therefore, love one another from the heart, and if a man sins against you, speak to him in peace (ἐν εἰρήνῃ), ..." For the translation, see Hollander-De Jonge, *The Testaments of the Twelve Patriarchs*, 331.

The Laws of Reproof in 4QBerakot 1-11, reconstructed by Bilhah Nitzan, show an analogous phraseology (for the text, see above, n. 43).

A comparable contrast and a phrasing similar to the one in 1QS 5:24-26a is also preserved in 4QD^a frag. 18 col II 6-10:

6 He will admonish their sons [and daughters] (וה[וא] ייסר את בניהם ובנותיהם)

7 [in a sp]irit of po[ve]rty and with [compassionate] lo[ve] ([ברו]ח ע[נ]וה ובא[הבת חסד])

8 He shall not bear a grudge against the[m ...] in anger and wra[th] ...

This manuscript 4QD^a has also been used by Elisha Qimron to restore the corrupted text of CD 13:17-19; see Broshi, *The Damascus Document Reconsidered*, 35.

[47] The lines about the examination of new members (5:20b-23a) are probably not reflected in *Did.* 14-15. Regulations for the admission of neophytes are also described in sections 5:7-20a and 6:13b-23. Since 5:20-23 covers the topic in general terms, reminiscences might not have been preserved in the Didache. Furthermore, the admission of new members to the Didache community is already treated in *Did.* 7.

conduct ("according to his insight and the perfection of his way") were promoted in rank while others who failed were demoted. While the rules in 1QS 5:20b-23a deal with an examination of aspirant members in general terms, the passage in 1QS 5:23b-24a refers to this annual examination and classification of full members.

At this point in the discussion, it may be useful to refer to *Did.* 15:1-2, a passage which is mostly regarded as suggesting an innovation of offices:

> (1) Select, then, for yourselves bishops and deacons worthy of the Lord, mild-tempered men who are not greedy, who are honest and have proved themselves, for they too perform the functions of prophets and teachers for you. (2) So do not disregard them, for they are the persons who hold a place of honour among you, together with the prophets and the teachers.

It is often believed that the decline of the authority and reputation of the itinerant charismatic leaders – the apostles, prophets, and teachers – and the decrease in their number caused them to be replaced by bishops and deacons. The view that *Did.* 15:1-2 indicates a new set of local offices, however, breaks down at several points. The purport of this section is not – as is frequently proposed – that bishops and deacons were to be elected for the first time, but that qualified men would be elected to whom the community was to accord an equally high esteem as it gave to the prophets and teachers.[48]

The enumeration of the qualities in *Did.* 15:1 for the selection of proper bishops and deacons fits in well with the perspective of 1QS 5:23b-24a. The "insight and the perfection of the way" of a high ranking official in the Qumran community is judged, as are the qualities required for the leadership roles of bishops and deacons. The examination of proselytes in 5:20b-23a is of less importance here since the admission of new members to the Didache community has already been dealt with in *Did.* 7. The instruction to elect bishops and deacons "worthy of the Lord" in *Did.* 15:1 and the subsequent mention of virtues and capacities are designed to prevent the appointment of unsuitable occupants for these offices. Just as the reference to the (annual) inspection of members (their ranks and gradation of authority) in 1QS 5:23b-24a led to the topic of reproof of offending members in general (1QS 5:24b-25), so the Didache by association with the emphasis on the criteria for office in 15:1-2 now turns to the reproof of trespassing Christians in general (*Did.* 15:3).

In *Did.* 14, it is the purity of the eucharistic offering which is central.[49] The issue

---

[48] See Schöllgen, "Die Didache als Kirchenordnung," 18-19. 23-25; cf. also Schöllgen-Geerlings, *Didache. Zwölf-Apostellehre*, 70-73; Van de Sandt-Flusser, *The Didache*, 335-40 and n. 27.

[49] On the face of it, one might assume that the topic of the failing fellow Christians echoes the warning against dissension in *Did.* 14:2. Pseudo-Cyprian, with a reference to the 'Doctrinae apostolorum' (Teachings of the Apostles), renders a quotation that conflates *Did.* 14:2 and 15:3 in Chap. 4 of his *De Aleatoribus* ("About Dice-players"): "Et in doctrinis apostolorum: si quis frater delinquit in ecclesia et non paret legi, hic nec colligatur donec poenitentiam agat, et non recipiatur, ne inquinetur et inpediatur oratio vestra" ("And in the teachings of the apostles: if a brother offends in the church and disobeys the law, let him not be considered until he does penance, nor received, lest he defile and obstruct your prayer"). Cf. Hartel, *S. Thasci Caecili Cypriani opera omnia* 3, 96. See also Von Harnack, *Die Lehre der zwölf Apostel*, Prolegomena, 20-21; Audet, *La Didachè*, 79-81 and Niederwimmer, *Die Didache*, 21-22.

of ritual purity and impurity brings us to a similar topic in 1QS 5:10b-20. A person entering the Qumran community was obliged to keep separate from the 'men of injustice' since non-members were believed to be unclean. The prohibition of contact with outsiders was based on a desire to avoid contamination. However, those who did not sincerely repent should not be permitted the rite of washing which entitled them to partake of the community's food. Washing as an instrument of moral cleansing gave access to the common meal eaten by the full members of Qumran:

> 13 ... He must not enter the water in order to touch the purity of the men of
> holiness (לגעת בטהרת אנשי הקודש).[50] For they cannot be cleansed
> 14 unless they turn away from their wickedness, for (he remains) impure among
> all those who transgress his words. No one must be united with him in his
> duty or his property, lest he burden him
> 15 (with) guilty iniquity. But he shall keep far away from him in everything, ...
> (1QS 5:13b-15a)

Only wholehearted repentance, the appropriate inner disposition, would cause the ritual of purification to be effective (13b-15a).[51] The section continues with a refusal to allow contact with outsiders, apparently with a concern to preserve the ritual purity of the community. After the statement that doing business with non-members is forbidden except in rare cases (16-17), the section closes with a suitable conclusion (18-20).[52]

The point of this section is much the same as that of *Did.* 14, in which the meal of the Eucharist (which is discussed in Chaps. 9-10) is associated with the idea of sacrifice:

> (1) Assembling on every Sunday of the Lord, break bread and give thanks,
> confessing your faults besides so that your sacrifice may be clean (ὅπως καθαρὰ
> ἡ θυσία ὑμῶν ᾖ). (2) Let no one engaged in a dispute with his comrade join
> you until they have been reconciled, lest your sacrifice be profaned (ἵνα μὴ
> κοινωθῇ ἡ θυσία ὑμῶν). (3) This is [the sacrifice] of which the Lord has
> said: "to offer me a clean sacrifice (θυσίαν καθαράν) in every place and time,
> because I am a great king," says the Lord, "and my name is held in wonder
> among the nations."

---

[50] For the expression of "the purity of the men of holiness" and the "purities of (the) many" (טהרת רבים) as referring to the 'pure food,' that is, the common meal eaten by the full members of Qumran, see Lieberman, "The Discipline in the so-called Dead Sea Manual of Discipline," 199-206; Licht, *The Rule Scroll*, 294-303; Schiffman, "The Sectarian Penal Code," 161-68. For the original text (and English translation), see Charlesworth, *The Dead Sea Scrolls*, 22-23.

[51] For further information, see Van de Sandt-Flusser, *The Didache*, 274-75. See also Klawans, *Impurity and Sin, passim*; id., "The Impurity of Immorality," 7-10; Neusner, *The Idea of Purity*, 78. 87. 119.

[52] For further details, see Wernberg-Møller, *The Manual of Discipline*, 94-98; Leaney, *The Rule of Qumran*, 173-75; Knibb, *The Qumran Community*, 108-112; Licht, *The Rule Scroll*, 131-34.

Like in 1QS 5:13b-15a, the implication is that a lustration does not purify people who have not repented. The description in *Did.* 14 focusses on the Eucharist, as a sacrifice, and the members of the community are to acknowledge their sins in order that the sacrifice will be ritually clean (14:1). This requirement of purity is corroborated by the additional cultic term κοινοῦσθαι ("to be profaned") in 14:2, expressing the opposite in the ritual domain of the key phrase θυσία καθαρά in 14:1 and 14:3. Cleanness involves morality, not merely taking a bath.[53] The purity required to approach the divine is only attained through the performance of ablutions in a state of moral blamelessness including a confession of sins and mutual reconciliation.

The evidence surveyed here shows that, in relatively extensive passages, the Didache and 1QS present similar materials in the same sequence (*Did.* 14:1-15:3 // 1QS 5:10a-6:1b) while both writings have almost identical wording in the clauses with which we are directly concerned (*Did.* 15:3a = 1QS 5:24b-25).

6 Conclusion

It can be established that the reproof passage in Matthew as well as the reproof verse in the Didache show clear indications of having been developed from a text like 1QS 5:23-6:1. It is not my contention, however, that the materials in Matthew and the Didache are to be considered as a direct derivation of the Manual of Discipline. The Manual is a composite work, compiled from several older sources originating from different times and different sources. The rules for the organization of the community in 1QS 5-7 may once have existed separately.[54] This basic tradition could have circulated apart from its eventual incorporation and modification in the Manual of Discipline. It might be more appropriate, therefore, to ascertain that the materials in Matthew and the Didache prove the influence of a tradition which is closely related to the one represented in 1QS.[55]

---

[53] See Van de Sandt-Flusser, *The Didache*, 281-83; 303-04; Van de Sandt, "'Do not Give,'" 242-45.

[54] Metso, *The Textual Development*, 120-24. 143-49; see also Murphy O'Connor, "La genèse littéraire," 528-49; Dimant, "Qumran Sectarian Literature," 501-02.

[55] Of course, there may be a number of oral and written stages between the primary shape of the rule and later versions reflected in Matthew and the Didache. Such a development accounts for the presence of expulsion in Matt 18:17b and *Did.* 15:3. A list of punishments (including expulsion) for the various offences is lacking in 1QS 5:23-6:1 and in the section immediately following 1QS 6:1. It is not until 1QS 6:24-7:25 and 8:16b-9:2 that penitential codes are found. On the other hand, the most customary punishment in Qumran is enforced removal from the community, which could range from a permanent to a limited expulsion (from a period of ten days to a period of two years). Each punishment, even that for unconscious sins, involved "separation from the purity," meaning exclusion from the common meal, and from public meetings for a certain span of time (see Licht, *The Rule Scroll*, 154-55; Weinfeld, *The Organizational Pattern*, 41-43; Knibb, *The Qumran Community*, 124-27). Since expulsion was also the usual punishment in Qumran and in the Manual of Discipline, the Jewish version underlying the reproof directives of Matthew and the Didache still betrays its nearness to the 1QS scroll. In this light, some other form of the reproof tradition attested to by 1QS 5:23b-6:1 may have mentioned the penalty of expulsion.

In Matthew 18 (as a whole) and *Did.* 15:3, we have two transparent windows providing us with an insight into the situation of one or more mutually interdependent communities. Two things are clear. First, Matthew's gospel does not present a credible setting for the origin of its reproof section.[56] *Did.* 15, on the other hand, appears to provide the key. In following the sequence of topics like the one in the community order of 1QS, the Chapters 14-15 of the Didache seem the more natural background of the reproof section. In the context of verses naming the qualities and capacities required for the offices of bishops and deacons in 15:1-2, the manual then turns to the correction of failing brothers in general.

Second, it is of particular interest to see that the revised form of the current tradition was not due to the peculiar views of the individual authors. The fact that Matthew and the Didache both independently transmuted and rewrote a common Jewish reproof tradition was a result of the immediate ties they had with the community where this tradition was transmitted. Rather than integrating the reproof tradition in a judicial format, each of the two editors chose to emphasize the merciful and benevolent manner in which reproach was administered. The transposition provides a glimpse of the development of their community's attitude towards its sinners. It no longer enforced the exclusion of its wicked members by avoiding and shunning them. The injunction may have been altered and adapted within Jewish or Jewish-Christian circles, which maintained highly refined ethical standards. The reproof passages in Matthew and the Didache are the product of a conscious modification of the form of basic materials in order to meet the new situation and the prevailing viewpoint in their community.

---

[56] The "gospel" referred to in *Did.* 15:3 must, therefore, have been some authoritative source. Since only 15:3a is connected with a reference to the gospel ("correct one another not in anger but in peace, as you have it in the gospel"), whereas the exclusion statement appears to be peculiar to the Didache itself (see above, p. 187), the "gospel" may have contained a friendly reproof, and a warm-hearted exhortation. The phrase in *Did.* 15:3a shows resemblance to Sir 19:13-17 and a distinct correspondence with *T. Gad* 6:1-5, the (hypothetical) reconstruction of 4QBerakot 1-11 (see above, n. 43), 4QD^a frag. 18 col II 6-10 (see above, n. 46), and with 1QS 5:24b-25 in particular. John S. Kloppenborg suggested to me that the "gospel" under discussion may have been part of the Q source which also displays points of contact with Qumran materials in other ways.

Chapter Eleven

Eschatology in the Didache and the Gospel of Matthew

Joseph Verheyden

Catholic University Leuven (Belgium)

Matthew and the author/compiler of the Didache both have incorporated towards or at the end of their composition a section dealing with the events of the end time (Matt 24–25; *Did.* 16), and what they have to say about it at least invites comparing the two. For both, too, their interest in eschatology is not limited to these sections. In addition, one finds a number of more or less isolated references to or uses of eschatological concepts. In *Did.* such references are found in Chapters 1, 3–5, and 8–11 (1:5; 3:7; 4:4, 7, 10; 5:2; 8:2; 9:4; 10:5, 6; 11:11). They have recently been studied by H. Lohmann.[1] In the following, however, I will concentrate above all on the material in the last chapter of *Did.* because it offers a more elaborate (coherent?) picture of the content of the eschatological scenario which *Did.* teaches and it is here that one finds the closest parallels to the eschatological discourse of Matt 24–25. There are also two negative reasons to do so: for some of the material in the earlier sections of *Did.* scholars have expressed doubts about whether it is indeed eschatological in nature (see 4:4)[2] or whether it actually reflects *Did.*'s own views since it is found as a part of the liturgical traditions of its community (10:6).[3]

I will first briefly refer to the discussion on how to assess the relationship of the latter part of *Did.* with Matthew's eschatological discourse and argue that the hypothesis of *Did.*'s acquaintance with Matt is convincing. Then I will explore the implications of this conclusion for understanding the content and composition of Chapter 16.

Before tackling these questions a word must be said about the composition history of *Did.* It is a given in Didache studies that the work is a compilation of material from different origins and of different purposes that circulated in the community.[4] This is most obvious for the liturgical section (prayers, prescriptions on sacraments).[5] It is also

---

[1] Lohmann, *Drohung und Verheissung*, 36-45.

[2] *Ibid.*, 39. Cf. Niederwimmer, *Die Didache*, 138, and with some hesitation also Wengst, *Didache (Apostellehre)*, 94-95.

[3] Lohmann, *Drohung und Verheissung*, 44-45. See also Wengst, *Didache (Apostellehre)*, 46-47; Niederwimmer, *Die Didache*, 201-03.

[4] A good survey of the discussion in Niederwimmer, *Die Didache*, 48-64 (Did 1–6) and 64-71. Cf. also Wengst, *Didache (Apostellehre)*, 20-23, and most recently Van de Sandt-Flusser, *The Didache*, 28-31, 35-40 (*Did.* 16), and 40-48 (*Did.* 1:3b–2:1).

[5] See, e.g., Wengst, *Didache (Apostellehre)*, 43-53; Rordorf-Tuilier, *La Doctrine des Douze Apôtres*, 38-48.

generally agreed that the Two Ways section existed in one or another form before it was incorporated in *Did.*[6] The stipulations and teaching on how to receive prophets may reflect, in part at least, ruling practice.[7] That a piece of teaching on eschatology such as 16:3-8 may once have existed as an autonomous piece of writing cannot be disproved.

It is, however, also widely accepted that *Did.* shows traces of redactional activity in the different sections (or stages) of its composition. Specifically with regard to Chap. 16, K. Niederwimmer assigns the addition of the quotation in 16:7 to the redactor and regards 16:1-2 as a composition based in part on Jesus tradition, "ohne dass man an eine schriftliche Vorlage denken müsste."[8] A. Lindemann allows for the possibility that the chapter was composed by the author/compiler of the Didache on the basis of traditional material, but with an individual touch. "Denkbar ist aber auch, dass *Did.* 16 vom Verfasser bzw. Redaktor der Didache selbst formuliert wurde, zwar unter Verwendung von alterer Überlieferung, aber doch so, dass er selbst die Weisung konzipierte, die seiner Meinung nach den Adressaten seiner Schrift auf deren Weg mitgegeben werden musste."[9] In any case one should reckon with the possibility that the redactor/compiler may have left his fingerprints, in style and in wording, in putting together the various parts of the document.

1   The Problem of the Relationship between *Did.* 16 and Matthew

Any discussion on the composition and the theology of *Did.* should begin by clarifying the question of its relationship to the earliest Christian tradition and writings. For the last chapter of the work this essentially means looking into the question of the connection the *Did.* has with the gospel of Matthew.

The Didache contains verbal and content parallels with passages from Matthew's eschatological discourse in all verses of Chapter 16 except v. 7 which is a quotation from the OT that is however probably also alluded to in the final section of Matthew's discourse (25:31). When looking at it from the perspective of Matt, the parallel material is found in four consecutive sections from the first half of the discourse (Chap. 24): 24:9-14, 15-22, 23-28, 29-31. The first and last of these sections show a larger concentration of parallels (vv. 10-12, 13, 30-31). For the other two sections the verbally parallel material is limited to one or another expression (from vv. 21 and 24). *Did.* has verbal parallels with material that is peculiar to Matt (16:3-5 par. Matt 24:10-12, 13 and 16:6 par. Matt 24:30a, 31a) and with material in which Matt agrees with Mark (16:4b par. Matt 24:21, 24 and 16:8 par. Matt 24:30b).

---

[6] Cf. Niederwimmer, *Die Didache*, 64-69; Id., "Der Didachist und seine Quellen," 15-36; Baudry, *La voie de la Vie*, 75-89; see now esp. also the detailed analysis by Van de Sandt-Flusser, *The Didache*, 55-80 and 140-90 (the Jewish source of *Did.* 1–6), 112-39 (reconstruction of the original form of the Two Ways document).

[7] See again Van de Sandt-Flusser, *The Didache*, 340-64.

[8] *Die Didache*, 70.

[9] "Die Endzeitrede in Didache 16," 156.

There are basically two options to deal with the source problem of *Did.* 16.[10] One can argue that *Did.* and Matt had access to a common tradition or source which they independently adapted to their own agenda. Or one can argue for the opposite position that there is a link of literary dependence of *Did.* upon Matt.[11] The latter has been the dominant hypothesis until the 1950s.[12] Whether we have since reached a new consensus, now for the alternative position,[13] is a rather less interesting issue than the discussion on the methods and criteria that can substantiate either of these hypotheses.

One can of course always postulate the existence of a common source or tradition to account for the parallels (and the differences?), but such a position also has something of an *ad hoc* solution. Moreover, attempts to further identify the source(s) or tradition in more detail either tend to explain only part of the evidence, or result in rather complicated reconstructions. Thus, R. Glover's suggestion that *Did.* had access to (some form of) Q (tradition) can be reasonably sustained for double tradition material only, if one does not want to destroy the very presuppositions on which the Q hypothesis is built.[14] The solution proposed by H. Koester with regard to *Did.* 16 suffers from the complication that it has to hypothesize, in addition to the common use of stock apocalyptic motifs, the combined influence, first on Matt and then again on *Did.*, of, on the one hand, an apocalyptic tract of Jewish origin that was also used by Mark in composing his eschatological discourse and, on the other, a piece of apocalyptic tradition that accounts for the parallels between Matt 24:10-12 and *Did.* 16:3-5.[15] This problem has well been sensed by J.S. Kloppenborg. He agrees with

---

[10] Unless, of course, one decides to remain uncommitted on the issue, as is, e.g., Jefford, *The Sayings of Jesus,* 85-90, esp. 90.

[11] Some sort of middle position was defended for *Did.* 16 by Drews, "Untersuchungen zur Didache," 68-73, who argued that this chapter was composed on the basis of the same source that underlied Mark 13, to which was added some material from Matt 24. For surveys of the earlier and the more recent discussion, see, a.o., Koester, *Synoptische Überlieferung,* 173-90, esp. 173-74 and 189-90; Tuckett, "Synoptic Tradition in the Didache," 197-200 / 92-95; Niederwimmer, *Die Didache,* 247-56; Jefford, *The Sayings of Jesus,* 4-17; Balabanski, *Eschatology in the Making,* 180-83.

[12] As a representative of this position, see above all Massaux, *Influence de l'Évangile,* 604-641. This chapter was originally published separately in *Ephemerides theologicae lovanienses* 25 (1949) 5-41. Köhler takes a quite different stand in *Die Rezeption des Matthäusevangeliums,* 51-55. See the assessment of Köhler's position in Balabanski, *Eschatology in the Making,* 189-91.

[13] Thus Tuilier, "Didache," 735. It should be noted that Tuilier's own solution for the sources of *Did.* is marred by his most singular position on the synoptic problem and the development of early Christian tradition: see his "La Didachè et le problème synoptique," 110-30.

[14] Cf. "The Didache's Quotations," 12-29, and "Patristic Quotations," 239.

[15] "Die mannigfachen Berührungen mit den Synoptikern beruhen 1. Auf dem Vorkommen auch sonst verbreiteter apokalyptischen Züge und Sätze (Did. 16,1.6.7), 2. Darauf, dass ein Teil der Did. 16 und Mark. 13 vorkommenden Stoffes aus ein und derselben jüdischen Apokalypse stammt (Did. 16,4b.5.8), 3. Darauf, dass ein weiteres apokalyptisches Traditionsstück sowohl von Did. 16 als auch von Mt. (24,10-12) benutzt wird (Did. 16,3.4a.5)" (*Synoptische Überlieferung,* 189).

This Jewish apocalypse receives a rather different content in Trevijano Etcheverria, "Discurso escatologico," 365-93. On the basis of a stichometric and stylistic analysis he reconstructs three strata: an apocalyptic document consisting of vv. 3-4a, 5 (but without the last four words), and 8; an addition by the Didachist (vv. 1-2); further explanatory additions by a "didaskalos" (vv. 4b, 5*fin,* 6-7). In a recent study Marcello Del Verme finds traces of such a Jewish apocalypse in a number of Hellenistic-Jewish writings and also in Qumran. His rather too

Koester that the parallels in Matt 24 and *Did.* 16 are best explained on the hypothesis that common tradition lies behind them, but he does not accept that (part of) this tradition can be identified with Mark's *Vorlage* in Chap. 13, "since Did 16 lacks most of the elements contained in that tradition."[16] He is also critical of how Koester manages to have the *Vorlage* fit the hypothesis when assuming that it read ἐπὶ τῶν νεφελῶν.[17] Kloppenborg himself prefers to speak of the common use by Matt and *Did.* of "free-floating apocalyptic tradition,"[18] but this may prove to be too general a way to account for all of the parallels and for the way they figure in Matt and in *Did.*

The hypothesis that *Did.* had access to the gospel of Matthew can of course not be built upon a mere listing of the parallels, as has sometimes been done in the past, but then this is certainly not the way it is currently argued for. In his fine analysis of the synoptic material in the Didache, C.M. Tuckett formulates as follows the principle that should decide on the matter: "if material which owes its origin to the redactional activity of a synoptic evangelist reappears in another work, then the latter presupposes the finished work of that evangelist."[19] Of course, "such a criterion must ... be applied with care," because it is always possible that two redactors have independently added the same or a similar phrase to the common tradition or source they are relying on. And it is also true that the criterion does not decide whether this dependence was direct or mediated. But, as Tuckett rightly concludes, "Nevertheless, this criterion is really the only one which ultimately can determine whether a text like the Didache presupposes the finished gospels or whether it uses traditions which lie behind our gospels."[20]

Koester built his case for the independent use by *Did.* and Matt of common tradition on the double observation that none of the parallel material in *Did.* 16:3-8 is of undisputably Matthean origin, and further also that no such elements can be found in this section of which it can be ascertained that Matt must have received them from Mark.[21] While the latter certainly is rather odd if Matt 24 is a major source of *Did.* in Chap. 16, the former part of the argument, if true, would be fatal for the hypothesis of literary dependence.

Tuckett takes issue with both aspects of Koester's argument. With regard to the material that is peculiar to Matt, Tuckett points out that several scholars now accept that vv. 10-12 may have been composed by Matt or at least show clear traces of

brief analysis of the NT data closely follows Koester's. Cf. "*Did.* 16 e la cosidetta 'apocalittica giudaica'," 68-71. A most useful tool (though with quite some typographical errors) is Del Verme's bibliography of *Did.* which covers a broader field than one would conclude from its subtitle: "*Didaché* e origini cristiane. Una bibliografia per lo studio della *Didaché* nel contesto del giudaismo cristiano," 5-39 and 223-45.

16 "Didache 16,6-8," 67.

17 "There is no sufficient evidence to conclude that Mk 13,26 originally read ἐπί, nor can 14,62 be called a witness, since the original reading there was undoubtedly μετά" ("Didache 16,6-8," 61).

18 *Ibid.*, 67.

19 "Synoptic Tradition in the Didache," 199 / 95.

20 *Ibid.*, 199-200 / 95.

21 *Synoptische Überlieferung*, 173-90. The second observation is repeated by Kloppenborg who speaks of "the presence of a disproportionately large amount of material in Did 16,3-8 which has parallels only in special Matthaean material and the corresponding lack of distinctively Marcan material as reproduced by Matthew" ("Didache 16,6-8," 66).

MattR.[22] The same can be argued, though perhaps less forcefully, for (some of) the elements from vv. 30-31 that have a parallel in *Did.*[23]

As for the second difficulty, Tuckett again answers by observing that some case can be made in favour of MarkR, if not for Mark 13:19 par. Matt 24:21 (οὐ γέγονεν), then at least for Mark 13:22 par. Matt 24:24, which both have a parallel in *Did.* 16.[24] However, this second part of the problem cannot be put on the same level with the first one. If it is correct that *Did.* in 16:3-5 is acquainted with a piece of Matthean composition, this conclusion has to be taken into account when assessing the Matthew-Mark agreements as well. If *Did.* had access, not to a tradition which it has in common with Matthew, but to the gospel itself (the "finished gospel" as Tuckett calls it), it may also well have taken the material which has a parallel in Matt and in Mark directly from Matthew's gospel, and there is no need then to speculate about Matt and *Did.* having used the same *Vorlage* of the discourse as Mark had done before him or to assign such material to the use of stock apocalyptic motifs.[25]

Tuckett concludes his study of *Did.* 16:3-8 with the observation that "there is nothing peculiar in the pattern of parallels with Did 16 in Matt 24. Did 16 shows verbal links with the material peculiar to Matthew in this chapter, with material common to Matthew and Mark and with Matthew's redaction of Mark. There is little convincing evidence to show that Matthew had access to any extensive source other than Mark for this chapter. The pattern of parallels between the Didache and Matthew is thus most easily explained if the Didache here presupposes Matthew's finished gospel."[26]

Tuckett's analysis has been called "– after that of H. Koester – incomparably the most careful and comprehensive study of the problem"[27] and "the best possible case for

---

[22] "Synoptic Tradition in the Didache," 205-07 / 101-03, and esp. n. 43. Tuckett calls it "a widespread agreement." It has become something of a common opinion in major recent commentaries. See Gnilka, *Das Matthäusevangelium* 2, 314-15. Harrington, *The Gospel of Matthew*, 332-33 (the false prophets of v. 11 and the persecution in v. 10 are "inspired" by Mark 13:6, 12). Luz, *Das Evangelium nach Matthäus* 3, 403: "Verse 24,9-14 sind eine von Mt recht frei geschriebene, sich aber an Mk 13,9-13 anlehnende Dublette;" cf. 422: "die von Matthäus neu geschriebenen V 10-12." Davies-Allison, *The Gospel According to Saint Matthew*, remain "unpersuaded" and suggest as "a guess" that "Matthew drew upon a small apocalypse akin to what appears in Did. 16.3-6," but they recognize that "most now attribute vv. 10-12 to redaction" (3, 327). They also point out that ἀνομία is a characteristic of Matt (343) and that v. 11, "if not independent tradition, … was probably composed from the elements of vv. 4-5, 23-4" (342-43).

[23] "Synoptic Tradition in the Didache," 207-08 / 103-04, and esp. n. 48. Tuckett ascribes the differences between Matt and Mark in the Daniel quotation in v. 30b to MattR (204 / 101 and n. 38). Cf. also Gnilka, *Das Matthäusevangelium* 2, 329 and 328 (on v. 30a): "Es besteht keine Veranlassung, den Satz wegen seiner Rätselhaftigkeit als alt anzusehen. Der Rückbezug auf 3b [σημεῖον] innerhalb der Rede und atl Anspielungen sprechen für MtR." Luz, *Das Evangelium nach Matthäus* 3, 434: "das von Mt selbst hinzugefügte Erscheinen des Zeichens des Menschensohns;" 436 (on the trumpet in v. 31).

[24] "Synoptic Tradition in the Didache," 200-02 / 96-98, and esp. n. 24.

[25] The discrepancy between the "amount" of special Matthean material and material which Matthew may have borrowed from Mark is thus less acute as Kloppenborg would have it and "disproportionately large" is a relative concept (see above n. 21). *Did.*'s preference for Matthew's special material can sufficiently be accounted for on the hypothesis that it was acquainted with this gospel and found in it the appropriate material to make its point (see the analysis below).

[26] "Synoptic Tradition in the Didache," 208 / 104.

[27] Rordorf, "Does the Didache Contain?," 400.

the literary dependence of the Did. upon the finished gospels of Matthew and Luke."[28] However, in academic discussions such words of praise can also function to introduce a more critical assessment.

Rordorf offers two kinds of criticism. The first one has to do with the precedence of the redactional-critical approach over the source-critical. Against Koester's claims that the verbal parallels in 16:3-5 with 24:10-12 are not impressive enough to support the conclusion that Did. depends directly upon Matt and that the parallel in Did. 16:3-5 can be used to hypothesize the existence of a tradition or source behind Matt 24:10-12 and Did. 16:3-5, Tuckett points out that, if one cannot on the sole basis of parallel vocabulary decide whether or not there is a direct literary dependence between Did. and Matt, the second of Koester's observations is a circular reasoning.[29] Rordorf objects, "I cannot see this," and continues, "The only procedure possible for me is to ask the question whether Matt 24,10-12 can be a self-sufficient Matthaean composition based on Mark 13,9-13."[30] But that is precisely the question Tuckett had asked and answered positively! And it is on the basis of this answer that the second of Koester's arguments can no longer function. The possibility that Did. and Matt made use of a common source (or tradition) and that Did. may provide additional evidence for its existence can only be maintained if the question of identifying MattR in 24:10-12 would have been answered negatively. The redaction-critical principle is the decisive factor in deciding on the relationship between two writings.[31]

The second criticism has to do with Tuckett's use of the concept of "free quotations" or allusions. In his analysis Tuckett repeatedly notes that Did. does not quote and did not want to quote the gospels, but that it alludes to certain passages or uses them freely. In four instances Did. at least explicitly refers to "the gospel" (8:2; 11:3; 15:3, 4). Apart from the first one, there does not follow a formal verbal quotation. Wengst has given great emphasis to these passages, which in his view are the corner stone for the dependence hypothesis.[32] Tuckett is more reserved, objecting that precedence should be given to the results gained through a redaction-critical study of the parallels and that one cannot exclude a late date for (some of) those references (15:3, 4).[33] Rordorf assigns the references in 15:3, 4 (what about the others?) to a redactor and finds in the distinction between explicit and allusive reference "a further decisive argument for the assumption that the Didachist did not have before him the completed Synoptic

---

[28] Henderson, "Style-Switching in the *Didache*," 179.

[29] "The claim that Did 16 itself may provide evidence that Mt 24,10-12 is pre-Matthean is a case of petitio principii here. If the question is whether the Didache depends on Matthew's gospel or on a pre-Matthean source, one cannot use the evidence of the Didache itself to solve the source problem of Matthew's text" ("Synoptic Tradition in the Didache," 208 / 103).

[30] "Does the Didache Contain?," 418.

[31] Compare the criticism of Rordorf in Balabanski, *Eschatology in the Making*, 183-85. Of course, one can dispute the redactional character of one or another element, but one cannot regard the redaction- and the source-critical solution as two equally valid alternatives as Jonathan Draper seems to suggest in a number of instances. See his "The Jesus Tradition in the Didache," 75-76.

[32] *Didache (Apostellehre)*, 24-32.

[33] "Synoptic Tradition in the Didache," 199 / 94 n. 10.

gospels, and he did not use them."[34] But can this negative evidence (the lack of explicit references) support the conclusion that at an earlier stage the *Did.* had no access yet to written but only to oral Jesus tradition?[35] After all, there may be two different authors at work. Tuckett, for one, has no problem with accepting that an (the same?) author or compiler can have used or referred to his sources in different ways.[36]

I.H. Henderson also concentrates his comments on the same problem of "deliberate non-quotation" as he rebaptizes Tuckett's "maxim" of the *Did.*'s freely using the gospel material.[37] Henderson asks two questions. First, "is it credible that someone who through direct access to Matthew and/or Luke was able to retain distinct impressions of Matthean or Lukan redactional choices would sometimes reproduce those impressions stylistically, but almost never reflect an understanding of the Matthean or Lukan argument?"[38] Questions about what is "credible" are by nature hard to answer. Moreover, it is quite an overstatement to say that *Did.* is "almost never" sensitive of Matthew's reasoning. Henderson's second, and in his view more important, question is, "why, after all, does the Didache quote when and as it does?"[39] Again, such a question might be inappropriate since an author does not have to follow a specific pattern. Henderson argues, that it must be "a conscious decision" on the part of the Didachist to use "non-quotations" along with "marked quotations."[40] The latter are not signaled out by a particularly greater concern for verbal precision when compared to some of the allusions.[41] Henderson suggests a plausible answer for the "marked" OT quotations. In *Did.* this form is apparently used to call upon an undisputed authority to promote some form of discrimination between in- and outsiders concerning social conduct (1:6; 9:4; 13:3) or the fate of humanity (16:7).[42] The same explanation would equally well apply for the most easily identifiable "marked" quotation from the gospels (8:2, the Lord's directions on prayer over against those of the "hypocrites"). In any case, Henderson admits that "non-quotations" reflect the author's "independence", but not for that reason "ignorance".[43]

Tuckett builds the case for literary dependence on the presence of verbal parallels that can be assigned to redaction in the source text. This case is further supported if particular combinations of verbal parallels or motifs occur. Thus with regard to 16:6-8 Tuckett rightly observes that if the indications for redaction of each of the verbal parallels taken separately may be not too impressive (stock apocalyptic motifs), "the connection between, for example, the eschatological trumpet and Dan 7:13, as in

---

[34] "Does the Didache Contain?," 420.

[35] So Rordorf, *Ibid.*, 421.

[36] "Synoptic Tradition in the Didache," 198 / 94.

[37] "Style-Switching in the *Didache*." A second "maxim" he discusses is that of "parsimony": the literary dependence hypothesis is a more economic solution (184-85).

[38] *Ibid.*, 183.

[39] *Ibid.*, 205.

[40] *Ibid.*, 182.

[41] *Ibid.*, 206-07.

[42] *Ibid.*, 206.

[43] *Ibid.*, 208.

both Did 16:6,8 and Mt 24:30, is not easy to attest elsewhere,"[44] thereby implying that this constellation of motifs cannot be regarded as the work of Mark which Matt took over. However, the situation seems to be rather different in 16:3-4a. There may be quite some verbal parallels with 24:10-12, but *Did.* seems to have mixed up all the phrases and also to have added some other material. Instead of Matt's πολλοὶ ψευδοπροφῆται ἐγερθήσονται, it is now said in 16:3a, πληθυνθήσονται οἱ ψευδοπροφῆται, which is the verb Matt used to describe the increase of lawlessness, for which *Did.* then has αὐξανούσης. Likewise, Matt's ψυγήσεται ἡ ἀγάπη has become καὶ ἡ ἀγάπη στραφήσεται εἰς μῖσος, which takes up the motif of "hatred" that is twice mentioned in 24:9-14. Matt's double triad of παραδώσουσιν ὑμᾶς ... – ἀποκτενοῦσιν ὑμᾶς – καὶ ἔσεσθε μισούμενοι ... (v. 9) and σκανδαλισθήσονται πολλοὶ καὶ παραδώσουσιν ... μισήσουσιν (v. 10) is rendered in one as μισήσουσιν ... καὶ διώξουσι καὶ παραδώσουσι in 16:4b, while σκανδαλισθήσονται πολλοί now shows up in 16:5 together with καὶ ἀπολοῦνται, a combination that recalls Matt 5:29, 30 and 18:9-11. Another such case of the "intrusion" of elements from another context in Matt is στραφήσονται τὰ πρόβατα εἰς λυκούς in 16:3a, which reminds one of the similar passage on the chaos caused by false prophets in Matt 7:15 where a variant but comparable form of the motif is used to characterize these prophets.

It looks as if *Did.* has done its best to destroy whatever evidence there can be found of its dependence on Matt's composition in 24:10-12. This may be the first impression, but not therefore the correct conclusion. Quite the opposite conclusion is reached indeed if one realizes that Matthew in rewriting 10:17-22 for his version of the eschatological discourse has used precisely the same double strategy of freely interchanging certain words and phrases, while occasionally also introducing a "new" motif from a related context. One has only to compare the change from παραδώσουσιν (– μαστιγώσουσιν – ἀχθήσεσθε) and θανατώσουσιν αὐτούς in 10:17, 21 to παραδώσουσιν – ἀποκτενοῦσιν in 24:9; the transfert from the concrete "brother – father – children" of 10:21 to the more general ἀλλήλους in 24:10; and the triad παραδώσει – ἐπαναστήσονται – θανατώσουσιν of 10:21 which has become σκανδαλισθήσονται – παραδώσουσιν – μισήσουσιν in 24:10. The pseudoprophets of 24:11 were not yet mentioned in 10:17-22, but they figure in the immediate context (v. 24), just as the ἀνομία motif was used before in 7:23 to condemn those who had falsely prophesied in Jesus' name (v. 22). It would appear then that the "inspiration" for *Did.*'s freely paraphrasing its source in this case may in part have come from the very similar way in which Matthew, when composing his second version of the persecution of the disciples, has handled the very same passage which would become *Did.*'s source text for 16:3-4a. As we will see below the result of this operation in *Did.* is less chaotic than it might seem.

[44] "Synoptic Tradition in the Didache," 208 / 104.

2 Reading the Didache's Eschatology with an Eye on the Gospel of Matthew

If a good case can be made for the hypothesis that *Did.* 16:3-8 shows traces of the use of Matthew's version of the discourse, it is a priori rather implausible that this can be taken in a minimalistic way, as if *Did.* recalled or borrowed a couple of expressions from Matt and then forgot about the rest of the discourse or the gospel. It is therefore a reasonable assumption to consider reading the eschatological scenario of *Did.* 16 with an eye on Matt. I do not want to argue that Matthew's gospel was *Did.*'s only source of inspiration for each and every detail of its composition. But I do think Matthew's discourse in Chap. 24 has guided and inspired the author/compiler of Chap. 16 to a greater extent than the somewhat oblique verbal parallels would suggest.[45]

Did. 16:1: When Shall the End Come and What Will It Be Like?

In Matt the disciples ask Jesus a double question: πότε ταῦτα ἔσται καὶ τί τὸ σημεῖον τῆς σῆς παρουσίας καὶ συντελείας τοῦ αἰῶνος (24:3). The answer to these questions does not follow immediately. It is embedded in a long discourse and it could perhaps have been formulated in a somewhat less complex way. The reader could indeed be tempted to find the answer to the first question in the description of the end time scenario in vv. 4-31, esp. if he identifies his own situation with one of the various tribulations that are described and then gives full weight to the εὐθέως of v. 29. He may realize that he is living on the doorstep of the final stage. But he will probably also be puzzled by how this εὐθέως is to be reconciled with the perspective that is opened in v. 14 and that apparently allows for a more or less long period of missionary activity throughout the world before the end comes. Some kind of clarification follows in vv. 34-36. It is now emphatically stated that "this generation will not pass away till all these things take place" (v. 34) and that only the Father knows "that day and hour" (v. 36). That seems to be the real answer to the "when" question and it is repeated again in vv. 42 and 44 and in the Parable of the Maidens. Yet the aporia that was created in the earlier half of the discourse is not solved.

The question of the sign is hardly more satisfactorily answered. The disciples/readers are given a detailed scenario of the events that will lead up to the parousia (vv. 4-31), but the structure is not as transparent as one would have wished. Jesus first tells the disciples about certain events that could be mistaken for the end but definitely are not, though they nevertheless are "the beginning of the birthpangs" (v. 8; cf. v. 6). There follows a description of troubles involving the faithful of which it is not clearly said how they relate to the previous section. They are obviously not the end yet, for that is mentioned only in v. 29. However, by the time the reader has reached v. 29 he has been taught that the kind of speculations that is linked to such scenarios will be

---

[45] In so far, my approach is comparable to Bentley Layton's analysis of *Did.* 1:3–2:1, which is conducted on the hypothesis that the author of this section was familiar with the gospel of Matthew: cf. his "The Sources, Date and Transmission." Only, Tuckett has now provided the necessary foundations for this hypothesis (see his comments on Layton's approach in "Synoptic Tradition in the Didache," 200 / 95).

rather useless for the coming of the Lord will be as obvious as the strike of lightning (v. 27). This idea is taken up again in vv. 32-33 and seems to be the real answer to the "what" question of the disciples.

Did. deals with the same two questions but in a much more direct way. The answer to the "when" is given right at the beginning of the chapter and it is clear and simple: οὐ γὰρ οἴδατε τὴν ὥραν (v. 1). And so is the answer to the "what". It is a fixed and simple scenario and there is no room for speculations about what has already happened or what is still to come, and even less about what does and what does not belong to the end. Vv. 3-8 are the scenario of what will happen "in the last days." No more talks of "beginnings of birthpangs." There will be an unspecified period of tribulations (16:3-5). Then there will appear three signs announcing the parousia (16:6-7). And finally the Lord will come (16:8). *Did.* has been true to Matthew's scenario but it has set the records straight. There is a clear answer to the "when" question, and it is the same as the one that really counts for Matt. By putting it right at the beginning the reader is no longer tempted to look for the answer at the wrong place. And there is also an equally clear answer to the "what" question, and it is one that integrates both parts of Matthew's answer for it describes in detail and without further complications what the signs of the parousia will be ("the signs of truth") and by the same token also illustrates that the parousia will be clearly recognizable.

Did. 16:3-5: Tribulations Ahead

As was said above, the structure of the discourse in Matt is a matter of dispute. The repetition of certain themes (false prophets are mentioned in v. 4 and v. 11 and again in vv. 24-26; war in v. 7 and in vv. 15-22) and the strange arrangement of the various motifs in vv. 4-28 (persecution – war – false prophets) argue against reading it as a straightforward description of a succession of events. Balabanski and Luz have recently proposed a double sequence division.[46] In Balabanski's proposal vv. 6-8 correspond to 15-20, vv. 9-12 to 21-28, and vv. 13-14 to 29-31, v. 4 being a sort of introduction. The first half describes the events of the Jewish war and the situation of the Matthean community from the perspective of those who did only hear about it, while the second half does so from the perspective of those who had eyewitnessed it and had found refuge in the community. Luz offers a modified form of this structure in which vv. 9-14 correspond to 21-28 and vv. 29-31 are regarded as the concluding description of the end. He also prefers to speak of an 'ecumenical' (universalistic) perspective and one that is limited to Judaea. Both proposals disregard, on the one hand, the function of v. 8, for which there is no real counterpart in v. 20, and on the other, the parallelism between vv. 21-22 and v. 13, as well as the difference between vv. 9-14 and (21-22,) 23-28, (29-31). These difficulties are (better) solved if vv. 4-8, taken together, are regarded as a general introductory description of the period "that is not yet the end" (v. 6, cf. 8), which is then "repeated" in more detail in the three scenes of vv. 9-14, 15-22, 23-28. The second (vv. 15-22) and third (vv. 23-28) take up, in inverted order,

---

[46] Balabanski, *Eschatology in the Making*, 153-162; Luz, *Das Evangelium nach Matthäus* 3, 407-08.

the motifs of wars and of false prophets misleading the faithful that are found in vv. 4-5, 6-7 (the false prophets also occur in v. 11, but only as a secondary element when compared to vv. 23-26). The first scene (vv. 9-14) adds something new and in so far it probably reflects a special concern of Matt. That may be the reason also why Matt, after having anticipated this passage in Chap. 10, nevertheless adds a second version of it in the discourse.

In *Did.* the period of tribulations that precedes the end is described in 16:3-5. The section is divided into three parts (3 ἐν ... 4b καὶ τότε ... 5 τότε), but these do not correspond to the three scenes of Matt 24:9-28, and as the analysis will show these three parts are most strongly interconnected and in fact describe only one type of tribulation.

Did. 16:3-4a: Persecution, Apostasy and Betrayal

The events that lead up to the end are dreadful. Matthew, following Mark, speaks of wars and warfare, of famine and earthquakes, of the destruction of the holy city, of chaos caused by false prophets, and of the persecution and suffering of the faithful. *Did.* takes up only this last motif.

In Matt 10:21 Jesus warns his disciples that they, and by extension Christians in general, will have to stand trial and even will be betrayed by members of their own family that have not converted.[47] The perspective is different, and in a sense more confused, in 24:9-14. On the one hand, Matthew repeats that the Christians will be hated by outsiders (he adds τῶν ἐθνῶν to ὑπὸ πάντων, diff. Mark 13:9 and Matt 10:22). But on the other hand, he now also introduces the motif of mutual hatred and strife (24:10b ἀλλήλους). Suffering will be brought upon the Christians by in- and outsiders alike. This scene is a more terrible one than that of 10:21. *Did.* even adds to it by omitting the outsider perspective of 24:9 and by focusing exclusively on what threatens to destroy the community from within.[48] Matthew further also introduces in 24:9-14 the motif of the false prophets deceiving many (24:11 πλανήσουσιν). *Did.* retains this motif but reformulates it: καὶ στραφήσονται τὰ πρόβατα εἰς λύκους, i.e., there will be a great apostasy of members of the community.[49] That στρέφω can have this meaning needs little comment. It is used in this way in the NT in Acts 7:39.[50]

---

47 Luz, *Das Evangelium nach Matthäus* 3, 422.

48 *Pace* Lindemann, "Die Endzeitrede in Didache 16," 162-63, who argues that ἀλλήλους does not specifically refer to Christians. But see Niederwimmer, *Die Didache*, 261: "Aus Brüdern werden Feinde, und das hat in der Situation, in der sich die Christen innerhalb der Gesellschaft befinden (nämlich in der Situation der ständigen Unsicherheit, die jederzeit in Verfolgung umschlagen kann), die Konsequenz, dass ein Bruder den anderen verfolgt und verrät. Mit παραδώσουσι ist gemeint, dass abgefallene Christen ihre ehemaligen Brüder bei den Behörden denunzieren."

49 The continuation of the verse (καὶ ἡ ἀγάπη στραφήσεται εἰς μῖσος) does not argue against this. There is no reason to omit the repetition of the verb as proposed by Wengst, *Didache (Apostellehre)*, 88; see Lindemann, "Die Endzeitrede in Didache 16," 161 n. 26.

50 Thus Haenchen, *The Acts of the Apostles*, 283: the verb alludes to Num 14:3, but "of course the present verse 'spiritualizes' this return ..., i.e. they fell into the idolatry which prevailed in Egypt." Cf. also Fitzmyer, *The Acts of the Apostles*, 380. This interpretation is to be preferred over the literal one that is too much influenced by Num 14:3. For the latter, see Barrett, *Commentary on the Acts of the Apostles* 1, 366.

The same connotation underlies the use of the verb in *Did.* 11:2a and this motif may then reflect a particular concern of *Did.*[51] The vocabulary of 16:3, and in part also the image itself, recalls Matt 7:15 and may have been inspired by πλανάω in 24:11 (cf. Matt 18:12-14 diff. Luke 15:4-7). Two dangers then will (are) threaten(ing) the community from within: apostasy and betrayal by fellow Christians.

Did. 16:4b: The Deceiver

With the appearance of the κοσμοπλανής in 16:4b the perspective moves from the level of the community to that of a suprahuman character, but the verse is still closely connected with the preceding as the analysis will show. The word κοσμοπλανής is not found elsewhere in early Christian literature.[52] This character calls forth associations with traditions on the Antichrist and Satan, but several aspects of *Did.*'s description seem to have been directly inspired by Matt. The deceiver will appear as "(a) son of God." As his name suggests, he will "lead astray" and he will do so by working "signs and wonders," as will do the pseudo-Christs and pseudoprophets of Matt 24:24 (see in vv. 4-5, 11). It is also said that "the earth will be given into his hands" and that "he will do godless things that have never been done."

The first of these motifs further characterizes the godlike aura of the deceiver. It can be compared with Rev 13:7,[53] but perhaps even better with the third and final offer in the temptation story (Matt 4:8-9), after the devil had already expressed doubts about whether Jesus really is the Son of God (4:3, 6).[54] The Deceiver is a parody of Christ. He will accept what the devil unsuccessfully offered to Jesus. The motif indirectly also introduces yet another character who is not mentioned by name. The Deceiver does not take his power from himself. It has been given to him (παραδοθήσεται). His appearance is in a sense orchestrated. A similar idea underlies Matt 24:21-22, 24. God will allow that a great tribulation and the appearance of false Christs and prophets threaten the faithful.[55] However, contrary to Matthew, who also says that there will be put an end to the affliction (v. 22) or implies that the pseudoprophets will not succeed (v. 24), *Did.* does not add here that the Deceiver's power will also again be taken away from him. It is possible that this was intended by the passive verb, but it is not said as such. It could be an indication that more was to follow in *Did.* after 16:8.[56]

---

[51] Cf. Niederwimmer, *Die Didache*, 212.

[52] The Apostolic Constitutions (CA) reads κοσμοπλάνος (thus Wengst also for *Did.*).

[53] Niederwimmer, *Die Didache*, 262 n. 9. Cf. Lietaert Peerbolte, *The Antecedents of Antichrist*, 182.

[54] Cf. Lindemann, "Die Endzeitrede in Didache 16," 163 n. 36: "In der synoptischen Tradition begegnet eine entsprechende Aussage nicht; vgl. aber Lk 4,6.9." See also Löfstedt, "A Message for the Last Days," 365 n. 41, who adds a reference to Matt 26:53, but is critical of the hypothesis that *Did.* may have had access to the gospel of Matthew. Giordano, "L' escatologia nella *Didaché*," 133, connects the phrase with imperial dominion.

[55] The connection between 24:21-22 and Dan 12:1-3 implies that God has "arranged" the apocalyptic timetable and the order of things; see Harrington, *The Gospel of Matthew*, 340.

[56] The Apostolic Constitutions (CA) VII, 32, 2, 4 mentions the defeat of the devil at the parousia of the Lord.

It is debated what is meant by ἀθέμιτα. It has been associated with the claims of the Deceiver that he is "son of God."[57] The parallelism between ποιήσει σημεῖα καὶ τέρατα and ποιήσει ἀθέμιτα rather invites to connect it with the activities of the false prophets. Niederwimmer comments, "Ob unser Apokalyptiker mit den ἀθέμιτα Christenverfolgungen meint, ist unsicher. Die Fortsetzung legt es nahe."[58] He also likens *Did.*'s ἀθέμιτα to the ἄνομα which according to Justin will be performed against Christians by the ἄνθρωπος τῆς ἀποστασίας.[59] In the two instances in which the word occurs in the NT (Acts 10:28 and 1 Pet 4:3) it has the same connotation of doing something that is at the same time unlawful and unholy.[60] The possible association between ἀθέμιτα and ἄνομα would create a link with 16:4a (ἀνομίας). The appearance of the Deceiver is thus probably best understood in light of the dangers that will threaten the community. *Did.* 16:4b points out who is behind them.

Did.'s ποιήσει ἀθέμιτα is often regarded as a kind of summary of the descriptions in 2 Thess 2:1-12 or Rev 13:1-10.[61] In Matt 24:24 (par. Mark 13:22) Matthew also offers "only" a summary of the activities of the false Christs in a form that is closely parallel to the way *Did.* describes the works of the Deceiver (working signs and wonders in order to deceive). Moreover, it is not impossible that even the character of the Deceiver himself has been inspired by Matthew's gospel. It has been argued that Matt's βδέλυγμα τῆς ἐρημώσεως (24:15) could refer to the Antichrist.[62] This interpretation is rather implausible because of the immediate context that speaks about those in Judaea and gives directions about how to flee from the chaos that is caused by the βδέλυγμα.[63] However, when making abstraction of the specific context in which the expression occurs in Matt, the word βδέλυγμα could certainly be associated with (the work of) the Antichrist.[64] It is in any case remarkable that *Did.* concludes precisely this part of the scenario with a phrase that contains a verbal parallel with Matt 24:21 that is found at the end of the section in which Matt mentions the βδέλυγμα.

---

[57] Thus Knopf, *Die Lehre der zwölf Apostel*, 39.

[58] Niederwimmer, *Die Didache*, p. 262.

[59] *Dial* 110:2 ὁ καὶ εἰς τὸν ὕψιστον ἔξαλλα λαλῶν, ἐπὶ τῆς γῆς ἄνομα τολμήσῃ εἰς ἡμᾶς τοὺς Χριστιανούς. Cf. Niederwimmer, *Die Didache*, p. 262 n. 12. See also Löfstedt, "A Message for the Last Days," 364: "It is roughly synonymous with ἀνομία."

[60] See, e.g., Fitzmyer, *The Acts of the Apostles*, 461. Elliott, *1 Peter*, 724.

[61] Cf. Lietaert Peerbolte, *The Antecedents of Antichrist*, 182; Lindemann, "Die Endzeitrede in Didache 16," 163 n. 38.

[62] See, e.g., Gnilka, *Das Matthäusevangelium* 2, 322-23. Davies-Allison, *The Gospel According to Saint Matthew*, 3, 345-46: "no less likely." Broer, "Redaktionsgeschichtliche Aspekte," 227-31, argues that v. 15 refers to a future tribulation, which he does not identify.

[63] Thus Lambrecht, "The Parousia Discourse," 321-22.

[64] Cf. Balabanski, *Eschatology in the Making*, 195. Whether *Did.* "could have done better than simply substitute the term κοσμοπλανής for βδέλυγμα τῆς ἐρημώσεως" (Löfstedt, "A Message for the Last Days," 365) is a matter of appreciation, but the word echoes Matthew's description in Chap. 24 of false prophets and Christs deceiving the faithful. We do not know whether *Did.* knew of an alternative (cf. ἀντίχριστος in 1 John 4:2-3 and Polycarp, *Phil* 7:1).

Did. 16:5: Passing or Failing the Test of Fire

With another τότε *Did.* introduces a new motif, but one that is also linked to 16:3. This is perhaps the most difficult verse of the whole chapter. It is also a crucial one for assessing the way in which *Did.* has handled Matt's scenario of the end time. It announces that "then human creation will pass into the testing fire and many will fall away and perish." The focus has shifted to mankind again. The major problem is whether the testing by fire is an eschatological tribulation that prepares for, and in any case precedes, the judgement that is still to come, or whether this testing is already a way to describe the final judgement itself. The latter view has recently been proposed by Lindemann on the basis of Paul's description in 1 Cor 3:13, of what follows in 16:6, and of ἡ κτίσις των ἀνθρώπων.[65]

In 1 Cor 3:13 Paul says that "the fire will test what sort of work each one has done" (καὶ ἑκάστου τὸ ἔργον ὁποῖόν ἐστιν τὸ πῦρ αὐτὸ δοκιμάσει). The testing here most probably coincides with the judgement,[66] but it does not prove that this must also be the case in *Did.* Apart from the broader question whether *Did.* may have been acquainted with Pauline traditions,[67] there is also a difference in presentation between Paul and *Did.* The latter speaks only of the alternative between perishing or salvation; for Paul, as a result of the testing, some will be rewarded and others will suffer a loss, but no one is lost (3:15).

As for the second argument, one cannot conclude from "the signs of truth" and the resurrection of the holy ones in 16:6 that the final judgement must already have taken place before the signs appear.[68] Nothing suggests that the (resurrected) "holy ones" of 16:7 are identical with those living in the final days who are addressed in 16:5.

The major difficulty is with the singular expression ἡ κτίσις τῶν ἀνθρώπων (the closest parallels in the NT are in Mark 16:15 and Col 1:23). Lindemann argues that the phrase better fits the perspective of the final judgement involving all mankind of which some will be saved and others will be scandalized and perish.[69] But 16:5b deals with the fate of the Christians only (ἐν τῇ πίστει αὐτῶν), as Niederwimmer rightly observes.[70] The contrast that is created is between those who are scandalized and those who endure in their faith. "To be scandalized" is contrasted to "to endure in the faith." Those who are scandalized have not endured; they have fallen away from the faith. Such a reasoning applies solely to Christians. *Did.* offers a double perspective. Mankind as a whole is put to the test, but what *Did.* itself is interested in is what will happen to the faithful. Such a double-level scene was already introduced

---

[65] "Die Endzeitrede in Didache 16," 164-66.

[66] So correctly Lindemann, *Der erste Korintherbrief*, 85-86.

[67] Which is answered negatively for *Did.*'s conception of judgement and salvation by Aono, *Die Entwicklung*, 163-210.

[68] *Ibid.*, 165: "in V. 6 (ist) das Gericht als bereits geschehen vorausgesetzt; jetzt nämlich werden 'die Zeichen der Wahrheit' offenbar werden."

[69] "Der Didachist redet in 16,5 vom eschatologischen Gericht, das für die einen den Untergang, für die anderen aber Rettung bedeutet" ("Die Endzeitrede in Didache 16,"165).

[70] *Die Didache*, 263.

in 16:3-4. The whole world is given into the hands of the Deceiver (4b), but the focus is on what this means for the Christian (3-4a).

In Lindemann's view judgement would already have been pronounced before the coming of the Lord. The parousia is the time of the gathering of the righteous. Hence the picture of *Did.* 16:3-8 is complete as it stands and there is no need to postulate a lost ending after v. 8.[71] While the judgement scenario is in itself perhaps not impossible, there does not follow from it that v. 8 is the authentic ending, for nothing is said yet about the gathering itself. Moreover, it is worth noting that at least one early reader of the *Did.* was troubled by 16:5, or had evidence that *Did.* originally followed a different pattern. The Apostolic Constitutions VII, 32, 5 does not mention the testing by fire but connects the judgement of the righteous and the wicked more directly with the parousia.[72] But there is also some indication in 16:5 itself that *Did.* is closer to the Matthean scenario of 24:9-14.

The meaning of ἡ πύρωσις τῆς δοκιμασίας is perhaps less evident than it might seem. A. Milavec has argued that the phrase has a double meaning pending on the result of the burning. The test means destruction for the many that are scandalized, but it also brings purification and hence salvation for those who endure in their faith.[73] *Did.* 16:5 would be a very early attestation of what would become the concept and doctrine of the Purgatory. There are a number of problems with this interpretation. First, there is no clear evidence for it in the writings of the New Testament. Milavec agrees that the meaning of οὕτως δὲ ὡς διὰ πυρός in 1 Cor 3:15 "must remain obscure."[74] The same is probably true for the two passages in 1 Pet 1:5-7 and 4:12-14 which, moreover, Milavec takes to allude to sufferings the Christians are already enduring ("this present testing …")[75]. Second, the motif of "purification", which is crucial to Milavec's reading and which is clearly expressed in the two parallels he can cite, one from the OT (Mal 3:2-3; 4:1) and the other from Hermas (4.3.2-5), is simply missing in *Did.*[76] And third, Milavec has to give up the common Christological understanding of ὑπὸ τοῦ καταθέματος, which is well documented in Christian tradition, and to accept that the phrase would refer to the fire itself.[77]

According to Niederwimmer the strange ἡ πύρωσις τῆς δοκιμασίας (why not simply ἡ δοκιμασία τῆς πυρώσεως?) refers to the tribulation that was mentioned in 16:3-4a.[78] That *Did.* in 16:5 had indeed still in mind the troubles of 16:3-4a can be

---

[71] Cf. Lindemann, "Die Endzeitrede in Didache 16," 171. See also Milavec, "The Saving Efficacy," 151-54.

[72] For a strong defense of CA offering at least "the *Didache's* proximate true ending," see now Aldridge, "The Lost Ending," 12. Aldridge also cites as further evidence the disputed Georgian version (of which he is rightly sceptical) and an eighth-century sermon on "Baptismal renunciation" by St Boniface. Of course one cannot simply substitute CA's text for the ending of *Did.* (*contra*: Wengst) and it is methodologically a much wiser procedure to cite CA as a kind of paraphrase (so Rordorf-Tuilier in their edition).

[73] "The Saving Efficacy," 137.

[74] *Ibid.*, 147.

[75] *Ibid.*

[76] Milavec also cites Sibylline Oracles 2, 252-54, though this text is not on purification but on escaping the fire (*ibid.*, 149).

[77] See the discussion on pp. 137-39.

[78] Which he regards as a situation of persecution (*Die Didache*, 263) and I have described above as one of betrayal and apostasy.

argued on the basis of the second half of the verse which takes up two more elements from Matt 24:9-14 that had not yet been used to further characterize this tribulation as a test. The first one is σκανδαλισθήσονται πολλοί (24:10), by which *Did.* re-uses in a sense the apostasy motif to describe the fate of those who do not endure. The other one is the motif of endurance that occurs in a form that is comparable to Matt 24:13 and in any case is true to the essence of Matthew's thought. Yet *Did.* has also made two remarkable changes. It explicitates, maybe somewhat redundantly, of what consists the endurance (ἐν τῇ πίστει αὐτῶν) and, in a quite peculiar way, it also says who will bring salvation (ὑπ' αὐτοῦ τοῦ καταθέματος instead of Matt's divine passive). These elements reflect the interests of *Did.*, but even now Matthew's gospel may have been in the background at one point.

"In the faith" occurs between οἱ ὑπομείναντες and σωθήσονται (at the same place as Matt's εἰς τέλος) which may be intentional, though it is commonly agreed that πίστις should be read with ὑπομένω. The phrase refers back to 16:2 where it was very much emphasized that one should stick to the faith until the final hour in order to be "perfected".

Those who hold on will be saved "by the Cursed One." This phrase must no doubt be taken to refer to Christ.[79] The motif of the cursing of the Lord is known in early Christianity from 1 Cor 12:3 and Gal 3:13, where it is linked to a typically Pauline reasoning. There is no reason to assume that a piece of Pauline theology has crept into *Did.*'s description in 16:5. *Did.* is not interested in Chap. 16 in opposing faith and law as ways of salvation or damnation, or in the motif of the curse of the cross (Gal), nor in the question of the criteria for deciding who speaks in the Spirit (1 Cor). The motif of cursing is found twice in other parts of *Did.* (1:3 and 5:1), though not with reference to Jesus and using the synonyms καταράομαι and κατάρα instead of κατάθεμα. In 5:1 κατάρα is one of two adjectives to describe the Way of Death: πρῶτον πάντων πονηρά ἐστι καὶ κατάρας μεστή. Of course, these parallels demonstrate that the motif was not unknown to *Did.*, but they do not yet explain the presence of the strange ὑπ' αὐτοῦ τοῦ καταθέματος in 16:5.[80] The combination of σκανδαλισθήσονται and ὑπ' αὐτοῦ τοῦ καταθέματος was probably intended (note the position at the beginning and the end of 16:5b). This most striking "Christological" title, which certainly contrasts with the threefold κύριος of 16:1, 7, 8, aptly describes what apostasy means: it is (like) cursing the Lord. In the gospel of Matthew and of Mark Peter has the dubious honour of denying Jesus while cursing (him?) and swearing, "I do not know this man" (26:74 τότε ἤρξατο καταθεματίζειν καὶ ὀμνύειν ὅτι οὐκ οἶδα τὸν ἄνθρωπον). He thereby fulfills the prophecy that Jesus had uttered in reply to Peter's fierce assertion that he at least would not be scandalized (26:33 εἰ πάντες σκανδαλισθήσονται ἐν σοί, ἐγὼ οὐδέποτε σκανδαλισθήσομαι). As for the cursing, Matthew has changed Mark's ἀναθεματίζειν into καταθεματίζειν (NT hapax).[81]

---

[79] See Pardee, "The Curse That Saves."

[80] Though the link between 5:1 and 16:3-5 may not be gratuitous, for the next verse in Chap. 5 contains a number of phrases that have a parallel also in the final chapter: note the play on μισέω – ἀγαπάω (see also 1:3; 2:7; 16:3), the rather unusual (not in NT) φθορεύς (in 5:2 to denote aborters; cf. 2:2; 16:3), and πενήτων ἄνομοι κριταί (cf. ἀνομία in 16:4a).

[81] Possibly assimilating to καταράομαι (cf. *Did.* 1:3), according to Senior, *The Passion of Jesus*, 206.

So *Did.*, far from putting upside down Matthew's arrangement by anticipating the execution of judgement before the announcement of the parousia, as would be the result of Lindemann's interpretation, rather keeps to a description that largely follows Matthew's, twice (in 16:5 and in 16:4, on the fate of the Deceiver) hinting at a sequel that is lost but most probably must have followed after v. 8.

To describe the period that precedes the end *Did.* does not refer to earthquakes or political and military disasters. Instead it has selected a tribulation that forms a constant threat for the community: the dangers of betrayal and of apostasy. By anticipating the section of the Christians suffering persecution and betrayal in 10:17-22 and then repeating it at 24:9-14, Matthew had already indicated that one of the dangers the community had certainly experienced indeed belongs to the troubles of the end time. *Did.* has emphasized this even more. In 16:3-4a the Didachist warns for the dangers of apostasy and betrayal by fellow members that will shake the community "in the last days." In v. 4b it is said that these tribulations are caused by the Deceiver. And in v. 5 they are further described as a test that decides on the fate of all Christians. In 16:5 *Did.* has not yet moved beyond the perspective of 16:3-4.[82]

Did. 16:6-8: The Signs of the Parousia and the Coming of the Lord

In Matt the disciples had asked Jesus what will be the sign (σημεῖον) of the parousia (24:3). The word occurs again in 24:29-31 in the mysterious "the sign of the Son of man in heaven." Not only is there discussion among Matthean scholars what this phrase might mean, but also whether it does refer to a sign at all.[83] *Did.* speaks of "the signs of truth" (τὰ σημεῖα τῆς ἀληθείας) that precede, and thus announce, the parousia. The qualification "of truth" could refer to the false "signs and wonders" that were wrought by the Deceiver (16:4b).[84] The series of three could be accidental (if this number ever is in biblical and Christian tradition), or perhaps also it was the result of a particular way of reading Matt 24:29-31![85]

Did. presents the three signs in an almost parallel form:
καὶ τότε φανήσεται τὰ σημεῖα τῆς ἀληθείας
πρῶτον σημεῖον ἐκπετάσεως ἐν οὐρανῷ,
εἶτα σημεῖον φωνῆς σάλπιγγος,
καὶ τὸ τρίτον ἀνάστασις νεκρῶν

---

[82] Balabanski, *Eschatology in the Making*, 191-94, puts great emphasis on the agreement in structure between *Did.* and Matt, but thinks v. 5 poses a problem. In so far as 16:5 looks back at 16:3-4a *Did.* has not really "disturbed" the structure of Matthew's discourse.

[83] See, e.g., Kloppenborg, "Didache 16.6-8," 64 n. 32; Luz, *Das Evangelium nach Matthäus* 3, 433-36.

[84] Niederwimmer, *Die Didache*, 265.

[85] Cf. Massaux, *Influence de l'Évangile*, 636-37: "Le didachiste paraît interpréter le texte de *Mt.*, xxiv, 30-31, où les trois signes qu'il donne peuvent aisément se retrouver" (in vv. 30a, 31a, 31b resp.). In his conclusion, Massaux is somewhat more reserved: "influence ... probable, mais non certaine, car la *Didachè* se conforme ici au schéma traditionnel de la présentation du tableau final de la parousie" (637).

I begin with the second sign, the sounding of the trumpet. If this was directly borrowed from Matt, it explains a lot on how *Did.* understood the passage in vv. 29-31 and composed its own version of "the signs of the parousia." In Matt the sounding of the trumpet occurs after the parousia is already mentioned and it is not called a sign (v. 31). But it is also obvious that for Matt it is part of the events involving the parousia and indeed can be taken as a sign announcing the execution of the command to gather the elect which will take place at the parousia.[86]

The sounding of the trumpet is preceded by the σημεῖον ἐκπετάσεως ἐν οὐρανῷ. Ἐκπέτασις is usually translated as "extension" or "opening". The latter of these translations is taken literally and would refer to the opening in or of heaven to prepare for the descent of the Lord and his angels. The former is to be taken in a metaphorical sense and would refer to either the appearance in heaven of the cross or of the "standard of the Lord."[87] None of these three interpretations can be linked in any way to Matt and each of them has its own difficulties. The second and third meaning derive from comparisons with other texts. There are a number of attestations, all of much later date and most of them in writings that were composed in Egypt, of the appearance of the cross in heaven at the parousia,[88] but in all of these texts the word "cross" is also explicitly mentioned. As Niederwimmer, who opts for this reading, observes: "Analog wäre nach σημεῖον ἐκπετάσεως zu ergänzen: ξύλου"[89] but this is a crucial element. The translation "standard" was suggested by A. Stuiber on the basis of his interpretation of σημεῖον τοῦ υἱοῦ τοῦ ἀνθρώπου in 24:30 which is, however, itself disputed.[90] Against the translation "opening" it has been said that it does not fit the preposition ἐν, but this is perhaps not so much of a problem.[91] However, "extension" or "opening" might be too weak as a translation. Ἐκπέτασις can also have the related but more vigorous, or violent, meaning of "a rift"[92] or (for the verb ἐκπετάννυμι) of "to scatter."[93] This rather recalls the image of the turmoils in heaven that are described in Matt 24:29, with the darkening of the sun and the moon and the stars falling out of the skies (πεσοῦνται ἀπὸ τοῦ οὐρανοῦ).[94] Was it this motif from 24:29 that *Did.* had in mind, and is the rare ἐκπέτασις perhaps in some way inspired by Matthew's πίπτω (subst. πτῶσις)?

---

[86] Cf. Davies-Allison, *The Gospel According to Saint Matthew* 3, 363.

[87] A survey of the various explanations in Niederwimmer, *Die Didache*, 265-66.

[88] References in Niederwimmer, *Die Didache*, 266.

[89] *Ibid.*

[90] See Stuiber, "Die drei σημεῖα," 442-44.

[91] Cf. Rengstorf, "σημεῖον," 260. Cf. Niederwimmer, *Die Didache*, 265 n. 48. The phrase σημεῖον ἐκπετάσεως does not have to mean "the sign of the opening" but can be translated merely as "the opening," just as σημεῖον φωνῆς σάλπιγγος means "the sounding" (which is being regarded as a sign) or as Matt's σημεῖον τοῦ υἱοῦ τοῦ ἀνθρώπου in 24:30 probably means "the Son of man."

[92] Cf. Lampe, *Patristic Greek Lexicon*, s.v.

[93] Cf. the reference in LSJ to the *Epitaphius Adonis* (l. 88) by the poet Bion of Smyrna (fl. late second century B.C.E.): ἔσβεσε λαμπάδα πᾶσαν ἐπὶ θλιαῖς Ὑμέναιος καὶ στέφος ἐξεπέτασσε γαμήλιον ("Hymenaeus has put out every torch at the doorposts and torn the nuptial garband asunder"); edited by Reed, *Bion of Smyrna*, 130. Cf. Hughes Fowler, *Hellenistic Poetry*, 271: "and scattered the bridal wreath."

[94] See the *v.l.* ἐκ (cf. Mark 13:25) and the *v.l.* with the composite ἐκπίπτοντες instead of the simplex in Mark 13:25. Note also how Luke in 21:25 has changed Mark (καὶ ἔσονται σημεῖα ἐν ἡλίῳ).

The third and final sign is that of the resurrection of the dead (τὸ τρίτον ἀνάστασις νεκρῶν). It is not itself called "a sign," but the numbering proves that it is regarded in this way by *Did.* In Matt 24:29-31 the parousia is the time when the angels will gather the elect of the Son of man from the four winds (καὶ ἐπισυνάξουσιν τοὺς ἐκλεκτοὺς αὐτοῦ ἐκ τῶν τεσσάρων ἀνέμων). In 25:31-32 it is said that "all the nations" will be gathered at the parousia of the Lord with His angels to prepare for the separation of the wicked and the righteous (see also 13:47). *Did.* does not speak of a gathering of the nations but of the resurrection of the holy ones (16:7). *Did.*'s presentation, while certainly not identical, may nevertheless have been inspired by Matthew's gospel in several ways. First, in describing the signs of the parousia, *Did.* concentrates on the fate of the righteous only, as does Matt in 24:31.[95] Second, that only the righteous will rise is motivated with a quotation from Zech 14:5. Matthew had alluded to this passage when referring to the parousia of the Lord in 25:31. In *Did.* the quotation receives a Christological touch ("the Lord," instead of Zech's "the Lord my God"), as is also the case in Matt 25:31 (ὁ υἱὸς τοῦ ἀνθρώπου ... καὶ πάντες οἱ ἄγγελοι μετ᾽ αὐτοῦ). Third, Matthew does not mention the resurrection of the dead in 24:31 (nor in 25:32), but most probably "the resurrection of the dead is presupposed."[96] But *Did.*'s decision to introduce a reference to the resurrection here may also have been inspired by the strange story in Matt 27:51-53 on the cosmic chaos and the resurrection of the holy ones that accompanied the death of Jesus (v. 52 καὶ πολλὰ σώματα τῶν κεκοιμημένων ἁγίων ἠγέρθησαν). These "saints" will wander to the holy city and will appear to many (ἐνεφανίσθησαν πολλοῖς).[97] The parousia completes the period that was inaugurated with the death and resurrection of Jesus.

And finally then there comes the parousia, and it looks very much the same in Matt and in *Did.*, including such "details" as the choice of a form of ἐπί with genitive (Matt ἐπί, *Did.* ἐπάνω; Mark ἐν with dative) and the addition of τοῦ οὐρανοῦ after τῶν νεφελῶν. The content and especially also the wording of what followed after v. 8 can only be guessed at, but the third sign may contain another indication that there probably did follow something, for if the fate of the deceased is mentioned nothing is said yet of those who will live to see the parousia.[98]

---

[95] Davies and Allison wonder whether "the elect" of 24:31 include only Christians (*The Gospel According to Saint Matthew* 3, 364), but they rightly point out that this was at least how *Did.* understood the eschatological gathering in 9:4 and 10:5. The motif is twice expressed in a form that is comparable to 24:31 (with ἀπὸ τῶν περάτων τῆς γῆς in 9:4, and with ἀπὸ τῶν τεσσάρων ἀνέμων in 10:5; note also τὴν ἁγιασθεῖσαν in 10:5 and cf. *Did.* 16:7). Was this the reason why the author/compiler of *Did.* opted for a different presentation in 16:7?

[96] Thus Davies-Allison in their laconic comment on 25:32 (*The Gospel According to Saint Matthew* 3, 421).

[97] Compare *Did.*'s τότε φανήσεται ... τότε ὄψεται ὁ κόσμος (16:6, 8).

[98] According to Kloppenborg ("Didache 16.6-8," 62), the agreement between Matt 24:30 and *Did.* 16:8 is probably not coincidental, but his conclusion that *Did.* cannot have been derived from Matt because it does not also cite the end of v. 30 rests upon an argument from silence (cf. Tuckett, "Synoptic Tradition in the Didache," 99: "precarious"). The substitution of τὸν κύριον for "Son of man" (Matt parr. and Dan) indicates that *Did.* was not concerned about exactly reproducing Matt 24:29-31. The change may have been motivated by the immediately preceding citation from Zech 14:5 in 16:7 where *Did.* left out ὁ θεός (see also 16:1). If so, *Did.* may also have felt that the reference to the Lord's glory of v. 30b was already anticipated in some way in the second half of the Zech quotation.

In her recent monograph on the development of eschatological expectations in Mark, Matt, and *Did.*, Balabanski concludes that Matt was actively upholding expectations of an imminent end for/in a community at a time that such hopes were fading.[99] In the discourse there are two indications in particular that support this conclusion. First there is the confident statement by Jesus in v. 34, which Matt took over from Mark, that "this generation will not pass away till all these things take place." When read in light of similar assertions by Jesus in Matt 10:23 and 16:28 (par. Mark 9:1) it is meant to be a most explicit assurance, on the level of the discourse and its addressees, that the parousia is thought to be near. Second, by adding εὐθέως in v. 29 Matt has significantly heightened the already dramatic connection in Mark between the section alluding to the destruction of the Temple and the parousia. The Lord will come "immediately" after "these days" of unprecedented tribulation (vv. 21-22).

Balabanski argues that *Did.* 16:3-8 shows "an interest in a paraenetic application of eschatology," both towards the individual and the community, but "it no longer reveals an imminent expectation of the End."[100] Lohmann does not exclude that the community still had a sense of imminency, but since *Did.* rather emphasizes that "the hour is unknown" he concludes, "die Naherwartung scheint bereits nachgelassen zu haben."[101] Lindemann objects that such a discussion is simply not on the agenda.[102] *Did.* has no strict parallel for Matt 24:34 and it does not mention the destruction of the Temple. Writing some decades after Matt, there was no need anymore for *Did.* to ponder about the destruction of the Temple and the city and to give this event a place in the scenario. But this must not necessarily mean that it also had forgotten about the Naherwartung. *Did.* 16:3-8 was written to further motivate the paraenesis of 16:1-2 "durch die Ankündigung der (zweifellos als nahe geglaubten) drohenden Endereignisse."[103] It is true that *Did.* does not explicitly say that its readers will actually live to "see" the parousia happen, but the association it makes between the warning that "the hour is unknown" and the emphasis on the test that will come in "the final hour" is comparable to what one reads (in inverted order) in Matt 24:34.36. One still needs a good deal of eschatological hope kept alive to make this presentation work.

A Double Purpose

Matthew's discourse is built of warnings and encouragements (note the imperatives) and of a description of what will happen in the end time. The discourse thus serves a double purpose. It instructs the disciples/readers about how their own time relates

---

[99] *Eschatology in the Making*, 173.

[100] *Ibid.*, 205.

[101] *Drohung und Verheissung*, 50. For a similar position, see Steimer, *Vertex Traditionis*, 209.

[102] "Die Endzeitrede in Didache 16," 155 n. 2: "die von Lohmann diskutierte Frage … liegt dem Text allerdings fern." A similar answer is given to Steimer (162, n. 28). See also, in line with Lindemann, Löfstedt, "A Message for the Last Days," 361.

[103] "Die Endzeitrede in Didache 16," 155.

to the end and about how the end will come and what it will be like. It also wants to encourage the reader to hold out and to offer directions about how to prepare for the coming of the Lord. Matthew goes beyond Mark (and Luke) in that he not only calls upon the reader to be watchful, but also very pointedly illustrates, in the parable of the Last Judgement, that the outcome of this judgement will depend on whether or not one has kept to the basic rules of Christian ethics. Ethics and eschatology are closely intertwined. Ultimately for Matthew the decision to live the life of a Christian is motivated by the expectation of the judgement that is soon to take place at the parousia of the Lord.

Both purposes (instruction and paraenesis) are also present in *Did.* One aspect of the paraenesis, the call for watchfulness, which is also an important theme in the eschatological discourse (Matt 24:42, 44; 25:13), is most prominently formulated in 16:1, at the beginning of the last chapter. Tuckett comments on the parallel of *Did.* 16:1 with Matt, "There is nothing here that is so clearly MattR that it could only have derived from Matthew's gospel."[104] But the combination of γρηγορεῖτε, γίνεσθε ἕτοιμοι, οὐκ οἴδατε, ὥρα, and ὁ κύριος (ἡ)μῶν ἔρχεται is found only in Matt (24:42, 44),[105] while that of γρηγορεῖτε, (οἱ λύχνοι ὑμῶν μὴ) σβεσθήτωσαν, ἕτοιμοι occurs only in the parable of 25:1-13 (vv. 8, 10, 13) and that of λύχνοι-ὀσφύες with γρηγορέω and ὁ κύριος ἔρχεται in its "parallel" in Luke 12:35-38 (see vv. 35, 37). *Did.* has added ὑπὲρ τῆς ζωῆς ὑμῶν to γρηγορεῖτε. It could be a reminiscence of the "way of life" motif that was developed in *Did.* 1–6, or it could have been inspired by the description of what will happen at the parousia in 24:40-41 (it is about life and dead). The images of keeping the lamps burning and the waists girded were commonly known in Christian tradition (see Eph 6:14). *Did.* formulates negatively (μή) and uses different verbs (in the imp. 3rd p.pl. as ἔστωσαν in Luke, but see also Matt 24:16-18),[106] the first of which is found in Matt 25:8 (αἱ λαμπάδες ἡμῶν σβέννυνται).

The other aspect, the emphasis on accepting Jesus' commandments because of what will come out of it ("life"), is most pregnantly expressed in the Two Ways section as Lohmann has argued.[107] But a variant form of this kind of paraenesis is also found in 16:2, in direct connection with the former one. The readers are called upon "to assemble frequently" and to seek for τὰ ἀνήκοντα ταῖς ψυχαῖς. In the motivation that follows it is stressed that a Christian life is profitable / rewarding in view of the perfection that will be required in the final hour but that can be reached only if one holds on to the end.[108]

As for the second purpose, there can be little discussion that Matt and *Did.* both wanted to instruct their readers about the end. It is more difficult to assess in how far they also wanted to remediate certain misunderstandings. Matt certainly shows this concern on the level of the story: Jesus corrects a possible misapprehension of the

---

[104] "Synoptic Tradition in the Didache," 212 / 108.

[105] The two verses are separated only by the short parable of the housekeeper's watch (v. 43).

[106] Cf. Giet, *L'énigme de la Didachè*, 255 n. 45.

[107] *Drohung und Verheissung*, 50.

[108] Cf. the comment by Audet, *La Didachè*, 470: "On a bien l'impression que συναχθήσεσθε est une particularisation de γρηγορεῖτε."

disciples on the fate of the Temple. The interest in the destruction of the Temple might also echo a burning question in the community. The way *Did.* specifies the motif of the resurrection in 16:7 by quoting from the OT could reflect a similar intention to answer questions that remained unsolved.[109] Likewise, the Deceiver in 16:4 could have been added to clarify a point that, if not missing, at least was present in Matt only in an indirect way, and to align the scenario with common Christian tradition.

In one respect, however, there is a difference between *Did.* and Matt, and that is the way in which they transmit their information. H.R. Seeliger has argued that the last chapter of *Did.* should better not be called an apocalypse because it lacks several features of the genre.[110] The same discussion about whether to speak of an apocalypse or an eschatological discourse has been going on in studies on Matt 24 parr. In Matt it is Jesus who teaches the disciples about the end and there are some features, such as the introductory scene in v. 3 or the confession in v. 36, that seem to present him as a kind of revealer or mediator of hidden wisdom. *Did.* on the contrary does not even mention Jesus. Rordorf wonders why *Did.*, if it depends on Matt, would have decided to appropriate for itself a task and position that Matt had said was Jesus's.[111] (Part of) the answer might be that the literary genre of *Did.* – a Church order[112] – hardly allows for the kind of narrative framework that is found in 24:1-3. But perhaps also it is not fully correct to speak of *Did.* accaparating the role of Jesus. In no way does it tell the reader that it is reworking Matt in this respect. It rather presents itself as the transmitter of a received body of teaching (from the Apostles!) on eschatology.[113]

3   Conclusion

What has *Did.* done to Matt? *Did.* 16 has variously been called a "sort of commentary" of Matthew's discourse,[114] a supplement to Matthew's version,[115] or an "aide-mémoire"

---

[109] It is rather unlikely that *Did.* was driven by an interest in millenarianism as was argued by O'Hagan, *Material Re-creation*, 25-30, esp. 29. Löfstedt, "A Message for the Last Days," 378, concludes that *Did.* was primarily written to encourage, but perhaps also "to guard against misunderstandings."

[110] "Erwägungen zur Hintergrund."

[111] "Does the Didache Contain?," 413: "the decisive difference between the *Didache* and the Synoptic Gospels is that the Gospels place the apocalyptic teaching on Jesus' lips, while the *Didache* forgoes this support. ... I find it very difficult to assume that the Didachist, if he had the completed text of the Synoptic Gospels before him, would have dared to take this doctrine, so to speak, out of Jesus' mouth again and present it as anonymous instruction."

[112] Cf. Steimer, *Vertex Traditionis*, 192-210.

[113] Cf. Koester, *Synoptische Überlieferung*, 190; Steimer, *Vertex Traditionis*, 20-27, esp. 26: "Der Titel stilisiert die Did zum Pseudepigraphon: Die Apostel sollen als Verfasser gelten, ihre Autorität das kompilierte Gut als apostolisches ausweisen."

[114] Cf. Massaux, *Influence de l'Évangile*, 637-38: "*Did.*, xvi dépend littérairement de *Mt.*, xxiv; le texte de *Mt.* a servi de base à notre auteur qui paraît en donner une sorte de commentaire." See also Lindemann, "Die Endzeitrede in Didache 16," 157: "eine Art 'Kommentierung' der Aussagen in Mt 24 (und 25)."

[115] Balabanski, *Eschatology in the Making*, p. 197: "the Didache does not aspire to comprehensiveness. Rather, its very selectivity presupposes the continued use of the Gospel, and implies that its *function was to serve as an adjunct*."

of apocalyptic teaching.[116] There may be some truth in all of these labels. As a commentary *Did.* has focused on the description of the sufferings by fellow Christians, but in doing so it has tried to preserve the essence and trust of the eschatological scenario and of the answers Matthew gives in his discourse, at times clearly reflecting the wording of its source and more than once also being inspired by it in a more general way. As a supplement it has added the motifs of the Deceiver and of the resurrection, though both are also partially modeled after Matt. As an "aide-mémoire" finally it has been concerned with simplifying the scenario and with introducing a more straightforward and resolutely eschatological perspective.[117] At the outset there is a strongly formulated paraenesis (16:1-2); then follows a description of the one tribulation that characterizes the sufferings of the last days: the double danger of apostasy and betrayal that continually threatens the community; and then there are three signs that announce the parousia (and what follows after it).

Eight verses, of which the last one is probably incomplete, is all there is left of *Did.*'s description of the end time. It is not much when compared to the 51 verses of Matthews discourse (or even 97 if one includes Chap. 25). Yet it was rewarding to read *Did.*'s Chap. 16 with an eye on Matt. His version of the eschatological discourse, and his gospel, has been the source and inspiration of *Did.* to a much larger degree than one would conclude from looking at the verbal parallels only. So here is a final warning and exhortation: when reading the Didache, watch Matthew!

---

[116] Cf. Seeliger, "Erwägungen zur Hintergrund," 187 (though without expressly pointing out on which source the summary was made). See already earlier, Vielhauer-Strecker, "Apokalypsen und Verwandtes. Einleitung," 536-37 ("ein katechismusartiges Stück").

[117] There is a certain danger with this third definition to disregard the function of 16,1-2. See the comment by Lindemann, "Die Endzeitrede in Didache 16," 162 n. 29.

Chapter Twelve

Do the Didache and Matthew Reflect an "Irrevocable Parting of the Ways" with Judaism?

Jonathan A. Draper

University of KwaZulu-Natal (South Africa)

1 Introduction

Most modern studies of the Didache have stressed the "Jewish" nature of the source material and orientation of this enigmatic early Christian writing.[1] The title I have been given thus raises one of the most intriguing questions facing the interpreters of the Didache, "When and how did the break come?" The answer to this question will, in some ways, determine the interpretation that follows. Adding the gospel of Matthew to the mix, adds an additional "wild card" to the pack, but is the logical corollary to the close connection that is seen between the two writings by many researchers, myself included. I have argued elsewhere that, while there is no literary dependency of the Didache on the current form of the gospel of Matthew,[2] the two writings come from the same community and the Didache represents the "community rule" of the Matthean community.[3] I have also argued that the Didache is concerned to define itself in two directions: over against the gentiles on the one side and over against other Jewish groups on the other.[4] The recent appearance of a new work on the Didache by Huub van de Sandt and David Flusser, *The Didache: Its Jewish Sources and its Place in Early Judaism and Christianity* (2002), raises these issues again in an acute form. In particular, their book lays the same charge of "virulent anti-Jewish polemic" against the Didache as is frequently laid against Matthew's gospel.

---

[1] So, for instance, Rordorf-Tuilier, *La Doctrine des douze Apôtres*: "son enseignement est principalement fondé sur la tradition judéo-chrétienne" (21) ; cf. Niederwimmer, *The Didache*, 44, and, most recently, Van de Sandt-Flusser, *The Didache, passim*.

[2] Draper, "The Jesus Tradition in the Didache," 269-89 / 72-91.

[3] Draper, "Torah and Troublesome Apostles," 347-72 / 340-63; Id., "The Genesis and Narrative Thrust," 25-48.

[4] Draper, "Christian Self-Definition," 362-77 / 223-43.

2   The Didache and Community Self-Definition

My earlier work rests on the conviction that the redactional composition of the Didache reveals successive stages of community self-definition. The only complete text of the Didache we possess, as opposed to various examples of the Two Ways teaching, proclaims itself as, "The Teaching of the Lord through the Twelve Apostles to the gentiles (τοῦς ἔθνεσιν)."[5] In other words, this is teaching given under the authority of the Jewish leaders of the Christian community and directed to gentile converts: it is designed by Jewish Christians for the initiation of gentiles into their community.[6] The instruction which follows: the Jewish tradition (written or oral) of the Two Ways or the *Derekh Erets*, consisting largely of ethical elaboration of the second table of the Decalogue, is taken up and used to instruct gentiles in the requirements for living in the community. There is a heavy emphasis, as Van de Sandt and Flusser have argued, following Alon,[7] on the "universal laws," which apply equally to gentiles and to Jews. Gentiles are admitted into the community of Jewish Christians in two categories: the "perfect" who are willing to be circumcised and keep the "whole yoke of the Lord," i.e. to become full Jews by conversion, and those who are unable to do this, but are admitted on the basis that they keep as much of the Torah as they can, including food laws, but keep strictly from eating *eidolothuton* (6:2-3). They are baptized and admitted to table fellowship with the other Jewish-Christian members of the community. Nevertheless, it is hoped that they will become "perfect" in the course of their life, as the eschatological warning in 16:2 shows, "For the whole time of you faith will not profit you, unless you are made perfect in the last time."

The instructions of the Two Ways ensure that a clean break is made with the gentile past of the converts. Moreover, the requirement to keep strictly from *eidolothuton* forces the converts to buy their meat, bread and drink from the *kosher* sources in the existing Jewish network.[8] The problem they would face is writ large from the different perspective of Paul in 1 Corinthians 10:25-30, where he rules against the strict prohibition on *eidolothuton*, a ruling which would inevitably have produced the kind of conflict between gentile and Jewish members of the Corinthian community which is depicted in 11:17-34. They would have been forced to sit at different tables or else abandon their faithfulness to the Torah-precisely the problem of Acts 15. On the other hand, there is in Didache 1-7 no such clear breach between converts to the community and other Jewish groups and parties. Those who converted to the community from paganism may have understood themselves as joining the Jewish community in general, albeit a party within it with a particular eschatological and messianic orientation. Some may even have been tempted to join other Jewish communities after their initiation.[9] Similar tensions and fears of defections from the nascent rabbinic community to

---

[5] Draper, "Ritual Process and Ritual Symbol," 121-22.
[6] Draper, "The Role of Ritual."
[7] Alon, "The Halacha," 165-94; cf. Segal, "Matthew's Jewish Voice," 17.
[8] Draper, "The Role of Ritual," 63-64.
[9] Cf. Kimelman, "Identifying Jews and Christians," 306-23.

Christianity can be shown to have existed in the early period.[10] Neither party had the power to enforce its will effectively on the other in the first century C.E.

However, at some stage, competition with another Christian grouping and simultaneously with another Jewish grouping becomes more intense and requires stronger definition of community boundaries. The Didache defines itself on the one hand against Christians depicted as sheep turned to wolves, led astray by the anti-Christ, who wish to lead the community away from its traditional way of teaching to a new teaching which "breaks down [Torah],"[11] and on the other hand against other Jews, labeled as "hypocrites". It is in this context that different days for public fasts are introduced and different public prayers (Chap. 8), which, by their very public nature, differentiate and distinguish membership of one or the other Jewish community. Yet this does not represent a break with the Jewish community as a whole.[12] It is an inner Jewish quarrel. The break is rather made with the community's competitors for ascendancy in Jewish society, namely the "hypocrites", whom I identify as the Pharisaic or emergent rabbinic community. These two communities are theologically close, which is what makes the contest bitter. Significantly, no theological rationale is given for their separation. It is thus not so much Christianity and Judaism that are at the parting of the ways at this stage but rather Christian Jewish and Pharisaic Jewish communities.[13]

While I have not done the same kind of study of Matthew's gospel, in terms of its self-definition over against other Jewish communities, my perspective on its social location would be the same. The strong agreements in source and redaction between Matthew and Didache indicate that they either come from the same community at a different stage of development or from closely related communities.[14] The excellent and focused study of Matthew by L. Michael White, "Crisis Management and Boundary Maintenance: The Social Location of the Matthean Community" (1991), concludes that, "Matthew's polemic against "*their* synagogues" cannot be understood as indicating he had broken away from the established order of Judaism in Jesus' day. Rather it was generated within the context and convulsions of an emerging new order, with both theological and social implications."[15] "The tension of the Matthean community with other Jewish groups (or to be more precise, the Pharisees and "their" synagogues) was born of proximity rather than distance, of similarity rather than difference."[16]

---

[10] *Ibid.*, 323-27.

[11] 6:1; 11:1-2; 16:3-5; cf. Draper, "Social Ambiguity," 284-312.

[12] "One should hesitate to say "separate themselves from Jewish society as a whole", since Jewish society was at this stage a very amorphous and multi-faceted affair. Ethnic Jews in the Diaspora could be observant or non-observant; they were also probably responsible for the development of strands of Gnosticism which rejected both the Torah and the God of the Torah. There was, at this stage, no single overall authority able or competent to determine who was or was not a Jew!" (Draper, "Christian Self-Definition," [1996] 230-31).

[13] Draper, "Christian Self-Definition," (1996) 242.

[14] Draper, "The Genesis and Narrative Thrust."

[15] White, "Crisis Management and Boundary Maintenance," 217.

[16] White, *Ibid.*, 241. Other papers in the collection edited by David Balch (1991, e.g. by Segal and Saldarini) maintain a similar position. Likewise, Wilson ("Related Strangers," 50-53) sees the conflict between Matthew and his Jewish contemporaries as that "of a sectarian minority, tenaciously defending its version of Judaism over and against other minorities or the Jewish community at large," which is essentially "the battle over common turf."

The new study of the Didache by Van de Sandt and Flusser (2002) makes similar claims in some respects, but shifts the focus from an inner Jewish conflict and division to that of a parting of the ways between Christianity and Judaism *per se*, the emergence of a new religion, which "appears to have alienated itself from its Jewish background and to have taken on the character of a primarily gentile Christian group," and which is also anti-Jewish.[17] This is a major shift and one with which I do not agree. However, I have come to feel that the question can only be answered if due attention is given to the three aspects of the problematic: Firstly, what is "Judaism"? Does it exist in the period under discussion? Was the community behind Matthew and the Didache aware of such an entity? Secondly, what constitutes an "irrevocable parting of the ways"? This will depend, to some extent on our answer to the first question. Thirdly, can we determine an evolution in the attitude of the community behind these writings, which can be demonstrated in terms of source and redaction? If there is a relationship between Matthew and the Didache, which the close parallels in some of the material they have in common seems to require, then it should be possible to determine in which direction the evolution runs? It cannot be assumed without further argument that the historical direction runs from Matthew to the Didache.

3   Are the Didache and Matthew "anti-Jewish" texts?

James Dunn begins his exploration of the "parting of the ways" between Christianity and Judaism, "Christianity is a movement which emerged from within first-century Judaism. That simple, uncontestable fact is crucial to our understanding of the beginnings of Christianity."[18] However, this is more problematic than it seems, since the very word "Judaism" is a major field of contestation today.[19]

The first knotted issue to be teased out in this paper is the question of what exactly is meant by "Jew" and "Judaism" in the Didache and Matthew.[20] In this case, it can be stated straight away that there is no mention of the word "Jew / Judaean" or "Judaism" in the former text at all. This rather obvious observation is nevertheless in itself extremely significant. Certainly, the community regards itself as different from "the hypocrites," but even here there is no definition of who these people are and almost no polemic against them. It is simply stated matter-of-factly that the hypocrites fast on Tuesdays and Thursdays, but you must fast on Wednesdays and Fridays (8:1), and you must not pray like the hypocrites but as follows . . . (8:2). The word "hypocrite"

---

[17] Van de Sandt-Flusser, *The Didache*, 329.

[18] Dunn, *The Parting of the Ways*, 1.

[19] Kimelman, "Identifying Jews and Christians," rightly observes, "The disagreement extends to almost every aspect of this relationship, including the facts, the interpretation of texts, the explanation of social phenomena, and even the definition of *Jew* and *Christian*" (301).

[20] Edward Said, *Orientalism*, points to the connection between the construction of "essentialisms" and imperialism. The construction of the "other" is really a construction of the self, and, once it is taken for granted, it obscures rather than illuminates the study of cultures other than one's own. Both Jewish and Christian traditions "have to be read against their rhetoric" if we are to understand their historical evolution (Kimelman, "Identifying Jews and Christians," 303).

appears to express opposition without particular content or vehemence. It is clearly going beyond the evidence to argue that this represents a violent "anti-Judaism", as suggested by Van de Sandt and Flusser.[21] They move from seeing the term "hypocrite" as "a general reference to (pious) Jews" to conclude that, "the sharp polemics against the ὑποκριταί seem to reflect the emergence of tensions between the Didache and Judaism....The whole section, in sum, reflects an attitude of animosity to Jews and Judaism; the unsubstantiated disparagement of the "hypocrites" does not seem to leave open any possibilities of reconciliation."[22] The failure to name the "Jews" or to provide specific charges of iniquity and wickedness against them seems to my reading to point in the other direction, that there was no such "Judaism" in the consciousness of this community. On this issue, at least, we need to reserve judgment for the moment, until we return to the issue of the "hypocrites".

What is true of the Didache is, by and large, true of Matthew as well. The word "Jew / Judaean" is only used five times, four referring to Jesus seriously or mockingly as "the king of the Jews / Judaeans" (2:2; 27:11; 27:29; 27:37) and one to a story concerning the tomb of Jesus circulating "among the Jews / Judaeans until this day" (28:15; cf. 26:8 – perhaps a "travelers' tale"). On the other hand, Matthew shows a strong consciousness of Judaea as a region (2:1, 5, 22; 3:1, 5; 4:25; 19:1). The birth of Jesus in Bethlehem of Judea seems connected to the concern to present him as "king of the Judaeans." There is no evidence here, either, that Matthew associated the word "Jew / Judaean" with anything negative or even that he was conscious of it as a category beyond the geographical / political reference to the land and kingdom of Judaea. Instead, the word used as a self-designation to describe the covenant people (twelve times: 2:6, 20, 21; 8:10; 9:33; 10:6, 23; 15:24, 31; 19:28; 27:9, 42) is "Israel".

Since the Didache does not use the term "Jews / Judaeans" at all, even though it is clearly critical of rival groups within Israel, there is a *prima facie* case for arguing that it is an "insider" quarrel and not an "outsider" quarrel. Gentiles who attacked Israelites called them "Jews" not "hypocrites"! It would indicate that they considered themselves (rival) members of the same socio-cultural grouping. The same must be said for Matthew's gospel, which nowhere targets its (often very venomous) rhetoric against "Jews / Judaeans." However violent the struggle and the language, this is an "insider" quarrel between social and political rivals from the same socio-cultural grouping.[23] We may dislike the intensity of Matthew's polemic, but there is no way that it could be called "anti-Jewish" and there is no way that it could be described as having "broken with Judaism," though these things do, sadly, belong to the history of the interpretation of Matthew. Graham Stanton has argued in a number of books and articles,[24] largely on the basis of Matthew 21:43 and 28:15, that such a split had indeed occurred

---

[21] Van de Sandt-Flusser, *The Didache*, 292-96.
[22] Van de Sandt-Flusser, *The Didache*, 296.
[23] For a summary of the research in this area, see Stanton, "The Origin and Purpose."
[24] "The Origin and Purpose;" *A Gospel for a New People; The Interpretation of Matthew.*

between Matthew and the synagogue, producing a "separate and quite distinct entity over against Judaism."[25] However, the evidence is better read when one sees Matthew's community as one among many competing sectarian groups in Israel of the first century C.E.[26]

Peter Tomson's[27] careful analysis of the designations "Jews" and "Israel" in the Second Temple period finds that there is a consistent usage: "Israel" is an "inner-Jewish" designation of the people within the community for themselves and in discussion with each other, while "Jew" is an "outside" designation of others for Jews, though it may be used by Jews of themselves where they are dealing with gentiles or have such relations in mind. Insiders who attacked other insiders preferred to retain the overarching self-designation "Israel" and "Israelites" for themselves.[28] Note, for instance, the way the Psalms of Solomon attack the "sons and daughters of Jerusalem" (e.g. Psalms 1, 8) for their iniquity and blame them for bringing disaster on the city and the land. Despite its destructive and shameful use in later Christian polemic, Matthew's account of the inhabitants of Jerusalem shouting to Pilate, "His blood be on us and on our children" (27:25) is only stating the same thing as the *Pss. Sol.* in dramatized form. On the other hand, God is implored to bless the "house of Israel" repeatedly throughout the *Pss. Sol.* The contest at this stage is not over, "Who is a Jew and who is not?" but over, "Who is an Israelite and who is not?"

Matthew clearly believed that the rulers in Jerusalem had committed iniquity and brought judgment on themselves and on the city of Jerusalem and the region of Judaea. The kingdom / rule of Judaea would be taken away from them (specifically the "chief priests and Pharisees" who saw the parable of the Vineyard as directed at them) and given to another *ethnos* who will "give [God] the fruits of it" (21:43). This and other references in Matthew to his community's belief that the wickedness of the rulers (and maybe people) of Jerusalem brought down on them the destruction of the city and temple (e.g. 22:7; 23:36-38), is nothing new. It is the message of the prophets in response to the destruction of Jerusalem in the Hebrew Scriptures. It is the message of the *Pss. Sol.*, the Dead Sea Scrolls[29] and many other Israelite writings from the Second Temple period. Certainly, Matthew saw the final straw, which brought on the judgment, as the murder of Jesus by the rulers of Jerusalem / Judaea, but then the Dead Sea Scrolls saw the treatment of the Teacher of Righteousness by the Wicked Priest in similar terms. This is a standard *topos* of the Israelite prophetic tradition, derived from an understanding of God's covenant with Israel as undergirded by blessings and curses attendant on keeping its legal provisions.

---

[25] Stanton, "The Origin and Purpose," 1914.

[26] As the recent work of Overman (*Matthew's Gospel and Formative Judaism*), Saldarini ("The Gospel of Matthew," [1991]; "The Gospel of Matthew," [1992]; *Matthew's Christian-Jewish Community*) and Sim ("The Gospel of Matthew;" "Christianity and Ethnicity;" *Apocalyptic Eschatology*, 182-198; *The Gospel of Matthew*) has shown.

[27] Tomson, "The Names Israel and Jew,"120-40; 266-89. Cf. Draper, "Holy Seed and the Return," 346-59, for an analysis of the terminology in John's gospel.

[28] Cf. Kuhn, "Ἰσραήλ, Ἰουδαῖος, Ἑβραῖος," 359-65; Dunn, *The Parting of the Ways*, 145.

[29] E.g. 1QpHab 10:1-13 where the wicked city built magnificently on wickedness will be burnt up with fire.

All of this serves to argue that there was no monolithic or uniform or orthodox "Judaism" in the first century of the Common Era. There were only competing factions within the socio-cultural grouping of Israel, which emerged as a result of the destruction of the central indigenous socio-political arrangements by successive empires. The Judaean temple-state system re-introduced by the Persian empire was only ever partial in establishing control over the old territory of the Davidic / Solomonic kingdom, even under the Maccabees. The Roman system of regular changes of the occupant of the High Priesthood and its subjugation alternately to the local Herodian dynasty or to direct rule, designed to prevent any indigenous institution from gaining a power centre from which they could be challenged, created insuperable ambiguities in the system. For this reason, the use of the term "Judaism" is inappropriate in discussions of the competition between emergent Christianity and early Rabbinism.[30] If we must have an overarching designation, it should be Israel / Israelite, the term the people used of themselves and not one so laden with two thousand years of conflictual history.[31]

4   What Constitutes a "Parting of the Ways?"

To take the discussion of the problematic further, we need to resolve the question of what would constitute a "parting of the ways." We have already resolved that the break cannot be with "Judaism", since this cannot be considered to exist as such in first century Syria-Palestine. Perhaps, on the one hand, we could rephrase the question as follows, "Did the community of the Didache and Matthew still consider both itself and its opponents to be members of the Israel of God?" This is important, since later Christian tradition came to claim the titles and privileges of Israel for itself, in light of the "failure" of "the Jews" to obey God's promised messiah. Such "supersessionism" then excludes ethnic Israel from the promises and the covenant, which had passed over to the gentiles. Such a position is clearly found, for instance, in the Epistle of Barnabas. Is it, however, anywhere apparent in Matthew or the Didache?

On the other hand, can we see any evidence in these writing that other Israelites considered the Israelite members of the communities of Matthew and the Didache to be outside the bounds of Israel, to be no longer members of the covenant people of God? Saldarini[32] rightly argues that when Matthew's community becomes "engulfed in their deviant role" to the point of according their deviance "master status," and when their opponents no longer view them as (deviant) members of Israel but outsid-

---

[30]   Even the use of the term "formative Judaism," which Andrew Overman (*Matthew's Gospel and Formative Judaism*) suggests in his excellent discussion of the social world of Matthew, surrenders far too much to the eventual triumph of the Rabbis as the leaders of the remnant of Israel, as does the suggestion of "middle Judaism" made by Boccaccini (*Middle Judaism*), who includes early Christianity within this designation.

[31]   The terms "sectarian" and "orthodox" should be avoided. Instead, the various movements within Israel should be seen as "different responses to imperial domination;" cf. Wilson, *Magic and the Millennium*; Ranger, "The Invention of Tradition;" Scott, *Domination and the Arts of Resistance*; Comaroff and Comaroff, *Of Revelation and Revolution*.

[32]   "The Gospel of Matthew" (1991), 60-61.

ers, this would be the decisive sign that a deviant community within an overarching society has become a separate competing society. Such a position was clearly adopted by some Israelite circles at a later stage, as evidenced by the much-debated rabbinic promulgation of the Birkat Ha-Minim at Yavneh (c 80 C.E.), which was understood to include Christians among other groups. It may be reflected also in the *aposynagogos* saying of John 9:34. The question remains whether there is evidence that this attitude was prevalent at the time of our texts.

5   Can We Trace Evolution on These Questions between the Didache and Matthew?

It is widely acknowledged that both the Didache and Matthew reflect sources drawn from earlier tradition that they redact according to the needs of their communities at the time of the final redaction. Unfortunately, in neither case do we have any clear indication of the dates or locations of their final redactions.

It is clear, most would agree, that Matthew was written after the fall of Jerusalem in 70 C.E. (both on the basis of his use of Mark and seeming reference to the Jewish War in Matt 22:7) but probably before 100 C.E. (in view of the probable use of Matthew by Ignatius), though this cannot address all the questions about further redactions.[33]

There is very little agreement on the dating of the Didache, with opinions varying from the middle to the end of the first century, with the balance of opinion having moved away from the very late date proposed by an influential group of English scholars in the early twentieth century[34] towards a date some time around the end of the first or beginning of the second century C.E. The only real issue is that of dependence on Matthew as an argument for a later date, but the balance of opinion is that no dependence on any canonical work of the New Testament can be demonstrated.[35] Little evidence is offered for any of the dates given, which usually depend on each scholars' reconstruction of Christian origins. It is generally agreed since Audet (1958) that Didache 1-6 uses and edits a Two Ways source, probably a "pre-Christian" one. In addition, it is likely that the

---

[33] E.g. the Trinitarian Baptismal Formula in Matthew 28:19, which is absent from Eusebius and for which the external textual attestation is not as prolific as for the rest of the gospel; see Lohmeyer, "Mir ist gegeben alle Gewalt!;" Green, "The Command to Baptize;" Kosmala, "The Conclusion of Matthew;" Flusser, "The Conclusion of Matthew;" Vööbus, *Liturgical Traditions*, 36-37. *Contra* Riggenbach, *Der trinitarische Taufbefehl*; Kertelge, "Der sogennante Taufbefehl;" Barth, *Die Taufe in frühchristliche Zeit*.

Interestingly, the same textual question emerges also in the contrast between the Trinitarian baptismal formula in *Did.* 7:1, 3 and the formula used in 9:5 ("in the Name of the Lord").

[34] See Robinson, *Barnabas, Hermas and the Didache*; Muilenburg, *The Literary Relations*; Connolly, "The Didache" (1932); Id., "The Didache" (1937) and Vokes, *The Riddle of the Didache*, though he later changed his position; cf. "The Didache and the Canon;" and "The Didache-Still Debated".

[35] Koester, *Synoptische Überlieferung*, 159-241; Rordorf, "Le problème de la transmission;" Audet, *La Didachè*; Draper, "The Jesus Tradition" (1996) 72-91; Kloppenborg "Didache 16:6-8;" Van de Sandt-Flusser, *The Didache*; et al. *Contra* Massaux, *The Influence*; Tuckett, "Synoptic Tradition in the Didache;" *et al.* Note, however, that Kloppenborg now seems to leave open the possibility of one direct dependence of the Didache on the Synoptics in his paper in this volume (pp. 105-29).

liturgical material may have been drawn from a prior source (7-10), that the material on apostles and prophets (11-13) originated elsewhere and that the Didache has made use of a pre-existing Apocalypse at the end (16). Attempts to establish the wording of the original sources for each of these sections have been numerous, as have the theories about the redaction of such sources. The problem is that the nature of source and redaction is heavily influenced by conceptions of the origin of Christianity and so analyses often end up being circular in nature, and I acknowledge that my own reconstructions are similarly influenced by my *Vorverständnis*, despite my best intentions!

In view of the uncertainty concerning the dating of both documents, the question of evolution from one to the other must be settled on the basis of internal evidence, that is, by a careful examination of the relevant texts where they overlap.

6 An Analysis of the Didache in terms of its Relation to Israel

In terms of the discussion provided by Van de Sandt and Flusser, the key terms which emerged for the relationship between the Didache and the Israel of God are δικαιοσύνη, τέλειος, ζυγός, ὑποκριταί, τὸ ἅγιον τοῖς κυσίν, ἐκκλησία, υἱὸς Δαυίδ. It is interesting and significant that each of the terms that relate to the problematic of the Didache's relations with Israel is found also as a significant term in Matthew's gospel, so that there is a clear overlap of source / redaction with Matthew.

I will leave aside in this paper, the discussion about Matthew 5:17-20, 21-48, which I have already explored elsewhere.[36] Van de Sandt and Flusser argue that this passage represents the original teaching of Jesus, who was promulgating the kind of Hassidic piety found in the *Derekh Erets*. Interesting again, though, that this is a point of close contact with the Didache 3:1-6; 11:1-2. It seems more likely to me that it represents the thinking of the community behind Matthew and the Didache than that it derives from Jesus himself. Instead, I will explore the terms mentioned above, in the light of the arguments of Van de Sandt and Flusser.

6.1 "Fulfill Righteousness," "Be Perfect"

The words δικαιοσύνη and τέλειος are key linked words for Matthew. Georg Strecker[37] has shown the way in which δικαιοσύνη recurs at key moments in the narrative framework (3:15; 5:6, 10, 20; 6:1, 33; 21:32), and represents a core value for Matthew's community. It is something to be fulfilled even by Jesus in accepting ritual purification in the baptism of John, which is also the "way of righteousness" (3:15; 21:32). It is something to hunger and thirst for, to be persecuted for. Matthew rejects the notion that the Torah has been "broken down" (καταλῦσαι), but asserts instead that it abides forever. Indeed, the righteousness of the community must abound more

---

[36] Draper, "Torah and Troublesome Apostles;" "The Genesis and Narrative Thrust."
[37] *Der Weg der Gerechtigkeit*; cf. Draper, "The Genesis and Narrative Thrust."

than that of the scribes and Pharisees (5:17-20). In other words, "righteousness" is a matter of obedience to Torah as understood by Matthew's community. Examples are then given of what it means to "abound" in righteousness more than them, with the five "you have heard that it was said but I say to you…" sayings (5:21-47). The whole section is then concluded with the saying: "You then shall be perfect (τέλειος) as your heavenly Father is perfect" (5:48), which occurs also in the Didache (1:4). For Matthew, the community is called to fulfill righteousness, that is, to keep the Torah better than other groups in Israel, and this is described as "being perfect." However, this righteousness is not to be done for human approval but in secret before God. Seeking God's righteousness is the priority for the community and is the same as seeking his kingdom (6:33), and leads to blessing.

The second occurrence of τέλειος in Matthew comes in the debate of Jesus with the Rich Young Man about the most important provision in the Torah, in 19:21, "What good thing must I do to inherit eternal life?" Jesus recognizes this as a question about Torah, since he says, "You know the commandments." When the young man claims to have kept all these, Jesus responds, "If you wish to be perfect (τέλειος), then go, sell all your possessions and give to the poor," something which goes beyond the minimum requirement of the Torah. In other words, this usage confirms the meaning of "being perfect" found in the Sermon on the Mount: it refers to doing more Torah than the minimum, more abundantly than the scribes and Pharisees, not less.

The word δικαιοσύνη occurs in Didache twice: the first time in conventional material from the Two Ways (5:2), but the second time (11:2) provides the expression εἰς δὲ προσθεῖναι δικαιοσύνη as a definition of teaching to be accepted as opposed to false teaching which "breaks down [Torah]" (διδάσκη ἄλλην διδαχὴν εἰς τὸ καταλῦσαι). What is significant is the idea that acceptable teachers help the community to do more righteousness not less. The thought world of requiring righteousness more abundant than that of the scribes and Pharisees lies behind this teaching in the Didache as much as in Matthew, in my opinion. It is interesting to note that the opponents of Paul in Corinth, who demand faithfulness to Torah observance, describe themselves as the διάκονοι δικαιοσύνης (2 Cor 11:15).[38] Paul may even be playing on the term τέλειος in his prediction that "their end (τέλος) will be according to their works" (cf. *Did.* 16:2).

Just as there are points of contact between Didache and Matthew in the concept of righteousness, so also with the concept of perfection. The collection of Jesus tradition in 1:3-6 is close in content to Matthew 5:38-48 and Luke 6:27-36, but follows the order and wording of neither, though it is closer to Matthew in wording. In *Did.* 1:4 the saying, "And you shall be perfect" follows the teaching on turning the other cheek, as if it is a conclusion to it, and is followed by the teaching on going the extra mile. In Luke it follows the teaching on lending without hope of return, as its conclusion, and is followed by the teaching on not judging others. In Matthew the teaching follows the teaching on loving one's enemies, and serves as both the capstone to this and as a final conclusion to the whole section of "greater righteousness." In none of these cases,

---

[38] Cf. Segal, "Matthew's Jewish Voice," 18.

it should be noted, is "And you shall be perfect" associated with keeping the ethical provisions of the Sermon on the Mount. In each case it serves as a summons to do more than the minimum required by the Torah, since even gentiles and sinners are capable of / required to do such deeds ("universal laws"). In other words, this little saying concerning perfection is already orientated towards ideas of minimum and maximum legal observation. The Israelite community(ies) of both Matthew and the Didache considers that its (their) fulfillment of the Torah goes beyond what its (their) Israelite opponents require.

This is important to note, since the second occurrence of the phrase in the Didache occurs in the context of whether the gentiles, who are admitted to the community, are required to keep the whole Torah, the whole "yoke of the Lord." The answer is that they are not. Perfection is only required of those within Israel, but it is recommended to those gentiles who join the community. If you are able to become full Jews and bear the burden of fulfilling the whole Torah, then you too will be perfect, as we are, more rigorous in keeping it than our opponents. However, the Torah is only required of Israel and not of the gentiles. Nevertheless, since the Torah is good and given by God, keep as much of it as you are able. Within these parameters, there are still minimum requirements to enable Israelites and gentiles to share table fellowship and community, namely a strict avoidance of what has been offered to idols. The hope is that at the end, all will be "perfected" (16:2).

The reference to "being perfect" in the Sermon on the Mount is attached to an example of generous behaviour, of doing more than the minimum, not to food laws or asceticism. In *Did.* 1:4, "being perfect" is attached to "going the extra mile," doing deeds which are over and above what is required. In 6:2 it is associated with gentiles doing more than the minimum requirements of the Noachic covenant which apply to them.

6.2 The whole Yoke of the Lord

Rordorf and Tuilier follow Stuiber[39] in seeing a Jewish source behind the expression, "the whole yoke of the Lord," but argue that the Christian editor of the Didache, who had already inserted "and you shall be perfect" in 1:4, has in mind here as well as there the "new law of Christ" as expressed in the Sermon on the Mount (as "being perfect") and not the Torah. [40] If this were the case, then the editor would in effect advocate the relaxation of the "difficult" teaching of Jesus: keep it all if you can, but if you cannot,

---

[39] Stuiber, "Das ganze Joch."

[40] Rordorf and Tuilier, *La Doctrine des douze Apôtres*, accept the Jewish source, but argue that, "Il est donc sûr que ce passage assimile la perfection morale à l'accomplissement des commandements du Sermon sur la montagne" (32-33). If one cannot live up to this impossible ethic, then at least one can keep the Two Ways (Niederwimmer, *The Didache*, 122-23). Cf. Theissen's theory that the simultaneous "intensification" and "relaxation" of norms in the Jesus movement leads to the collapse of legalism: "If it becomes clear that everyone must inevitably fall short of the intensified norms, all moral self-righteousness must appear to be hypocrisy" (*Sociology of Early Palestinian Christianity*, 77-95, esp. 79). This is a common perception of the ethic of the Sermon on the Mount, but mistaken in my opinion.

do what you can. This seems unlikely. Rather, "being perfect" in both 1:4 and 6:2 refers to doing righteousness over and above what is required by the Torah.

The reference to the "yoke of the Lord" in 6:2 in the context of food laws in 6:3 seems indeed to point unequivocally to the Torah, as argued by Stuiber[41] and Flusser,[42] so that the passage originates in a Jewish-Christian community. The evidence seems compelling.[43] In 2 Baruch the sage prophesies, "For behold, I see many of your people who separated themselves from your statues and who have cast away from them the yoke of your law."[44] R. Nehunya b. Ha-Kanah (T1-2) states, "He that takes upon himself the yoke of the law (עֹל תורה), from him shall be taken the yoke of the kingdom and the yoke of worldly care" (*m.Abot* 3:5; cf. 6:2; *b.B.Metsi'a* 85b). Although it is used in various combinations, in this passage, the foundational reference, on which the word plays depend, is the "yoke of the law." So too the saying in *t.Sotah* 14:4, "Those who cast off the yoke of Heaven, there will reign over them the yoke of a king of flesh and blood."

All the references to the "yoke" in the earliest Christian material, if we put aside the gospel of Matthew for the moment, refer unambiguously to the Torah, mostly conceived in a negative sense. So Paul, in polemical fashion refers to the Torah as a yoke of slavery (Gal 5:1: μὴ πάλιν ζυγῷ δουλείας ἐνέχεσθε). Likewise Acts 15:10 uses the expression in the context of conflict over the Torah and it is clearly a reference to the Torah as a yoke upon the neck of the people of Israel. The Epistle of Barnabas 2:6 rejects the Torah as a "yoke of necessity" (ζυγὸς ἀνάγκης), as opposed to the "new law of our Lord Jesus Christ" (ὁ καινὸς νόμος). My own opinion[45] is that Barnabas deliberately attempts to undermine an aspect of the Two Ways tradition which he rejects, namely covenantal nomism. An echo remains in Justin *Dial.* 53:1, which has many other echoes of the Two Ways tradition, where the gentiles are unharnessed foals until they receive the "yoke of the word" (τὸν ζυγὸν τοῦ λόγου). So too *Didascalia* LII,17-35, which has a complicated argument concerning the two yokes, one, natural law, given to all human beings before the Golden Calf and the second one, Torah, given to the Jews as a punishment for idolatry.

The evidence for Matthew 11:28-30 has been examined again by Celia Deutsch, whose real interest is in the theme of Wisdom. Nevertheless, the evidence she examines confirms that the primary reference is to the Torah:

> In most of these passages the negative use of 'yoke' occurs over against a positive use; that is, it is usually set in contrast to the 'yoke of Torah' or 'the yoke of Heaven.' 'The yoke of the commandments' is synonymous with 'the yoke of Torah'. Passages such as *m.Abot* 3.6 and *t.Sotah* 14.4 do not mean that 'there is no place for political or economic care'. Rather they imply that the burden of domination and mundane worry are relieved by obedient devotion to Torah–that obedience and devotion to Torah help one to carry those burdens.[46]

---

[41] "Das ganze Joch."

[42] "Paul's Jewish-Christian Opponents," 195-211; Van de Sandt-Flusser, *The Didache*, 238-42.

[43] Cf. Strack-Billerbeck, *Kommentar zum Neuen Testament* 1, 176-77; 608-10.

[44] Translation in Charlesworth, *The Old Testament Pseudepigrapha* 1, 633.

[45] Draper, "Barnabas."

[46] *Hidden Wisdom and the Easy Yoke*, 127.

Taking on oneself the "yoke" refers to obedient performance of Torah and breaking the "yoke" refers to disobedient rejection of Torah: "One can break off the yoke by transgressing specific *mitzvoth*, as well as by rejecting the entire Torah."[47]

Deutsch[48] explores the contrast between the yoke of care, the difficulty of obeying Torah from day to day, and the understanding of the words of Torah as the source of life and refreshment, of water and milk (see especially Sifrei Deuteronomy 317, 321). It is in this context, she suggests that Sirach 51:13-30 understands the teacher's call to seek Wisdom, "understood as Torah." This then can be seen as a parallel to Jesus' usage of the terminology of "the yoke" in Matt 11:28-30, whom the evangelist presents "as Wisdom incarnate" and "as the Sage, the Teacher of wisdom,"[49] as in the saying of Q 10:21-22 with which Matthew prefaces this saying on the "yoke". Despite this, "the yoke" never loses its primary reference to Torah.[50]

To sum up, both the Didache and Matthew use the terminology of the yoke to refer to Torah. Since the Didache is directed to gentiles, the performance of the full Torah is not an obligation but a goal towards which one should strive. Matthew contrasts the performance of Torah as interpreted by Jesus with the performance of Torah as interpreted by other Sages to argue that his way is easy and light. Matthew's use of the terminology represents reflective and mature theological development of the concept of legal interpretation, possibly along the lines of Wisdom traditions, whereas the usage in the Didache is matter of fact and literal. While agreeing with Van de Sandt and Flusser that *Did.* 6:2-3 represents the perspective of Jewish Christianity, since it allows voluntary performance of aspects of Torah like the dietary laws, I disagree that this marks the passage out as a foreign body in the Two Ways tradition. They argue:

> Whereas the prohibitions in Chapters 1-5 (and the verse in 6:1 as well) suggest a morality which applies to a community within the boundaries of Judaism proper, Did 6:2-3 has all the marking of an address to non-Jewish Christians. The passage represents an adjustment to the perspective of gentile believers who are not capable of bearing the entire "yoke of the Lord" and may have difficulties in observing Jewish dietary laws. An observant Jew does not have the choice mentioned here. Thus, there is a strong possibility--and this position reflects a broad scholarly consensus--that these two verses originally did not belong to the teaching of the Two Ways.[51]

The Two Ways instruction consists largely of haggadic expansion of the second table of the Decalogue, the Noachic Covenant and the "universal laws" which apply to all humankind. Moreover, the instructions are specifically said to be directed to the gentiles in the second of the titles, which belong with the Two Ways. The teaching of the Two Ways in the Didache would seem to be that the ethical parts of the Torah apply

---

[47] Deutsch, *Hidden Wisdom and the Easy Yoke*, 128.
[48] *Ibid.*,128-30.
[49] *Ibid.*,130
[50] *Ibid.*,143.
[51] Van de Sandt-Flusser, *The Didache*, 238.

to gentiles, whereas the purity laws and circumcision are optional but desirable. I see no contradiction with the obligations of Israelites to keep the whole Torah here. I also do not agree that the repetition of καὶ ἔσῃ τέλειος (1:4b) and τέλειος ἔσῃ (6:2) necessarily represents the hand of a still later "Didachist", an "anti-Jewish" redactor of the document as a whole, who advocated "a two tier ethic of perfection and mediocrity,"[52] and who was ignorant of its "Jewish character" and what it meant (Torah). The editor of the Apostolic Constitutions seems to have known what it meant, as does the author of Barnabas. In both *Did.* 1:4b and in Matthew the exhortation to "be perfect" is an exhortation to do more than necessary, to perform righteousness over and above the minimum which is required by the letter of the Torah. In effect, it is an appeal for exactly the kind of "hassidic piety" which Van de Sandt and Flusser[53] see as characteristic of the Two Ways. The Torah itself does not obligate the gentiles to observe it. Most rabbis then and now would agree with that sentiment. Nevertheless, to be "perfect" for a gentile would be to take on the Covenant of God with Israel as far as possible, ultimately to become part of the people of the Covenant in a full sense, even though this is not required by the Torah. This is how the righteousness of the Christian community exceeds that of the scribes and Pharisees!

6.3 "Hypocrites"

The real test case for Didache with regard to its putative "anti-Jewishness," or as to whether it is looking from beyond the great divide between "Christianity" and "Judaism," is the use of the term "hypocrite" (ὑποκριτῶν) in 8:1-2. I have written on this matter a couple of times already, and here need only state that, in agreement with Moshe Weinfeld and Kurt Niederwimmer,[54] I believe that this term has no fixed content beyond an accusation of impiety, ungodliness, apostasy.[55] The Septuagint shows that ὑποκριτῶν is derived from the Hebrew roots ענה or חנף. Weinfeld argues that the accusation of "preaching well but not practicing well" is a common charge leveled by rabbis of rival schools against each other. חנף is used in this way in the Scrolls to attack their opponents, "those who seek smooth things," that is, those whose interpretations of the Torah are regarded as being too liberal, e.g. 1QS 4:10 and 4QTest (4Q175) 28. However, it seems that it could mean little more than a charge of "hypocrisy, dishonesty, flattery" or simply "faithlessness to religion, apostasy."[56] Calling someone a "hypocrite" is a feature of "inner Jewish debate,"[57] a charge that would be laid against someone close, not against someone unrelated: it is a matter of "when

---

[52] *Ibid.*, 240

[53] *Ibid.*, 172-90.

[54] Weinfeld, "The Charge of Hypocrisy;" Niederwimmer, *The Didache*, 131.

[55] "With few exceptions the term is employed *in sensu malo*. The ὑποκριτής is bad as such and ὑπόκρισις is a form of wrongdoing. In this respect there is no question of presenting a righteous appearance so that the true face of evil is disguised. Hence the translation 'hypocrisy' is hardly apt" (Wilckens, "ὑποκρίνομαι, κτλ.," 569).

[56] Jastrow, *A Dictionary of the Targumim*, 482.

[57] Weinfeld, "The Charge of Hypocrisy," 52-58.

brothers fall out." I think there is no evidence at all to suggest that "all [pious] Jews" are implied by the word "hypocrites".[58] While I agree that the term is the kind of "blanket condemnation" typical of "the expression of the contrast between two groups,"[59] it is illegitimate to apply it to a "Christian" versus "Jewish" split, since this is anachronistic in assuming that "Judaism" existed in any kind of definitive or normative form in the first century C.E.

In Matthew, the ὑποκριτῶν become major players. The word occurs 13 times with a virulence that is striking in comparison with the Didache. They are specifically identified as the "scribes and Pharisees" in the series of woes in Chapter 23. The charge is not always specifically that they say one thing and do another, although that is a strong component of Matthew's attack. They criticize others but are blind to their own shortcomings (7:5). Their teachings on purity ("the precepts of men") go beyond the requirements of the Torah (15:7), and, indeed, their teachings prevent people from entering the kingdom (23:13). They are interested in gentile converts, but only to make them more evil than they are themselves (23:15). They fuss about tithes but ignore fundamental justice (23:23). They keep outward purity but are inwardly defiled by wickedness (23:25; 27). They maintain the tombs of the prophets but share guilt for the blood of the righteous (23:29). Leaders in Matthew's community who are unfaithful stewards of those in their care will be cast out "with the hypocrites" when the Lord returns to judge (24:51). In this last case, it is significant that "defective" leaders of the Christian party are seen as sharing the same designation and fate as the leaders of the nascent rabbinic party.

In Didache 8, there is no characterization of the charges laid against the community's opponents at all. The purpose of this section of the text is clearly to differentiate members of the community from those of another community. I have argued[60] that fasts and prayers were very public affairs, much as in the Muslim world today, possibly commenced and concluded with a blast on the *shofar*,[61] and that this is what made them such a mark of differentiation in a fragmented society such as Israel in the first century C.E., a kind of test of which group within Israel a person identified with.

Firstly, they fast on Mondays and Thursdays, while the Didache community fasts on Wednesdays and Fridays. No reasons given. However, the evidence we have suggests that the opponents are Pharisees or nascent Rabbinism, since there is no evidence for a general acceptance of these as set days for "stationary" fasting among all parties in Israel in the first century C.E., as opposed to fasting called publicly to respond to a particular crisis. However, these days were clearly promulgated by the rabbis (*m.Meg.* 3:6, 4:1; *m.Ta'an.* 4:2; *b.Ta'an* 12a).[62] Tertullian (*De ieiunio* 16; cf. *Ad nationes* 1:13) describes "all Jews everywhere" fasting on these days, but he writes from the beginning of the third century in the West, when the rabbis had established their hegemony and

---

[58] As argued by Von Harnack (*Die Lehre der zwölf Apostel*, 24-25), Audet (*La Didachè*, 367-68), Niederwimmer (*The Didache*, 131).

[59] Niederwimmer, *The Didache*, 132.

[60] Draper, "Christian Self-Definition" (1996), 233-38.

[61] See Schürer, *The History of the Jewish People* 3/1, 446-47.

[62] Cf. *Ibid.*, 483-84.

when the great "separation" between rabbinic and Christian Israelites was already a thing of the past. We have little evidence for the nature of fasting at Qumran, though Jaubert[63] claims that the Wednesday fast of the early Christian movement originates with the Essenes. Nevertheless, it is clear that they observed a Day of Fasting which was different from the party of the Wicked Priest in Jerusalem, since he used the opportunity of their fasting associated with the Day of Atonement to "cause them to stumble" (1QpHab 11:8). The fragmentary 4Q525 [fragm. 15 line 7] (= 4QBeat) claims that the fasts of the opponents of the community were "fasts of the pit" (צומי שחת). By contrast, the Didache is rather restrained, simply stating that its community fasts on different days to the nascent rabbinic community, without giving reasons or any negative characterization than designating them "hypocrites". I have previously suggested[64] that the community of the Didache had previously fasted on the same days as the "hypocrites", but that the days were changed deliberately to make a distinction. It could be, however, that the emergence of the "stationary fasts" was more muddled than that, perhaps even that they were a response to the fall of the Temple and were in contention from the beginning between the different parties of Israel. In any case, while the reason for the choice of Wednesdays and Fridays is obscure, it seems likely to be related in some way to loyalty to Jesus as messiah, if the rationale given for the different prayers in 8:2-3 lies also behind this change.

Second, the community does not pray the same prayers as the "hypocrites", but instead the Lord's Prayer, as commanded "in his gospel" (8:2). This characterizes the prayer of the community as eschatological and messianic and links it to Jesus. This prayer is to be repeated three times a day, in the same manner as nascent Rabbinism required its community to recite the daily *Tefilla*, which crystallized into the *Shemoneh Esreh* (*b.Ber.* 26b; *t.Ber.* 3:6).[65] The publicly recited prayers, which would have occasioned a cessation of activity and an audible recital, would again have marked one community off from another in Israel. There is nothing close to the *Shemoneh Esreh*, for instance, in the Dead Sea Scrolls, but many other prayers marked by adherence to the theology of the group. It appears, instead that the community prayed twice a day, morning and evening, varying their prayers with the season:

> He shall bless Him [with the offering] of the lips at the times ordained by Him: at the beginning of the dominion of light, and at its end when it retires to its appointed place; at the beginning of the watches of darkness when He unlocks their storehouse and spreads them out, and also at their end when they retire before the light; when the heavenly lights shine out from the dwelling-place of Holiness, and also when they retire to the place of Glory; at the entry of the (monthly) seasons on the days of new moon and also at their end when they

---

[63] "Jesus et le Calendrier." *Contra* Braun, *Qumran und das Neue Testament* 2, 51-52.
[64] Draper, "Christian Self-Definition" (1996), 238.
[65] So Drews, "Untersuchungen zur Didache," 74ff; Klein, *Der Älteste Christliche Katechismus*, 215; Knopf, *Die Lehre der zwölf Apostel*, 23; Rordorf-Tuilier, *La Doctrine des douze Apôtres*, 175; Schöllgen, *Didache. Zwölf-Apostellehre*, 48-49.

succeed to one another. Their renewal is a great day for the Holy of Holies and a sign for the unlocking of everlasting mercies at the beginning of seasons in all times to come (1QS 9:26-10:5).

This instruction to twice daily prayer is followed by a number of set hymns and prayers, which may have formed the content of this practice. There are many morning and evening prayers from Qumran (4Q503), which survive in fragmentary form and follow a monthly cycle.[66] Once again, it is not the practice of the "Jews" in general which is targeted by the Didache community, but the practice of nascent Rabbinism in particular.

The situation in Matthew 6 is similar to that found in the Didache 8, but with significant changes. Firstly, the order is reversed and instructions on almsgiving are added. Secondly, the trilogy is placed under the theological rationale of secrecy, which is found only in Matthew: "Beware of practicing your piety before men in order to be seen by them; for you will have no reward from your Father who is in heaven" (6:1). This theology is reaffirmed at the end of the group of sayings: "Do not lay up for yourselves treasures on earth, where moth and rust consume and where thieves break in and steal, but lay up for yourselves treasures in heaven, where neither moth nor rust consumes and where thieves do not break in and steal. For where your treasure is, there will your heart be also" (6:19-21). The latter saying is found in simpler form and in a different context in Luke 12:33-34, where it is wedged between an admonition not to worry about material necessities and an eschatological warning to be ready. In other words, the theological framework is clearly a Matthean redaction, particularly since the ring composition / inclusion form is characteristic of his narrative style, even though the collection of material relating to differentiation of the community from the "hypocrites" may be earlier.

The group of sayings in Matthew emphasizes that good works should be done in secret because God sees what is done in secret (ἐν τῷ κρυπτῷ or ἐν τῷ κρυφαίῳ 6:4, 6, 18) and will give a heavenly reward, and not publicly in order to obtain human approval.

Obviously, almsgiving can easily be done discretely and without public display. However, the logic of the public display of generosity lies in its orientation towards public office and therefore community control. In the ancient Hellenistic world, public benefactions were important requirements for extending a person's influence, preparing for public office and exercising patronage.[67] Clearly, the community of the "hypocrites" was engaged in this form of public benefaction as part of a concerted effort to win public office. The community of Matthew, by way of contrast, has given up the attempt to win public control and has retreated into the confidence that the real measure of "righteousness" lies with God. The passage indicates to me that the Matthean community has lost or is losing the battle for the public sphere in its com-

---

[66] See Davila, *Liturgical Works*, 213-38.
[67] See, for example, Malina, "Patron and Client;" Id., *The New Testament World*; Crossan, *The Historical Jesus*, 59-71; Hanson-Oakman, *Palestine in the Time of Jesus*, 63-97.

petition with nascent Rabbinism and is retreating into the sphere of the private, into a sectarian consciousness, if we may use that word in the sense given above.

Again, the instruction concerning praying in secret and not in public relates to the same dynamic. If the "hypocrites" pray ostentatiously in the synagogue and on the street corners, it probably relates to their gaining or having gained control of the public expressions of community worship, to the exclusion or diminishing of the influence of the community of Matthew. It seems likely also that their public presence in places where prayer was being offered was an aspect of the monitoring of public praxis. We have the same description of their public influence in Matthew 23:1-12, where they are specifically called "Pharisees", and where they "sit on Moses' seat," have the places of honour at feasts, the chief seats in the public assembly (synagogue) and are called "sir" ("rabbi"). In that passage, the Matthean community are commanded to avoid such titles and to practice humility, and to do what the leaders of the local community of Israel tell them to do, bitter as that may be, considering they are "hypocrites". As far as prayer is concerned, the recital of the Lord's Prayer, the public prayer of the Matthean community, is now to be practiced in secret. Followers of Jesus must shut themselves away in their inner room and pray in secret. This is because people did not have the possibility of silent prayer, of "reading in one's head," which is widely practiced today, but could only recite out loud. Hence retreating to an inner room avoids the possibility of being overheard and identified as a member of the community. Again, this seems to indicate that Matthew's community, bitter as that truth may be, has lost its battle for the public sphere and risks expulsion or public consequences for being identified as members. It is a retreat from the kind of public identification seen in the instructions of the Didache.

The same things can be observed with regard to the stationary fast (6:16-18). The public nature of a fast, with sackcloth and ashes, unkempt hair and unshavenness and other easily visible signs, is rejected. Instead, the face must be washed and the head anointed, traditional signs of celebration, so that no one will know that the member of Matthew's community is fasting. It seems to me that the problem around the public nature of the fast is understandable if Matthew's community was observing the fast on different days to the nascent rabbinic community, and if their opponents were now gaining control of the public sphere and could punish "deviants". In that case, the public consequences of differentiation would become severe. On the other hand, it is unlikely that nascent Rabbinism had the authority to force compliance with their own party practice of fasting, prayer and almsgiving at this stage either, so that members of Matthew's community would have been "virtually invisible"[68] if they avoided public displays of their allegiance.

To sum up, Matthew's community is facing extreme pressure. On the one hand, they are determined to maintain their position within Israel, within the covenant people. They respect the office of those who sit on the seat of Moses, even if they regard them as wicked "hypocrites". They have lost the struggle for pre-eminence in the community in the vacuum left by the Roman destruction of Jerusalem in 70 C.E.

---

[68] Segal, "Matthew's Jewish Voice," 31.

The public assemblies and public occasions in the public squares are controlled by nascent Rabbinism. Confrontation is now likely to invite retribution from that quarter. The "hypocrites" not only have the power to try and punish members of Matthew's community publicly *within* Israel ("handing over to councils" and "beatings in the synagogue"), but also the power to hand over known followers of Jesus to the Roman authorities ("governors and kings") for further punishment (Matt 10:17-23). In response to this, Matthew's community can be seen turning inward, to practice their messianic faith "in secret," safe in the knowledge that their cause is in the hands of God who sees in secret. The "parting of the ways" with an Israel now dominated by nascent Rabbinism has not yet occurred, but it is certainly on the horizon, even inevitable. The concern of Matthew's community is to ward off that moment by avoiding public confrontation wherever possible in the new and dangerous world in which it finds itself.

No such concern appears in the Didache, which emphasizes the differentiation with respect to fasting and prayers without any caution. This would appear to suggest that the "hypocrites" do not have as much power to harm the community at this stage or in this place. Clearly there is an evolution in practice between Matthew and Didache, even as there is clearly a major connection between these two writings. Much depends on the relative dating of the two documents. My own feeling is that the line runs from the situation described by the Didache, which has an archaic feel at every point of contact with the tradition found in both, to that described by Matthew. The former sets out the instructions for public differentiation between the rival groups within Israel. It may even represent the beginning of these practices that later become the norm within the Christian church. The latter responds to the consequence of this differentiation once the "hypocrites" have gained a broad measure of control over the community of Israel. It seeks to avoid conflict and confrontation in public in order to avoid punitive measures. It is possible that the Didache dates from a later time when the Christian community has been irrevocably separated / expelled from the community of Israel, and from a situation where the "hypocrites" have no authority, but I would then expect more explicit polemic and warning against "the Jews." As it stands, there is nothing in the document, which could really be classed as a virulent attack on the "hypocrites" let alone "the Jews." The real attack is reserved for the community's Christian rivals who advocate relaxing the Torah.[69]

6.4 *"You shall not give what is holy to the dogs"*

The Didache instructs members of the community not to admit any to the eucharistic meal "except those who are baptized in the Name of the Lord" (9:5). This is re-inforced with a saying of "the Lord" that "You shall not give what is holy to the dogs." The background to this saying in Didache and Matthew has been ably researched recently by Huub van de Sandt,[70] who points to its close parallel with rabbinic (e.g.

---

[69] Draper, "Torah and Troublesome Apostles" (1996), 340-63; "Social Ambiguity," 284-312.
[70] "Do not give what is holy;" cf. Draper, *A Commentary on the Didache*, 198-203.

m. Tem. 6:5) and Qumran material concerning what has been offered in the temple. What has been offered in the temple is holy and remains holy and therefore cannot be redeemed in case it is subjected to impurity, in the extreme case, that of being eaten by an unclean animal such as a dog. I would add to this background the saying in Lev 22:10, where it is gentiles who are prohibited from τὸ ἅγιον: καὶ πᾶς ἀλλογενὴς οὐ φάγεται ἅγια. Thus, it seems not unlikely that the saying was associated with gentiles at a stage already prior to its usage in Didache. "Dogs" is a widely used term of abuse leveled by Israel against gentiles.[71] Van de Sandt argues that Didache is close in conception to rabbinic usage here, since its community meal is holy and must be kept from falling into the hands of those who are impure, either because they are unbaptised gentiles (9:5) or because they are impenitent sinners (14:2). It spiritualizes the saying in a way similar to the way the טהרות of the community at Qumran is preserved from the uninitiated in Israel (1QS 3:4-6) and also from community members under discipline (1QS 6:24-25; 7:2-3; 8:16-17).

By way of contrast, the saying in Matthew 7:6 is coupled with a saying about throwing pearls before pigs, and uses the material metaphorically. It is likely, then, that Didache preserves the saying in its earlier form.[72] Perhaps this indicates that the community of Matthew is less concerned with ritual impurity and with the danger of contacting impurity through the presence of gentiles in the community, and that it is more concerned with the presence of unworthy members of the community (cf. the parable of the Wheat and the Tares, as well as the Parable of the Wedding Feast).

In any case, once the community of the Didache embarks on the process of differentiation of its community definitively from that of the "hypocrites", this kind of exclusion rule would presumably apply equally to non-members from Israel, in the way it does also at Qumran. However, in both cases, of Didache and Qumran, the hope presumably remained that members of Israel belonging to other groups would join and become pure!

For the rest of the eucharistic prayers, I do not think it is really profitable to discuss whether the Didache has separated from "Judaism" on the basis of its "profound Christianization" of the "sequence (cup-bread) of mainstream Judaism,"[73] since there is a methodological problem speaking of "redaction" of a later third or fourth century C.E. work (Birkat Ha-Mazon) by a first or early second century C.E. work (Didache).[74] I do not believe that one can demonstrate any firm wording or pattern for the *berakot* in the first century C.E.[75]

---

[71] Michel, "Κύων, κυνάριον," 1101-1104; Strack-Billerbeck, *Kommentar zum Neuen Testament* 1, 722-26; Böcher, "Wölfe im Schafspelzen."
[72] Van de Sandt, "Do not give what is holy," 229-31.
[73] Van de Sandt-Flusser, *The Didache*, 312-13.
[74] Cf. the warning given by Segal, "Matthew's Jewish Voice," 3-4.
[75] Cf. Heinemann, *Prayer in the Talmud*; Hoffman, "Reconstructing Ritual;" Reif, "The Early History of Jewish Worship." I have argued this already at length ("Ritual Process and Ritual Symbol") and see no reason to change my opinion on this.

6.5 "So also let your ekklesia be gathered together from the four corners of the earth into your kingdom"

Van de Sandt and Flusser have argued that the reference to the gathering in of the "ekklesia" into the kingdom from the four corners of the earth represents a mark of anti-Judaism and of irrevocable separation between the community of the Didache and "the Jews."[76] This assertion does not appear to me to be capable of being substantiated. As Schrage[77] has demonstrated, the words συναγωγή and ἐκκλησία are used interchangeably in the Septuagint for קהל and עדה, and both simply refer to the "assembly of Israel." There is no question of buildings being referred to by either term, nor is there any evidence in the earliest material of either being confined to the use of one particular party in Israel. However, it is a different matter with regard to the possibility that one group within Israel might designate itself "the true Israel." Clearly the party at Qumran regarded themselves as "all Israel," since the anointed priest "shall come [at] the head of the whole congregation of Israel with all [his brethren, the sons] of Aaron the Priests, [those called] to the assembly, the men of renown; and they shall sit [before him, each man] in the order of his dignity" (1QSa 2:12-14). Indeed, they are the only ones who would be gathered into the eschatological kingdom, "Look on [our affliction] and trouble and distress, and deliver Thy people Israel [from all] the lands, near and far [to which thou has banished them], every man who is inscribed in the Book of Life" (4QDibHam 6:11-14). The rabbis in their turn also took it upon themselves to decide, when they had the power to do so, what constituted "all Israel" (*m.Sanh.* 10:3)[78] and who was excluded, including those members of Israel who followed Jesus as Messiah and other parties who may have constituted the *minim*.

Competing parties within an overarching society will commonly compete over ownership of the things everyone holds dear. Some terms may become associated in the end with those who claim them the most vigorously. For instance, designations, which really characterize all Christian churches, may come to be accepted as referring to sectional interests: there is no inherent difference between "Assembly" and "Congregation", or between "Catholic" and "Universal", but the existence of two different words in English can provide titles for different churches making the same claims. Likewise, the existence of two terms for the same expression claimed by all parties in Israel, the "assembly of Israel," enabled competing parties to appropriate one or other of them to define themselves: nascent Rabbinism appropriated the term συναγωγή while nascent Christianity appropriated the term ἐκκλησία, even though they essentially mean the same thing and make the same claim. Qumran also regarded itself as both קהל יהוה and עדה ישראל. The Didache simply makes the prayer that all who are members of its community will be gathered up into the eschatological community of God's people. Of course, it also signals its belief that membership of its community guarantees a place in that final gathering.

---

[76] Van de Sandt-Flusser, *The Didache*, 325-29.
[77] Schrage, "συναγωγή κτλ. "
[78] Cf. Draper, "The Genesis and Narrative Thrust."

Matthew's community, like that of the Didache, regards itself as the "assembly of God," but defines it more narrowly than the latter. For the community of Matthew the ἐκκλησία θεοῦ is founded on Peter (Matt 16:17); membership is the only guarantee against the powers of death, and it is given the authority of binding and loosing (probably a Semitic expression)[79], no matter what authority may be officially claimed and exercised by those in the "seat of Moses." This is a similar pattern, again, to what we have already observed of Matthew's attitude to the power held by the "hypocrites" who "sit on the seat of Moses." Moreover, the use of ἐκκλησία in 18:17 shows that it is closely identified with the gathering of the community and/or its leadership. Quarrels should be resolved privately, but if they cannot be, then the assembly has the final authority of binding and loosing (18:18). The "church" is emerging as an institution in the same way as the "synagogue", and in opposition to it.

When do such party claims become irrevocable? That is a difficult question to answer. I suppose when one of the parties ceases to regard itself as part of the overarching culture altogether, or when it ceases to be recognized as such by the power holders in the overarching culture. But even then, assuming that they still have to live together in the same society, there are always interactions and compromises and hopes that the claims of the party will be recognized by all. Children intermarry or cross the lines; people move to areas where there is no existing community of their preference. Perhaps it is only the writing of new holy books not recognized by the other parties which would constitute a final separation, as perhaps with the promulgation of the Book of Mormon as Scripture or the New World Translation of the Bible as non-negotiable. This seems to constitute an insurmountable barrier to reconciliation between members of the Church of Jesus Christ of Latter Day Saints or Jehovah's Witnesses and other Christians. Yet people still come and go between groupings and sects within the same culture (even, for example, between Mormons and Jehovah's Witnesses and other Christian groupings). Maybe when the writing of new books, and claims to exclusivism, coincide with changes in political boundaries and control the change may become permanent? Certainly this has not yet happened between the community(ies) of the Didache / Matthew and the community of the "hypocrites".

6.6 "The Holy Vine of David your servant / son which you made known to us through Jesus your servant / son"

As I have argued elsewhere,[80] the symbol of the cup as the "vine of David your servant / son," made known through Jesus "your servant / son," is a highly significant one. The vine's symbolic referent is both to David as king, and therefore to Jesus as the successor of David, the one who revives his kingdom which is fallen, and to Israel as the people / kingdom of David. Israel is "made known" by Jesus to the gentiles, who are addressed by the Didache. This cannot be construed as supersessionism, since it is not that the gentiles have replaced the people of Israel as heirs of the covenant, but that Israel is

---

[79] Cf. Segal, "Matthew's Jewish Voice," 10
[80] Draper, "Ritual Process and Ritual Symbol."

238

"made known to them" by their baptism. In other words, they become members of Israel by adoption through Jesus as the heir of David. The kingdom echoes through the ritual section of the text, in the Lord's Prayer (8:2), in the prayer before the meal (9:4), and in the prayer after the meal (10:5). The assembly is to be snatched from evil and gathered into the eschatological kingdom. The eucharistic prayer concludes with a hymn of praise to the "house of David" (the older Coptic version is to be preferred to the "sanitized" versions in H, "God of David" and CA, "son of David"): "Let the Lord come and let this world pass away. Hosanna to the house of David!" In other words, the only really tangible Christology identifiable in the Didache is a Davidic Christology of Jesus as the heir of David and restorer of the Kingdom of Israel, the Kingdom of God. Gentiles receive the promise and privilege of entering that kingdom through their baptism in the "Name of the Lord" (9:5).

The situation seems a little more complex in Matthew, where "son of David" is also important. The concern with Bethlehem shows already the concern with Jesus as David's heir. "Son of David" is the designation given to Jesus by the crowds (12:23; 21:15; 22:42) and by the two blind men (20:30). However, it is a problematic designation for Matthew also, since Jesus is more than the son of David. When the crowds assert that the Christ is "son of David," Jesus replies, "Why then does David call him Lord?" citing Psalm 110:1.

It is the same thing with the title Kingdom of Israel, since Matthew's Jesus warns repeatedly of the rejection of "the sons of the kingdom:" "Many will come from east and west and sit down with Abraham and Isaac and Jacob in the kingdom of heaven, but the sons of the kingdom will be cast out into the outer darkness, where there will be wailing and gnashing of teeth" (8:11-12). Likewise in the parable of the wicked tenants, the vineyard will be taken away from the chief priests and the Pharisees and given to a people producing the fruits of it" (21:43). The same message is conveyed by the Parable of the Wedding Feast (22:1-10). While I do not wish to argue for Matthew's innocence before the tribunal of history, I still believe that this can be explained in terms of the prophetic *topos* of the "guilt of the people of Jerusalem" or the "guilt of the kingdom of Judah / Judaea," and does not represent supersessionism *per se*. The Judaeans, or particularly their rulers, are blamed as the ones who crucified Jesus and brought their own blood down on their heads through their wickedness. This probably represents the perspective of an Israelite from outside of Judaea. Yet there is a significant development and problematization of the relationship between the people of Israel and the kingdom. There is an enhancement in the position of gentiles within the eschatological kingdom in Matthew. It seems to me that the Didache stands at the beginning of a process and Matthew further down the line!

7 Conclusion

Let me summarize my findings briefly and somewhat tentatively. Didache and Matthew in their final forms, represent different stages of development in the process of alienation from Israel. Neither community is external to Israel. Their enemies are members of the same socio-cultural universe, competitors for the same space. If we might quote Mary Douglas, "If two symbolic systems are confronted, they begin to form, even by their opposition, a single whole. In this totality each half may be represented to the other by a single element that is made to jump out of context to perform this role. Other people select among our external symbols of allegiance those which offend or amuse them most."[81] This is how Christianity and Judaism ultimately come to relate to each other. In this case, however, it is a matter of a contest over the *same symbolic elements* represented by both sides as significant at every point. I see nothing to indicate the emergence of Didache / Matthew on the one side and the rabbis on the other as two different symbolic universes constructed in opposition to each other. Not yet!

The position in the Didache seems to me to reflect a time when the followers of Jesus as Messiah have accepted gentiles as members of their community, provided that they adopt the minimum of cultic purity to enable them to share fellowship with Israelites, specifically that they avoid food offered to idols and keep the ethical or universal laws found in the second table of the Decalogue, as this is interpreted in the traditions of Israel of the Second Temple period. Gentiles are only obligated to keep the rules of God's covenant made with Noah and therefore with all the descendants of Noah. However, this observance is regarded by the Didache as only a minimum for gentiles: Israelite members of the community continued to observe the Torah in its fullness ("perfectly") and encouraged gentiles also to become "perfect" by circumcision and by taking on themselves the full culture and identity of Israel ("the whole yoke of the Lord"). The community of the Didache understood Jesus as son of David and king of the eschatologically restored Israel. The arrival of the eschatological age meant that the gentiles would come in, as promised by the prophets. The arrival of gentiles in their midst led first to the need to negotiate the terms of entry for them and then, naturally, to characterize the relationship between followers of Jesus from Israel and followers of Jesus from among the gentiles. They were engaged also in a process of differentiating themselves not only from the gentile society from whom their converts came, but also from a rival community in Israel, namely nascent Rabbinism, the successors of the scribes and the Pharisees ("hypocrites"). To this end they fasted publicly on two different days of the week and prayed publicly different prayers three times a day. They permitted only those baptized to share their eucharistic meal, a prohibition initially aimed at gentile outsiders, but which had the obvious potential to apply to other Israelites also, if they too were required to be baptized. There is little polemic, however, concerning the "hypocrites". Most of the anxiety expressed in the Didache seems to relate to rival communities who accepted Jesus as the Lord but advocated a different teaching around the Torah. Thus, in addition to the two aspects of "self-definition" against gentiles and other Jews, and associated with them, was the third aspect of "self-definition" against other Christian grouping(s) which had resolved the problematic in different ways.

---

[81] *In the Active Voice*, 41; cf. Jaffee, "Rabbinic Oral Tradition."

Matthew's gospel also insists that the Torah has not passed away and never will "until the end of the age," and also insists on a prioritization of the ethical half of the Decalogue, summarized in the Love Commandments (as in the Didache). He too polemicizes against abandoning the Torah (Matt 5:17-20), which he, like the Didache, rejects as "lawlessness" (ἀνομία). However, gentiles seem to play a stronger role in Matthew's community. There is no suggestion that it would be a good thing if gentiles should keep the Torah as such, so presumably Israelite members carried on with the full observance of the Torah but gentiles kept only the Noachic commandments. The yoke of Jesus is easy and gives rest, whereas in Didache it is experienced as a burden. One gets the feeling that, in Matthew, the understanding of the "yoke" as Torah observance by gentiles has shifted away from ritual observance towards an understanding of Torah as "wisdom" (which also has roots in the traditions of Israel). Torah can be summarized and fulfilled by the double command to love God and love one's neighbour.[82] There is a strong feeling expressed in Matthew that the Judaean leaders and people had acted wickedly in crucifying God's messiah and had brought their judgment on themselves. The kingdom is now taken from them and given to others who will bear the fruit, who will sit at table with the patriarchs, who will share the wedding feast of the messiah. The polemic against the "hypocrites" is now strident and unambiguously directed against the scribes and the Pharisees. The position of the "hypocrites" in the public sphere in Matthew appears to have become overwhelmingly powerful, so that the marks of differentiation in fasting, prayer and almsgiving must now be kept secret. The "hypocrites" are seated on the chair of Moses and must be obeyed, but not respected since they are wicked whatever their appearance.

Perhaps we can see in the Didache, which survived in its current form by accident, an earlier stage of the conflict between members of Israel who accepted Jesus and the successors of the Pharisees who did not and who were growing in power and influence in the wake of the destruction of the Temple. That conflict comes to full flower in the gospel of Matthew, which represents a further step of alienation and rejection. The break is not complete, since members are still required to obey the successors of Moses, the nascent rabbinic movement, but the bitterness and blame make it difficult to see how a final break could have been avoided at some stage.

---

[82] Cf. Segal, "Matthew's Jewish Voice," 22.

Cumulative Bibliography

Achtemeier, P.J., "*Omne verbum sonat*: The New Testament and the Oral Environment of Late Western Antiquity." *Journal of Biblical Literature* 109 (1990) 3-27

Alexander, P.S., "Jesus and the Golden Rule." In *Hillel and Jesus: Comparative Studies of Two Major Religious Leaders*, edited by J.H. Charlesworth and L.L. Johns. Minneapolis 1997, 363-88

– "'The Parting of the Ways' from the Perspective of Rabbinic Judaism." In *Jews and Christians*, edited by J.D.G. Dunn, 1–25

Allison, D.C., *The Jesus Tradition in Q.* Valley Forge (Pa.) 1997

Alon, G., *Studies in Jewish History in the Times of the Second Temple, the Mishna and the Talmud* 1-2. Tel Aviv 1958-61 (Hebr)

– "Ha-halakha ba-Torat 12 ha-Shelihim." *Tarbiz* 11 (1939-40) 127-45; repr. in id., *Studies in Jewish History* 1, 274-94 (Hebr). ET: "The Halacha in the Teaching of the Twelve Apostles." In *The Didache in Modern Research*, edited by J.A. Draper, 165-94

– "Le-yishuva shel baraita ahat." In Alon, *Studies in Jewish History* 2, 120-27 (Hebr)

– "Ha-halakha ba-Iggeret Bar-Nava." *Tarbiz* 12 (1940-41) 23-38. 223; repr. in Alon, *Studies in Jewish History* 1, 295-312 (Hebr)

– *The Jews in Their Land in the Talmudic Age (70-640 CE)* 1-2. Jerusalem 1980-84

Aldridge, R.E., "The Lost Ending of the *Didache*." *Vigiliae Christianae* 53 (1999) 1-15

Aono, T. *Die Entwicklung des paulinischen Gerichtsgedankens bei den Apostolischen Vätern* (Europäische Hochschulschriften 23/Theologie 137). Frankfurt am Main-Bern-New York, 1979

Audet, J.P., *La Didachè: Instructions des apôtres* (Études Bibliques). Paris 1958

Avigad, N., *The Herodian Quarter in Jerusalem.* Jerusalem 1991

Baarda, T., "Thomas and Tatian." In *Early Transmission of Words of Jesus: Thomas, Tatian and the Text of the New Testament. A Collection of Studies*, edited by T. Baarda, J. Helderman and S.J. Noorda. Amsterdam 1983, 37–49

Balabanski, V., *Eschatology in the Making. Mark, Matthew and the Didache* (Society for New Testament Studies Monograph Series 97). Cambridge 1997

Balch, D.L., (ed.), *Social History of the Matthean Community: Cross-Disciplinary Approaches.* Minneapolis 1991

Ball, W., *Rome in the East: The Transformation of an Empire.* London 2000

Bardy, G., (ed.), *Eusèbe de Césarée: Histoire ecclésiastique* 1-4 (Sources Chrétiennes 31, 41, 55, 73). Paris 1952-1960

Barnard, L.W., "The Dead Sea Scrolls, Barnabas, the *Didache* and the Later History of the 'Two Ways'." In Id., *Studies in the Apostolic Fathers and Their Background.* Oxford 1966, 87–107

– *Studies in the Apostolic Fathers and their Background.* Oxford 1966

Barr, J., "Hebrew, Aramaic and Greek in the Hellenistic Age." In *The Cambridge History of Judaism* 2, edited by W.D. Davies, L. Finkelstein *et al.* Cambridge 1989, 79–114

Barrett, C.K., *A Critical and Exegetical Commentary on the Acts of the Apostles* 1-2 (International Critical Commentary). Edinburgh 1994-98

Barth, G., *Die Taufe in frühchristliche Zeit.* Neukirchen-Vluyn 1981

Bartlet, J.V., and K. Lake, *The New Testament in the Apostolic Fathers.* Oxford 1905

Bauckham, R. (ed.), *The Gospels for All Christians. Rethinking the Gospel Audiences.* Edinburgh 1998

Baudry, G.-H., *La voie de la Vie. Étude sur la catéchèse des Pères de l'Église* (Théologie historique 110). Paris 1999

Bauer, W., *Rechtgläubigkeit und Ketzerei im ältesten Christentum* (Beiträge zur historischen Theologie 10). 2nd rev. ed. Tübingen 1964

Baumgarten, J.M., "Halakhic Polemics in New Fragments from Qumran Cave 4." In *Biblical Archaeology Today: Proceedings of the International Congress on Biblical Archaeology Jerusalem, April 1984*, edited by J. Amitai. Jerusalem 1985, 390-99

Beare, F.W., *The Gospel According to Matthew.* Peabody 1981

Belkin, S., *The Alexandrian Halakah in Apologetic Literature of the First Century C.E.* Philadelphia (Pa.) n.d. [1936]

Bellinzoni, A.J., *The Sayings of Jesus in the Writings of Justin Martyr* (Supplements to Novum Testamentum 17). Leiden 1967

Benoit, A., *Le Baptême Chrétien au second siècle: La théologie des Pères* (Études d'histoire et de philosophie religieuses publiées par la Faculté de Théologie protestante de l'Université de Strasbourg 43). Paris 1953

Bergemann, Th., *Q auf dem Prüfstand: Die Zuordnung des Mt/Lk-Stoffes zu Q am Beispiel der Bergpredigt* (Forschungen zur Religion und Literatur des Alten und Neuen Testaments 158). Göttingen 1993

Betz, J., "Die Eucharistie in der Didache." In *Archiv für Liturgiewissenschaft* 11 (1969) 10-39; ET: "The Eucharist in the Didache." In *The Didache in Modern Research,* edited by J.A. Draper, 244-75

Beyer, K., *Die aramäischen Inschriften aus Assur, Hatra und dem übrigen Ostmesopotamien (datiert 44 v. Chr. bis 238 n.Chr.).* Göttingen 1998

Boccaccini, G., *Middle Judaism: Jewish Thought, 300 B.C.E. to 200 C.E.* Minneapolis 1991

Böcher, O., "Wölfe im Schafspelzen: zum religionsgeschichtlichen Hintergrund von Matth. 7,15." *Theologische Zeitschrift* 24 (1968) 406-26

Botte, B. (ed.), *La Tradition Apostolique d'après les anciennes versions.* (Sources Chrétiennes 11 bis) Paris 1984

Bover, J.M., "Si peccaverit in te frater tuus ... Mt 18,15." *Estudios Bíblicos* 12 (1953) 195-98

Bradshaw, P., "The Problems of a New Edition of the *Apostolic Tradition.*" In *Acts of the International Congress 'Comparative Liturgy' Fifty Years after Anton Baumstark (1872-1948),* edited by R.Taft and G. Winkler (Orientalia Christiana Analecta 265). Rome 2001, 613-22

– "Parallels between Early Jewish and Christian Prayers: Some Methodological Issues." In *Identität durch Gebet,* edited by A. Gerhards, A. Doeker, P. Ebenbauer, 21-36

– M.E. Johnson, L.E. Philips, *The Apostolic Tradition: A Commentary* (Hermeneia). Minneapolis 2002

– *The Search for the Origins of Christian Worship.* London 1992

Braun, H., *Qumran und das Neue Testament* 1-2. Tübingen 1966

Brennecke, H.C., "Lucian von Antiochien." In *Theologische Realenzyklopädie* 21. Berlin 1991, 474–79

Brock, S.P., *Studies in Syriac Christianity.* Aldershot 1992

– *From Ephrem to Romanos: Interactions between Syriac and Greek in Late Antiquity.* Aldershot 1999

– "Eusebius and Syriac Christianity." In *Josephus, Judaism, and Christianity,* edited by L.H. Feldman and G. Hata, 212–34; repr. as Chapter II of his *From Ephrem to Romanos*

– "Greek and Syriac in Late Antique Syria." In *Literacy and Power in The Ancient World,* edited by A.K. Bowman and G. Woolf. Cambridge 1994, 149–60; repr. as Chapter I of his *From Ephrem to Romanos*

– "Jewish Traditions in Syriac Sources." *Journal of Jewish Studies* 30 (1979) 212–32; repr. as Chapter IV of his *Studies in Syriac Christianity*

– "A Palestinian Targum Feature in Syriac." *Journal of Jewish Studies* 46 (1995) 271–82

– "Limitations of Syriac in Representing Greek." In S.P. Brock and B.M. Metzger, *The Early Versions of the New Testament: Their Origin, Transmission, and Limitations.* Oxford 1977, 83–98

Broer, I., "Redaktionsgeschichtliche Aspekte von Mt. 24:1-28." *Novum Testamentum* 35 (1993) 209-33

Brooks, S.H., *Matthew's Community. The Evidence of His Special Sayings Material* (Journal for the Study of the New Testament-Supplement Series 16). Sheffield 1987

Broshi, M. (ed.), *The Damascus Document Reconsidered.* Jerusalem 1992

Brown, R.E., and J.P. Meier, *Antioch and Rome: New Testament Cradles of Catholic Christianity.* New York 1983

Bryennios, Ph., Διδαχὴ τῶν δώδεκα ἀποστόλων ἐκ τοῦ ἱεροσολυμιτικοῦ χειρογράφου νῦν πρῶτον ἐκδιδομένη μετὰ προλεγομένων καὶ σημειώσεων ἐν οἷς καὶ τῆς Συνόψεως τῆς Π.Δ., τῆς ὑπὸ ᾿Ιωάνν. τοῦ Χρυσοστόμου, σύγκρισις καὶ μέρος ἀνέκδοτον ἀπὸ τοῦ αὐτοῦ χειρογράφου. Constantinople 1883

Bultmann, R., *Die Geschichte der synoptischen Tradition* (Forschungen zur Religion und Literatur des Alten und Neuen Testaments 29). 6th ed. Göttingen 1964

Butler, B.C., "The Literary Relations of Didache, Ch. XVI." *Journal of Theological Studies* N.S. 11 (1960) 265–83

– "The 'Two Ways' in the Didache." *Journal of Theological Studies* N.S. 12 (1961) 27–38

Cadbury, H.J., *The Style and Literary Method of Luke* (Harvard Theological Studies 6). Cambridge (Mass.) 1920

Carleton Paget, J., "Jewish Christianity." In *Cambridge History of Judaism* 3, 731–75

– "Anti-Judaism and Early Christian Identity." *Zeitschrift für Antikes Christentum* 1 (1997) 195–225

Carmody, T.R., "Matt 18:15-17 in Relation to Three Texts from Qumran Literature (CD 9:2-8, 16-22; 1QS 5:25-6:1)." In *To Touch the Text. Biblical and Related Studies in Honor of Joseph A. Fitzmyer, S.J.*, edited by M.P. Horgan, and P.J. Kobelski. New York 1989, 142-50

Catchpole, D., "Reproof and Reconciliation in the Q community: A study of the tradition-history of Mt 18,15-17. 21-22 / Lk 17,3-4." In *Studien zum Neuen Testament und seiner Umwelt.* Aufsätze 8, edited by A. Fuchs. Linz 1983, 79-90

Charlesworth, J.H., *The Old Testament Pseudepigrapha* 1-2. London 1983-85

– *The Dead Sea Scrolls: Hebrew, Aramaic, and Greek Texts with English Translations.* 1: *Rule of the Community and Related Documents*; 2: *Damascus Document, War Scroll, and Related Documents*, Tübingen-Louisville 1994-1995

Cody, A., "The Didache: An English Translation." In *The Didache in Context*, edited by C.N. Jefford, 3-14

Comaroff, J., and J. Comaroff, *Of Revelation and Revolution: Colonialism and Consciousness in South Africa* 1. Chicago 1991

Connolly, R.H., "The Didache in Relation to the Epistle of Barnabas." *Journal of Theological Studies* 33 (1932) 327-53

– "The Didache and Montanism." *Downside Review* 55 (1937) 339-47

Corbo, V.C., *Cafarnao 1: Gli edifici della città* (Pubblicazioni dello Studium Biblicum Franciscanum 19). Jerusalem 1975

Court, J.M., "The Didache and St. Matthew's Gospel." *Scottish Journal of Theology* 34 (1981) 109-20

Crossan, J.D., *The Historical Jesus: the Life of a Mediteranean Jewish Peasant.* New York 1991

– *Jesus: A Revolutionary Biography.* San Francisco 1994

– *The Birth of Christianity: Discovering What Happened in the Years Immediately After the Execution of Jesus.* San Francisco 1998

Cullmann, O., *Urchristentum und Gottesdienst* (Abhandlungen zur Theologie des Alten und Neuen Testaments 3). Zürich 1950

Daniélou, J., "Le traité De centesima, sexagesima, tricesima et le judéo-christianisme latin avant Tertullien." *Vigiliae christianae* 25 (1971) 171-81

Davies, W.D., and D.C. Allison, *A Critical and Exegetical Commentary on the Gospel According to Saint Matthew* 1-3 (International Critical Commentary). Edinburgh, 1988-1997

Davila, J.R., *Liturgical Works* (Eerdmans Commentaries on the Dead Sea Scrolls 6). Grand Rapids (Mich.) - Cambridge 2000

Del Verme, M., "*Did.* 16 e la cosidetta 'apocalittica giudaica'." *Orpheus* 22 (2001) 39-76

– "*Didaché* e origini cristiane. Una bibliografia per lo studio della *Didaché* nel contesto del giudaismo cristiano.» *Vetera Christianorum* 38 (2001) 5-39 and 223-45

Desreumaux, A., "La doctrine d'Addaï, l'image du Christ et les monophysites." In *Nicée II, 787–1987: Douze siècles d'images religieuses. Actes du colloque international Nicée II*, edited by F. Bœspflug and N. Lossky. Paris 1987, 73–79

Deutsch, C., *Hidden Wisdom and the Easy Yoke: Wisdom, Torah and Discipleship in Matthew 11.25-30* (Journal for the Study of the New Testament-Supplement Series 18). Sheffield 1987

Dibelius, M., "Die Mahl-Gebete der Didache." *Zeitschrift für die neutestamentliche Wissenschaft* 37 (1938) 32-41; repr. in *Botschaft und Geschichte: Gesammelte Aufätze von Martin Dibelius 2: Zum Urchristentum und zur hellenistischen Religionsgeschichte*, edited by H. Kraft and G. Bornkamm. Tübingen 1956, 117-27

Dimant, D., "Qumran Sectarian Literature." In *Jewish Writings of the Second Temple Period: Apocrypha, Pseudepigrapha, Qumran Sectarian Writings, Philo, Josephus*, edited by M.E. Stone (Compendia rerum iudaicarum ad Novum Testamentum 2/2). Assen-Philadelphia 1984, 483-550

Dirksen, P.B., "The Old Testament Peshitta." In *Mikra*, edited by M.J. Mulder, 255–97

Dörrie, H., "Zur Geschichte der Septuaginta im Jahrhundert Konstantins." *Zeitschrift für die neutestamentliche Wissenschaft* 39 (1940) 57–110

Douglas, M., *In the Active Voice*. London-Boston 1982

– *Natural Symbols: Explorations in Cosmology.* New ed. New York 1982

Downey, G., *A History of Antioch in Syria from Seleucus to the Arab Conquest*. Princeton (N.J.) 1961

Downing, F.G., "Word-Processing in the Ancient World: The Social Production and Performance of Q." *Journal for the Study of the New Testament* 64 (1996) 29–48

Draper, J. A., "Confessional Western Text Centered Biblical Interpretation and an Oral or Residual Oral Context." *Semeia* 73 (1996) 59-77

– (ed.), *The Didache in Modern Research* (Arbeiten zur Geschichte des antiken Judentums und des Urchristentums 37). Leiden-New York-Köln 1996

– "The Jesus Tradition in the Didache." In *The Jesus Tradition Outside the Gospels*, edited by D. Wenham (Gospel Perspectives 5). Sheffield 1985, 269-89. Revised and reprinted in J.A. Draper, *The Didache in Modern Research*, 72-91

– *A Commentary on the Didache in the Light of the Dead Sea Scrolls and Related Documents*. Unpublished PhD Thesis, Cambridge University 1984

– "Torah and Troublesome Apostles in the Didache Community." *Novum Testamentum* 33 (1991) 347-72; rev. and repr. in Id., *The Didache in Modern Research*, 340-63

– "'Korah' and the Second Temple." In *Templum Amicitiae: Essays on the Second Temple presented to Ernst Bammel*, edited by W. Horbury (Journal for the Study of the New Testament-Supplement Series 48). Sheffield 1991, 150-74

– "Christian Self-Definition against the 'Hypocrites' in Didache 8." In *Society of Biblical Literature 1992 Seminar Papers*, edited by E. H. Lovering. Atlanta (Ga.) 1992, 362-377. Rev. and repr. in J.A. Draper, *The Didache in Modern Research*, 223-43

– "Social Ambiguity and the Production of Text: Prophets, Teachers, Bishops and Deacons and the Development of the Jesus Tradition in the Community of the Didache." In *The Didache in Context*, edited by C.N. Jefford, 284-312

– "Barnabas and the Riddle of the Didache Revisited." *Journal for the Study of the New Testament* 58 (1995) 89-113

– "Resurrection and the Cult of Martyrdom in the Didache Apocalypse." *Journal of Early Christian Studies* 5 (1997) 155-79

– "The Role of Ritual in the Alternation of Social Universe: Jewish Christian Initiation of Gentiles in the Didache." *Listening* 37 (1997) 48-67

– "The Genesis and Narrative Thrust of the Paraenesis in the Sermon on the Mount." *Journal for the Study of the New Testament* 75 (1999) 25-48

- "Ritual Process and Ritual Symbol in Didache 7-10." *Vigiliae Christianae* 54 (2000) 121-58
- "Holy Seed and the Return of the Diaspora in John 12:24." *Neotestamentica* 34 (2000) 346-59
- "The Didache in Modern Research: an Overview." In Id. (ed.), *The Didache in Modern Research*, 1-42
- "A Continuing Enigma: The 'Yoke of the Lord' in Didache 6:2-3 and Early Jewish-Christian relations." In *The Image of the Judaeo-Christians in Early Jewish and Christian Literature; Papers Delivered at the Colloquium of the Institutum Iudaicum, Brussels, 18-19 November 2001*, edited by P.J. Tomson and D. Lambers-Petry (Wissenschaftliche Untersuchungen zum Neuen Testament 158). Tübingen 2003, 106-123 (forthcoming)

Drews, P., "Apostellehre (Didache)." In *Handbuch zu den Neutestamentlichen Apokryphen*, edited by E. Hennecke. Tübingen 1904, 256-83
- "Untersuchungen zur Didache." *Zeitschrift für die neutestamentliche Wissenschaft* 5 (1904) 53-79

Drijvers, H.J.W., *Bardaiṣan of Edessa* (Ph.D. diss.). Assen 1966
- *Cults and Beliefs at Edessa* (Etudes préliminaires aux religions orientales dans l'empire romain 82). Leiden 1980
- *East of Antioch: Studies in Early Syriac Christianity*. London 1984
- *History and Religion in Late Antique Syria*. Aldershot 1994
- "Marcionism in Syria: Principles, Problems, Polemics." *Second Century* 6 (1987–88) 153–72; repr. as Chapter XI of his *History and Religion*
- "Syrian Christianity and Judaism." In *The Jews among Pagans and Christians in the Roman Empire*, edited by J. Lieu, J. North, and T. Rajak. London 1992, 124–46; repr. as Chapter II of his *History and Religion*
- "Early Syriac Christianity: Some Recent Publications." *Vigiliae Christianae* 50 (1996) 159–77
- "Edessa und das jüdische Christentum." *Vigiliae Christianae* 24 (1970) 4–33; repr. as Chapter II of his *East of Antioch*
- "Facts and Problems in Early Syriac-Speaking Christianity." *Second Century* 2 (1982) 157–75; repr. as Chapter VI of his *East of Antioch*
- "Addai und Mani: Christentum und Manichäismus im dritten Jahrhundert in Syrien." In *IIIᵉ Symposium Syriacum 1980*, edited by R. Lavenant (Orientalia christiana analecta 221). Rome 1983, 171–85; repr. as Chapter XV of his *History and Religion*
- "Rechtgläubigkeit und Ketzerei im ältesten Syrischen Christentum." In *Symposium Syriacum 1972*, edited by I. Ortiz de Urbina (Orientalia christiana analecta 197). Rome 1974, 291–308; repr. as Chapter III of his *East of Antioch*
- "Jews and Christians at Edessa." *Journal of Jewish Studies* 36 (1985) 88–102; reprinted as Chapter I of his *History and Religion*
- "The Peshitta of Sapientia Salomonis." In *Scripta Signa Vocis: Studies about Scripts, Scriptures, Scribes and Languages in the Near East Presented to J.H. Hospers*, edited by H.L.J. Vanstiphout *et al.* Groningen 1986, 15–30; repr. as Chapter VI of his *History and Religion*
- "The Persistence of Pagan Cults and Practices in Christian Syria." In *East of Byzantium*, edited by N.G. Garsoïan *et al.*, 35–43; repr. as Chapter XVI of his *East of Antioch*

Drijvers, H.J.W., and J.F. Healey, *The Old Syriac Inscriptions of Edessa and Osrhoene: Texts, Translations and Commentary* (Handbuch der Orientalistik 1/42). Leiden 1999

Driver, G.R., *Aramaic Documents of the Fifth Century B.C.* Oxford 1957

Duling, D.C., "Matthew 18:15-17: Conflict, Confrontation, and Conflict Resolution in a 'Fictive Kin' Association." *Biblical Theology Bulletin* 29 (1999) 4-22

Dunn, J.D.G., *The Partings of the Ways between Christianity and Judaism and their Significance for the Character of Christianity*. London-Philadelphia 1991
- (ed.), *Jews and Christians: The Parting of the Ways A.D. 70 to 135* (Wissenschaftliche Untersuchungen zum Neuen Testament 66). Tübingen 1992
- "The Incident at Antioch (Gal. 2:11-18)." *Journal for the Study of the New Testament* 18 (1983) 3-57

Elliott, J.H., *1 Peter* (Anchor Bible 37B). New York 2000

Epstein, J.N., *Introduction to Tannaitic Literature: Mishna, Tosephta and Halakhic Midrashim*, edited by E.Z. Melamed. Jerusalem 1957 (Hebr)

Eshel, E., "4Q477: The Rebukes by the Overseer." *Journal of Jewish Studies* 45 (1994) 111-22

Falk, D.K., *Daily, Sabbath, and Festival Prayers in the Dead Sea Scrolls* (Studies on the Texts of the Desert of Judah 27). Leiden 1998

- "Jewish Prayer Literature and the Jerusalem Church in Acts." In *The Book of Acts in Its First Century Setting* 4: *The Book of Acts in its Palestinian Setting*, edited by R. Bauckham. Grand Rapids-Carlisle 1995, 267–301

Farrar, F.W., "The Bearing of the 'Teaching' on the Canon." *The Expositor* 8 (1884) 81-91

Feneberg, R., *Christliche Passafeier und Abendmahl: eine biblisch-hermeneutische Untersuchung der neutestamentlichen Einsetzungsberichte* (Studien zum Alten und Neuen Testament 27). München 1971

Fitzmyer, J.A., *The Acts of the Apostles* (Anchor Bible 31). New York, 1997

Fleischer, E., "On the Beginnings of Obligatory Jewish Prayer." *Tarbiz* 59 (1989-90) 397-441 (Hebr)

Flusser, D., "Paul's Jewish-Christian Opponents in the Didache." In *Gilgul. Essays on Transformation, Revolution and Permanence in the history of Religions*, edited by S. Shaked, D. Shulman, and G.G. Stroumsa (FS. Z. Werblowski). Leiden-New York-Copenhagen 1987, 71-90; repr in *The Didache in Modern Research*, edited by J.A. Draper, 195-211

- "The Conclusion of Matthew in a New Jewish Christian Source." *Annual of the Swedish Theological Institute* 5 (1966) 110-20

Forkman, G., *The Limits of the Religious Community: Expulsion from the Religious Community within the Qumran Sect, within Rabbinic Judaism, and within Primitive Christianity* (Coniectanea Biblica - New Testament Series 5). Lund 1972

Fredriksen, P., "Judaism, the Circumcision of Gentiles, and Apocalyptic Hope: Another Look at Galatians 1 and 2." *Journal of Theological Studies* 42 (1991) 532-64

Freedman, D.N. (ed.), *Anchor Bible Dictionary* 1-6. New York 1992

Frey, J.-B., *Corpus inscriptionum iudaicarum: recueil des inscriptions juives qui vont du IIIe siècle avant Jésus-Christ au VIIe siècle de notre ère* 2: *Asie–Afrique* (Sussidi allo studio delle antichità cristiane 3). Città del Vaticano 1952

Freyne, S., "The Geography, Politics, and Economics of Galilee and the Quest for the Historical Jesus." In *Studying the Historical Jesus: Evaluations of the State of Current Research*, edited by B. Chilton and C.A. Evans (New Testament Tools and Studies 19). Leiden 1994, 75–121

Frye, R.N., *The Heritage of Persia*. London 1962

Funk, F.X., *Didascalia et Constitutiones Apostolorum* 1. Paderborn, 1905; repr Turin 1962

Gafni, I.M., "The Historical Background." In *The Literature of the Sages*, edited by S. Safrai, 1-34

García Martínez, F., "La Represión fraterna en Qumrán y Mt 18,15-17." *Filologia Neotestamentaria* 2 (1989) 23-40; ET: "Brotherly Rebuke in Qumran and Mt 18:15-17." In *The People of the Dead Sea Scrolls: Their Writings, Beliefs and Practices*, edited by F. García Martínez and J. Trebolle Barrera. Leiden-New York-Cologne 1995, 221-32

García Martínez, F., and E.J.C. Tigchelaar, *The Dead Sea Scrolls; Study Edition* 1-2. Leiden-New York-Köln 1997-1998

Garrow, A.J.P., *The Gospel of Matthew's Dependence on the Didache* (Journal for the Study of the New Testament-Supplement Series 254). London-New York 2004

Garsky, A., Ch. Heil, T. Hieke, and J. Amon, *Q 12:49–59*. In *Documenta Q: Reconstructions of Q Through Two Centuries of Gospel Research Excerpted, Sorted and Evaluated*. Edited by S. Carruth, J.M. Robinson, P. Hoffmann, and J.S. Kloppenborg (gen. eds.). Leuven 1997

Garsoïan, N.G. , Th.F. Mathews, and R.W. Thomson (eds.), *East of Byzantium: Syria and Armenia in the Formative Period*. Washington (D.C.) 1982

Gerhards, A, A. Doeker, P. Ebenbauer (eds.), *Identität durch Gebet: Zur gemeinschaftsbildenden Funktion institutionalisierten Betens in Judentum und Christentum*. Paderborn 2003

Giesen, H., "Zum Problem der Exkommunikation nach dem Matthäus-Evangelium." *Studia Moralia* 8 (1970) 185-269; repr. in Id., *Glaube und Handeln*. 1: *Beiträge zur Exegese und*

Theologie des Matthäus- und Markus-Evangeliums (Europäische Hochschulschriften 23: Theologie 205). Frankfurt a. M.-Bern-New York 1983, 17-72 (expanded with an 'Excursus' on pp. 72-83)

Giet, St., *L'énigme de la Didachè* (Publications de la Faculté des Lettres de l'Université de Strasbourg 149). Paris 1970

Ginzberg, L., *A Commentary on the Palestinian Talmud: a study of the development of the Halakah and Haggadah in Palestine and Babylonia* 1-4. New York 1941-61 (Hebr)

– *Die Haggada bei den Kirchenvätern* 1: *Die Haggada in den pseudo-hieronymianischen 'Quaestiones'*. Amsterdam 1899

– *On Jewish Law and Lore*. Philadelphia 1955; repr. New York 1977

– *The Legends of the Jews* 1-6. Philadelphia 1909-28. Vol. 7, Index (B. Cohen). Philadelphia 1938; and repr.

– *An Unknown Jewish Sect* (Moreshet 1). New York 1976

– *Yerushalmi fragments from the Genizah* 1: *Text with various readings from the editio princeps*. New York 1909; repr. Jerusalem 1969

Giordano, O., "L' escatologia nella *Didaché*." In *Oikoumene. Studi paleocristiani pubblicati in onore del Concilio Ecumenico Vaticano II*. Catania 1964, 121-39

Glover, R., "The Didache's Quotations and the Synoptic Gospels." *New Testament Studies* 5 (1958) 12-29

– "Patristic Quotations and Gospel Sources." *New Testament Studies* 31 (1985) 234–51

Gnilka, J., *Das Matthäusevangelium* 2: *Kommentar zu Kap. 14,1 - 28,20* (Herders theologischer Kommentar zum Neuen Testament 1/2). 2nd ed. Freiburg 1992

Goldenberg, D.M., *Halakhah in Josephus and in Tannaitic Literature: A Comparative Study* (Ph. D. diss. Dropsie University). Philadelphia (Pa.) 1978

Goldhahn-Müller, I., *Die Grenze der Gemeinde: Studien zum Problem der Zweiten Busse im Neuen Testament unter Berücksichtigung der Entwicklung im 2. Jh. bis Tertullian* (Göttinger theologische Arbeiten 39). Göttingen 1989

Goodman, M., "The First Jewish Revolt: Social Conflict and the Problem of Debt." In *Essays in Honour of Yigael Yadin*, edited by Géza Vermès and Jacob Neusner (= Journal of Jewish Studies 33). Totawa (N.J.) 1982, 417–27

– *Josephus and Variety in First-Century Judaism* (Proceedings of the Israel Academy of Sciences and Humanities 7/6). Jerusalem 2000

– (ed.), "Jews, Greeks, and Romans." In *Jews in a Graeco-Roman world*. Oxford 1998, 3–14

– "Diaspora Reactions to the Destruction of the Temple." In *Jews and Christians*, edited by J.D.G. Dunn, 27–38

– *State and Society in Roman Galilee, A.D. 132–212* (Oxford Centre for Postgraduate Hebrew Studies Series). Totawa (N.J.) 1983

Goodspeed, E. J., "The Didache, Barnabas and the Doctrina." *Anglican Theological Review* 27 (1945) 228-47

Grant, R.M., "The Early Antiochene Antiphon." *Anglican Theological Review* 30 (1948) 91-94

– "Jewish Christianity at Antioch in the Second Century." In *Judéo-christianisme*, edited by J. Moignt. Paris 1972, 97-108

Green, H. B.. "The Command to Baptize and Other Matthaean Interpolations." In *Studia Evangelica* 4 (Texte und Untersuchungen 102). Berlin 1968, 60-63

Greyvenstein, J., *The Original 'Teaching of the Twelve Apostles'* (Ph.D. diss.). Chicago 1919

Griffith, S.H., "The Doctrina Addai as a Paradigm of Christian Thought in Edessa in the Fifth Century." *Hugoye* (http://syrcom.cua.edu/hugoye) 6/2 (2003)

Grundmann, W. , *Das Evangelium nach Matthäus* (Theologischer Handkommentar zum Neuen Testament 1). 5th ed . Berlin 1981

Gundry, R.H., *Matthew. A Commentary on His Literary and Theological Art*. Grand Rapids (Mich.) 1983 (repr.)

Guttmann, A., "The End of the Jewish Sacrificial Cult." *Hebrew Union College Annual* 38 (1967) 137–48

Haar Romeny, B. ter, *A Syrian in Greek Dress: The Use of Greek, Hebrew, and Syriac Biblical Texts in Eusebius of Emesa's Commentary on Genesis* (Traditio exegetica graeca 6). Leuven 1997
– "The Peshitta and its Rivals: On the Assessment of the Peshitta and Other Versions of the Old Testament in Syriac Exegetical Literature." *The Harp* 11–12 (1998–99) 21–31
Haenchen, E. *The Acts of the Apostles. A Commentary.* Philadelphia (Pa.) 1971
Halleux, A. de, "Les ministères dans la Didachè." *Irénikon* 53 (1980) 4-29; ET: "Ministers in the Didache." In *The Didache in Modern Research*, edited by J.A. Draper, 300-320
Hamel, G.H., *Poverty and Charity in Roman Palestine: First Three Centuries C.E.* (Near Eastern Studies 23). Berkeley 1990
Hanson, K.C. and D.E. Oakman, *Palestine in the Time of Jesus.* Minneapolis 1998
Hare, D., and D. Harrington, "Make Disciples of all the Gentiles (Mt. 28:19)." *Catholic Biblical Quarterly* 37 (1975) 359-69
Harnack, A. von, *Die Lehre der zwölf Apostel nebst Untersuchungen zur ältesten Geschichte der Kirchenverfassung und des Kirchenrechts* (Texte und Untersuchungen 2/1). Leipzig 1884; repr. Leipzig 1893
– *Die Apostellehrre und die jüdischen beiden Wege*, Leipzig 1886
– *Die Mission und Ausbreitung des Christentums in den ersten drei Jahrhunderten.* 4th enl. ed. Leipzig 1924; ET: *The Mission and Expansion of Christianity in the First Three Centuries* 1-2 (Theological Translation Library 19). New York 1908
Harrak, A., "Trade Routes and the Christianization of the Near East." *Journal of the Canadian Society for Syriac Studies* 2 (2002) 46–61
Harrington, D.J., *The Gospel of Matthew* (Sacra Pagina 1). Collegeville (Minn.) 1991
Hartel, W., *S. Thasci Caecili Cypriani opera omnia. 3: Opera spuria. Indices. Praefatio* (Corpus scriptorum ecclesiasticorum latinorum 3/3). Vienna 1871, 92-104
Heinemann, J., *Prayer in the Talmud: Forms and Patterns*, Berlin-New York 1977
Hempel, C., *The Laws of the Damascus Document: Sources, Tradition and Redaction* (Studies on the Texts of the Desert of Judah 29). Leiden 1998
Henderson, I.H., "Didache and Orality in Synoptic Comparison." *Journal of Biblical Literature* 111 (1992) 283-306
– "Style-Switching in the *Didache*: Fingerprint or Argument?" In *The Didache in Context*, edited by C.N. Jefford, 177-209
Hoffman, L.A., "Reconstructing Ritual as Identity and Culture." In *The Making of Jewish and Christian Worship*, edited by P. F. Bradshaw and L.A. Hoffman. Notre Dame 1991, 23-41
Hoffmann, P., "Der Petrus-Primat im Matthäusevangelium." In *Neues Testament und Kirche*, edited by J. Gnilka. Freiburg 1974, 94-114
Hollander, H.W., and M. de Jonge, *The Testaments of the Twelve Patriarchs: A Commentary* (Studia in Veteris Testamenti pseudepigrapha 8). Leiden 1985
Horsley, R.A., and J.A. Draper, *Whoever Hears You Hears Me: Prophets, Performance, and Tradition in Q.* Harrisburg (Pa.) 1999
– "Synagogues in Galilee and the Gospels." In *Evolution of the Synagogue: Problems and Progress*, edited by H.C. Kee and L.H. Cohick. Harrisburg (Pa.) 1999, 46-72
Hughes-Fowler, B., *Hellenistic Poetry. An Anthology.* Madison (Wisc.) 1990
Hultgren, A.J., "Liturgy and Literature: The Liturgical Factor in Matthew's Literary and Communicative Art." In *Texts and Contexts: Biblical Texts in their Textual and Situational Contexts*, Essays in Honor of Lars Hartman, edited by T. Fornberg and D. Hellholm. Oslo-Copenhagen-Stockholm 1995, 659-73
Hummel, R., *Die Auseinandersetzung zwischen Kirche und Judentum im Matthäusevangelium* (Beiträge zur evangelischen Theologie 33). 2nd ed. München 1966
Hunt, E.J., *Christianity in the Second Century: The Case of Tatian.* London 2003
Hvalvik, R., *The Struggle for Scripture and Covenant: The Purpose of the Epistle of Barnabas and Jewish-Christian Competition in the Second Century* (Wissenschaftliche Untersuchungen zum Neuen Testament 2/82). Tübingen 1996

Isaac, B., "Judaea after A.D. 70." *Journal of Jewish Studies* 35 (1984) 44–50; repr. with postscript in Id., *The Near East under Roman Rule: Selected Papers* (Mnemosyne Supplements 177). Leiden 1998, 112–21

Jaffee, M. S., "Rabbinic Oral Tradition in Late Byzantine Galilee: Christian Empire and Rabbinic Ideological Resistance." In *Orality, Literacy, and Colonialism in Antiquity*, edited by J.A. Draper (Semeia Studies 47). Atlanta 2004, 171-91

Jackson, B.S., "*Testes singulares* in Early Jewish Law and the New Testament." In Id., *Essays in Jewish and Comparative Legal History* (Studies in Judaism in Late Antiquity 10). Leiden 1975, 172-201

Jacobson, A.D., *The First Gospel: An Introduction to Q* (Foundations and Facets - Reference Series). Sonoma (Calif.) 1992

Jansma, T., *Natuur, lot en vrijheid: Bardesanes, de filosoof der Arameeërs en zijn images* (Cahiers bij Nederlands Theologisch Tijdschrift 6). Wageningen 1969

– "The Book of the Laws of Countries and the Peshitta Text of Genesis IX, 6." *Parole de l'Orient* 1 (1970) 409–14

Janson, A.G.P., *De Abrahamcyclus in de Genesiscommentaar van Efrem de Syriër* (Leiden Ph.D. diss.). Zoetermeer 1998

Jastrow, M., *A Dictionary of the Targumim, the Talmud Babli and Yerushalmi, and the Midrashic Literature*. Brooklyn (N.Y.) 1950

Jaubert, A., *La date de la Cène: calendrier biblique et liturgie chrétienne*, Paris 1957

– "Jesus et le Calendrier de Qumran," *New Testament Studies* 7 (1960-1961) 1-30

Jefford, C.N., *The Sayings of Jesus in the Teaching of the Twelve Apostles* (Supplements to Vigiliae Christianae 11). Leiden 1989

– "Ignatius of Antioch and the Rhetoric of Christian Freedom." In *Christian Freedom. Essays by the Faculty of the Saint Meinrad School of Theology*, edited by C.N. Jefford (American University Studies 7: Theology and Religion 144). New York 1993, 25-39

– (ed.), *The Didache in Context. Essays on Its Text, History and Transmission* (Supplements to Novum Testamentum 77). Leiden-New York-Köln 1995

– "Did Ignatius of Antioch Know the *Didache?*" In Id. (ed.), *The Didache in Context*, 330-51

– "Reflections on the Role of Jewish Christianity in Second-Century Antioch." In *Le Judéo-christianisme dans tous ses états*, edited by S.C. Mimouni, 147-67

Jeremias, J., *Die Abendmahlsworte Jesu*. 4th ed. Göttingen 1967; ET (from the 2nd ed): *The Eucharistic Words of Jesus*. Oxford 1955

– *Die Sprache des Lukasevangeliums: Redaktion und Tradition im Nicht-Markusstoff des dritten Evangeliums* (Kritisch-exegetischer Kommentar über das Neue Testament; Sonderband). Göttingen 1980

Joannou, P.P., *Discipline générale antique (IIe-IXe siècles) 2: Les canons des Pères grecs (IV-IXe s.)* (Fonti 9). Rome 1963, 71-76

Johnson, L.T., *The Writings of the New Testament*. Philadelphia 1986

Johnson, M.E. *The Rites of Christian Initiation: Their Evolution and Interpretation*. Collegeville 1999

Johnson, Sh.E., "A Subsidiary Motive for the Writing of the Didache." In *Munera Studiosa: Studies Presented to W.H.P. Hatch on the Occasion of His Seventieth Birthday*, edited by M.H. Shepherd and Sh. Johnson. Cambridge (Mass.) 1946, 107-22

Jones, F.S., "The Pseudo-Clementines: A History of Research, Part I." *Second Century* 1 (1982) 1-33

Jonge, H.J. de, "The Early History of the Lord's Supper." In *Religious Identity and the Invention of Tradition*, edited by J.W. van Henten and A. Houtepen (Studies in Theology and Religion 3). Assen 2001, 209-37

Jonge, M. de, "The Two Great Commandments in the Testaments of the Twelve Patriarchs." *Novum Testamentum* 44 (2002) 371-92

Joosten, J., "The Old Testament Quotations in the Old Syriac and Peshitta Gospels: A Contribution to the Study of the Diatessaron." *Textus* 15 (1990) 55–76

Kähler, Ch., "Zur Form- und Traditionsgeschichte von Matth. XVI. 17-19." *New Testament Studies* 23 (1977) 36-46

Kamesar, A., *Jerome, Greek Scholarship, and the Hebrew Bible: A Study of the Quaestiones hebraicae in Genesim* (Oxford Classical Monographs). Oxford 1993

Kee, H. C. "Defining the First-Century C. E. Synagogue: Problems and Progress." In *Evolution of the Synagogue: Problems and Progress*, edited by H. C. Kee and L. H. Cohick. Harrisburg (Pa.) 1999, 7-26

Kelber, W.H., *The Oral and the Written Gospel: the hermeneutics of speaking and writing in the synoptic tradition, Mark, Paul, and Q*. Philadelphia 1983

Kertelge, K., "Der sogennante Taufbefehl Jesu (Mt 28,19)." *Zeichen der Glaubens. Studien zu Taufe und Firmung* (FS Balthazar). Freiburg im Breisgau 1972, 29-40

Khan, G., "Some Remarks on Linguistic and Lexical Change in the North Eastern Neo-Aramaic Dialects." *Aramaic Studies* 1 (2003) 179–90

Kimelman, R., "Identifying Jews and Christians in Roman Syria-Palestine." In *Galilee through the Centuries: Confluence of Cultures*, edited by E. M. Meyers. Winona Lake (Ind.) 1999, 301-33

Kirk, A., *The Composition of the Sayings Source: Genre, Synchrony, and Wisdom Redaction in Q* (Supplements to Novum Testamentum 91). Leiden 1998

Klawans, J., *Impurity and Sin in Ancient Judaism*. New York 2000

– "The Impurity of Immorality in Ancient Judaism." *Journal of Jewish Studies* 48 (1997) 1-16

Klein, G., *Der Älteste Christliche Katechismus und die Jüdische Propaganda-Literatur*, Berlin 1909

Klijn, A.F.J., and G.J. Reinink, *Patristic Evidence for Jewish-Christian Sects* (Supplements to Novum Testamentum 36). Leiden 1973

Klinghardt, M., *Gemeinschaftsmahl und Mahlgemeinschaft: Soziologie und Liturgie frühchristlicher Mahlfeiern* (Texte und Arbeiten zum neutestamentlichen Zeitalter 13). Tübingen 1996

Kloppenborg, J.S., "Didache 16,6–8 and Special Matthaean Tradition." *Zeitschrift für die neutestamentliche Wissenschaft* 70 (1979) 54-67

– *Excavating Q: The History and Setting of the Sayings Gospel*. Minneapolis 2000

– *The Formation of Q: Trajectories in Ancient Wisdom Collections* (Studies in Antiquity and Christianity). Philadelphia 1987

– "The Sayings of Jesus in the Didache: A Redaction-Critical Approach." M.A. thesis, University of St. Michael's College 1976

– "The Transformation of Moral Exhortation in Didache 1–5." In *The Didache in Context*, edited by C.N. Jefford, 88–109

– "The Sayings Gospel Q: Literary and Stratigraphic Problems." In *Symbols and Strata: Essays on the Sayings Gospel Q*, edited by R. Uro (Suomen Eksegeettisen Seuran julkaisuja 65). Helsinki-Göttingen 1996, 1-66

Klugkist, A.C., *Midden-Aramese Schriften in Syrië, Mesopotamië, Perzië en Aangrenzende Gebieden* (Ph.D. diss.). Groningen 1982

Knibb, M., *The Qumran Community* (Cambridge Commentaries on Writings of the Jewish and Christian World 200 BC to AD 200). Cambridge-London-New York 1987

Knopf, R., *Die Lehre der zwölf Apostel; Die zwei Clemensbriefe* (Handbuch zum Neuen Testament, Ergänzungsband 1). Tübingen 1920

Köhler, W.-D., *Die Rezeption des Matthäusevangeliums in der Zeit vor Irenäus* (Wissenschaftliche Untersuchungen zum Neuen Testament 24). Tübingen 1987

Koehler, L., and W. Baumgartner, *Lexicon in Veteris Testamenti libros*, and *Supplementum*. Leiden 1958

Koester, H., *Synoptische Überlieferung bei den apostolischen Vätern* (Texte und Untersuchungen 65). Berlin 1957

– "The Text of the Synoptic Gospels in the Second Century." In *Gospel Traditions in the Second Century: Origins, Recensions, Text, and Transmission*, edited by William L. Petersen (Christianity and Judaism in Antiquity 3). Notre Dame-London 1989, 19–37

– *Introduction to the New Testament* 2. Philadelphia-Berlin 1982

– *Ancient Christian Gospels: Their History and Development.* Harrisburg (Pa.) 1990

Kooij, A. van der, *Die alten Textzeugen des Jesajabuches: ein Beitrag zur Textgeschichte des Alten Testaments* (Orbis biblicus et orientalis 35). Freiburg-Göttingen 1981

– "Peshitta Genesis 6: 'Sons of God'—Angels or Judges." *Journal of Northwest Semitic Languages* 23 (1997) 43–51

Kosmala, H., "The Conclusion of Matthew." *Annual of the Swedish Theological Institute* 4 (1965) 132–47

Kraeling, C.H., "The Jewish Community in Antioch." *Journal of Biblical Literature* 51 (1932) 130–60

Kraeling, C.H., and C.B. Welles, *The Christian Building.* In A.R. Bellinger (ed.), *The Excavations at Dura-Europos Conducted by Yale University and the French Academy of Inscriptions and Letters: Final Report* 8.2. New Haven 1967

Kraft, R.A., "Setting the Stage and Framing some Central Questions." *Journal for the Study of Judaism* 32 (2001) 371-96

Kümmel, W.G., *Einleitung in das Neue Testament.* 20th ed. Heidelberg 1980

Kugel, J.L., "On Hidden Hatred and Open Reproach: Early Exegesis of Leviticus 19:17." *Harvard Theological Review* 80 (1987) 43-61

Kuhn, K.G., " ʾΙσραήλ, ʾΙουδαῖος, ʾΕβραῖος in Jewish Literature after the OT." In *Theological Dictionary of the New Testament* 3, 359-69

Lambrecht, J., "The Parousia Discourse. Composition and Content in Mt. xxiv-xxv." In *L'Évangile selon Matthieu. Rédaction et théologie,* edited by M. Didier (Bibliotheca ephemeridum theologicarum lovaniensium 29). Gembloux 1972, 309-42

– "'Du bist Petrus'. Mt 16:16-19 und das Papsttum." *Studien zum Neuen Testament und seiner Umwelt* 11 (1986) 5-32

Lampe, G.W.H., *A Patristic Greek Lexicon.* Oxford 1978

Langer, R., "The 'Amidah as Formative Rabbinic Prayer." In *Identität durch Gebet: Zur gemeinschaftsbildenden Funktion institutionalisierten Betens in Judentum und Christentum,* edited by A. Gerhards, A. Doeker, P. Ebenbauer. Paderborn 2003, 127-56

Layton, B., "The Sources, Date and Transmission of Didache 1.3b–2.1." *Harvard Theological Review* 61 (1968) 343-83

Leaney, A.R.C., *The Rule of Qumran and Its Meaning: Introduction, Translation and Commentary* (The New Testament Library). London 1966

Levine, B., "Damascus Document IX, 17-22: A New Translation and Comments." *Revue de Qumran* 8 (1972-75) 195-96

Licht, J., *The Rule Scroll: A Scroll from the Wilderness of Judaea: 1QS - 1QSa - 1QSb.* Jerusalem 1965 (Hebr.)

Liddell, H.G., and R. Scott and H.S. Jones, *A Greek-English Lexicon: with a Supplement.* 9th ed. Oxford 1968

Lieberman, S., "The Discipline in the so-called Dead Sea Manual of Discipline." *Journal of Biblical Literature* 71 (1952) 199-206

– *Greek in Jewish Palestine: Studies in the Life and Manners of Jewish Palestine in the II-IV Centuries C.E..* New York 1965

– *Hellenism in Jewish Palestine: Studies in the Literary Transmission, Beliefs and Manners of Palestine in the I Century B.C.E. - IV Century C.E.* (Texts and Studies of the Jewish Theological Seminary of America 18). 2nd ed. New York 1962

Lietaert Peerbolte, L.J., *The Antecedents of Antichrist. A Traditio-Historical Study of the Earliest Christian Views on Eschatological Opponents* (Supplements to the journal for the study of Judaism 49). Leiden 1996

Lietzmann, H., *Messe und Herrenmahl. Eine Studie zur Geschichte der Liturgie* (Arbeiten zur Kirchengeschichte 8) Berlin 1926; ET: *Mass and Lord's Supper. A Study in the History of the Liturgy,* with Introduction and Further Inquiry by R.D. Richardson. Leiden 1979

Lindemann, A., "Die Endzeitrede in Didache 16 und die Jesu-Apokalypse in Matthäus 24-25." In *Sayings of Jesus. Canonical and Non-Canonical. Essays in Honour of Tjitze Baarda,* edited by W.L. Petersen *et al.* (Supplements to Novum Testamentum 89). Leiden 1997, 155-74

– *Der erste Korintherbrief* (Handbuch zum Neuen Testament 9/1). Tübingen 2000

Linder, A., *The Jews in Roman Imperial Legislation*. Detroit-Jerusalem 1987

Lieu, J., *Image and Reality: The Jews in the World of the Christians in the Second Century*. Edinburgh 1996

Llewelyn, S.R., *New Documents Illustrating Early Christianity* 9: *A Review of Inscriptions and Papyri Published in 1986–87*. Grand Rapids (Mich.) 2002

Löfstedt, T., "A Message for the Last Days: Didache 16.1-8 and the New Testament Traditions." *Estudios Biblicos* 60 (2002) 351-80

Lohmann, H., *Drohung und Verheissung. Exegetische Untersuchungen zur Eschatologie bei den Apostolischen Vätern* (Beihefte zur Zeitschrift für die Neutestamentliche Wissenschaft 55). Berlin 1989

Lohmeyer, E.. "Mir ist gegeben alle Gewalt!" In *In Memoriam Ernst Lohmeyer*, edited by W. Schmauch. Stuttgart 1951, 22-49

Lührmann, D., *Fragmente apokryph gewordener Evangelien in griechischer und lateinischer Sprache* (Marburger Theologische Studien 59). Marburg 2000

Luomanen, P., *Entering the Kingdom of Heaven. A Study on the Structure of Matthew's View of Salvation* (Wissenschaftliche Untersuchungen zum Neuen Testament 2/101). Tübingen 1998

Lust, J., and E. Eynikel and K. Hauspie, *A Greek-English Lexicon of the Septuagint* 1, Stuttgart 1992

Luz, U., *Das Evangelium nach Matthäus* 1-3 (Evangelisch-katholischer Kommentar zum Neuen Testament 1/1-3) Zürich 1985-1997; ET: *Matthew* 3 vols. Minneapolis 1989-2005

– "Der Antijudaismus im Matthäusevangelium als historisches und theologisches Problem. Eine Skizze," *Evangelische Theologie* 53 (1993) 310-27

– *The Theology of the Gospel of Matthew*. Cambridge 1995

– "Das Matthäusevangelium und die Perspektive einer biblischen Theologie." In *‚Gesetz‘ als Thema biblischer Theologie*, edited by D.R. Daniels (Jahrbuch für Biblische Theologie 4). Neukirchen-Vluyn 1989, 233-48

Malina, B. J., "Patron and Client: The Analogy behind Synoptic Theology." *Forum* 4.1 (1988) 2-32

– *The New Testament World: Insights from Cultural Anthropology*. 2nd ed. Louisville 1993

Malcolm X, *Autobiography of Malcolm X*. New York 1965

Markschies, C., "Wer schrieb die sogenannte *Traditio Apostolica?*" In W. Kinzig, C. Markschies, M.Vinzent, *Tauffragen und Bekenntnis* (Arbeiten zur Kirchengeschichte 74). Berlin 1999, 1-74

– "Neue Forschungen zur sogenannten 'Traditio apostolica.'" In *Acts of the International Congress 'Comparative Liturgy' Fifty Years after Anton Baumstark (1872-1948)*, edited by R.Taft and G. Winkler (Orientalia Christiana Analecta 265). Rome 2001, 583-98

Massaux, É., *Influence de l'Évangile de saint Matthieu sur la littérature chrétienne avant saint Irénée*. Leuven 1950; repr. by F. Neirynck, suppl. Bibliogr. 1950-1985 by B. Dehandschutter (Bibliotheca ephemeridum theologicarum lovaniensium 75). Leuven 1986. ET: *The Influence of the Gospel of Saint Matthew on Christian Literature before Saint Irenaeus* 1-3. Macon (Ga.) 1993

Mazza, E., "L'eucaristia di «1 Cor 10, 16-17» in rapporto a «Didachè 9-10»." In Id., *L'anafora eucaristica: Studi sulle origini* (B.E.L. Subsidia 62). Roma 1992, 77-109

– "Didache IX-X: Elementi per una interpretazione eucaristica." *Ephemerides Liturgicae* 92 (1979) 393-419; ET: "Didache 9-10: Elements of a Eucharistic Interpretation." In *The Didache in Modern Research*, edited by J.A. Draper, 276-99

McGowan, A., *Ascetic Eucharists: Food and Drink in Early Christian Ritual Meals*, Oxford 1999

– "Is there a Liturgical Text in this Gospel? The Institution Narratives and their Early Interpretive Communities." *Journal of Biblical Literature* 118 (1999) 73-87

Mees, M., "Die Bedeutung der Sentenzen und ihrer auxesis für die Formung der Jesuworte nach Didaché 1,3b-2,1." *Vetera Christianorum* 8 (1971) 55–76

Meier, J.P., *Matthew*. Wilmington 1980

– "Nations or Gentiles in Matthew." *Catholic Biblical Quarterly* 39 (1977) 94-102

Messner, R., "Zur Eucharistie in den Thomasakten, Zugleich ein Beitrag zur Frühgeschichte der eucharistischen Epiklese." In *Crossroads of Cultures: Studies in Liturgy and Patristics in Honor of Gabriele Winkler*, edited by H.-J. Feulner, E. Velkovska, R. Taft (Orientalia Christiana Analecta 260). Rome 2000, 493-513

Metso, S., *The Textual Development of the Qumran Community Rule* (Studies on the Texts of the Desert of Judah 21). Leiden-New York-Köln 1997

Metzger, B.M., *A Textual Commentary on the Greek New Testament* (United Bible Societies). 3rd ed. Stuttgart 1975

Metzger, B.M., and M.D. Coogan (eds.), *The Oxford Companion to the Bible*. New York 1993

Metzger, M., "Enquêtes autour de la prétendue *Tradition apostolique*." In *Ecclesia orans* 5 (1992) 7-36

– (ed.), *Les constitutions apostoliques* 1-3 (Sources Chrétiennes 320, 329, 336). Paris 1985-87

Michel, O., "Κύων, κυνάριον." In *Theological Dictionary of the New Testament* 3, 1101-04

Migne, J.P. (ed.), *Patrologia cursus completus, Series graeca* (= *PG*). Paris 1857ff

Milavec, A., *The Didache: Faith, Hope, and Life of the Earliest Christian Communities*. New York 2003

– "The Social Setting of 'Turning the Other Cheek' and 'Loving One's Enemies' in Light of the Didache." *Biblical Theology Bulletin* 25 (1995) 131-43

– "Synoptic Tradition in the Didache Revisited." *Journal of Early Christian Studies* 10 (2003) 443-80

– *To Empower as Jesus Did: Acquiring Spiritual Power Through Apprenticeship*. Lewiston 1982

– "The Saving Efficacy of the Burning Process in Didache 16.5." In *The Didache in Context*, edited by C.N. Jefford, 131-55

– "Distinguishing True and False prophets. The Protective Wisdom of the Didache." *Journal of Early Christian Studies* 2 (1994) 117-36

Millar, F., *The Roman Near East: 31 BC–AD 337*. Cambridge (MA) 1993

– "The Problem of Hellenistic Syria." In *Hellenism in the East: The Interaction of Greek and Non-Greek Civilizations from Syria to Central Asia after Alexander*, edited by A. Kuhrt and S. Sherwin-White. Berkeley 1987, 110–33

Mimouni, S.C., *Le Judéo-christianisme dans tous ses états. Actes du colloque de Jérusalem 6-10 juillet 1998* (Lectio divina, hors série). Paris 2001

Mitchell, M.M., "Concerning *PERI DE* in 1 Corinthians." *Novum Testamentum* 31 (1989) 229-56

Mitchell, N., "Baptism in the Didache." In *The Didache in Context*, edited by C.N. Jefford, 226-55

Moreland, M.C., and J.M. Robinson. "The International Q Project Work Sessions 6–8 August, 18–19 November 1993." *Journal of Biblical Literature* 113 (1994) 495–99

Muilenburg, J., *The Literary Relations of the Epistle of Barnabas and the Teaching of the Twelve Apostles*. Marburg 1929

Mulder, M.J. (ed.), *Mikra: Text, Translation, Reading and Interpretation of the Hebrew Bible in Ancient Judaism and Early Christianity* (Compendia rerum iudaicarum ad Novum Testamentum 2/1). Assen- Philadelphia 1988

Murphy O'Connor, J., "La genèse littéraire de la Règle de la Communauté." *Revue Biblique* 76 (1969) 528-49

Murray, R., "The Characteristics of the Earliest Syriac Christianity." In *East of Byzantium*, edited by N.G. Garsoïan *et al.*, 3–16

Mussies, G., "Greek in Palestine and the Diaspora." In *The Jewish People in the First Century: Historical Geography, Political History, Social, Cultural and Religious Life and Institutions* 2, edited by S. Safrai and M. Stern (Compendia rerum iudaicarum ad Novum Testamentum 1/2). Assen 1976, 1040–64

Nautin, P., "Notes critiques sur la Didachê." *Vigiliae Christianae* 13 (1959) 118-20

Naveh, J., *Early History of the Alphabet: An Introduction to West Semitic Epigraphy and Palaeography*. 2nd rev. ed. Jerusalem 1987

Neufeld, E., "Self-Help in Ancient Hebrew Law." *Revue internationale des droits de l'antiquité* 3/5 (1958) 291–98

Neusner, J., *Why No Gospels in Talmudic Judaism?* (Brown Judaic studies 135). Atlanta (Ga.) 1988

— *The Idea of Purity in Ancient Judaism: The Haskell Lectures 1972-1973* (Studies in Judaism in Late Antiquity 1). Leiden 1973

— *A History of the Jews in Babylonia* 1 (Studia post-biblica 9). Leiden 1965

— *Aphrahat and Judaism: The Christian-Jewish Argument in Fourth-Century Iran* (Studia post-biblica 19). Leiden 1971

Neymeyr, U., *Die Christlichen Lehrer im zweiten Jahrhundert: Ihre Lehrtätigkeit, ihr Selbstverständnis und ihre Geschichte* (Supplements to Vigiliae Christianae 4). Leiden-New York-København 1989

Nicklas, T., and M. Tilly (eds.), *The Book of Acts as Church History: Text, Textual Traditions and Ancient Interpretations /Apostelgeschichte als Kirchengeschichte: Text, Texttraditionen und antike Auslegungen* (Beihefte zur Zeitschrift für die Neutestamentliche Wissenschaft 120). Berlin 2003

Niederwimmer, K., *Die Didache* (Kommentar zu den Apostolischen Vätern 1). 2nd ed. Göttingen 1993 (1989). ET: *The Didache* (Hermeneia). Minneapolis 1998

— "Zur Entwicklungsgeschichte des Wanderradikalismus im Traditionsbereich des Didache." *Wiener Studien* N.F. 11 (1977) 145-67

— „Der Didachist und seine Quellen." In *The Didache in Context*, edited by C.N. Jefford, 15-36

Nitzan, B., "The Laws of Reproof in 4QBerakhot (4Q286-290) in Light of their Parallels in the Damascus Covenant and other Texts from Qumran." In *Legal Texts and Legal Issues: Proceedings of the Second Meeting of the International Organization for Qumran Studies Cambridge 1995*, edited by M. Bernstein, F. García Martínez, and J. Kampen (Studies on the Texts of the Desert of Judah 23). Leiden-New York-Köln 1997, 149-65

— "4QBerakhot^{a -e} (4Q286-290): A Covenantal Ceremony in the Light of Related Texts." *Revue de Qumran* 16 (1995) 487-506

— "The Dead Sea Scrolls and the Jewish Liturgy." In *The Dead Sea Scrolls as Background to Postbiblical Judaism and Early Christianity: Papers from an International Conference at St. Andrews in 2001*, edited by J.R. Davila (Studies on the Texts of the Desert of Judah 46). Leiden 2003, 195–219

Nocent, A., "Christian Initiation During the First Four Centuries." In *Sacraments and Sacramentals*, edited by A. Chupungco (Handbook for Liturgical Studies 4). Collegeville 2000, 5-28

Nöldeke, Th., " Ἀσσύριος Σύριος Σύρος." *Hermes* 5 (1871), 443-68

Novak, D., *The Image of the Non-Jew in Judaism: An Historical and Constructive Study of the Noahide Laws* (Toronto Studies in Theology 14). New York-Toronto 1983

O'Hagan, A.P., *Material Re-creation in the Apostolic Fathers* (Texte und Untersuchungen 100). Berlin 1968

Ong, W., *The Presence of the Word: Some Prolegomena for Cultural and Religious History*. New Haven 1967

Overman, J. A., *Matthew's Gospel and Formative Judaism: The Social World of the Matthean Community*. Minneapolis 1990

Pardee, N., "The Curse That Saves (Didache 16.5)." In *The Didache in Context*, edited by C.N. Jefford, 156-76

Perrin, N., *Thomas and Tatian: The Relationship between the Gospel of Thomas and the Diatessaron* (Society of Biblical Literature Academia Biblica 5). Atlanta 2002

Pesch, R., *Das Abendmahl und Jesu Todesverständnis* (Quaestiones disputatae 80). Freiburg 1978

Pesch, W., "Die sogenannte Gemeindeordnung Mt 18." *Biblische Zeitschrift* NF 7 (1963) 220-35

Petersen, W.L., *Tatian's Diatessaron: Its Creation, Dissemination, Significance, and History in Scholarship* (Supplements to Vigiliae Christianae 25). Leiden 1994
- "The Christology of Aphrahat, the Persian Sage: An Excursus on the 17th Demonstration." *Vigiliae christianae* 46 (1992) 241–56
- "Constructing the Matrix of Judaic Christianity from Texts." In *Le Judéo-Christianisme dans tous ses états*, edited by S. Mimouni, 126–44
Pognon, H., *Inscriptions sémitiques de la Syrie, de la Mésopotamie et de la région de Mossoul*. Paris 1907
Polanyi, M., *The Tacit Dimension* (The Terry lectures at Yale University). Garden City 1966
- *Personal Knowledge: Towards a Post-critical Philosophy*. Chicago 1958
Prostmeier, F.R., *Der Barnabasbrief* (Kommentar zu den Apostolischen Vätern 8). Göttingen 1999
Ranger, T., "The Invention of Tradition in Colonial Africa." In *The Invention of Tradition*, edited by T. Ranger and E. Hobsbawm. Cambridge 1983, 211-62
Reed, J.D., *Bion of Smyrna. The Fragments and the 'Adonis'* (Cambridge Classical Texts and Commentaries 33). Cambridge 1997
Reed, S.A., "Genre, Setting and Title of 4Q477." *Journal of Jewish Studies* 47 (1996) 147-48
Rehm, B., J. Irmscher and F. Paschke, *Die Pseudoklementinen* 1: *Homilien* (Griechischen christlichen Schriftsteller 42). Berlin-Leipzig 1969
Reid, J.S., "Charity, Almsgiving (Roman)", *Encyclopedia of Religion and Ethics* 3, edited by J. Hastings. Edinburgh 1922, 391-92
Reif, S.C., *Judaism and Hebrew Prayer: New Perspectives on Jewish Liturgical History*. Cambridge 1993
- "The Early History of Jewish Worship." In *The Making of Jewish and Christian Worship*, edited by P. F. Bradshaw and L. A. Hoffman. Notre Dame 1991, 109-36.
Rengstorf, K.H., "σημεῖον" In *Theologisches Wörterbuch zum Neuen Testament* 7, 199-268
- "διδάσκω, διδάσκαλος, νομοδιδάσκαλος, κτλ." In *Theologisches Wörterbuch zum Neuen Testament* 2, 138-68 (= *Theological Dictionary of the New Testament* 2, 135-65)
Restle, M., "Les monuments chrétiens de la Syrie du Sud." In *La Syrie de l'époque achéménide à l'avènement de l'Islam*, edited by J.-M. Dentzer and W. Orthmann (Archéologie et histoire de la Syrie; Schriften zur vorderasiatischen Archäologie 1/2). Saarbrücken 1989, 373–84
Richardson, C.C., "The Teaching of the Twelve Apostles, commonly called the Didache." In *The Early Christian Fathers* (Library of Christian Classics 1). Philadelphia 1953, 161-79
Riggenbach, E., *Der trinitarische Taufbefehl Matth. 28,19 nach seiner ursprünglichen Textgestalt und seiner Authentie untersucht* (Beiträge zur Förderung christlicher Theologie 7). Gütersloh 1903
Robinson, B.P., "Peter and His Successors. Tradition and Redaction in Matthew 16:17-19." *Journal for the Study of the New Testament* 21 (1984) 85-104
Robinson, J. A., *Barnabas, Hermas and the Didache: Being the Donnellan Lectures Delivered before the University of Dublin in 1920*. London 1920
Robinson, J.M., P. Hoffmann, and J.S. Kloppenborg (eds.), *The Critical Edition of Q: A Synopsis, Including the Gospels of Matthew and Luke, Mark and Thomas, with English, German and French Translations of Q and Thomas*. Gen. ed. Milton C. Moreland (Hermeneia Supplements). Leuven-Minneapolis 2000
- (eds.), *Die Logienquelle Q. Der griechische Text in der Rekonstruktion des Internationalen Q-Projekts mit deutscher Übersetzung*, edited by Ch. Heil. Darmstadt 2002
- (eds.), *The Sayings Gospel Q in Greek and English with Parallels from the Gospels of Mark and Thomas* (Contributions to Biblical Exegesis and Theology 30). Leuven 2002
Robinson, J.M., P. Hoffmann, J.S. Kloppenborg, and M.C. Moreland (eds.), *El Documento Q en griego y en español con paralelos del evangelio de Marcos y del evangelio de Tomás*, edited by Santiago Guijarro (Biblioteca de Estudios Bíblicos 107). Salamanca-Leuven 2002

Rordorf, W., "Does the Didache Contain Jesus Tradition Independently of the Synoptic Gospels?" In *Jesus and the Oral Gospel Tradition*, edited by H. Wansbrough (Journal for the Study of the Old Testament, Supplement Series 64). Sheffield 1991, 394-423
- "Le problème de la transmission textuelle de Didache 1,3b-2,1." In *Überlieferungsgeschichtliche Untersuchungen*, edited by F. Paschke (Texte und Untersuchungen 125). Berlin 1981, 499–513
- "Baptism according to the Didache." In *The Didache in Modern Research*, edited by J.A. Draper, 212-22
- "Die Mahlgebete in der Didache Kap. 9-10. Ein neuer *status quaestionis*." *Vigiliae Christianae* 51 (1997) 229-46
Rordorf, W., and A. Tuilier, *La Doctrine des douze Apôtres (Didachè)* (Sources Chrétiennes 248). Paris 1978; 2ⁿᵈ ed. (Sources Chrétiennes 248 bis). Paris 1998
Ross, S.K., *Roman Edessa: Politics and Culture on the Eastern Fringes of the Roman Empire, 114–242 CE.* London 2001
Rouwhorst, G. "La célébration de l'Eucharistie dans l'Eglise primitive." *Questions liturgiques* 74 (1993) 89-112
- "La célébration de l'Eucharistie selon les Actes de Thomas." In *Omnes circumadstantes: Contributions towards a History of the Role of the People in the Liturgy* edited by C. Caspers and M.Schneiders (FS Herman Wegman). Kampen 1990, 51-77
- "Identität durch Gebet. Gebetstexte als Zeugen eines jahrhundertelangen Ringens um Kontinuität und Differenz zwischen Judentum und Christentum." In *Identität durch Gebet*, edited by A. Gerhards, A. Doeker, P. Ebenbauer, 37-55
- "The Quartodeciman Passover and the Jewish Pesach," *Questions liturgiques* 77 (1996) 152-173
Sabatier, P., ΔΙΔΑΧΗ ΤΩΝ ΙΒ' ΑΠΟΣΤΟΛΩΝ: *La Didachè ou l'enseignement des douze apôtres.* Thèse présentée à la faculté de Théologie protestante de Paris. Paris 1885
Safrai, S., "Gathering in the Synagogues on Festivals, Sabbaths and Weekdays." In *Biblical Archaeology Review: International Series* 499 (1989) 7-15
- "Halakha." In Id. (ed.), *The Literature of the Sages. First Part: Oral Tora, Halakha, Mishna, Tosefta, Talmud, External Tractates* (Compendia rerum iudaicarum ad Novum Testamentum 2/3a). Assen – Philadelphia 1987, 121-209
- "Religion in Everyday Life." In *The Jewish People in the First Century. Historical Geography, Political History, Social, Cultural and Religious Life and Institutions*, edited by S. Safrai and S. Stern (Compendia rerum iudaicarum ad Novum Testamentum 1/2) Assen-Philadelphia 1976, 793-833
- "The Decision according to the School of Hillel in Yavneh." In *Proceedings of the Seventh World Congress of Jewish Studies: Studies in Talmud, Halacha and Midrash.* Jerusalem 1981, 21-44; repr. in Id. *In Times of Temple and Mishnah: Studies in Jewish History* 2. Jerusalem 1996, 382-405 (Hebr.)
Said, E., *Orientalism.* London 1978
- *Culture and Imperialism.* New York 1993
Sainte Croix, G.E.M. de, *The Class Struggle in the Ancient Greek World from the Archaic Age to the Arab Conquests.* Ithaca 1981
Saldarini, A. J., "The Gospel of Matthew and Jewish Christian Conflict." In *Social History of the Matthean Community: Cross-Disciplinary Approaches,* edited by D. L. Balch. Minneapolis 1991, 38-61
- "The Gospel of Matthew and Jewish Christian Conflict in Galilee." In *The Galilee in Late Antiquity*, edited by L.I. Levine. Cambridge (Mass.) 1992, 23-38
- *Matthew's Christian-Jewish Community* (Chicago Studies in Judaism). Chicago 1994
Sand, A., *Das Evangelium nach Matthäus* (Regensburger Neues Testament). Regensburg 1986
Sanders, E.P., *Jesus and Judaism.* 3ʳᵈ pr. London 1991
Sanders, J. T., *Schismatics, Sectarians, Dissidents, Deviants: The First One Hundred Years of Jewish-Christian Relations.* Valley Forge (Pa.) 1993

Sandt, H. van de, "'Do not Give What is Holy to the Dogs' (Did 9:5d and Matt 7:6a): the Eucharistic Food of the Didache in its Jewish Purity Setting." *Vigiliae Christianae* 56 (2002) 223-46

– "The Gathering of the Church in the Kingdom: The Self-Understanding of the *Didache* Community in the Eucharistic Prayers." In *Society of Biblical Literature 2003 Seminar Papers*, Atlanta (Ga) 2003, 69-88

– "Didache 3:1–6: A Transformation of an Existing Jewish Hortatory Pattern." *Journal for the Study of Judaism* 23 (1992) 21–41

Sandt, H. van de, and D. Flusser, *The Didache: Its Jewish Sources and its Place in Early Judaism and Christianity* (Compendia rerum iudaicarum ad Novum Testamentum 3/5). Assen-Minneapolis 2002

Sardar, Z., *Orientalism*. Buckingham 1999

Sartre-Fauriat, A., "Culture et société dans le Hauran (Syrie du Sud) d'après les épigrammes funéraires (IIIe–Ve siècles ap. J.-C.)." *Syria* 75 (1998) 213–24

Sato, M., *Q und Prophetie: Studien zur Gattungs- und Traditionsgeschichte der Quelle Q* (Wissenschaftliche Untersuchungen zum Neuen Testament 2/29). Tübingen 1988

Schaff, Ph., *The Oldest Church Manual Called the Teaching of the Twelve Apostles*. Edinburgh 1885

Schenk-Ziegler, A., *Correctio fraterna im Neuen Testament: Die "brüderliche Zurechtweisung" in biblischen, frühjüdischen und hellenistischen Schriften* (Forschung zur Bibel 84). Würzburg 1997

Schermann, Th., *Die allgemeine Kirchenordnung, frühchristliche Liturgien und kirchliche Überlieferung* 1: *Die allgemeine Kirchenordnung des zweiten Jahrhunderts* (Studien zur Geschichte und Kultur des Altertums. Ergänzungsband 3/1). Paderborn 1914

– *Eine Elfapostelmoral oder die X-Rezension der "Beiden Wege"* (Veröffentlichungen aus dem kirchenshistorischen Seminar 2/2). München 1903

Scheuermann, G., *Gemeinde im Umbruch. Eine sozialgeschichtliche Studie zum Matthäusevangelium* (Forschung zur Bibel 77). Würzburg 1996

Schiffman, L.H., "Reproof as a Requisite for Punishment." In Id., *Sectarian Law in the Dead Sea Scrolls: Courts, Testimony and the Penal Code* (Brown Judaic Studies 33). Chico (Calif.) 1983, 89-109

– "Reproof as a Requisite for Punishment in the Law of the Dead Sea Scrolls." In *Jewish Law Association Studies 2: The Jerusalem Conference Volume*, edited by B.S. Jackson (The Jewish Law Association. Papers and Proceedings). Atlanta (Ga) 1986, 59-74

– "The Qumran Law of Testimony." *Revue de Qumran* 8 (1972-75) 603-12 and *Revue de Qumran* 9 (1977) 261-62

– *The Halakhah at Qumran* (Studies in Judaism in Late Antiquity 16). Leiden 1975

Schoedel, W.R., *Ignatius of Antioch. A Commentary on the Letters of Ignatius of Antioch* (Hermeneia). Philadelphia 1985

Schöllgen, G., "Die Didache als Kirchenordnung: Zur Frage des Abfassungszweckes und seinen Konsequenzen für die Interpretation." *Jahrbuch für Antike und Christentum* 29 (1986) 5-26. ET: "The Didache as a Church Order: An Examination of the Purpose for the Composition of the Didache and its Consequences for its Interpretation." In *The Didache in Modern Research*, edited by J.A. Draper, 43-71

– "Die Didache - ein frühes Zeugnis für Landgemeinden?" *Zeitschrift für die neutestamentliche Wissenschaft* 76 (1985) 140-43

– "Wandernde oder sesshafte Lehrer in der Didache?" *Biblische Notizen* 52 (1990) 19-26

Schöllgen, G. und W. Geerlings (eds.), *Didache. Zwölf-Apostellehre / Traditio Apostolica. Apostolische Überlieferung*. (Fontes christiani 1) Freiburg-Basel-Wien 1991

Schreckenberg, H., "The Works of Josephus and the Early Christian Church." In *Josephus, Judaism, and Christianity*, edited by L.H. Feldman and G. Hata. Leiden 1987, 315–24

Schreckenberg, H., and K. Schubert, *Jewish Historiography and Iconography in Early and Medieval Christianity* (Compendia rerum iudaicarum ad Novum Testamentum 3/2). Assen-Minneapolis 1992

Schwartz, E. (ed.), *Eusebius II: Die Kirchengeschichte*: II/1-2: *Die Bücher I-V. VI-X.* (GCS 9,1-2) Leipzig 1903-08

Schweizer, E., *Matthäus und seine Gemeinde* (Stuttgarter Bibelstudien 71). Stuttgart 1974

Schrage, W., "συναγωγή κτλ." In *Theological Dictionary of the New Testament* 7, 798-852

Schürer, E., *The History of the Jewish People in the Age of Jesus Christ (175 B.C.-A.D. 135)* 1-3/2, revised by G. Vermes, F. Millar and M. Goodman. Edinburgh 1973-1987

Scott, J. C., *Domination and the Arts of Resistance: Hidden Transcripts*. New Haven 1990

Seeliger, H.R., "Erwägungen zur Hintergrund und Zweck des apokalyptischen Schlusskapittels der Didache." In *Studia Patristica* 21: *Papers presented to the Tenth International Conference on Patristic Studies held in Oxford 1987*, edited by E.A. Livingstone. Leuven 1989, 185-92; ET: "Considerations on the Background and Purpose of the Apocalyptic Conclusion of the Didache." In *The Didache in Modern Research*, edited by J.A. Draper, 373-82

Segal, A., "Matthew's Jewish Voice." In *Social History of the Matthean Community: Cross-Disciplinary Processes*, edited by D. L. Balch. Minneapolis 1991, 3-37

Segal, J.B., *Edessa: "The Blessed City."* Oxford 1970

Senior, D., *The Passion of Jesus in Matthew*. Wilmington (Del.) 1985

Shedinger, R.F., *Tatian and the Jewish Scriptures: A Textual and Philological Analysis of the Old Testament Citations in Tatian's Diatessaron* (Corpus scriptorum christianorum orientalium 591/Subs. 109). Leuven 2001

Sim, D.C., "The Gospel of Matthew and the Gentiles." *Journal for the Study of the New Testament* 57 (1995) 19-48

– "Christianity and Ethnicity in the Gospel of Matthew." In *Ethnicity and the Bible*, edited by M. G. Brett. Leiden 1996, 171-95

– *Apocalyptic Eschatology in the Gospel of Matthew* (Society for New Testament Studies Monograph Series 88). Cambridge 1996

– *The Gospel of Matthew and Christian Judaism: The History and Social Setting of the Matthean Community* (Studies of the New Testament and Its World). Edinburgh 1998

Simon, M., *Verus Israel: étude sur les relations entre chrétiens et juifs dans l'Empire romain (135-425)*. 2nd ed. Paris 1964

Skehan, P.W., "Didache 1,6 and Sirach 12,1." *Biblica* 44 (1963) 533–36

Slee, M., *The Church in Antioch in the First Century CE. Communion and Conflict* (Journal for the Study of the New Testament, Supplement Series 244). Sheffield 2003

Slingerland, H.D., "The Transjordanian Origin of Matthew's Gospel." *Journal for the Study of the New Testament* 3 (1979) 18-28

Sodini, J.-P., "Les églises de Syrie du Nord." In *La Syrie de l'époque achéménide à l'avènement de l'Islam*, edited by J.-M. Dentzer and W. Orthmann (Archéologie et histoire de la Syrie; Schriften zur vorderasiatischen Archäologie 1/2); Saarbrücken 1989, 347–72

Spence, C., *The Teaching of the Twelve Apostles.* Διδαχὴ τῶν δώδεκα ἀποστόλων. *A Translation with Notes; And Excursus (I. to IX.) Illustrative of the "Teaching;" and the Greek text.* London 1885

Stanton, G. N., "The Origin and Purpose of Matthew's Gospel: Matthean Scholarship from 1945-1980." In *Aufstieg und Niedergang der römischen Welt*, II, 25, 3, edited by H. Temporini and W. Haase. Berlin 1985, 1889-1951

– *A Gospel for a New People: Studies in Matthew*. Edinburgh 1992; repr 1993

– *The Interpretation of Matthew*. Edinburgh 1995

– "Revisiting Matthew's Communities." *Hervormde teologiese studies* 52 (1996) 376-94

Steimer, B., *Vertex Traditionis. Die Gattung der altchristlichen Kirchenordnungen* (Beihefte zur Zeitschrift für die Neutestamentliche Wissenschaft 63). Berlin 1992

Stemberger, G., "Reaktionen auf die Tempelzerstörung in der rabbinischen Literatur." In *Zerstörungen des Jerusalemer Tempels: Geschehen – Wahrnehmung – Bewältigung*, edited by Johannes Hahn (Wissenschaftliche Untersuchungen zum Neuen Testament 147). Tübingen 2002, 207–236

Stendahl, K., *The School of St. Matthew and its Use of the Old Testament* (Acta Seminarii Neotestamentici Upsaliensis 20). 2nd ed. Lund 1968

- "Hate, Non-Retaliation and Love, 1QS X,17–20 and Romans 12:19–21." *Harvard Theological Review* 55 (1962) 343–55
Stewart-Sykes, A., *Hippolytus: On the Apostolic Tradition. An English Version with Introduction and Commentary.* New York 2001
- *The Lamb's High Feast. Melito, Peri Pascha and the Quartodeciman Paschal Liturgy at Sardis* (Supplements to Vigiliae Christianae 43). Leiden 1998
Stolper, M.W., *Management and Politics in Later Achaemenid Babylonia: New Texts from the Murašu Archives* (microfilmed Ph.D. diss.). Michigan 1974
Strack, H.L. und P. Billerbeck, *Kommentar zum neuen Testament aus Talmud und Midrasch* 1-4/2. München 1922-28
Strecker, G., *Der Weg der Gerechtigkeit: Untersuchung zur Theologie des Matthäus* (Forschungen zur Religion und Literatur des Alten und Neuen Testaments 82). 2nd ed. Göttingen 1966; 3rd ed. Göttingen 1971
- "Die Kerygmata Petrou." In *Neutestamentliche Apokryphen* 2, edited by E. Hennecke and W. Schneemelcher. 4th ed. Tübingen 1971, 63-80
Streeter, B.H., *The Four Gospels: A Study of Origins, Treating of the Manuscript Tradition, Sources, Authorship, and Dates.* London 1924; 5th ed. London 1936
Stuiber, A., "Das ganze Joch des Herrn (Didache 6:2-3)." In *Studia Patristica* 4, edited by F. L. Cross (Texte und Untersuchungen 79). Berlin 1961, 323-29
- "Die drei σημεῖα von Didache xvi." *Jahrbuch für Antike und Christentum* 24 (1981) 442-44
Suggs, M.J., "The Christian Two Ways Tradition: Its Antiquity, Form, and Function." In *Studies in New Testament and Early Christian Literature*, Essays in Honour of A.P. Wikgren, edited by D.E. Aune (Supplements to Novum Testamentum 33). Leiden 1972, 60-74
Syreeni, K., *The Making of the Sermon on the Mount: A procedural analysis of Matthew's redactoral activity* 1: *Methodology & Compositional Analysis* (Annales Academiae Scientiarum Fennicae Diss. 44). Helsinki 1987
- "Peter as Character and Symbol in the Gospel of Matthew." In *Characterization in the Gospels. Reconceiving Narrative Criticism*, edited by D. Rhoads and K. Syreeni (Journal for the Study of the New Testament-Supplement Series 184). Sheffield 1999, 106-52
- "Separation and Identity: Aspects of the Symbolic World of Matt 6:1-18." *New Testament Studies* 40 (1994) 522-41
- "James and the Pauline Legacy: Power Play in Corinth?" In *Fair Play: Diversity and Conflict in early Christianity*, Essays in Honour of Heikki Räisänen, edited by I. Dunderberg, C. Tuckett and K. Syreeni. Leiden-Boston-Köln 2002, 397-437
- "A Single Eye: Aspects of the Symbolic World of Matt 6:22-23." *Studia Theologica* 53 (1999) 97-118
Talley, T., "From Berakah to Eucharistia." *Worship* 50 (1976) 115-37
Taylor, M.S., *Anti-Judaism and Early Christian Identity: A Critique of the Scholarly Consensus* (Studia post-biblica 46). Leiden 1995
Telfer, W., "The *Didache* and the Apostolic Synod of Antioch." *Journal of Theological Studies* 40 (1939) 133-46
Theissen, G., *Sociology of Early Palestinian Christianity.* Phildelphia 1978
Thompson, W.G., *Matthew's Advice to a Divided Community: Mt. 17,22-18,35* (Analecta Biblica 44). Rome 1970
Tomson, P. J., "The Names Israel and Jew in Ancient Judaism and in the New Testament." *Bijdragen, tijdschrift voor filosofie en theologie* 47 (1986) 120-40. 266-89
- "'Jews' in the Gospel of John as Compared with the Palestinian Talmud, the Synoptics and Some New Testament Apocrypha." In *Anti-Judaism and the Fourth Gospel: Papers of the Leuven Colloquium, 2000*, edited by R. Bieringer, D. Pollefeyt and F. Vandecasteele-Vanneuville (Jewish and Christian Heritage 1). Assen 2000, 301-40
- *"If this be from Heaven...". Jesus and the New Testament Authors in their Relationship to Judaism* (The Biblical Seminar 76). Sheffield 2001

- "Les systèmes de halakha du *Contre Apion* et des *Antiquités*." In *Internationales Josephus-Kolloquium Paris 2001: Studies on the Antiquities of Josephus: Études sur les Antiquités de Josèphe*, edited by F. Siegert and J.U. Kalms (Münsteraner judaistische Studien 12). Münster 2002, 189-220
- *Paul and the Jewish Law: Halakha in the Letters of the Apostle to the Gentiles* (Compendia rerum iudaicarum ad Novum Testamentum 3/1). Assen-Minneapolis 1990
- "Paul's Jewish Background in View of His Law Teaching in 1 Cor 7." In *Paul and the Mosaic Law*, edited by J.D.G. Dunn (Wissenschaftliche Untersuchungen zum Neuen Testament 89). Tübingen 1996, 251-70
- "The wars against Rome, the rise of Rabbinic Judaism and of Apostolic Gentile Christianity, and the Judaeo-Christians: Elements for a synthesis." In *The Image of the Judaeo-Christians in Ancient Jewish and Christian Literature*, edited by P.J. Tomson and D. Lambers-Petry (Wissenschaftliche Untersuchungen zum Neuen Testament 158). Tübingen 2003, 1-31
Trevijano Etcheverria, R., "Discurso escatologico y relato apocaliptico en Didakhe 16." *Burgense* 17 (1976) 365-93
Trilling, W., *Das wahre Israel: Studien zur Theologie des Matthäus-Evangeliums* (Studien zum Alten und Neuen Testaments 10). 3rd ed. München 1964
Tsafrir, Y., "The Development of Ecclesiastical Architecture in Palestine." In Id. (ed.), *Ancient Churches Revealed*. Jerusalem 1993, 1–16
Tuckett, C.M., "Synoptic Tradition in the Didache." In *The New Testament in Early Christianity: La réception des écrits néotestamentaires dans le christianisme primitif*, edited by J.M. Sevrin (Bibliotheca ephemeridum theologicarum lovaniensium 86). Leuven 1989, 197–230; repr. in *The Didache in Modern Research*, edited by J.A. Draper, 92-128
Tuilier, A., "Didache." In *Theologische Realenzyklopädie* 8. Berlin 1981, 731-36
- «La Didachè et le problème synoptique.» In *The Didache in Context*, edited by C.N. Jefford, 110-30
Ulrichsen, J.H., *Die Grundschrift der Testamente der Zwölf Patriarchen: Eine Untersuchung zu Umfang, Inhalt und Eigenart der ursprünglichen Schrift* (Uppsala universitet, Historia Religionum 10). Uppsala 1991
Unnik, W.C. van, "Die Motivierung der Feindesliebe in Lk 6.32–35." *Novum Testamentum* 8 (1966) 284–300
- "The Teaching of Good Works in I Peter." *New Testament Studies* 1 (1954) 92–110
Vaganay, L., "Matthieu." In *Dictionnaire de la Bible: Supplément* 5, edited by L. Pirot et H. Cazelles. Paris 1957, 940-56
VanderKam, J.C., "The Calendar, 4Q327, and 4Q394." In *Legal Texts and Legal Issues: Proceedings of the Second Meeting of the International Organization for Qumran Studies Cambridge 1995: Published in Honour of J.M. Baumgarten*, edited by M. Bernstein, F. García Martínez, J. Kampen (Studies on the Texts of the Desert of Judah 23). Leiden 1997, 179-94
Van Rompay, L, "Antiochene Biblical Interpretation: Greek and Syriac." In *The Book of Genesis in Jewish and Oriental Christian Interpretation: A Collection of Essays*, edited by J. Frishman and L. van Rompay (Traditio exegetica graeca 5). Leuven 1997, 101–23
Vielhauer, Ph., *Geschichte der urchristlichen Literatur. Einleitung in das Neue Testament, die Apokryphen und die Apostolischen Väter*. Berlin 1975
Vielhauer, Ph., and G. Strecker, "Apokalypsen und Verwandtes. Einleitung." In *Neutestamentliche Apokryphen in deutscher Übersetzung* 2, edited by W. Schneemelcher. Tübingen, 1989, 536-37
Viviano, B.T., "Where was the Gospel according to St. Matthew Written?" *Catholic Biblical Quarterly* 41 (1979) 533-46
Vööbus, A., *History of Asceticism in the Syrian Orient: A Contribution to the History of Culture in the Near East* 1 (Corpus scriptorum christianorum orientalium 184/Subs. 14). Leuven 1958
- *Liturgical Traditions in the Didache* (Papers of the Estonian Theological Society in Exile 16). Stockholm 1968

Vokes, F.E., *The Riddle of the Didache. Fact or Fiction, Heresy or Catholicism?* London-New York 1938

– "The Didache and the Canon of the New Testament." In *Studia Evangelica* 3. Berlin 1964, 427-36

– "The Didache-Still Debated," *Church Quarterly* 3 (1970) 57-62

Weinfeld, M., "The Charge of Hypocrisy in Matthew 23 and in Jewish Sources." *Immanuel* 24/25 (1990) 52-58

– *The Organizational Pattern and the Penal Code of the Qumran Sect: A Comparison with Guilds and Religious Associations of the Hellenistic-Roman Period* (Novum Testamentum et Orbis Antiquus 2). Göttingen 1986

Weitzman, M.P., *The Syriac Version of the Old Testament: An Introduction* (University of Cambridge Oriental Publications 56). Cambridge 1999

Wenger, A. (ed.), *Jean Chrysostome: Huit catéchèses baptismales inédites* (Sources Chrétiennes 50). Paris 1957

Wengst, K., *Didache (Apostellehre), Barnabasbrief, Zweiter Klemensbrief, Schrift an Diognet* (Schriften des Urchristentums 2). Darmstadt 1984

– *Tradition und Theologie des Barnabasbriefes* (Arbeiten zur Kirchengeschichte 42). Berlin-New York 1971

Wernberg-Møller, P., *The Manual of Discipline* (Studies on the Texts of the Desert of Judah 1). Leiden 1957

White, L.M.. "Crisis Management and Boundary Maintenance: The Social Location of the Matthean Community." In *Social History of the Matthean Community: Cross-Disciplinary Approaches*, edited by D.L. Balch. Minneapolis 1991, 211-47

– "Shifting Sectarian Boundaries in Early Christianity." *Bulletin of the John Rylands University Library of Manchester* 70 (1988) 7-24

Whittaker, M. (ed.), *Tatian: Oratio ad Graecos and Fragments* (Oxford Early Christian Texts). Oxford 1982

Wilckens, U., "ὑποκρίνομαι, κτλ." In *Theological Dictionary of the New Testament* 8, 559-71

Willis, W.L., *Idol Meat in Corinth. The Pauline Argument in 1 Corinthians 8 and 10* (Society of Biblical Literature - Dissertation Series 68). Chico 1985

Wilson, B. R., *Magic and the Millennium: A Sociological Study of Religious Movements of Protest among Tribal and Third-World Peoples.* London 1973

Wilson, S.G., *Related Strangers: Jews and Christians 70-170 C.E.* Minneapolis 1995

Wohlenberg, G., *Die Lehre der zwölf Apostel in ihre Verhältnis zum neutestamentlichen Schrifttum.* Erlangen 1888

Wrege, H.-Th., *Die Überlieferungsgeschichte der Bergpredigt* (Wissenschaftliche Untersuchungen zum Neuen Testament 9). Tübingen 1968

Ysebaert, J., *Die Amtsterminologie im Neuen Testament und in der Alten Kirche: Eine lexikographische Untersuchung.* Breda 1994

Zerbe, G.M., *Non-Retaliation in Early Jewish and New Testament Texts: Ethical Themes in Social Contexts* (Journal for the Study of the Pseudepigrapha: Supplement Series 13). Sheffield 1993

Zetterholm, M., *The Formation of Christianity in Antioch: a social-scientific approach to the separation between Judaism and Christianity.* London 2003

Indices

Division: 1. Index of Sources
2. Index of Subjects
3. Index of Ancient Personal Names
4. Index of Geographical Names
5. Index of Modern Authors

1. Index of Sources

Hebrew Bible

Septuagint

OT Syriac Translation

OT Pseudepigrapha

Qumran

Greek Jewish Writers

Sayings 'Source' (Q)

Didache

Other Early Christian Writings

Inscriptions, Manuscripts, and Papyri

Pagan Greek Authors

2. Index of Subjects

3. Index of Ancient Personal Names

4. Index of Geographical Names

5. Index of Modern Authors